PELICAN BOOKS

A 431

THE USES OF LITERACY

RICHARD HOGGART

RICHARD HOGGART

THE USES OF LITERACY

Aspects of working-class life
with special reference to publications
and entertainments

PENGUIN BOOKS

IN ASSOCIATION WITH
CHATTO AND WINDUS

Penguin Books Ltd, Harmondsworth, Middlesex

CANADA: Penguin Books (Canada) Ltd, 178 Norseman Street
Toronto 18, Ontario

AUSTRALIA: Penguin Books Pty Ltd, 762 Whitehorse Road,
Mitcham, Victoria

—

First published by Chatto and Windus 1957
Published in Pelican Books 1958

Made and printed in Great Britain
by Butler and Tanner Ltd
Frome and London

TO MARY, WITH LOVE

ACKNOWLEDGEMENTS

I should like to express very warmly my sense of gratitude to the following friends and colleagues, who have given extensive, detailed, and ungrudging help in the preparation of this book. I need hardly add that the errors and weaknesses which remain are all my own:

A. Atkinson, H. L. Beales, A. Briggs, J. M. Cameron, D. G. Charlton, J. F. C. Harrison, the late F. D. Klingender, G. E. T. Mayfield, R. Nettel, S. G. Raybould, R. Shaw, A. Shonfield, E. J. Tinsley, my brother Tom, and my wife.

For much secretarial help I am greatly indebted also to Mrs E. Clayton, Miss M. Downs, Mrs J. Graves, Mr F. Nicholson, Mr V. Waterhouse, Miss J. Woodhead, and Miss N. Young.

Among the several libraries consulted, I should like to mention particularly Hull Public Library, whose officials, always willingly, gave the most substantial assistance.

I wish to express my thanks also to all those authors and publishers whose works have been quoted. The sources of these quotations have been separately acknowledged in the Notes and Bibliography. If any prove to have been omitted I apologize to the authors and publishers concerned, and shall be glad to make good the deficiencies in any future editions.

CONTENTS

PREFACE

This book is about changes in working-class culture during the last thirty or forty years, in particular as they are being encouraged by mass publications. I imagine that similar results would be gained if some other forms of entertainment, notably the cinema and commercial broadcasting, were used for illustration.

I am inclined to think that books on popular culture often lose some of their force by not making sufficiently clear who is meant by 'the people', by inadequately relating their examinations of particular aspects of 'the people's' life to the wider life they live, and to the attitudes they bring to their entertainments. I have therefore tried to give such a setting, and so far as I could, to describe characteristic working-class relationships and attitudes. Where it is presenting background, this book is based to a large extent on personal experience, and does not purport to have the scientifically-tested character of a sociological survey. There is an obvious danger of generalization from limited experience. I have therefore included, chiefly in the notes, some of the findings of sociologists where they seemed necessary, either as support or as qualification of the text. I have also noted one or two instances in which others, with experience similar to mine, think differently.

It will be seen that two kinds of writing are to be found in the following pages: that of the kind described above, and the more specific literary analysis of popular publications. The two may seem at first glance uneasy companions, and the change of approach in the second half is certainly sharp; but I hope the two approaches will be found by the reader, as they seem to me, mutually illuminating.

I have thought of myself as addressing first of all the serious 'common reader' or 'intelligent layman' from any class. By this I do not mean that I have tried to adopt any particular tone of voice, or that I have avoided using any technical terms and all but the most obvious allusions. But I have written as clearly as my understanding of the subject allowed, and used technical terms and allusions only when they seemed likely, once known, to prove helpful and suggestive. The 'intelligent layman' is an elusive figure, and popularization a dangerous undertaking: but it seems to me that those of us who feel that writing for him is an urgent necessity must go on trying to reach him. For one of the most striking and ominous features of our present cultural situation is the division between the technical languages of the experts and the extraordinarily low level of the organs of mass communication.

University of Hull, 1952–6

R. H.

The men of our age of critical realism, goaded by mass-stupidity and mass-tyranny, have protested against the common people to the point of losing all direct knowledge and vision of it. . . . And perhaps – strange that it should be left for me to make this observation – they have not affected their folk more profoundly because they have not loved it enough.

LUDWIG LEWISHOHN

and a warning against romanticism;

There is peasant blood in my veins, and you cannot astonish me with peasant virtues.

TCHEKOV

PART ONE

AN 'OLDER' ORDER

CHAPTER I

WHO ARE 'THE WORKING-CLASSES'?

A. *Questions of Approach*

IT is often said that there are no working-classes in England now, that a 'bloodless revolution' has taken place which has so reduced social differences that already most of us inhabit an almost flat plain, the plain of the lower middle- to middle-classes. I can see the truth in such a statement, within its proper contexts, and do not wish to under-estimate the extent or the value of many recent social changes. To appreciate afresh the scope of these changes as they affect working-class people in particular, we need only read again a social survey or a few novels from, say, the turn of the century. We are likely to be struck by the extent to which working-class people have not only improved their lot, acquired more power and more possessions, but especially by the degree to which they no longer feel themselves members of 'the lower orders', with a sense of other classes, each above them and each superior in the way the world judges. Some of this remains, but it has been greatly reduced.

In spite of these changes, attitudes alter more slowly than we always realize, as the first half of this book seeks to show. Attitudes alter slowly, but obviously a great number of complex forces are bringing about changes here too: the second half of this book discusses some ways in which a change, towards a culturally 'classless' society, is being brought about.

It will be necessary to define rather more specifically what I mean by 'the working-classes', but difficulties of definition are less troublesome than are those of avoiding the romanticisms which tempt anyone who discusses 'the workers' or 'the common people', and these romanticisms deserve to be mentioned first. For they increase the danger of over-stressing the admirable qualities of earlier working-class culture and its debased condition today. The two over-emphases tend to reinforce each other, and so the contrast is often exaggerated. We may have serious doubts about the quality of working-class life today, and especially about the speed with which it may seem to deteriorate. But some of the more debilitating invitations have been successful only because they have been able to appeal to established attitudes which were not wholly admirable; and though the contemporary ills which particularly strike an observer from outside certainly exist, their effects are not always as consider-able as a diagnosis from outside would suggest, if only because working-class people still possess some older and inner resistances.

No doubt such an over-emphasis is often inspired by a strong admiration for the potentialities of working-class people and a consequent pity for their situation. Related to it is a more positive over-expectation which one frequently finds among middle-class intellectuals with strong social consciences. Some people of this kind have for a long time tended to see every second working-class man as a Felix Holt or a Jude the Obscure. Perhaps this is because most of the working-class people they have known closely have been of an unusual and self-selected kind, and in special circumstances, young men and women at Summer Schools and the like, exceptional individuals whom the chance of birth has deprived of their proper intellectual inheritance, and who have made remarkable efforts to gain it. Naturally, I do not intend in any way to limit their importance as individuals. They are exceptional, in their nature untypical of working-class people ; their very presence at Summer Schools, at meetings of learned societies and courses of lectures, is the result of a moving-away from the landscape which the majority of their fellows inhabit without much apparent strain. They would be exceptional people in any class: they reveal less about their class than about themselves.

From the pity – 'How fine they would be if only . . .', to the praise – 'How fine they are simply because . . .': here we encounter pastoral myths and 'Wife of Bath' admirations. The working-classes are at bottom in excellent health – so the pastoral descriptions run – in better health than other classes; rough and unpolished perhaps, but diamonds nevertheless; rugged, but 'of sterling worth': not refined, not intellectual, but with both feet on the ground; capable of a good belly-laugh, charitable and forthright. They are, moreover, possessed of a racy and salty speech, touched with wit, but always with its hard grain of common sense. These over-emphases vary in strength, from the slight over-stressing of the quaint aspects of working-class life to be found in many major novelists to the threadbare fancies of popular contemporary writers. How many major English writers are there who do not, however slightly, over-emphasize the salty features of working-class life? George Eliot does so, unusually brilliant though her observation of workers is; and the bias is more evident in Hardy. When we come to our own much more consciously manipulative times, we meet the popular novelists' patronizingly flattered little men with their flat caps and flat vowels, their well-scrubbed wives with well-scrubbed doorsteps; fine stock – and amusing too! Even a writer as astringent and seemingly unromantic as George Orwell never quite lost the habit of seeing the working-classes through the cosy fug of an Edwardian music-hall. There is a wide range of similar attitudes running down to the folksy ballyhoo of the Sunday columnists, the journalists who always remember to quote with admiration the latest bon-mot of their pub-pal 'Alf'. They have to be rejected more forcefully, I think, because there is an element of truth in what they say and it is a pity to see it inflated for display.

Again, one has sometimes to be cautious of the interpretations given by historians of the working-class movement. The subject is fascinating and moving; there is a vast amount of important and inspiring material about working-class social and political aspirations. But it is easy for a reader to be led into at least a half-assumption that these are histories of the working-classes rather than, primarily, histories of the activities – and the valuable consequences for almost every member of the working-classes – of a minority. Probably the authors would specifically claim no more for them, and these aims are important enough. But from such books I do sometimes bring away an impression that their authors overrate the place of political activity in working-class life, that they do not always have an adequate sense of the grass-roots of that life.

A middle-class Marxist's view of the working-classes often includes something of each of the foregoing errors. He pities the betrayed and debased worker, whose faults he sees as almost entirely the result of the grinding system which controls him. He admires the remnants of the noble savage, and has a nostalgia for those 'best of all' kinds of art, rural folk-art or genuinely popular urban art, and a special enthusiasm for such scraps of them as he thinks he can detect today. He pities and admires the Jude-the-Obscure aspect of working-people. Usually, he succeeds in part-pitying and part-patronizing working-class people beyond any semblance of reality.

It is some novels, after all, that may bring us really close to the quality of working-class life – such a novel as Lawrence's *Sons and Lovers*, at least, rather than more popular or more consciously proletarian fiction. And so, in their own way, do some of the detailed surveys of working-class life which sociologists have made during the last twenty years. These books convey powerfully the complex and claustrophobic impression which working-class life can make on an observer who tries to know it in all its concreteness. I mean the impression of being immersed in an endless forest, full of the most minute detail, all of it different and yet all of it similar; a great mass of faces and habits and actions, yet most of them apparently not very meaningful. The impression seems to me both right and wrong: right in that it indicates the sprawling and multitudinous and infinitely detailed character of working-class life, and the sense – often depressing to an outsider – of an immense uniformity, of always being part of a huge and seething crowd of people, all very similar even in the most important and individual matters. I think such an impression is wrong if it leads us to construct an image of working-class people only from adding together the variety of statistics given in some of these sociological works, from the numbers who do this or do not do that, from the percentage who said that they believe in God, or who thought free-love was 'all right in its way'. A sociological survey may or may not assist us here, but clearly we have to try to see beyond the habits to what the habits stand for, to see through the statements to what the statements really mean (which may be the opposite of the statements themselves), to detect the differing pressures of emotion behind idiomatic phrases and ritualistic observances.

A writer who is himself from the working-classes has his own temptations to error, somewhat different from but no less than those of a writer from another class. I am from the working-classes and feel even now both close to them and apart from them. In a few more years this double relationship may not, I suppose, be so apparent to me; but it is bound to affect what I say. It may help me to come nearer to giving a felt sense of working-class life, to avoid some of an outsider's more obvious risks of misinterpretation. On the other hand, this very emotional involvement presents considerable dangers. Thus it seems to me that the changes described in the second half of this book are, so far, tending to cause the working-classes to lose, culturally, much that was valuable and to gain less than their new situation should have allowed. To the extent that I can judge the matter objectively, that is my belief. Yet in writing I found myself constantly having to resist a strong inner pressure to make the old much more admirable than the new, and the new more to be condemned, than my conscious understanding of the material gave me grounds for. Presumably some kind of nostalgia was colouring the material in advance: I have done what I could to remove its effects.

In both halves of the book I discovered a tendency in myself, because the subject is so much part of my origins and growth, to be unwarrantedly sharp towards those features in working-class life of which I disapprove. Related to this is the urge to lay one's ghosts; at the worst, it can be a temptation to 'do down' one's class, out of a pressing ambiguity in one's attitudes to it. Conversely, I found a tendency to over-value those features in working-class life of which I approve, and this tempted towards a sentimentality, a romanticizing of my background, as though I were subconsciously saying to my present acquaintance – see, in spite of all, such a childhood is richer than yours.

A writer has to meet these dangers as he can and in the very process of writing, as he struggles to find out what it is that he truly has to say. I suppose it is unlikely that he will ever quite succeed. But his reader is in a luckier position, like Marlowe's hearers in Conrad's *Heart of Darkness*:

Of course in this you fellows see more than I could see. You see me.

The reader sees what is intended to be said and also, from tone, from the unconscious emphases and the rest, he comes to know the man saying it.

B. *A Rough Definition*

In deciding who would be 'the working-classes' for the purposes of this survey my problem, as I saw it, was this: the mass publications from which I draw most of my evidence affect far more than those working-class groups of which I have a close knowledge; in fact, in so far as they tend to be 'classless' publications, they affect all classes in society. But in order to discuss the way in which these publications affect attitudes and to avoid the vagueness which almost inevitably results from talking about 'the common people', it was necessary to find a focus. I have therefore taken one fairly homogeneous group of working-class people, have tried to evoke the atmosphere, the quality, of their lives by describing their setting and their attitudes. Against this background may be seen how the much more generally diffused appeals of the mass publications connect with commonly accepted attitudes, how they are altering those attitudes and how they are meeting resistance. Unless I am much-mistaken, the attitudes described in this first part will be sufficiently shared by many other groups which go to make up 'the common people', to give the analysis a wider relevance. In particular, many of the attitudes I describe as 'working-class' might also be attributed to what are often called the 'lower middle-classes'. I cannot see how this kind of overlapping is to be avoided, and hope readers will feel, as I do, that it does not weaken the main lines of my argument.

The setting and the evidence as to attitudes are drawn mainly from experience in the urban North, from a childhood during the twenties and thirties and an almost continuous if somewhat different kind of contact since then.

I admitted earlier that working-class people probably do not feel themselves to be members of a 'lower' group as strongly as they did a generation or two ago. Yet those I have in mind still to a considerable extent retain a sense of being in a group of their own, and this without there being necessarily implied any feeling of inferiority or pride; they feel rather that they are 'working-class' in the things they admire and dislike, in 'belonging'. Such a distinction does not go far, but it is important; others may be added, none of them definitive but each of them helping to give the greater degree of definition which is needed.

The 'working-classes' described here live in districts such as Hunslet (Leeds), Ancoats (Manchester), Brightside and Attercliffe (Sheffield), and off the Hessle and Holderness Roads (Hull). My fullest experience is of those who live in the miles of smoking and huddled working-class houses in Leeds. Such people have their own recognizable parts of the towns; they have, almost city by city, their own recognizable styles of housing – backs-to-backs here or tunnels-backs there; their houses are usually rented, not owned. They are increasingly being moved on to the new estates now, but this does not seem to me at present to affect strongly my main contentions as to their attitudes.

Most of the employed inhabitants of these areas work for a wage, not a salary, and the wage is paid weekly: most have no other sources of income. Some are self-employed; they may keep a small shop for members of the group to which, culturally, they belong or supply a service to the group, for example as a 'cobbler', 'barber', 'grocer', 'bike-mender' or 'cast-off clothing dealer'. One cannot firmly distinguish workers from others by the amount of money earned, since there are enormous variations in wages among working-class people; and most steel-workers, for instance, are plainly working-class though some earn more than many teachers who are not. But I suppose that in most of the families described here a wage of about £9 or £10 a week for the chief wage-earner, at 1954 rates, would be regarded as roughly normal.

Most of them were educated at what ought now to be called a secondary modern school, but is still popularly known as 'elementary' school. In occupation they are usually labourers, skilled or unskilled, or craftsmen and perhaps apprentice-trained. This loose boundary includes, therefore, men who do what used to be called 'navvying' and other outdoor manual work, commercial and public transport workers, men and girls on routine jobs in factories, as well as skilled tradesmen, from plumbers to those who perform the more difficult tasks in heavy industries. Foremen are included, but office-clerks and employees in large shops, though they may live in these areas, are on the whole better regarded as members of the lower middle-classes.

Since this essay is concerned with cultural change, my main means of definition will be less tangible features of a working-class way of life than those named above. Speech will indicate a great deal, in particular the host of phrases in common use. Manners of speaking, the use of urban dialects, accents, and intonations, could probably indicate even more. There is the cracked but warm-hearted voice, slightly spitting through all-too-regular false teeth, of some women in their forties. The comedians often adopt it; it suggests a heart which, without illusions or regrets about life, is nevertheless in the right place. There is a husky voice which I have often heard, and heard only there, among working-class girls of the rougher sort; it is known among the more 'respectable' working-classes as a 'common' voice. But unfortunately, I have not sufficient knowledge to pursue this examination of manners of speaking.

Cheap mass-produced clothing has reduced the immediately recognizable differences between classes, but not as greatly as many think. A Saturday-night crowd leaving the cinemas in the city centre may look superficially one. A closer glance from an expert of either sex, from a middle-class woman or a man particularly conscious of clothes, will usually be sufficient even nowadays for them to 'place' most people around them.

There are thousands of other items from daily experience which, as will be seen, help to distinguish this recognizably working-class life, such as the habit of paying out money in small instalments over month after month; or the fact that, for as long as anyone except the old can now remember, almost every worker has been on the 'panel' at the local doctor's, and so on.

To isolate the working-classes in this rough way is not to forget the great number of differences, the subtle shades, the class distinctions, within the working-classes themselves. To the inhabitants there is a fine range of distinctions in prestige from street to street. Inside the single streets there are elaborate differences of status, of 'standing', between the houses themselves; this is a slightly better house because it has a separate kitchen, or is at the terrace end, has a bit of a yard, and is rented at ninepence a week more. There are differences of grade between the occupants; this family is doing well because the husband is a skilled man and there is a big order in at the works; the wife here is a good manager and very houseproud, whereas the one opposite is a slattern; these have been a 'Hunslet family' for generations, and belong to the hereditary aristocracy of the neighbourhood.

To some extent there is, also, a hierarchy of specialization in any group of streets. This man is known to be something of a 'scholar' and has a bound set of encyclopedias which he will always gladly refer to when asked; another is a good 'penman' and very helpful at filling in forms; another is particularly 'good with his hands', in wood or metal or as a general repairer; this woman is expert at fine needlework and will be called in on special occasions. All these are group services before they are professional services, even though some of the workers may be professionally engaged on the same work during the day. This kind of specialization seemed, though, to be dying out in the large urban working-class centres I knew even when I was a boy. A friend who knows well the smaller West Riding urban working-class centres (such as Keighley, Bingley, and Heck-mondwike) thinks it is still quite strong there.

Yet one may fairly make generalizations about attitudes without implying that everyone in the working-classes believes or does this or this about work or marriage or religion. (Perhaps I should add here that my experience is of predominantly Protestant areas.) The implication of my generalizations throughout the book is rather that this or this is what most working-class people assume should be believed or done about such matters. I am writing particularly of the majority who take their lives much as they find them, and in that way are not different from the majority in other classes; of what some trade union leaders, when they are regretting a lack of interest in their movement, call 'the vast apathetic mass'; of what song-writers call, by way of compliment, 'just plain folk'; of what the working-classes themselves describe, more soberly, as 'the general run of people'. Within that majority there is obviously a very wide range of attitudes, and yet there is a centre at which a great number of people are represented.

It follows that I shall give less attention to, for example, the purposive, the political, the pious, and the self-improving minorities in the working-classes. This is not because I underrate their value but because the appeals made by the mass publicists are not primarily to their kinds of mind. Nor is the amount of attention which I give to different attitudes that which would be required if this survey aimed to be a complete account of working-class life. I lay emphasis on those elements which are especially exploited (as I would say) by the mass publicists. Thus, certain strains often found among the majority – the self-respecting, the thrifty, for instance – though they are given a place, do not receive the same weight of attention as some others, such as the tolerant, or that which insists on the need to have a good time while one can.

The fairly strict division into 'older' and 'newer' attitudes is made largely for the sake of clarity, and does not imply a strict chronological succession. Obviously, elements as subtle as attitudes could never be attributed to one generation or one decade. Of what are called the 'older' attitudes some features have existed for a very long time, are indeed part of the outlook of 'the common people' in any generation and in almost any land. Some have persisted, very little changed, from a rural into an urban England; others were given special emphasis by the challenges of urbanization. Yet in describing the 'older' attitudes I have drawn to a large extent on memories of my childhood about twenty years ago, because I personally saw these attitudes at their strongest in the generation which was adult when I was a child. This was a generation which grew up in an urban environment and amid many difficulties but did not experience, whilst growing up, the assault of the mass Press as it is known today, of the wireless and television, of the ubiquitous cheap cinemas, and so on. But clearly these 'older' attitudes exist not only in the middle-aged or elderly; they form a background to much in the lives of younger people. What I am questioning throughout is how long they will continue to be as powerful as they are now, and in what ways they are being altered.

Similarly, much in what are here called the 'newer' appeals and in the attitudes encouraged by them, was evident in that earlier generation and before. Indeed, the three ideas of which the misuse is shown later to reinforce these appeals have a long European history. My argument is not that there was, in England one generation ago, an urban culture still very much 'of the people' and that now there is only a mass urban culture. It is rather that the appeals made by the mass publicists are for a great number of reasons made more insistently, effectively, and in a more comprehensive and centralized form today than they were earlier; that we are moving towards the creation of a mass culture; that the remnants of what was at least in parts an urban culture 'of the people' are being destroyed; and that the new mass culture is in some important ways less healthy than the often crude culture it is replacing.

The distinction between the 'old' and the 'new' attitudes, therefore, whilst it cannot be clear-cut, seems to be firm enough to be useful. In particular, it should be firm enough to make clear at the outset that, when I speak of 'older' attitudes, I am not invoking some rather mistily conceived pastoral tradition the better to assault the present.

An even clearer chronological background may be gained by thinking briefly of the history of one family, and my own will perhaps serve as well as any. It is generally agreed that the main pattern of future development in the urbanization of England was clear by about 1830. My family came rather later in the process.

My grandmother married a cousin and at that time their family was still rural, living in a village about a dozen miles from Leeds. Sometime in the seventies she and her young husband were drawn to that expanding city, into the service of the steelworks on the south side. She set about raising a growing family – ten were born but some were 'lost' – in the vast new brick acres of Hunslet. All over the North and Midlands the same thing was happening, the villages losing their young people, the towns staining the countryside around with raw cheap housing. They were insufficiently provided with medical, educational, and other social facilities; their streets, inadequately cleansed and lighted, were being packed with families whose pattern of life was still to a large extent rural. Many died young (the plaque commemorating a cholera epidemic used still to stand in a railway shunting-yard that I passed each day on my way to the secondary school); 'T.B.' took a heavy toll.

My grandmother lived through all this and on through the First World War until almost the beginning of the Second; she learned to become a city-dweller. Yet in every line of her body and in many of her attitudes her country background spoke. Her house, still rented at nine shillings a week in 1939, was never truly urban. Newspaper-packets of home-dried herbs hung from the scullery ceiling; a pot of goose-grease lay always on the shelf there, in case anyone 'got a bad chest'. She retained in the vitality of her spirit, in the vigour of her language, in the occasional peasant quality of her humour, a strength which her children had not and towards which they had at times something of a sophisticated and urbanized 'neshness' (soft squeamish-ness). She called you a 'corf-eerd' (calf-head) without any conscious archaism; she was full of pithy aphorisms, such as 'as t'owd cock crows, t'yung un larns' (of a cheeky boy whose mother did not control him); she had a wealth of superstitious tags and old remedies to fall back upon in emergencies. Occasionally, when the arrival of an illegitimate child in the neighbourhood was remarked, she would recount with rough amusement the story of a scandal in a working-class district (of Sheffield, I think, where she had spent some years), where irregular intercourse behind the pulpit at chapel became popu-lar. She had only been, and that occasionally, to a dame school. When I was in the sixth form she read, without spectacles, many of the books I brought home. I remember especially her reaction to D. H. Lawrence; much of it she admired, and she was not shocked.

But of his descriptions of physical sex she said, "'E makes a lot of fuss and lah-de-dah about it.'

For our family she was a first-generation townswoman and therefore only partly a townswoman. Meanwhile the second generation, her children, were growing up. They were growing up from the time of the Third Reform Act, through the series of Education Acts, the various Housing Acts, the Factory Acts and Public Health Acts, through the Boer War; and the youngest was just old enough to serve in the First World War. The boys went to 'Board' school and so into steelworks or, since we had white-collar leanings, into the more genteel openings, as grocery assistants or salesmen in town shops, though this was regarded as almost a step up in class. The girls were swallowed one after the other into the always-demanding, because always-changing, population of tailoresses, those girls who were and are the foundation of Leeds' predominance as a centre for ready-made clothing.

This generation – my parents, uncles, and aunts – did retain a few rural habits, though now with a touch of nostalgia, of veneration for their parents who 'knew what was right when all's said and done'; it was not so much in the blood as something remembered, regretted in its passing, and so slightly consciously held on to. Much more, and here their attitude to their parents was often jollying, they were of the newer world. That world had many advantages to offer; cheaper and more varied clothes, cheaper and more varied food; frozen meat at a few pence the pound, tinned pineapples for next to nothing, cheap tinned savouries, fish-and-chips round the corner. It had cheap and easy travel on the new trams, and ready-packeted proprietary drugs from the corner-shops.

This second generation had fewer children, and on their account, in particular, felt the pressure of the greater organization of urban life: they were glad that 'the lad's chances in life' had improved, but they began to worry about whether he would get his scholarship. 'The lad' and his sister were my cousins, my brother and sister, myself. We had been from the beginning fully of the towns, of the trams and buses, of the elaborate network of social services, of the chain-stores, the picture-palaces, the trips to the seaside. For us the country is not, after all, home; nor even the place where Father and Mother were so healthily reared. It is an occasionally remembered backcloth, a place you sometimes visit.

CHAPTER 2

LANDSCAPE WITH FIGURES – A SETTING

'What are the roots that clutch . . .?'

A. *An Oral Tradition: Resistance and Adaptation: A Formal Way of Life*

A great deal has been written about the effect on the working-classes of the modern 'mass media of communication'. But if we listen to working-class people at work and at home we are likely to be struck first, not so much by the evidence of fifty years of popular papers and cinema, as by the slight effect these things have had upon the common speech, by the degree to which working-people still draw, in speech and in the assumptions to which speech is a guide, on oral and local tradition. That tradition is no doubt weakening, but if we are to understand the present situation of the working-classes we must not pronounce it dead when it still has remarkable life.

These examples were all collected in a deliberately short period, the first from a bright, pastel-shade distempered and tubular furnished waiting-room of a children's clinic. A handful of drab and untidy mothers were waiting with their children, and the conversation dribbled on aimlessly but easily about their habits. In three minutes two women used these phrases:

' 'E shows well for it anyway' (of a well-nourished child).
'If it's not there y' can't put it there' (of the intelligence needed to pass the scholarship examination).
'Aye, they're good alarm clocks aren't they?' (of early waking by children).
'Y' can't lay in where bairns are.'
'Well, 'unger's t'best sauce.'

Soon afterwards, a few shops where housewives meet in the mornings, produced:

'She gave me a meaning look.'
'We're not as well lined as we were: we 'aven't got enough lining' (on the shortage of meat, in particular of English beef).

'Did yer 'ear about t'schoolmaster? 'e went eerie.'

'Ah'm all dressed up today. Ah've got me 'ypocrite on' (of a false front to a blouse).

Round the basic features of life – birth, marriage, copulation, children, death – the old phrases cluster most thickly. On sex:

'A slice off a cut cake is never missed' (on the easy sexual habits of some married women).

'Y' don't look at the mantelpiece when y' poke the fire' (a woman doesn't need to be pretty to make sexual intercourse with her enjoyable).

'Ah'd rather 'ave a good meal any day' (debunking comment on a woman whose physical attractions are all too noticeable).

'Y'll last a man a lifetime with care' (for sex and housework – to a young wife ill in bed and feeling a bit sorry for herself).

'Nay, they don't oppen t'oven for one loaf' (a middle-aged mother to a young wife expecting her first baby, who had said that she would be happy to have only one child).

Most of these are the remnants of a more muscular tradition of speech; the use of 'hypocrite', for instance, clearly depended on a moral sense naturally felt to inform everyday life. I have little evidence that such phrases are being newly minted. During the last war the services created a few, but scarcely one has passed into common speech. Periodically, and for a period, one is taken from a popular wireless programme; we have already had twenty years of those, from 'Can yer 'ear me, Muther?' to 'Right, Munkey!' For the rest, young working-class people seem increasingly to make do with a few blanket epithets in addition to those of the older phrases they have taken over: most admired things are 'luvly', most disliked things 'awful'; what is particularly admired is 'grand' or, more recently, 'smashing' (though this last is one of the newer 'classless' epithets).

Still strongly in middle-aged people, and more strongly than we often think in those younger, the old forms of speech persist. They persist not in a racy or lively but in a formal manner: the phrases are used like counters, 'click-click-click'. If we listen only to their tone we might conclude that they are used simply by rote, flatly and mean-inglessly, that they have no connexion at all with the way life is lived, are used and yet somehow do not connect. If we notice only their subject-matter – the acceptance of death, laughter at marriage but yet an acceptance of it, making the best of your lot – we might conjure up a pretty picture of the way in which old attitudes, simple but healthy, remain unaffected. The truth lies between the two extremes: the persistence in so strong a measure of older forms of speech does not indicate a powerful and vibrant continuance of an earlier tradition, but the tradition is not altogether dead. It is harked back to, leaned upon as a fixed and still largely trustworthy field of reference in a world now difficult to understand. The aphorisms are drawn as a kind of comfort; 'ah well, good and bad go in cycles', people say, and there are a dozen variants of that phrase. It should cause no surprise, and at the level at which such speech has its effect it is not paradoxical, that these tags often contradict one another, that in any lengthy conversation they will be brought out to prove opposing views: they are not used as parts of intellectual constructions.

Much the same is true of the hold of superstition and myth. The world of experience is mapped at every point, particularly closely at the great nodes, in two colours, into those things which 'mean good luck' and those which 'mean bad luck'. These divisions are invoked daily and automatically. To put shoes on the table, to walk under a ladder, to spill salt, to bring certain flowers indoors, to burn 'green stuff', to bring holly into the house before Christmas, to break a mirror, to give a knife without receiving a coin, to cross knives at table, are unlucky: to have a black cat cross one's path, to put on stockings the wrong way out, to have a dark man enter the house first at Christmas and the New Year, to touch wood after tempting misfortune, all these are lucky. A bride must not see her groom before the ceremony on her wedding-day, and should wear – and still usually does – 'Something old, something new,/Something borrowed, something blue.' A baby should cry at its baptism, as that means luck; the day of birth and a baby's physical features will prompt any one of a score of rhyming tags, like 'A dimple in your chin/ Your living brought in'. Dreams are not to be ignored, not because they help to explain something in the past or indicate some hidden worry, but because they *foretell*: and they 'go by contraries'; if you cry in a dream that means something pleasant. But you must really cry and not just dream that you were crying and wake dry-eyed.

Superstition clings particularly to anything affecting health. 'I don't believe in doctors' is still a common expression, and supporting it are a crowd of old saws and modern instances, mostly apocryphal.

My generation is probably the last to be dosed with brimstone and treacle for most of the occasional ailments of childhood, but the recipe still lingers. There are others much stranger. I know of two recent urban experiments with horsehair and steak to remove warts: the steak is buried in the ground with the hair tied round it, and the wart thereafter withers and finally drops off. A few years ago the story went round some Leeds clothing factories that to wash in one's own urine was good for the complexion. It is still commonly believed that weakness in young children can be due to the hair being too long and thick; the 'goodness' of the hair is gained at the expense of the body. Each separate activity, no matter how minor, has its folk-lore: thus, at whist-drives some women always carry a coin issued in the year of their birth, some will only mark the score with red pencils, some will not wear black shoes.

Most of these myths have existed for a long time and some are slowly dying; but occasional new ones are created. I notice particularly those about great figures in the world outside: in the more elementary folk-lore of the working-classes, as distinct from their comic art, great public figures are more likely to be inflated than reduced. There are fabulous stories of how this film-star died (she tried to slim by standing in a refrigerator and was frozen to death) or how that princess lives. It was popularly said that Stalin had 'had injections' to make him live until a hundred and fifty. The process sometimes works the other way round: 'They' are reported to order that out of every ten contraceptive sheaths manufactured, one should be punctured; and 'They' put bromide in servicemen's tea, to reduce the sexual urges.

Some of all this, notably the instances of good and bad luck, is also believed, in a sense, by other classes. In what way exactly can working-class people be said to believe in it? They repeat the phrases, but often with a saving prefatory: 'They say that . . .' They do not intellectually examine them: yet on certain occasions they laugh readily at them as 'old wives' tales'. But usually they take care to obey their directions. They say 'Oh, it's all superstition', and look at popular-magazine articles which discount them; but still they pick them up verbally and pass them on, and this applies to young people almost as much as to the old. Is there a working-class magazine without its horoscope? Change is very slow, and people are not troubled by inconsistencies; they believe and do not believe. They go on repeating the old tags and practising their sanctions and permissions: the oral tradition is still strong.

So it is in many other parts of working-class life. The world of many a middle-aged working-class couple is still largely Edwardian, their living-rooms little changed from the time they equipped them or took them over from their parents, except for the addition of an occasional ornament or chair. Young couples like to go out and buy everything new when they 'set up', and the furniture salesmen often do their best to persuade them to buy, by hire-purchase, more new furniture than they need. But though the furniture calls itself modern and may use new materials, it must embody the same assumptions as to the furnishing of a 'really homely' room as the older things, bought by the customers' grandparents. Much the same is true of the pottery trade, of the fun-fairs, of popular-song writing.

This is not simply a power of passive resistance, but something which, though not articulate, is positive. The working-classes have a strong natural ability to survive change by adapting or assimilating what they want in the new and ignoring the rest.

To live in the working-classes is even now to belong to an all-pervading culture, one in some ways as formal and stylized as any that is attributed to, say, the upper-classes. A working-class man would come to grief over the right way to move through a seven-course dinner: an upper middle-class man among working-class people would just as surely reveal his foreign background by the way he made conversation (the tempo of conversation, not only the matter or idiom), used his hands and feet, ordered drinks or tried to stand drinks. Recall for a moment some of the routines of working-class life: as to clothes, the persistence of the Sunday suit, the 'best clothes' for children newly bought at Whitsun and the round tour on Whit Sunday morning to show these clothes to relatives and receive a present of money, the intricate system of clothes renewal by the use of 'club checks': or the elaboration of formalities, from a simple 'passing of the time of day', a 'paying of respects' to a dead neighbour by standing at the cemetery gates at the time of the funeral, to the rituals of the 'Buffs' and Odd Fellows. Or the fifty-year-old formality of seaside postcards: most of the year 'decent' working-class people would hardly approve of them, but on holiday they are likely to 'let up a bit' and send a few to friends – cards showing fat mothers-in-law and fat policemen, weedy little men with huge-bottomed wives, ubiquitous bottles of beer and chamber-pots, with their endless repetition of beer-bottom-and-lavatory humour, their extraordinary changelessness.

Thus, many of the newer approaches to working-class people do not deeply affect them. They are less affected than might be assumed from a consideration only of the great extent to which they are approached today. There may be some prophetic truth in discussions about 'the vast anonymous masses with their thoroughly dulled responses'. But so far working-class people are by no means as badly affected as that sentence suggests, because with a large part of themselves they are just 'not there', are living elsewhere, living intuitively, habitually, verbally, drawing on myth, aphorism, and ritual. This saves them from some of the worst effects of the present approaches; it also makes them, in other ways, easier subjects for those approaches. In so far as they have been affected by modern conditions, they have been affected along lines on which their older traditions made them most open and undefended.

B. 'There's No Place Like Home'

The more we look at working-class life, the more we try to reach the core of working-class attitudes, the more surely does it appear that the core is a sense of the personal, the concrete, the local: it is embodied in the idea of, first, the family and, second, the neighbourhood. This remains, though much works against it, and partly because so much works against it.

In magazines published for working-class girls and housewives there is a frequent use of the word 'sin'. The word is little used in more sophisticated literature today except by those writers who specifically want to recall their readers to 'man's metaphysical condition'. But working-class magazines do not use 'sin' in a metaphysical sense, they are not thinking of man's fallen nature and his duty to God. 'Sin' is getting a girl with child before marriage and then not marrying her, 'sin' is allowing yourself to be put into such a position, 'getting yourself into trouble' (abortion is rarely suggested and practically never condoned), 'sin' is risking the break-up of your marriage by messing around with some other man or woman, 'sin' is breaking some other person's marriage. 'Sin' is any act against the idea of home and family, against the sense of the importance of 'keeping the home together'. Where almost everything else is ruled from outside, is chancy and likely to knock you down when you least expect it, the home is yours and real: the warmest welcome is still 'Mek y'self at 'ome'.

Working-class people have always hated the thought of 'ending up in the work'ouse' for several good reasons, and of these the deepest is the sense of the inalienable quality of home life. A widow will 'work 'erself to death' as a charwoman rather than accept offers of places even in a comfortable orphanage for her children. If she dies, the family, some of whom may well have done nothing for her earlier and do not much want to look after a child, will split the children between them. My mother was left with three, aged one, three, and five; when she died after five years of struggle, I remember a previously unknown aunt from some distance away saying that 'orphanages are different nowadays'. She cut no ice; we were taken severally then and there by various members of the family, each of them poorer than she was.

The insistence on the privacy of home arises from this feeling, reinforced by the knowledge that, though the neighbours are 'your sort' and will rally round in trouble, they are always ready for a gossip and perhaps a mean-minded gossip. 'What will the neighbours think?' Usually they think that two and two make six; their gossip may 'mean no harm' but it can be unconscionably brutal. They may be able to 'hear everything going on' through the thin party-wall, but you can shut the front door, 'live yer own life', 'keep y'self to y'self' – that is, to the immediate members of the household which includes the married sons and daughters with their families from the streets nearby, and extends to the few friends who are on 'popping-in' terms. You want good neighbours but a good neighbour is not always 'coming in and out': if she does that, she may have to be 'frozen off'. The half-length lace curtains keep out most of what little sun there is, but they establish your privacy: the window-ledges and doorsteps scrubbed and yellowed with scouring-stone further establish that you are a 'decent' family, that you believe in 'bottoming' the house each week.

Inside, the aspidistra has gone in favour of the ragged-country-lad-eating-cherries and the little-girl-coyly-holding-her-skirt or the big-girl-in-a-picture-hat-holding-two-Borzois or a single Alsation. Chain-store modernismus, all bad veneer and sprayed-on-varnish-stain, is replacing the old mahogany; multi-coloured plastic and chrome biscuit barrels and bird-cages have come in. This is more than keeping up with the Joneses; these things subserve the domestic values, full and rich. So, many prefabs now have leaded and coloured window-panes provided by the owners: in the older houses the deep window-sills give the opportunity for some exterior colour, for a box of rank and colourful nasturtiums or of even more dazzling geraniums.

Looking back on years of living in one, I should say that a good 'living-room' must provide three principal things: gregariousness, warmth, and plenty of good food. The living-room is the warm heart of the family and therefore often slightly stuffy to a middle-class visitor. It is not a social centre but a family centre; little entertaining goes on there or in the front room, if there happens to be one: you do not entertain in anything approaching the middle-class sense. The wife's social life outside her immediate family is found over the washing-line, at the corner-shop, visiting relatives at a moderate distance occasionally, and perhaps now and again going with her husband to his pub or club. He has his pub or club, his work, his foot-ball matches. The friends of either at all these places may well not know what the inside of their house is like, may never have 'stepped across the threshold'. The hearth is reserved for the family, whether living at home or nearby, and those who are 'something to us', and look in for a talk or just to sit. Much of the free time of a man and his wife will usually be passed at that hearth; 'just staying-in' is still one of the most common leisure-time occupations.

It is a cluttered and congested setting, a burrow deeply away from the outside world. There is no telephone to ring, and knocks at the door in the evening are rare. But the group, though restricted, is not private: it is a gregarious group, in which most things are shared, including personality; 'our Mam', 'our Dad', 'our Alice' are normal forms of address. To be alone, to think alone, to read quietly is difficult. There is the wireless or television, things being done in odd bouts, or intermittent snatches of talk (but rarely a sustained conversation); the iron thumps on the table, the dog scratches and yawns or the cat miaows to be let out; the son, drying himself on the family towel near the fire, whistles, or rustles the communal letter from his brother in the army which has been lying on the mantel-piece behind the photo of his sister's wedding; the little girl bursts into a whine because she is too tired to be up at all, the budgerigar twitters.

In a few of the more careful homes this unity is still objectified in the making of a clip-rug by the hearth. Clippings of old clothes are prepared, sorted into rough colour groups and punched singly through a piece of harding (sacking). Patterns are traditional and simple, usually a centre circle or diamond with the remainder an unrelieved navy blue except for the edging) or that greyish-blue which mixed shoddy usually produces; most of us knew it years ago in army blankets. The rug will replace at the fireside one made a long time ago and will have cost little more than the price of the harding unless it is decided to have a vivid centre and colour is short. Then prepared clippings in, say, red can be bought at about half a crown the pound.

Is it to be wondered that married sons and daughters take a few years to wean themselves from their mother's hearth? Until the needs of their own children make evening visits practically impossible, and this will be a long time after a mother with views on the healthy rearing of children would think it reasonable, the son or daughter with whatever children they have will be around in the evenings. A son-in-law will tend to drop in straight from work and be fed at a table more often laid than not. He may well join Grandad and Grandma, who are permanent residents (though most old people hate the thought of 'giving up me 'ome' and only do so as a last resort; they much prefer the younger people and their children to join them).

Warmth, to be 'as snug as a bug in a rug', is of the first importance. Seventy years of cheap coal have ensured that most people have learned to use it lavishly, by most foreign standards. A good house-wife knows that she must 'keep a good fire', and is likely to pay more attention to securing that than to buying the better qualities of warm woollen underclothing: a fire is shared and seen.

'A good table' is equally important, and this still means a fully-stocked table rather than one which presents a balanced diet. Thus, many families seem to buy less milk than they should and salads are not popular. Around this there clusters a whole group of attitudes, some of them plainly sensible, some founded on myth. 'Home-cooking' is always better than any other; café food is almost always adulterated. Small confectioners know they will fare better if they put 'Home-made Bread and Cakes' over their windows; in a sense the claim is still likely to be true, though huge electric ovens have probably replaced the original range in what was once the family kitchen behind the shop. The mistrust of cafés has been reinforced by the knowledge that they can hardly be afforded anyway, but much the same resistance often arises to the cheap works' canteens. A husband will complain that the food there 'has no body' and the wife has to 'pack something up', which usually means a pile of sandwiches with 'something tasty' in them, and she prepares a big hot meal for the evening.

'Something tasty' is the key-phrase in feeding: something solid, preferably meaty, and with a well-defined flavour. The tastiness is increased by a liberal use of sauces and pickles, notably tomato sauce and piccalilli. I used to notice that in the flusher early years of married life my relatives were often frying at tea-times – chops, steak, kidney, chips. By contrast, poor old-age pensioners used sometimes to simulate a tasty meal by dissolving a penny Oxo in warm water, and having it with bread. Meat has been much relied upon since it first became really cheap, and any working-class wife who has known thin times will have a fine knowledge of those cuts which are inexpensive and nourishing and also tasty. The emphasis on tastiness shows itself most clearly in the need to provide 'something for tea', at weekends if not each day. There is a great range of favourite savouries, often by-products – black-puddings, pig's feet, liver, cowheel, tripe, polony, 'ducks', chitterlings (and for special occasions pork-pies, which are extremely popular); and the fishmongers' savouries – shrimps, roe, kippers, and mussels. In our house we lived simply for most of the week; breakfast was usually bread and beef-dripping, dinner a good simple stew; something tasty was provided for the workers at tea-time, but nothing costing more than a few coppers. At the week-end we lived largely, like everyone else except the very poor, and Sunday tea was the peak. By six on that evening the middens up the back had a fine topcoat of empty salmon and fruit tins. Pineapple was the most popular because, in that period of what now seems extraordinarily cheap canned fruit, it could be bought for a few pence (there was a recurrent story that it was really flavoured turnip). Peaches and apricots were more expensive, and needed something approaching an occasion – a birthday or a sudden visit by relatives from a few miles away. The salmon was delicious, especially the red middle-cut; I still find it far 'tastier' than fresh salmon.

During the years in which meat was short, the newer spiced-meat products seem to have been adopted by a large public. I know a family of five where they buy their meat-loaf by the four pound tin; one son-in-law who has his meals there will eat no fresh meat, only a version of Spam, cold or fried. It is not a cheap food, any more than boiled ham or fish-and-chips, which retain their high favour.

The insistence on food which is both solid and enjoyable is not difficult to appreciate – 'as long as y' get some good food inside y', y' can't complain'; you have to ensure plenty of bulk and protein for the heavy workers and as high a measure of tastiness as can be managed. No doubt the effects are less admirable than the aims. When I was a boy my aunts and uncles, in their thirties and forties, all seemed to have false teeth. Was this only due to neglect? (They had corn-trouble, too, from years of ill-fitting shoes.) Yet I remember also that a regular topic of conversation was this one's constipation and that one's 'heartburn': we bought bicarbonate of soda as regularly as firewood. This may be a fancy, but I am often struck by an apparent difference in the fatness of the different classes, say between that of a middle-aged working-class woman and that of a prosperous middle-aged business-man. One has a white and matt quality, the other is tightly rounded, shiny and polished; one makes me think of gallons of tea, hundredweights of bread, and plates of fish-and-chips; the other of steaks in station hotels.

I could continue almost endlessly recalling other individual details which give this kind of domestic life a recognizable quality of its own; the steam-and-soda-and-hashed-meat smell of wash-day, or the smell of clothes drying by the fireside; the Sunday smell of the *News of the World*-mingled-with-roast-beef; the intermittent reading of pieces of old newspaper in the lavatory; the waste of Sunday afternoon, relieved by occasional visits to relatives or to the cemetery, whose gates are flanked by the stalls of flower-sellers and by the workshops of those who sell expensive headstones. Like any life with a firm centre, it has a powerful hold: working-class people themselves are often sentimental about it. In the excesses of poker-work or the ornately frilled cards and hankies sold even today at fairs and seaside booths, there is still embroidered 'Home, sweet Home', or 'Home – the place where we grumble the most and are treated the best'.

This description and the later descriptive passages in this chapter are largely based on memories of twenty years ago, as I have said. I say little about the increased spending-power of working-class people and so about, for example, the effects of labour-saving devices in the home, and so on. This is chiefly because many of us assume today that the effects of these changes on our attitudes are greater than they are. It therefore seems important to stress first how large a part of the basic pattern of working-class life remains as it has been for many years.

This is in many respects a good and comely life, one founded on care, affection, a sense of the small group if not of the individual. It is elaborate and disorderly and yet sober: it is not chintzy or kittenish or whimsical or 'feminized'. The father is a part of the inner life of the home, not someone who spends most of his time miles away earning the money to keep the establishment going: the mother is the working-centre, always with too much to do and with her thoughts revolving almost entirely around the life of this family room (bedrooms are simply places you sleep in). Her 'one hope', as she puts it, is that her daughters and sons will 'soon find a nice lad or lass and make homes of their own'.

Though it may seem muddled and sprawling, the design can be seen, ensured by an unsophisticated and unconscious but still strong sense of what a home is for. Compare it with the kind of public room which may be found in many a café or small hotel today – the walls in several hostile shades of distemper, clashing strips of colour along their centres; cold and ugly plastic door-handles; fussy and meaningless wall lamp-holders; metal tables which invite no one and have their over-vivid colours kicked and scratched away: all tawdry and gimcrack. The materials need not produce this effect; but when they are used by people who have rejected what sense of a whole they had and have no feeling for the new materials, the collapse is evident. In homes, the new things are absorbed into the kind of whole instinctively reached after. The old tradition is being encroached upon, here as in so many other areas. But the strong sense of the importance of home ensures that change is taken slowly: generations of opposing the chief home-breaker – drink – have helped to build a solid resist-ance to new potential destroyers.

c. *Mother*

> I know her scrubbed and sour humble hands
> . . . this monumental
> Argument of the hewn voice, gesture . . .

To write of a working-class mother is to run peculiar risks. We know, if only from the profusion of novels published during the documentary thirties, that she has an honoured place in most accounts of working-class childhoods. Her own menfolk may appear careless of her for much of the time, but like to buy ornaments inscribed 'What is home without a mother', and for years after she has 'gone' will speak lovingly of 'me mam'.

Yet one can have little but admiration for the position such a mother naturally assumes in her household. I am thinking of her chiefly in early-middle or middle age, when she has fully established herself as the mother of the family, when she comes into her own. She is then the pivot of the home, as it is practically the whole of her world. She, more than the father, holds it together; writes with difficulty to a son in the Services or to a daughter working away. She keeps close contact with those other members of the family who live near, with the grandparents, brothers, sisters, and cousins; occasionally she may go to sit with one of them or with a neighbour for an hour. She leaves the outer world of politics and even of the 'news' to her husband; she knows little about his job; such friends as she has from outside are usually his, since on marriage she drops her own.

So far this is too boldly drawn, but it is necessary to establish first the close, the myopic nature of the lives of most working-class mothers. The pressure is so strong that in those who have special troubles or are very poorly gifted imaginatively it can produce a turned-in-upon-itself world into which nothing which does not concern the family penetrates.

It is a hard life, in which it is assumed that the mother will be 'at it' from getting up to going to bed: she will cook, mend, scrub, wash, see to the children, shop, and satisfy her husband's desires. Even today, it is often a life with few modern aids such as vacuum cleaners and electric washers, and yet with more dirt to fight than in the more prosperous districts. Curtains can hardly be kept 'a good colour' even with frequent washing in dolly blue or cream; the fireplace and range may need blackleading and hard 'nursing'. Everywhere the smoke and soot from the nearby factories and railway lines creep in, and most women 'can't abide the thought of dirt getting a hold'.

Some free time can be occupied with darning and patching, rarely with making new clothing for the children. Not many mothers, even if they have worked in a clothing factory, are trained in the making of complete garments. In any case, sewing-machines are expensive and working-class people do not seem to buy them, even by hire-purchase, as readily as they buy articles which more obviously give pleasure to the whole family. Ready-made clothing is inexpensive and attractive. The husband's clothes are knocked about at work, and so the endless patching-up goes on, interspersed with the buying of new articles which, because they are cheap, are not economical and soon show wear.

Partly because the husband is at work but also because women are simply expected to look after such things, it will be the mother who has the long waits in public places, at the doctor's for 'a bottle', at the clinic with a child who has eye-trouble, at the municipal offices to see about the instalment on the electricity bill.

All this is made more difficult because there is in most cases, or has been until the last few years, little room for manoeuvre financially, only just enough to 'wag on'; the housekeeping money is usually 'mortgaged' to a penny or so. To manage on a tight string like this requires considerable skill, and that often comes hard, but come it must or the family is likely to be in trouble. A wife soon takes it for granted – indeed, assumes with marriage – that she will have to 'fadge' to make ends meet. Rowntree pointed out years ago that there is often a period between the growing-up of the children and going on to the old-age pension during which matters are easier. But, in the main, it is a life of 'tightness' and 'contriving'. I often noticed that some of the happier wives were those whose husbands earned just a few shillings above the average for the street, but who in other respects lived in the same manner as the rest. If the husband were a decent sort and let his wife have an extra shilling or two, then she could be relieved of a deal of fine calculation; a sudden call for an electric-light bulb, shoe repairs or a boy's Scout outfit did not cause her serious worry. Partly because ready money in any substantial amount is hard to come by, partly because housewives often do not see just how awkward a position they are putting themselves into by the slow mounting of a debt, the most elaborate shifts and devices can be carried out with pathetic concentration. I know one housewife who now spends about eight pounds a week at the grocer's and could in these easier days pay it off weekly: but the habits of the thirties cannot be shaken off and she can never bring herself to clear it; she is happier on the 'paying something off' system than she would be in paying outright. At my grandmother's we were not living 'on relief' but, like many around us, we were 'a bit short'. For years during the early thirties, I queued on Friday evenings for the family groceries; each weekly bill was between fifteen and twenty shillings, and always we carried something over. In my self-conscious teens I had a regular sick envy of those who paid off cheerfully, a horrid shyness at going through the weekly form of words, 'Grandma says she'll leave five shillings till next week'. More recently, I know of one woman who slowly built up a debt of about one pound at the butcher's and then suddenly realized how large it was. She saw no way of finding a spare pound all at once, and simply stopped going for meat. But her family was still registered with him, so that she must have found it difficult to manage through the winter of 1952, when meat was none too plentiful. The butcher, meanwhile, would have been glad to see her and suggest an arrangement, but he knew she would not come. Any similar shopkeeper can give plenty of other examples. This is a situation which full employment and Welfare State arrangements have done a great deal to alter, but not as much as might be thought; the old habits persist.

Usually the wife has to operate on her own this narrow system of weekly finance. That is why there is still strong competition between small shopkeepers over a penny off this or the willingness to make up small portions of that; these things may decide a sale. Twopence a pound on meat may seem negligible but can cause a bad wobble in the week's planning; so can the sudden call to 'rig out' a boy for school camp or a girl for the Sunday-school concert, or for a present to a cousin who is getting married. There are always the clubs, or those drapers and fancy-goods shops which, whether they take agents' checks or not, are a shilling cheaper than the big shops in town and may let you take articles away on a small payment. Almost always their materials are by no means as good as those which do cost only a shilling more: presents are shoddy and break, chromium is thin and peels soon. The clubs, or check-trading, tend to become a habit and the house-to-house agents are adept at persuading clients to 'keep the account open' continuously, so that in many cases more money is leaking away weekly in this way than can really be spared. The cycle goes on: if the family is suddenly hard-up, then it is usually the mother who goes short, who 'pinches herself' on food or clothes.

Life is very much a week-by-week affair, with little likelihood of saving a lump sum to 'fall back upon'. There may be a tin box on the mantelpiece in which savings for the holiday are put, but this is not usual. There is no bank acount, no sick pay except that from the 'National Health' and perhaps something from a club, and these come to little enough. You may still see housewives queueing at a quarter to nine each Tuesday outside the post-offices to claim their family allowances. If 'the mester is laid off' there may be real distress. The old habit of looking well after the wage-earners, particularly in food, is still alive; so is the stress on the need for all to 'pull together': the boat is likely to founder quickly otherwise. A wife is happy if she can 'manage' or 'get along'; if she can find something left over for extras at the end of the week, she is very content.

Here, as in most aspects of domestic life, the wife is by tradition responsible; the husband is out, wage-earning. He wants food and his own sort of relaxation when he comes home. I suppose this explains why, as it seems to me, the wife is often expected to be responsible for contraceptive practice. Most non-Catholic working-class families accept contraception as an obvious convenience, but both husbands and wives are shy of clinics where advice is given, unless they are driven there by near-desperation. The husband's shyness and an assumption that this is really her affair often ensure that he expects her to take care of it, that he 'can't be bothered with it'. She has rarely been told anything before marriage, and the amount she has picked up from older girls or married women at work or nearby varies enormously. She must take what advice she can early unless there are to be more children than either she or her husband want. When she has done that her knowledge of the possibilities is likely to be limited to coitus interruptus, the best-known type of pessary, and the sheath. Husbands tend not to like sheaths – 'they take away the pleasure'; she may be embarrassed in buying either those or pessaries, and both are dear; coitus interruptus is probably the commonest practice.

But to use any of these methods requires a rigid discipline, a degree of sustained competence many wives are hardly capable of. She forgets just once or 'lets herself go', or a sheath is cheap and bursts or the husband demands awkwardly after a night at the club. How often, therefore, it is assumed that any children after the first one or two were 'not intended'. I am inclined to think that among, say, the middle-classes the child who was 'not intended' is apt to arrive when the parents are about forty. They have had two or three children during their late twenties and early thirties and their contraceptive practice has thereafter been effective. Perhaps by the time they reach forty they feel safer and grow careless. With the working-classes the pattern seems to be different: unless a miscarriage is procured, the first unintended child is likely to arrive only a year or two after the others. It is usually accepted 'philosophically'; after all, 'what did yer get married for?' It is a 'philosophic' acceptance but one without much sentimentality; 'kids are a trouble', they mean more work and less money to go round. But they receive the same indulgences and smothering attention.

It is evident that a working-class mother will age early, that at thirty, after having two or three children, she will have lost most of her sexual attraction; that between thirty-five and forty she rapidly becomes the shapeless figure the family know as 'our mam'. She went into the world earlier than girls of other classes, began going around with boys at sixteen and was probably 'courting regular' at eighteen. At that time she was using freely a cheap and restricted range of cosmetics – lipstick, 'rouge' and the cheaper perfumes, powders and creams. She may practise some of this simple cosmetic routine for a time after marriage, but it fairly soon ends, except for a rather heavy and crude 'rouging' on special occasions – a 'rouging' that gives to faces insufficiently prepared the faintly Grock-like quality which some people take as evidence of the coarseness of the working-classes when they see them on holiday.

By forty-five or fifty, ailments begin: you hear during the poorer periods that she is 'nobbut middling' just now. There may be rheumatism, or a regular back-ache from a twenty-year-old undetected prolapse. The big fear, one which recurs constantly in conversation, is of a growth, visualized as some huge and ramping cancerous organism; or of a 'stone', imagined as a great hard pebble. I remember watching a middle-aged mother with a full shopping-basket passing through Hunslet Feast (fair) one Friday obviously 'ailing' and worried. She was attracted by the patter of a vast, screamingly and coarsely opulent woman in a herbalist stall. After a few moments of hesitation she went nearer and whispered her problem. She was sold for six shillings a packet of some sort of crystals . . . 'Never mind what the doctors tell you, me dear. Take these twice a day in a tumbler of warm water and they'll wash the stone away. You'll know no more about it. It'll all come away in the toilet, dear.'

There is little time for 'doctoring'; if things are bad she might get a bottle from the surgery, but usually the long wait there or a disinclination to keep on troubling the doctor (and something of a doubt that he can really do much to help) ensure that most times nothing is done. Now and again there will be trials of recommended patent medicines. Most doctors in working-class districts know that there is usually little they can do. Their middle-aged housewife patients look after themselves badly, work too long or hard, do not know how to relax, take insufficient sleep, have a badly balanced diet. They expect to have to go on all the time, 'fadging', often muddling because the demands are complex and heavy and yet must be met somehow. Always at the back of the wife's mind, though probably not consciously, is the knowledge that if 'anything happens' to the husband she will have to 'turn to' and manage on her own, finding what 'charring' she can to supplement her pension.

During the years in which my mother had the three of us on her own, she was never strong enough, since she had acute bronchial trouble, to do any outside work. She managed with surprising skill on a weekly twenty-odd shillings from 'the Guardians' (some of this was in the form of coupons exchangeable at specified grocers'). Surprising to a spectator, but not to her: she had been a gay young girl, I believe, but by this time had lost most of her high spirits. She was well past the striking of attitudes about her situation, and though she would gladly take a pair of old shoes or a coat, she thanked no one for their pity or their admiration; she was without sentimentality about her position and never pretended to do more than go through with it. It was too much an unrelieved struggle to be at all enjoyable, and three young children, always hungry for more food and pleasures than she could afford, were not – except occasionally – rewarding companions. She helped herself along by smoking Woodbines – furtively, in case 'They' found out: my brother was trained to put the twopenny packet in the drawer without a word if he came back from the shop to find a visitor at home. The tiny house was damp and swarming with cockroaches; the earth-closet was a stinking mire in bad weather. Food was unvaried but a lot more nourishing than it would have been with many mothers in that situation. My mother had firmness and intelligence enough to resist all our demands for fish-and-chips and tea, and we drank nothing but cocoa. We had a succession of cheap stews with vegetables throughout each week: I remember someone bringing (I must have been about six at the time) a small box of assorted biscuits to the house, and how dazzled we were by them. For a tea-time treat, we occasionally had sweetened condensed milk on bread. Pocket-money was one penny a week for the whole family, so our separate turns came up every three weeks. We were usually advised to buy something that could be shared, and we usually objected. We were always 'well turned out', well darned throughout the year, and had new outfits at Whitsun; the last I remember were sailor-suits with whistles for the two boys.

On one occasion my mother, fresh from drawing her money, bought herself a small treat, something which must have been a reminder of earlier pleasures – a slice or two of boiled ham or a few shrimps. We watched her like sparrows and besieged her all through tea-time until she shocked us by bursting out in real rage. There was no compensation; she did not want to give us this, and there could be no easy generosity in the giving. We got some, though we sensed that we had stumbled into something bigger than we understood.

This is an extreme case, though one in the true line of the tradition. We need to avoid any suggestion of a sense of heroism in the people (and there are men, as well as women) who actually live this kind of life. It is challenging, and the lines on the face of an old working-class woman are often magnificently expressive – but they are hard earned. We should not try to add a glamour to such a face ; it has its fineness without any artificial light. It is often a face with a scaly texture and the lines, looked at closely, have grime in them; the hands are bony claws covered with densely lined skin, and again the dirt is well-ingrained there: years of snatched washes, usually in cold water, have caused that. The face has two marked lines of force – from the sides of the nose down to the compressed lips; they tell of years of 'calculating'. Or notice that many old working-class women have an habitual gesture which illuminates the years of their life behind. D. H. Lawrence remarked it in his mother: my grandmother's was a repeated tapping of her fingers on the arm of her chair, a tapping which accompanied an endless working out of something in her head; she had had years of making out for a large number on very little. In others you see a rhythmic smoothing of the hand down the chair-arm, as though to smooth everything out and make it workable; in others there is a working of the lips or a steady rocking. None of these could be called neurotic gestures, nor are they symptoms of acute fear; they help the constant calculation.

Today, if I hear someone using words like 'sorrow' and 'misery' freely, they usually sound slightly archaic; they are to be reserved for special events. To my grandmother they were regular words, together with 'care' and 'hardship', used as often and as meaningfully as 'nuisance' and 'awkward' among many of the people I know today. When my grandmother spoke of someone 'taking the bread from her mouth' she was not being dramatic or merely figurative; she was speaking from an unbroken and still relevant tradition, and her speech at such times had something of the elemental quality of Anglo-Saxon poetry:

I can utter a true song about myself . . . how in toilsome days I often suffered a time of hardship, how I have borne bitter sorrow in my breast.

So a working-class mother carries on. She has her 'treats' occasionally, as the men do. Her greatest pleasure, as Dr Zweig notes, is to be 'waited upon' in some way; it may be by the daughters and the father taking over the house for a day, it may be by going on a day trip, with large knife-and-fork meals laid on at intervals: it may be simply that she is taken to the pictures by the father. But in general she carries on with work until she becomes a grandmother, and then she has new calls for her help.

There are some who become bitten-in and make it all a harsh ritual and their toil a badge of dreadful honour; there are some who are shiftless: for most there is, in varying degrees, a steady and self-forgetful routine, one devoted to the family and beyond proud self-regard. Behind it, making any vague pity irrelevant, is pride in the knowledge that so much revolves around them. This can make the most unpromising and unprepossessing young woman arrive at a middle-age in which she is, when in the midst of her home and family, splendidly 'there' and, under all the troubles, content. Her husband may be the 'mester' in the household, but she is not a door-mat; she and he know her value and virtue if she is, in her way, a 'good mother'. The nagging wife is still one of the major villains in truly popular art.

But how far is all this being transmitted, it may be asked, to the teen-age girls who walk the streets in the evening? They seem to fill the space between leaving school and marriage with thrice-weekly visits to 'musicals' and 'romantic dramas' at the pictures, with fantasy love-stories, and with successive hops at the 'Palais', the 'Mecca', the 'Locarno', or the Public Baths. Their jobs rarely engage more than a small portion of their personalities, they seem to have little interest as committed individuals in anything, they take no interest in Trade Union activities and little in the home. Surely they are most of them flighty, careless, and inane?

I shall be discussing that aspect in later chapters. Here the emphasis is on the other side, on why matters are not always as bad as they at first appear. Girls like these have only a brief flowering period, only a few years during which they have no responsibilities and some spare money. A surprisingly high proportion of them, in view of the forces which discourage it, take up healthy outdoor activity. For most, what is so conveniently and insistently offered is sufficient, and these are indoor activities. These girls are often bored by their work; there are plenty of people who know the easier ways of winning from them the money in their pockets. They seem soon to be enveloped in the chrysalis of an adolescent daydream. Everything they choose to do seems urban and trivial; it would be difficult to hold their attention for long to anything not part of the dream.

Yet there is rarely any revolt against home, even though there may be little apparent positive response to it. Home's 'alright' (the adjective is used to indicate something you accept but have no enthusiasm for); you live there; you do not usually leave it; nor do you think about it or stay in it if you can get out at nights. But it seems to me that this gay, and it is in many ways gay, life of the teens is not regarded as finally 'real', as the real business of life. It is enjoyed and not regretted; it rarely affects the sense that, after all, the real business of life is getting married and having a family. It is certainly 'life' in a sense that school never was; you learn a lot in this period about what life really is and means, through gossip and the talk at work; you enjoy yourself. But real life, questions of fun apart, is marriage: for both sexes the main dividing-line in a working-class life is this, not a change of job or town or going up to a university or qualifying in a profession. Marriage is the end of this temporary freedom for a woman and the beginning of a life in which 'scraping' will be normal. With most this pattern is taken for granted; the free period is a kind of butterfly flight, giddy while it lasts but short. There is a wealth of meaning in the phrase used as soon as a girl has found a man she is going to marry, 'I'm going steady now'.

Once that happens, she begins to draw upon her older roots. She has some hard lessons to learn and there are bound to be awkward periods before she finally settles. The more careless refuse to learn, go on smoking and 'picture-going' while the kids knock around scruffily. Most pick up a rhythm which goes back beyond the dance-tunes and the cinema's lovers. Watch the way a girl who, in view of the extent to which her taste is assaulted by the flashy and trivial, should have an appalling sense of style can impose on even the individually ugly items she buys that sense of what it is important to re-create in a living-room. Watch the way she handles a baby; not the more obvious features, the carelessness of hygiene and the trivialities, but the acceptance of a child in the crook of the arm or in a bath by the fire.

She has usually had some training before leaving school, helping a little with the cleaning at home, looking after younger brothers, pushing out their own or the neighbour's baby. But this may not amount to a lot, and after six or seven years of determined trivialization the surprising fact is that she takes up the threads so well. That is because they have never been broken, but only casually covered over. Those young wives who stay at work until the children come, or after, if grandma or a nursery will look after them, are not usually revolting against the demands of marriage but rather prolonging, for what they know must be a limited period, the time when they can have spare money for little luxuries – fairly frequent boiled ham at two shillings a quarter or fish-and-chips for supper two or three nights a week. When that goes, it goes : most working-class girls do not much pine for their lost freedom; they never regarded it as other than temporary.

They do mishandle their children by 'educated' standards; I mean by the standards usually advocated in modern books on child-care. It is a working-class tradition of long standing to indulge not only children but young people all the way up to marriage. Babies are smothered with love and attention, not allowed to cry, stuffed till their little bellies ache and then given dubious remedies in sixpenny packets; even today many of them are rarely left without a 'dummy' and that probably dipped in syrup, jogged continually in their magnificent prams, hardly ever left alone by mother, by father when he gets home from work, by grandparents, and kept up far too late. Later, though sometimes the girls may be expected to help a little in the house and the boys may take on a 'newspaper-round', the remarkable feature, in view of how much the mother has to do and how short is spare money, is that they are asked to do so little and that spare-time money-making is so often regarded as for their own pockets. How often do the children wash up? How often are they bought disproportionately expensive presents – bikes of the most splendid kind and prams almost full-size? Parents expect and encourage the children, even in adolescence, to do little to support the house in labour or money. Most of what a working-class girl knows on marrying about the running of a home she has usually assimilated unconsciously. She may be 'earning good money' and costing a lot to keep, but she is probably paying less than she costs to her mother. If this is a blind selfishness, it is a selfishness which the parents condone and support; there is all the rest of life to come and you cannot do much about that; you must let them "ave a good time while they can'; after all, 'yer' only young once'.

D. *Father*

Like his wife, a working-class man often seems to me almost physically recognizable. He tends to be small and dark, lined and sallow about the face by the time he has passed thirty. The bone-structure of the face and neck then shows clearly, with a suggestion of the whippet about it. In general, these physical marks are observable early, and remain throughout life. Thus – though this is lightly put – if I or some of my professional acquaintances who were born into the working-classes put on the sort of flat cap and neckerchief which go with looking 'county', or if we leave our collars open, the sit of the cap and the neckerchief, or the structure of the bones round the neck make us look, not like the sporting middle-classes, but like working-men on a day off.

The point of departure for an understanding of the position of the working-class father in his home is that he is the boss there, the 'master in his own house'. This he is by tradition, and neither he nor his wife would want the tradition changed. She will often refer to him before others as 'Mr W.' or 'the mester'. This does not mean that he is by any means an absolute ruler or that he gets or expects his own way in everything. It often accompanies a carefulness, a willingness to help and be 'considerate', to be 'a good husband'. In the lazy or insensitive, it may support a considerable selfishness or near-brutality. In either case, there is likely to be a deference to him as the main breadwinner and heavy worker, even though these assumptions are not always correct today. He remains the chief contact with the outer world which puts the money into the house.

There is often a kind of roughness in his manner which a middle-class wife would find insupportable. A wife will say how worried she is because something is amiss, and 'the mester will be mad' when he gets home; he may 'tell yer off' harshly or in a few cases may even 'bash' you, especially if he has had a couple of pints on the way from work. Or middle-aged wives will say to a younger one, "'e's good to yer, i'n't 'e?', meaning that he is not likely to become violent in word or act, or that he does not leave his wife alone almost every-night, or that he will 'see 'er out' if she gets into difficulties with the housekeeping allowance. This is in part a heavy peasant crudeness in personal relations and expression, and clearly does not necessarily indicate a lack of affection, or a helplessness on the wife's part. The man who is able to growl is also able to defend; he has something of the cock about him. Hence, rough boys are often admired; the head-shaking over them is as proud as it is rueful – "'e's a real *lad*,' people say.

A husband is therefore not really expected to help about the house. If he does, his wife is pleased; but she is unlikely to harbour a grudge if he does not. 'When all's said and done', most things about a house are woman's work: 'Oh, that's not a man's job,' a woman will say, and would not want him to do too much of that kind of thing for fear he is thought womanish. Or the highest praise will take the form, "'E's ever so good about the 'ouse. Just like a woman': if he does help much he is doing it in place of the woman whose job it should be; the household chores are not joint responsibilities.

So it is a positive act of helpfulness if he decides to help with washing up or the baby. In many cases a wife would not only 'never dream' of having his help with the washing, but does not feel that she can ''ave the washing around' when he is at home. There are often difficulties of drying-space, especially on rainy days, that are aggravated by the need for a complicated system of putting the damp stuff round the fire on a clothes-horse and taking it off again into a basket or zinc bath at the times when the husband wants to 'see t'fire'.

There are many husbands who regard all the family's money affairs as a shared concern, who hand over their wage-packet on Friday night and leave its disposition to their wives. But an assumption just as characteristic, in my experience, is that the wage-packet is the husband's, and that he gives his wife a fixed amount for housekeeping each week. There are many households where the wife does not know how much her husband earns. This does not necessarily mean that she is poorly treated. 'Oh, 'e sees me alright,' or ''e treats me alright,' she will say, meaning that she is not left short but implying, in the phrasing itself, that the distribution of the wage lies with him. The wife is often responsible, out of this fixed amount, for any replacements – of crockery, furnishings, and so on; the more thoughtful of these husbands will be open to suggestion, will promise something out of the next payment of overtime. Quite often the wife's share of any overtime money only arrives quixotically. Sometimes she feels unable to discuss family financial problems with her husband, and this may extend even to such a question as whether it is possible to send a child to the grammar-school. There will be discussion of a kind, and particularly if it has to be decided whether a child can be kept at a grammar-school after sixteen, but it is not usually a precise discussion of financial ways and means, of how this can be cut here or that pleasure reduced there.

If he is on the dole, and the same assumptions naturally apply whether he is in that position through ill health or ill luck or shiftlessness, both husband and wife assume that he must still have his pocket-money. Self-respect is involved; 'a man can't be without money in 'is pocket'; he would then feel less than a man, feel 'tied to' his wife and inferior to her, and such a situation is against nature. He must have money for cigarettes and beer, perhaps even for an occasional bet; the amount regularly spent each week, even by men out of work, would seem in many cases excessive to, say, the professional middle-classes. Fifteen cheap cigarettes a day seems normal, and those cost about thirteen shillings a week; for a man out of work and drawing the dole, one pound a week for pocket-money is the figure I most commonly hear nowadays. Such things as cigarettes and beer, it is felt, are part of life; without them, life would not be life ; there are rarely any other major interests to make these pleasures less relevant and worth forgoing. It is, I suppose, the sense that such things are part of the minimum staple of life which makes many families, even where the husband is working well and has plenty of money in his pocket, maintain the old arrangement whereby the wife buys 'with the groceries' – that is, out of the housekeeping money – a proportion of the husband's weekly cigarettes.

I noted that girls are usually indulged by parents, but that, especially before they leave school, they are expected to do more about the house than their brothers. A boy soon acquires something of the feeling that 'it's different for men' which he will have in greater strength when he is grown-up. On leaving school the attitude quickly strengthens; he is, probably for the first time, close to his father and finds his father ready to be close to him; they now share the real world of work and men's pleasures.

All this is still largely true and must be put first, but has much too strongly implied that the husband is selfish and leaves all the troubles to his wife. The basic assumption is that the man is master of the house. Some of the expressions of this assumption, and these not the more unusual ones, might seem grossly unfair to the women. Yet there are a great many husbands who are thoughtful and helpful, who spend much of their free time at home, making and mending. Even so, there is the sense that the father occupies a special position. There are some things, difficult and men's things – such as chopping wood – which only he can do; there are others which he may do without undermining the order, such as getting himself off to work or bringing his wife a cup of tea in bed occasionally.

Among some younger husbands there are signs of a striking change in the basic attitude. Some wives press for it and find their husbands ready to modify the outlook they inherited from their fathers. Here as elsewhere, no doubt, educational improvements are quietly but pervasively promoting a different attitude among those who are ready to be affected. More particularly, a few husbands and wives may be influenced by the example of some young professional and lower-middle-class husbands who have learned, especially since the war, to help their wives as partial substitute for the daily help their class can no longer always afford. Some working-class husbands will share the washing up if their wives go out to work, or will take turns with the baby if their job releases them early and not too tired. But many wives come home from work just as tired as their husbands and 'set to' to do all the housework without help from them. And not many working-class husbands will help their wives by pushing the baby round the streets in its pram. That is still thought 'soft', and most wives would sympathize with the view.

If a wife has a conscious wish, it is probably not for a husband who does such things, but rather for one who remains a husband in much the old sense, yet 'a good one' in the old sense, for one who is 'steady' and 'a good worker', one who is not likely to land her suddenly in poverty, who is likely to be kept on if sackings begin, who brings home his money regularly, who is generous with his bonuses.

Emotionally, his best contribution is to be, without being soft or 'womanish', ready to agree, to live according to the idea that happy married life is 'a matter of give and take'. A great many, perhaps most, husbands do this: working-class people have a host of jokes about marriage, but not against marriage. They are not harassed by the ambivalences of some more self-conscious people who are so shocked at the thought that they may end up in the bourgeois satisfaction of their parents that it takes them years to realize that they like being married, and even enjoy its ordinary duties and everyday necessities. Working-class men and women still accept marriage as normal and 'right', and that in their early twenties. What a husband is earning at twenty-one, he is likely to be earning at fifty-one; he probably married a girl from exactly his own class, and they set about 'getting a home of their own together' and living their lives inside it.

E. *The Neighbourhood*

Home may be private, but the front door opens out of the living-room on to the street, and when you go down the one step or use it as a seat on a warm evening you become part of the life of the neighbourhood.

To a visitor they are understandably depressing, these massed proletarian areas; street after regular street of shoddily uniform houses intersected by a dark pattern of ginnels and snickets (alley-ways) and courts; mean, squalid, and in a permanent half-fog; a study in shades of dirty-grey, without greenness or the blueness of sky; degrees darker than the north or west of the town, than 'the better end'. The brickwork and the woodwork are cheap; the wood goes too long between repaintings – landlords are not as anxious to keep up the value of the property as are owner-occupiers. The nearest park or green open space is some distance away, but the terraces are gap-toothed with sour and brick-bespattered bits of waste-ground and there is a piece of free ground half a mile away, called 't' Moor'. Evocative name: it is a clinkered six-acre stretch surrounded by works and grimy pubs, with a large red-brick urinal at its edge.

The houses are fitted into the dark and lowering canyons between the giant factories and the services which attend them; 'the barracks of an industry' the Hammonds called them. The goods-lines pass on embankments in and around, level with many of the bedroom windows, carrying the products of the men's work to South Africa, Nigeria, Australia. The viaducts interweave with the railway lines and with the canals below; the gas-works fit into a space somewhere between them all, and the pubs and graceless Methodist chapels stick up at intervals throughout. The green stuff of the region forces its way where it can – and that is almost everywhere – in stunted patches. Rough sooty grass pushes through the cobbles; dock and nettle insist on a defiant life in the rough and trampled earth-heaps at the corners of the waste-pieces, undeterred by 'dog-muck', cigarette packets, old ashes; rank elder, dirty privet, and rosebay willow-herb take hold in some of the 'backs' or in the walled-off space behind the Corporation Baths. All day and all night the noises and smells of the district – factory hooters, trains shunting, the stink of the gas-works – remind you that life is a matter of shifts and clockings-in-and-out. The children look improperly fed, inappropriately clothed, and as though they could do with more sunlight and green fields.

But to the insider, these are small worlds, each as homogeneous and well-defined as a village. Down below, on the main road running straight into town, the bosses' cars whirr away at five o'clock to converted farm-houses ten miles out in the hills; the men stream up into their district. They know it, as do all its inhabitants, in intimate detail – automatically slipping up a snicket here or through a shared lavatory block there; they know it as a group of tribal areas. Pitt Street is certainly one of ours; just as certainly as Prince Consort Street next to it is not, is over the boundary in another parish. In my own part of Leeds I knew at ten years old, as did all my contemporaries, both the relative status of all the streets around us and where one part shaded into another. Our gang fights were tribal fights, between streets or groups of streets.

Similarly, one knows practically everybody, with an intimacy of detail – that these people have a son who 'got on' or emigrated; that those have a daughter who went wrong or one who married away and is doing well; that this old man living alone on his pension shops at the horsemeat place in town and smokes a sixpenny mixture of herbs; that this old housewife is a fusspot and scours her window-ledges and steps twice a week, on her knees on a bit of old harding, and even washes the brick-work up to shoulder height; that this young woman had her black child after the annual visit of the circus a few years ago; that this woman's idiot child can be trusted to run errands; that that old woman is always ready to sit up with an invalid for 'a consideration'; that this man is a specially skilled worker and has been doing well for some time, so that he takes his family for a lavish week at Blackpool each summer and bought a television set before anyone else; they have weekly booked seats at the Empire Theatre, the lad gets more ice-cream than any of his mates, and more than usually expensive presents at Christmas and birthdays.

This is an extremely local life, in which everything is remarkably near. The houses, I said, open on to the street; the street itself, compared with those of suburbia or the new housing-estates, is narrow; the houses opposite are only just over the cobbles and the shops not much farther. For the things you want only periodically you may drop down two or three hundred yards to the shops on the main tram-route or go into town; day-to-day services are just over the road or round the corner, and practically every street has its corner-shop, usually a general grocer's or paper-shop. The paper-shop window is a litter of odds-and-bobs; if the light is kept on at nights the children make it a meeting-place; a frame-full of little sixpence-a-week advertisements on the wall at the side makes an exchange and mart for the area, full of items 'in v.g. condition' or 'cheap for quick sale' or 'almost new': 'Blue Court Shoes, almost new, 10/-'; 'Boy's

Tweed Coat (fit 14 years), 12/6; 3 ft Divan (cost £12), £4 – apply after 7'.

The grocer, whose corner-shop is the housewives' club as it is in most kinds of district, will hardly prosper unless he respects the forms of the neighbourhood. Newcomers may pin to the shelf at the back of the counter one of those notices which the local jobbing printers produce, 'Please Do Not Ask for Credit As A Refusal Might Offend', but whether the notice stays up or not most of them have to start giving 'tick' before long. Many housewives remember how obliging their grocer was during the depression: he knew they had not enough money to pay off the bill each week, that he might have to wait for months; but if he did not serve them there would have been no customers, so he kept on and weathered it, or shut up shop after a time. Now he goes on providing an almost seven-days-a-week service, with Sunday morning as one of the busiest; and if you do find him shut, you can go round to the house-door.

He may be honest or up to all sorts of shifty tricks, but his relation to his customers is different from that of the shop-keeper in middle-class areas. There he tends to assume, in manner at least, a lower status than his customers; he may earn more than many of them do but he acts as their servant and calls them 'madam'. Here the shop-keeper is among his own class, though his income may sometimes be above the average for the neighbourhood. In such a case, since he has the tastes and habits of the neighbourhood, he is a lucky man, one of the 'better-off'; he lives in the same kind of house, sends his children to the same school, dresses similarly, but has money to save or for extra pleasures.

Unless he gets a council-house, a working-class man is likely to live in his local area, perhaps even in the house he 'got the keys for' the night before his wedding, all his life. He has little call to move if he is a general labourer, and perhaps hardly more if he is skilled, since his skill is likely to be in a trade for which several nearby works, or some only a tram-ride away, provide vacancies. He is very unlikely to be the only one doing his kind of job in the area. He is more likely to change his place of work than his place of living; he belongs to a district more than to one works. He may have a cousin who teaches, married a girl in Nottingham and settled there; he may have a brother who met a girl in Scotland during the war and brought her down here. But by and large the family live near and have 'always' lived near: each Christmas Day they all go to tea at Grandma's.

Nor does he travel a great deal, in spite of the great changes in transport during the last fifty years. There are 'chara' trips, football excursions and perhaps an annual holiday, and occasional train trips to the funeral or wedding of some member of a branch of the family forty or fifty miles away. Before he married, he may possibly have gone to the Continent, or seen some distant parts of England by push-bike; he probably travelled a great deal during war-service or National Service. But after marriage, and if we leave aside the occasions just mentioned, the speed and the extent of his travel are not much different from what they would have been thirty years ago. The car has not reduced distance for him; the trains are no faster than they were three-quarters of a century ago. True, he will usually travel by bus if he has to travel, but the point is that he normally has to undertake very little travel except within a mile or two. The local quality of the day-to-day life of a working-class man is well-illustrated by the way he will still trudge half-way across town with a handcart or old pram, transporting a sixth-hand kitchen table he has picked up cheap from someone who knew someone. It will take the better part of an evening, but seems normal procedure. One is reminded of Tess of the d'Urbervilles moving from one valley to another and seeming, to herself, to move from one country to another. The contrast is not so acute, but the working-man in this instance is nearer Tess than he is to the city solicitor who runs out seven miles for a round of golf. For plenty of working-class people a bus journey to relatives half-way across the county is still a matter for considerable thought and upheaval.

Their experience of public transport is so often hectic. If a man travels to work, he probably goes on a crowded workmen's train; or he goes on an equally crowded tram to the football match. If his wife goes shopping in town, she usually goes at just the time when lots of others from her neighbourhood are free to do the same – that is, on Saturday afternoon; if the family go to the sea they will travel on a packed 'trip' or Bank Holiday train. Working-class men are likely to have quiet transport only when they are off work through illness, and the rest are still working.

Life centres on the groups of known streets, on their complex and active group life. Think, for example, of the mass of financial arrangements which are transacted between house and house, the insurance collectors, the clothing clubs, the 'diddlems', the Christmas clubs, the 'Snowballs', the 'draws' of all kinds. Sixpence a week is given to a man known for years who comes on his bike in a worn mackintosh and remembers to ask how the rheumatism is; the woman three doors up is paid a shilling a week for a chromium lamp chosen from a colourful catalogue, or for a 'check' taken out to get someone a set of clothes. The check scheme may be managed from an office in town or fifty miles away; what these people know is that Mrs Jackson, who has been a neighbour for years, is running it and 'speaks well of it'.

There are the men's Masonic-type organizations, the Royal and Antediluvian Order of Buffaloes and the Independent Order of Odd Fellows, with complicated systems of dues and payments out. There are numerous whist-drives, arranged by a variety of organizations; they seem to attract particularly housewives over thirty-five, those whose children can be left on their own or whose husbands have died and left them lonely. They sit very happily, talking in the intervals and enjoying the mild excitement of the chance of a prize. There is usually a sharp-eyed woman who is all out for prizes, who sets an uncomfortable pace and is likely to 'tell off' her partners if they are silly enough to revoke. As they come home you will almost certainly hear someone say, 'Did y' see that woman in dark blue? Wasn't she *keen*? Ah go for the company and ah like a game . . . ah can't abide these *keen* women.' There are the Coronation and Victory parties, arranged by single streets. A village may have a Coronation festival and still manage to act roughly as a unit; in cities the County Borough Council will organize festivities in the parks, and the working-classes will partake of them. But they never feel that it is really their show; it may be a democratic item of organization, but is not a really communal act: for that one must, in these cities, think by streets.

We may come closer by looking through the eyes of the child glanced at earlier. He is, say, a boy of eleven going to the paper-shop for his Saturday magazine, for the *Wizard* or the *Hotspur*. Here he passes a shop where they never grumble at being asked to sell penny-worths of sweets, here a pal's father smoking in the doorway in his shirtsleeves, after the last shift before the weekend; here a broken-down wooden fence out of which large spiders can be teased; here the off-licence with its bell clanging as someone comes out with a small jug of vinegar.

There are the varieties of light he will know: the sun forcing its way down as far as the ground-floor windows on a very sunny afternoon, the foggy grey of November over the slates and chimneys, the misty evenings of March when the gangs congregate in the watery yellow light of the kicked and scratched gas-lamp. Or the smells: the beer-and-Woodbine smell of the men on Saturday nights, the cheap-powder-and-cream smell of his grown-up sisters, fish-and-chips, the fresh starchiness of new clothes at Whitsun, the pervasive aura of urine – dog, cat, and human. Most attractive of all, a scene with noise, light, and smell – between eleven and twelve on a sunny Sunday morning, when all doors are open and most steps occupied; the roast beef gives out its flavour from almost every house, the wirelesses mix their noises with each other, you can hear families talking or laughing or quarrelling. But there is little quarrelling just now; over almost all is a sense of ease, recreation, and good food to come.

A few years ago he would have known the 'tingle-aireys' (barrel-organs or street-pianos); they were hired by the day from a depot in town by seedy old men, and provided working-class housewives with their morning music before the wireless made the Light Pro-gramme and Radio Luxembourg available. They had a flighty and apparently uncertain manner of playing, all runs and cascades inside a regular series of great swings of melody; every tune was translated into an affair of burplings and flutings, of trollopy flirtings and gurgly runs, with a particularly skittish twirl at the end of each movement. If I hear *Valencia* or *I left my heart in Avalon* nowadays, no matter how played, I hear it poignantly as the street-pianos played it. They have gone, but little hand-operated roundabouts on carts still come round, announced by a great clanging bell; and the rag-and-bone men still shout out offers of goldfish for old clothes and jam-jars.

There are the boy's odder pleasures of taste, not so much the ordinary toffees and boiled sweets, nor even the sherbet-fountains, monkey nuts, and aniseed balls, but the stuff of which each generation of boys transmits the secret – a penny stick of licorice or some cin-namon root from the chemist, two pennyworth of broken locust, a portion of chips 'with some scraps, please', well soused with salt and vinegar and eaten out of a piece of newspaper which is licked at the end. Eaten in this way, as you slowly walk down the pavement at night, they are delicious.

There is the animal life of the neighbourhood: the crowd of domestic pets, with mongrel dogs the most interesting, though cats are more numerous than dogs. The starlings occupy the public buildings in town, but sparrows abound here and occasional pigeons raid the cobblestones; mice can be found in the communal middens, and ladybirds have a way of appearing in the mucky bits of back-garden; at the end of the yard may be an orange-box for a few rabbits or an elaborately tiered series of crates housing budgerigars.

There are the occasional special excitements – a funeral or a wedding in the street, a chimney on fire, a coalman's horse down on the icy cobbles, an attempted gassing in the kitchen oven, a family row which can be heard from half a dozen doors away on each side. Most absorbing of all to a boy are the games of the street, with the lamp-post taking the place of the tree on a village green. Between five and thirteen, roughly, you play with your own sex. Games change as the year unfolds, following the products of the season (e.g. 'conkers'), or simply by the boys' own intuitively followed rhythm. At one time everyone is playing 'taws', with his marbles ranked in prestige according to age and killing power; quite suddenly marbles go and everybody wants a threepenny peashooter. Occasionally new amusements have a vogue, like the yo-yo of the thirties, but usually these are only temporary. Games should normally require no equipment other than a ball or stick; they should make use of available materials, of the lamp-posts, the flagstones, and the flat ends of houses. Hoops and shuttlecocks have almost entirely gone, and whips-and-tops are not so popular now; but 'piseball', 'tig', hopscotch across the flags and a great number of games involving running round the lamp-posts or in and out of the closet-areas, such as 'Cowboys and Indians', are still popular. Girls still like skipping-ropes, and almost peculiar to them is the game of dressing-up – trailing round the streets in grown-ups' cast-off clothes and old lace, as 'a wedding'. Now and again a couple of boys set to work in a back-yard and make a 'bogey' out of a couple of planks and the wheels off an old pram: then they race down the pavements or on the nearest bit of tarmac'd road, operating the wooden hand-brake as they approach the tram-route.

Rhyming chants survive, to accompany the games – 'eeny-meeny – miny – mo': 'one-two-three-a'lairy': 'tinker – tailor – soldier – sailor': 'I like coffee, I like tea. I like sitting on a black man's knee'. For the rest, there are songs on only a few occasions – the voting song, 'Vote, Vote, Vote for Mister...'; an occasional Bonfire Night collecting song; and the chants used, in a flat sing-song, after a few carols at a house-door:

> Christmas is coming; the goose is getting fat,
> Please put a penny in the old man's hat.
> If you haven't got a penny a ha'penny will do,
> If you haven't got a ha'penny – God bless you.

or

We wish you a merry Christmas; we wish you a merry Christmas;
We wish you a merry Christmas, and a Happy New Year.

Of 'outings', those recreations which involve spending a few coppers or leaving the home-ground, the sequence is determined almost entirely by the seasons. There are outings with jam-jars to a dirty stream a mile or so away, for sticklebacks and red-throats; blackberrying, also with jam-jars, even farther afield, past the church with the whalebone arches; raids on the nearest rhubarb and turnip fields, or a little birds'-nesting. Those who can cadge a few coppers from their mothers go to the public baths; or occasionally catch a tram to some remote part of the city where the children's playground is said to be good, and spend the whole day there with a few sandwiches and a bottle of pop between the lot of them. In autumn, whole days can be passed watching the 'feast' set up, and working out what it will be possible to go on.

So the days and the weeks succeed one another, often dull and grey, but relieved by all kinds of excitements. There is a rhythm, but it is the rhythm of a brick-world, to which those of the seasons or of the great religious festivals are only incidental. At each week-end, perhaps, there is Friday night's shopping with Mother down a shopping street that is all bustle and warmth and gregarious spending, and the trams rattle and flash past constantly. There is the whole weekend ahead, with the pictures on Saturday, or a chapel concert with a hot supper in the Sunday school room; bacon and eggs for Sunday breakfast, the big Sunday tea. Then, throughout the year, Pancake Tuesday, Voting Day, which is always a holiday, Hotcross Buns on Good Friday, the Autumn 'Feast', Mischief Night, and all the weeks of cadging and collecting for Bonfire Night. It is a truly urban fire, with very little wood that has known a tree for the last few years, a fire composed of old mattresses and chairs – replaced now that someone's club turn has come up – or a horsehair sofa displaced by a modern one on hire purchase. As the fireworks run out, you bake potatoes round the fire's edges.

It is because for all ages such a life can have a peculiarly gripping wholeness, that after twenty-five it can be difficult for a working-class person either to move into another kind of area or even in-to another area of the same kind. We all know of working-class people's difficulties in settling into the new council-house estates. Most react instinctively against consciously planned group activities; they are used to a group life, but one which has started from the home and worked outwards in response to the common needs and amusements of a densely packed neighbourhood. In these brick and concrete wastes they feel too exposed and cold at first, they suffer from agoraphobia; they do not feel 'it's homely' or 'neighbourly', feel 'too far from everything', from their relatives and from the shops; they do not much take to gardening unless they have been used to running an allotment, and not always then; they long to put up hen-huts, and they acquire dogs and cats.

[margin note: morbid dread of public places]

The strength of this sense of home and neighbourhood may be seen at its most pathetic in those old men who fill the reading-rooms of the branch public libraries. They are often the solitaries, men whose families have grown up and left them, whose wives have died or are bedridden, and who are no longer at work. If they are lucky they may still live in their old house or lodge with a son or daughter; a few scrabble along on a pension in a common lodging-house or in one room of an apartment-house in a démodé district. Even those in their own area are especially lost during the working day when the streets are occupied only by infants and a few busy, if kindly, housewives. The older ones haunt the railway-stations along with some of the mentally-deficient. Many come daily to the reading-room, where it is warm and there are seats. It all sadly recalls those hidden inlets which the smaller detritus of a river eventually reaches, held there in a yeasty scum – old sticks, bits of torn paper, a few withered leaves, a matchbox. But the reading-rooms themselves have a syringed and workhouse air (I am thinking of the old ones, many of which remain): the newspapers stretch bleakly round the walls, heavily clamped and with the sporting-pages carefully pasted over, so as to discourage punters; the magazines lie on dark-oak desks across which green-shaded lamps throw so narrow a beam that the whole of the room above elbow height is in permanent shadow by the late afternoon.

The shadow helps to soften the insistence of the many notices, heavy black on white, all prohibitive and most imperative, which alternate with the newspapers on the walls. In one I know there are eight major injunctions, varying in length from SILENCE in letters nine inches high and four inches across to NO PERSON IS ALLOWED TO BRING READING MATTER INTO THIS ROOM FOR PERUSAL BUT READERS MUST CONFINE THEMSELVES TO THE PUBLI-CATIONS HEREIN DISPLAYED. They range in tone from the curtly peremptory to the diffusely interdictory. After a while the atmosphere is so depressing that you begin to think that NO AUDIBLE CON-VERSATIONS ALLOWED is an instance of warm-heartedness in the midst of officialdom, a sensible allowance for the fact that so many of the regulars talk to themselves.

This is the special refuge of the misfits and left-overs, of the hollow-cheeked, watery-eyed, shabby, and furtively sad. An eccentric ab-sorbed in the rituals of his monomania sits between a pinched unmarried brother, kept by a married sister for the sake of his war-pension, and an aged widower from a cheap lodging or a house smell-ing permanently of old tea and the frying-pan. They come in off the streets, on to which they had gone after swilling under a cold-tap and twisting scarves round collarless necks; they come in after walking round a bit, watching other people doing things, belonging some-where. If a bench in the paper-strewn square is too chilly, they come in after a while to the warmth they have been looking forward to. A few make for one of the items of sect-journalism and resume their endless cult-reading; some – shifty and nervous of detection, or with a bland and cheeky skill – plot how to win on the pools or mumble through a rough sandwich; some turn leaves aimlessly or stare blankly for ten minutes at one page; some just sit and look at nothing, picking their noses. They exist on the periphery of life, seeing each other daily but with no contact.   Reduced to a handful of clothes, a few primary needs and a persistent lack, they have been disconnected from the only kind of life in which they ever had a part, and that was a part unconsciously accepted; they have no conscious arts for social intercourse.

There is usually one who comes into this resort of the unpossessed as though it were a Conservative Club and he the town's senior alderman. Threadbare but jaunty, he moves down the aisle to his favourite chair with nods and smiles which are none the less assured for being nowhere acknowledged. He has brazened out some terms with circumstance, and in his own eyes is a happy man. Most look inwards to a dream of life as a vista of warm fires, big and regular meals, a wife to listen to your talk, money for cigarettes and beer, a little 'standing'. No wonder the reading-room attendant inspires deference; some of them have so far surrendered self-respect as to retain no power either to resent or be cocky towards him.

CHAPTER 3

'THEM' AND 'US'

A. *'Them': 'Self-Respect'*

Presumably most groups gain some of their strength from their exclusiveness, from a sense of people outside who are not 'Us'. How does this express itself in working-class people? I have emphasized the strength of home and neighbourhood, and have suggested that this strength arises partly from a feeling that the world outside is strange and often unhelpful, that it has most of the counters stacked on its side, that to meet it on its own terms is difficult. One may call this, making use of a word commonly used by the working-classes, the world of 'Them'. 'Them' is a composite dramatic figure, the chief character in modern urban forms of the rural peasant – big-house relationships. The world of 'Them' is the world of the bosses, whether those bosses are private individuals or, as is increasingly the case today, public officials. 'Them' may be, as occasion requires, anyone from the classes outside other than the few individuals from those classes whom working-people know as individuals. A general practitioner, if he wins his way by his devotion to his patients, is not as a general practitioner, one of 'Them'; he and his wife, as social beings, are. A parson may or may not be regarded as one of 'Them', according to his behaviour. 'Them' includes the policemen and those civil servants or local-authority employees whom the working-classes meet – teachers, the school attendance man, 'the Corporation', the local bench. Once the Means Test Official, the man from 'the Guardians', and the Employment Exchange officer were notable figures here. To the very poor, especially, they compose a shadowy but numerous and powerful group affecting their lives at almost every point: the world is divided into 'Them' and 'Us'.

'They' are 'the people at the top', 'the higher-ups', the people who give you your dole, call you up, tell you to go to war, fine you, made you split the family in the thirties to avoid a reduction in the Means Test allowance, 'get yer in the end', 'aren't really to be trusted', 'talk posh', 'are all twisters really', 'never tell yer owt' (e.g. about a relative in hospital), 'clap yer in clink', 'will do y' down if they can',

53

'summons yer', 'are all in a click [clique] together', 'treat y' like muck'.

There has been plenty of violent action by the authorities in England, especially during the first half of the nineteenth century. But on the whole, and particularly in this century, the sense of 'Them' among working-class people is not of a violent or harsh thing. This is not the 'Them' of some European proletariats, of secret police, open brutality, and sudden disappearances. Yet there exists, with some reason, a feeling among working-class people that they are often at a disadvantage, that the law is in some things readier against them than against others, and that petty laws weigh more heavily against them than against some other groups. Their street-corner betting, it is often remarked, is a risky business; if they ran an account with a 'Commission Agent' it would not be. If they celebrate and get drunk they are likely to do so in a public bar, and run more risk of being picked up than the man who keeps his drinks at home. Their relations with the police tend to be rather different from those of the middle-classes. Often they are good, but good or bad, they tend to regard the policeman primarily as someone who is watching them, who represents the authority which has its eye on them, rather than as a member of the public services whose job it is to help and protect them. They are close to the police and know something of the bullying and petty corruption that can sometimes exist. 'Oh, the police always look after themselves. They'll stick by one another till they're blue in the face, and the magistrates always believe them,' they have said for years, and go on saying.

Towards 'Them' generally, as towards the police, the primary attitude is not so much fear as mistrust: mistrust accompanied by a lack of illusions about what 'They' will do for one, and for the complicated way – the apparently unnecessarily complicated way – in which 'They' order one's life when it touches them. Working-class people have had years of experience of waiting at labour-exchanges, at the panel doctor's and at hospitals. They get something of their own back by always blaming the experts, with or without justifica-tion, if something goes wrong – 'Ah never ought to 'ave lost that child if that doctor 'ad known what 'e was doing.' They suspect that public services are not so readily and effectively given to them as to the people who can telephone or send a stiff letter.

So often their contacts are with the minor officials, with those in the lower grades of uniformed and pensioned jobs. Again, as with the police, these may be to other classes servants, but to the working-classes they seem the agents of 'Them' and are mistrusted, even though they may be kindly and well disposed. If they are ill disposed, they can display to working-class people all the insolence of minor office, the brusqueness of the pettily uniformed; they can be 'bosses' men'. So, when working-class people are asked to become foremen or N.C.O.s they often hesitate. Whatever their motives, they will be regarded now as on the side of 'Them'. Some minor officials have a doubleness in their attitudes. They tend to be sharp towards the working-classes because they would like to feel more securely separate from them; they know in their hearts by just how little they are separated and do not like to think of dropping back. Their deference towards the middle-classes can conceal an animosity; they would like to be one of them but realize they are not.

By all this working-class women are easily made unhappy, and so are usually more deferential than their menfolk towards small officials. A man is more likely to kick against it, and his kicking often takes the form of becoming really 'vulgar'. He is liable, if driven, to offer to 'knock 'is bloody block off if 'e doesn't cut out 'is bloody chelp'.

Perhaps no place so well illustrates the division into 'Them' and 'Us' as a typical North Country Magistrates' Court. It so often has an air of sour, scrubbed, provincial puritanism and mortification, from the stench of carbolic which meets you at the door, past the lavatories still marked MALES and FEMALES, to the huge pitch-pine bench lighted by high and narrow windows. The policemen may themselves feel nervously under the eye of superior officials, but to the working-class people in the well of the court they look like the hired and menacing – the more menacing because now on their own ground, with their helmets off – assistants of that anonymous authority which the bench symbolizes. The magistrates' clerk may be one who likes to 'run people around a bit'; the figures on the bench seem to peer down from a distant world of middle-class security and local importance. Listening to a series of cases I usually find myself admiring the success of the bench in seeing through the incapacity and often evasiveness of working-class witnesses to a genuinely human view of the cases. They have to make most of the allowances, since the working-class people involved are aware of almost nothing but the vast apparatus of authority which has somehow got hold of them, and which they cannot understand.

To these major attitudes towards 'Them' may be added one or two minor but recurrent ones. The 'Orlick' spirit first, the 'I ain't a gentleman, you see' attitude; a dull dog-in-the-manger refusal to accept anything higher than one's own level of response, which throws out decent attempts at using authority and debases them with the rest. Or the peculiarly mean form of trickery which goes with some forms of working-class deference, the kind of obvious 'fiddling' of someone from another class which accompanies an over-readiness to say 'sir', but assumes – in the very obviousness with which it is practised – that it is all a contemptuous game, that one can rely on the middle-class distaste for a scene to allow one to cheat easily. Or the attitude which grows when self-respect is low, and results in a series of 'They oughts'. Like primitive kings, 'They ought' to bring rain when it is needed, and are to be blamed if rain comes inopportunely; after all, 'that's what They're there for'. 'They' ought to look after you when you are in trouble, to 'do something about it', 'take care that sort of thing doesn't happen', to 'lock 'em up'. The contrast is sharp with that much more common attitude which causes working-class people only to make use of 'Them' when absolutely forced: if things go wrong, people feel then, put up with them: don't get into the hands of authority, and, if you must have help, only 'trust yer own sort'.

The 'Them/Us' attitudes seem to me strongest in those over thirty-five, those with memories of unemployment in the thirties and of all the 'Thems' of those days. Younger people, even if they are not active in the unions, here inhabit a different atmosphere from that their fathers grew up in: at least, the atmosphere has a different emotional temperature. At bottom the division is still there, and little changed in its sharpness. Young people are likely to be less actively hostile, or contemptuous, or fearful towards the bosses' world; nor are they likely to be deferential. But this is not always because they are better able than their parents to cope with that world, that they have come to terms with the great outside in a way their parents have not: they often seem to be simply ignoring it, to have 'contracted out' of any belief in its importance; they have gone into their own worlds, supported now by a greater body of entertaining and flattering provision than their parents knew. When they have to meet the other world sharply, as on many occasions after marriage, they often do their best to go on ignoring it, or draw upon attitudes similar to those of their parents. Ask at a baby clinic what proportion of working-class mothers can even now be persuaded to take full advantage of the services. I know some who will not 'go near' the clinic, not even for their orange juice; they mistrust anything authority provides and prefer to go to the chemists', even though this is more expensive.

Behind all this is a problem of which we are acutely conscious today – that everyone is expected to have a double eye, one for his duties as an individual person, and another for those as a citizen in a democracy. Most of us, even the more-or-less intellectual, find it difficult to relate these worlds to each other. Working-class people, with their roots so strongly in the homely and personal and local, and with little training in more general thinking, are even less likely to be able to bring the two worlds into focus. They are, if they think of it, ill at ease; this second and complex world cannot easily be dramatized, is too vast, too much 'beyond' them. They do much to bring it within their own scope, usually by simplification: for the rest they continue to say, as their grandparents said, 'I don't know what the world's coming to.'

One traditional release of working-class people in their dealings with authority is more positive than this. I mean their debunking-art, their putting-a-finger-to-the-nose at authority by deflating it, by guying it. The policeman may sometimes be a trouble; he can also have songs written about his feet. My impression is that this reaction is less strong than it used to be. No doubt the change is due in part to the greatly improved position of working-class people in society. It can also be an expression of the 'contracting-out' mentioned earlier, of a feeling that 'we get on alright as we are'; we ask 'Them' for nothing and feel no particular resentment towards them. Such an attitude may be encouraged by the great quantity of entertainment offered today. These entertainments are of such a kind that they render their consumers less likely to make the ironically vigorous protest contained in debunking-art.

The old manner survives to some degree in the Services, where the division between 'Them' and 'Us' is still clear and formal.

Most of the debunking songs heard there are at least forty years old. I have in mind songs such as, 'Left, left. I had a good job when I left', 'When this bloody war is over', and 'I don't want to be a soldier'.

More than vigour, there is a clear dignity in that reaction to the pressures of the outside world which takes the form of insisting on 'keeping y' self-respect'. And the moment this idea of 'self-respect' and 'self-reliance' comes to mind, it begins to flower into related ideas: into that of 'respectability' first, which itself spreads outwards and upwards from some thin-lipped forms, through the pride of a skilled workman, to the integrity of those who have practically nothing except a determination not to allow themselves to be dragged down by circumstances. At the centre is a resolution to hold on to that of which one can be rightly proud; in a world which puts so many stumbling-blocks in the way, to hold on at least to 'self-respect'. 'At least, ah've got me self-respect'; the right to be able to say that, though it can be said meanly, makes up for a lot. It is at work constantly in the hatred of 'going on the parish', in the worry to keep up sick payments, in the big insurances to avoid a parish burial, in thrift and the cult of cleanliness. There is, I think, a tendency among some writers on the working-classes to think of all those who aim at thrift and cleanliness as imitators of the lower middle-classes, as in some way traitors to their own class, anxious to get out of it. Conversely, those who do not make this effort tend to be regarded as more honest and less servile than those who do. But cleanliness, thrift, and self-respect arise more from a concern not to drop down, not to succumb to the environment, than from an anxiety to go up; and among those who altogether ignore these criteria, the uninhibited, generous, and carefree spirits are outnumbered by the slovenly and shiftless whose homes and habits reflect their inner lack of grip. Even the urge for children to 'get on' and the respect for the value of 'book-learning' is not most importantly produced by the wish to reach another class out of snobbery. It is associated much more with the thought of a reduction in the numerous troubles which the poor have to meet, simply because they are poor:

I have seen him that is beaten, him that is beaten: thou art to set thine heart on books. I have beheld him that is set free from forced labour: behold, nothing surpasseth books.

'How narrow the gap, how slight the chance', for keeping the raft afloat and being able to 'look people in the face'. It is therefore important to have that sense of independence which arises from a respect for oneself, because that is what no one can physically take away. 'Ah've worked 'ard all me life,' people will say, 'and ah owe no man anything.' They own nothing either, except a few sticks of furniture, but they never expected to own more. Hence the survival of all kinds of apparent oddities, especially among those now over fifty. I know several families which have elected to keep their electricity supply on the shilling-in-the-slot system. They pay more that way and frequently find themselves in the dark because no one has a shilling; they have enough money coming in now to pay quarterly bills easily. But they cannot bear the thought of having a debt outstanding longer than a week. (Clothing club 'draws' and the grocery bill often come in another category – they do not seem like debts owed to 'Them'.)

Here, too, lies the origin of the clinging, whatever straits people have reached, to the 'little bit of something' which speaks of a time when they had tastes of their own and the freedom to make gestures. No doubt these things are better arranged now, but when I was a boy our area was shocked by the clumsiness of a Board of Guardians visitor who suggested to an old woman that, since she was living on charity, she ought to sell a fine teapot she never used but always had on show. 'Just fancy', people went around saying, and no further analysis was needed. Everyone knew that the man had been guilty of an insensitive affront to human dignity . . . 'Oh, reason not the need; . . ./ . . . Allow not nature more than nature needs,/ Man's life is cheap as beast's.'

We may understand why working-class people often seem not 'oncoming' to social workers, seem evasive and prepared to give answers designed to put off rather than to clarify. At the back of the announcement that 'Ah keep meself to meself' there can be a hurt pride. It is difficult to believe that a visitor from another class could ever realize all the ins-and-outs of one's difficulties – there is an anxiety not to 'show y'self up', to defend oneself against patronage.

It is still important to 'have a trade in your hands', and this not merely because a skilled tradesman has, until recently, almost always earned more. The skilled workman can say more firmly than the unskilled labourer that he is 'as good as the next chap'. He is out of the ruck of those who receive the first shock of large labour cuts; he has remnants of a journeyman's pride. He may never seriously think of moving, but at the back of his mind is the idea that he is at liberty to pack his tools and go. Fathers who are anxious to 'do right' by their boys still try to have them apprenticed.

B. 'Us' – the Best and the Worst of It

In any discussion of working-class attitudes much is said about the group-sense, that feeling of being not so much an individual with 'a way to make' as one of a group whose members are all roughly level and likely to remain so. I avoid the word 'community' at this stage because its overtones seem too simply favourable; they may lead to an under-estimation of the harsher tensions and sanctions of working-class groups.

Certainly working-class people have a strong sense of being members of a group, and just as certainly that sense involves the assumption that it is important to be friendly, co-operative, neighbourly. 'We are all in the same boat'; 'it is no use fighting one another'; but 'in unity is strength'. One's mind goes back to the movements of the last century, to the hundreds of friendly societies, to the mottoes of the unions: the Amalgamated Society of Engineers, with 'Be United and Industrious'; the Provisional Committee of the National Union of Gas Workers and General Labourers choosing, in the late nineties, 'Love, Unity and Fidelity'. And the 'Love' in the last recalls the strength which this sense of unity acquired from a Christian background.

The friendly group tradition seems to me to have its strength initially from the ever-present evidence, in the close, huddled, intimate conditions of life, that we are, in fact, all in the same position. You are bound to be close to people with whom, for example, you share a lavatory in a common yard. That 'luv' which is still the most common form of address, and not only to people in their own class, by tram and bus conductors and by shop-keepers, is used automatically, but still indicates something. To call anyone 'neighbourly' or 'right sociable' is to offer a high compliment; a club may be praised because it is a 'real sociable place'; the most important recommendation for lodgings or seaside 'digs' is that they are 'sociable', and this outweighs over-crowding; and a church is just as likely to be weighed in the same scales. 'Ar' Elsie got married at All Saints',' they will say, of the church they chose from several nearby, not one of which can claim them as parishioners – 'it's a nice friendly church.' The story of a Christmas party at the local will end, 'It was a luvly night. Everybody got real friendly.' Good neighbourliness consists not just in 'doing fair by each other', but in being 'obliging' or 'always ready to oblige'. If the neighbours in a new area seem to lack the right kind of neighbourliness, the newcomer will insist that she 'just can't settle'.

The sense of a group warmth exercises a powerful hold, and continues to be missed when individuals have moved, financially and probably geographically, out of the working-classes. I have noticed that self-made men now living in villas – grocers who have done well and own a small chain of local shops; jobbing builders who have advanced so far as to be putting up fields of private 'semis' – like to join the crowd at football matches. They drive up in a car now and wear shaggily prosperous Harris tweed, but many of them still go on the terraces rather than in the stands. I imagine they enjoy recapturing something of the mateyness of the ranks, much as a commissioned Q.M. will usually be found in the non-commissioned bar at a unit dance.

This is not a very self-conscious sense of community; it is worlds away from the 'fellowship in service' of some of the socially pur-posive movements. It does not draw its main strength from – indeed, it precedes, and is more elementary than – the belief in the need to improve each other's lot jointly which gave rise to such organizations as the Co-operative movement. It arises chiefly from a knowledge, born of living close together, that one is inescapably part of a group, from the warmth and security that knowledge can give, from the lack of change in the group and from the frequent need to 'turn to a neighbour' since services cannot often be bought. It starts from the feeling that life is hard, and that 'our sort' will usually get 'the dirty end of the stick'. In most people it does not develop into a conscious sense of being part of 'the working-class movement': the 'Co-ops' are today less typical of the outlook of the majority in the working-classes than the small privately-owned corner-shops serving a couple of streets. The attitude finds expression in a great number of formal phrases – 'Y've got to share and share alike'; 'y've got to 'elp one another out'; 'y've got to 'elp lame dogs'; 'we must all pull together'; 'it's sink or swim together'. But for the most part these are actually spoken only on special occasions, at singsongs and festivals.

The solidarity is helped by the lack of scope for the growth of ambition. After the age of eleven, when the scholarship boys and girls go off to the grammar-school, the rest look increasingly outward to the real life which will begin at fifteen, to the life with the group of older men and woman which, for the first few years after school, forms the most powerfully educative force they know. Once at work there is for most no sense of a career, of the possibilities of promotion. Jobs are spread around horizontally, not vertically; life is not seen as a climb, nor work as the main interest in it. There is still a respect for the good craftsman. But the man on the next bench is not regarded as an actual or potential competitor. It is not difficult to understand, therefore, the strong emotional hold of the 'go slow – don't put the other man out of a job' attitude. Working-class people number several vices among their occupational attitudes, but not those of the 'go-getter' or the 'livewire', nor those of 'the successful smilers the city can use'; 'keen types' are mistrusted.

Whatever one does, horizons are likely to be limited; in any case, working-class people add quickly, money doesn't seem to make people happier, nor does power. The 'real' things are the human and companionable things – home and family affection, friendship and being able to say 'enjoy y'self': 'money's not the real thing', they say, and 'Life isn't worth living if y'sweating for extra money all t' time.' Working-class songs often ask for love, friends, a good home; they always insist that money does not matter.

There are exceptions: those who still hold to the line Matthew Arnold satirized – 'Ever remember, my dear Dan, that you should look forward to being one day manager of that concern.' Among some of the more avidly respectable this shows in the way boys are urged to 'get on', to pass that scholarship, to be careful of their 'penmanship' since gentlemen in offices like 'a neat hand'. And there are sharp-eyed little men whom the rest regard with charity as wrong-headed, who 'never let a penny go'. They take on extra work at nights and weekends and are always anxious to make an extra bob-or-two at the hour when others are having a good time.

These people are not usually moving upward or out of their class; they are running agitatedly round inside it, amassing the unconsidered trifles which are always about.

The attitude to bachelors probably shows as well as anything the tolerance which is extended to established exceptions within the group. The occasional bachelor in any neighbourhood is likely to be living at home with a widowed mother or in the family of a married sister. Such a bachelor can usually be found on most nights in a fixed corner of the local pub or club, since he is likely to be quiet and regular in his habits. Perhaps a certain kind of shyness has helped to make him a bachelor; he is in some ways a lone bird, but he cannot be called lonely. He is respected in the neighbourhood. He is not thought of as a man-on-the-loose and therefore as a potential Don Juan. He probably figures, rather, as a harmless uncle of indeterminate age, who is 'always very polite' and 'quiet-spoken' and is said to be good to his mother or sister. There is sometimes a touch of amusement in this attitude, as though behind it is a feeling that old So-and-so has been a little scared of the physical relations with a woman which marriage entails. But this is not normally an expression of scorn; nor is such a bachelor likely to be regarded as selfish or queer or anti-social. Some men, it is felt, are born bachelors; they are therefore a real part of the neighbourhood.

That minority who become conscious of their class-limitations and take up some educational activity – so as to 'work for their class' or 'improve themselves' – tend to be ambiguously regarded. The respect for the 'scholar' (like the doctor and the parson) to some extent remains. I remember sitting, not long after I had won a scholarship, next to a middle-aged bachelor miner in a working-men's club. Whenever he paid for his rum-and-hot milk he passed me a half-crown from the change. I tried to refuse: 'Tek it, lad, and use it for thee education,' he said. 'Ah'm like all miners. Ah only waste t'bluddy stuff.' On the other hand, there is often a mistrust of 'book-learning'. What good does it do you? Are you any better off (i.e. happier) as a clerk? or as a teacher? Parents who refuse, as a few still do, to allow their children to take up scholarships are not always thinking of the fact that they would have to be fed and clothed for much longer; at the back is this vaguely formulated but strong doubt of the value of education. That doubt acquires some of its force from the group-sense itself: for the group seeks to conserve, and may impede an inclination in any of its members to make a change, to leave the group, to be different.

The group, I suggested, works against the idea of change. It does more than this: it imposes on its members an extensive and sometimes harsh pressure to conform. Those who become different, through education and in one or two other ways, may often be allowed for, and I do not want to suggest a strong automatic hostility to any departure at all from the group or its attitudes. Indeed, one of the marked qualities of working-class groups is a wide tolerance in some things; but it is a tolerance which works freely only if the chief class assumptions are shared.

The group is close: it is likely to regard someone originally from a town forty miles away as 'not one of us' for years; and I have seen it unconsciously and insensitively cruel for a long time – and kind, too, in many things – towards a foreign wife. The group watches, often with a low unallowingness, an unimaginative cruelty which can make for much unhappiness. 'Ah wunder what she meant by that?'; 'Ooh, don't things get about!'; 'It doesn't do to let others know too much' are common phrases. Wondering what the neighbours will say is as common here as elsewhere; perhaps more common, in its own way. Working-class people watch and are watched in a manner which, because horizons are limited, will often result in a mistaken, and lowering, interpretation of what the neighbours do. A working-class woman may be known to act as a 'sitter-in' at the place where she cleans all day; but if she is brought home at the end of the evening she is likely to ask to be left a couple of streets away. What would the neighbours say if they saw her coming home with a man?

The group does not like to be shocked or attacked from within. There may be little of the competitive urge to keep up with the Joneses, but just as powerful can be the pressure to keep down with the Atkinses. Hence the frequent use, long before advertisers made so much of its value, of the appeal to the ordinary and the unextreme, 'any decent man would . . .', 'it's not natural', 'I like 'im; 'e's always the same'. If you want to be one of the group you must not try to 'alter people's ways', and you will be disliked if you imply a criticism of their ways by acting differently yourself; if you infringe the taboos you will run into disfavour:

There's such a thing as mass thought, you know. If you think the same as the man next to you, you're all right. But if you don't, if you're seen bringing in a book [i.e. into work] or anything like that, you're not. It's very difficult to stand up to ridicule.

All classes require conformity to some degree; it needs to be stressed here because there is a tendency to stress upper- and middle-class conformity and to regard the working-classes as more free from it.

Acting beyond the ideas of the group, 'acting posh', 'giving y'self airs', 'getting above y'self', 'being lah-de-dah', 'thinking y'self too good for other people', 'being stuck-up', 'turning y'nose up at other people', 'acting like Lady Muck' – all these are much disliked and not very sensitively discriminated. The genuine 'toff' might be found amusing, as he was fifty years ago, and the 'real gentleman' (who will talk to you 'just like I'm talking to you now') is still likely to be admired, even though he is obviously one of 'Them'. Neither inspires a feeling as strong as that aroused by the person who is putting on 'posh' airs because he thinks they are better than working-class airs. 'Ay, and what do you dislike most, then?' asks Wilfred Pickles. 'Stuck-up fowk.' Roars of applause. 'Jolly good! and will you just tell me what you like most?' 'Good neighbourly fowk.' Increased applause. '. . . and very right too. Give her the money.'

Whatever their origins, Gracie Fields and Wilfred Pickles hardly qualify as members of the working-classes now. But both are still warmly 'alright' because they remain of them in spirit and have conquered the 'moneyed classes' with their working-class wit and attitudes. 'They love Wilfred Pickles down South,' working-class people will say, meaning that people not of their class love him: there is some pride that their values, those of the unpolished and 'straight', are appreciated by other classes. Their 'comics' have stormed the posh citadels; 'good luck to 'em!'

We frequently hear that the English working-classes are gentle, gentler than those of almost any other country, gentler today than their own parents and grandparents. Undoubtedly there has been a decrease in the amount of sheer brutality in the towns during the last fifty years, a decline in the rough and savage stuff which some-times made the streets at night and particularly at weekends places to avoid. The hooliganism and rowdyism which caused the police to work in pairs in several areas of many towns have almost gone. We no longer hear, except very occasionally, of bare-fist fights on bits of waste-ground, of broken-bottle fights inside bars, of regular assaults by gangs on girls at fairgrounds, of so much animal drunkenness.

It would be a deluding and foolish archaism which regretted the loss of all this, which assumed that its decline meant the loss of some gusto among the working-classes, that the gentleness is merely a passivity. But that same generation which was often coarse and savage could also be gentle: I think again of my grandmother, who saw brutalities which would shock a woman of almost any class today and was herself often harshly crude. But she, in common with many of her generation, had in some things an admirable gentleness and fineness of discrimination. Perhaps the gentleness we notice is not so much a new feature as an old strain which is more evident, has been allowed more room to operate today. It must have taken generations to develop, is the product of centuries in which people got along pretty well together, were not persistently harassed by the more violent evidences of the powers above them, and felt – however severe their troubles – that law was fairly generally applicable and authority not hopelessly corrupt. I have not forgotten the experiences of the 'Hungry Forties' of the last century; but I think also of the Russian serfs and of the Italian attitude towards civil servants even today. All this has no doubt bred a reasonableness, a remarkably quiet assumption that violence is the last ditch.

If I draw further attention, then, to the strain of coarseness and insensitivity running through working-class life, I do so not to infer that other classes have not their own forms, nor to deny all that is usually said about gentleness, but to restore a balance which we have been inclined to lose during the last twenty years. The evidence must be chosen with unusual care, must not include habits which simply seem coarse by the usage of other classes. Thus, working-class speech and manners in conversation are more abrupt, less provided with emollient phrases than those of other groups: their arguments are often conducted in so rude a way that a stranger might well think that after this, at the worst, fighting would follow, and at the best a permanent ending of relations. I find that even now, if I am not to be misunderstood, I have to modify a habit of carrying on discussion in an 'unlubricated' way, in short sharp jabs that are meant to go home – and yet not meant really to hurt. Neither the phrasing nor the rhythms of working-class speech have the easing and modified quality which, in varying degrees, is characteristic of other classes. The pattern of their speech follows more closely the pattern of emotions they are feeling at the time, whether it be exasperation, as in the rows, or gaiety, as in that occasional shrieking of working-class housewives out for a day at the sea which dismays some who sit in the front gardens of private hotels. There is, of course, a 'calling a spade a spade' arrogance which makes a few working-class people overdo the rougher elements in their speech when with others from a different class.

But working-class life, whatever changes there may have been, is still closer to the ground than that of most other people. The prevalent grime, the closeness and the difficulties of home life, I have sufficiently described; we have to remember as well that the physical conditions of the working-lives of men, and of some women, are often noisy, dirty, and smelly. We all know this in our heads, but realize it freshly only if we have to pass through some of those deep caverns in Leeds where the engines clang and hammer ceaselessly and the sparks fly out of huge doorways and men can be seen, black to the shoulders, heaving and straining at hot pieces of metal: or through the huge area in Hull which has a permanent pall of cooking fish-meal over it, seeping through the packed houses. The heavy, rough, and beast-of-burden work is still there to be done and working-class people do it. These are not conditions which produce measured tones or the more padded conversational allowances.

Thus the rows which are so much a part of the life of any working-class neighbourhood, and of many working-class families, can be easily misinterpreted. They are understandably a part of the neighbourhood's life: in narrow, terraced streets, with thin party-walls, they could hardly be kept private anyhow, unless they were conducted in very subdued voices. They certainly are not quietly conducted, and so they become one of the interests of the neighbourhood. Children, hearing that 'Old So-and-so's up t'street are 'aving a right row', will gather in a group as near as they can. And if a row goes on too long or too noisily for the patience of a neighbour, he can always hammer on the party-wall or rattle a poker on the fire-back.

It would be wrong to assume from this that working-class people

are congenitally quarrelsome and continually rowing. Some rows
are nasty and distressing, and some families are known to be 'always
'aving rows', and these will probably not be regarded as the most
respectable. Many families – perhaps most – will have an occasional
row. All this will not be automatically regarded as bringing dis-
repute to the neighbourhood. It is accepted that disputes – perhaps
about the amount of money spent on drinking, perhaps among
womenfolk about the sharing of household duties, perhaps about
'another woman' – will arise from time to time, and that they will
erupt into vivid, quick, noisy war. In my experience, rows about
drinking are the most common, and those about the 'other woman'
(or man) the least common.

If I may digress for a moment on this latter aspect: these affairs,
as I knew them, seemed generally to concern a man in his late
thirties or early forties, a man who was slightly more dapper than
his acquaintances, though in the same sort of work. His wife would
have lost her physical appeal, so he sought interest elsewhere. Yet
the woman he 'took up with' was likely enough to be married
herself and of roughly the same age as his own wife – and to a
stranger no more attractive physically. The two would probably
become drinking companions in a known place. The wife would
soon learn what was going on and fierce rows would blow up (on
more than one occasion I remember a much more serious development – an early-morning 'bashing' of the man by the injured husband
on a piece of waste-ground). The oddest feature of all was that
sometimes the two women became friendly, and settled into a
relationship which the connexions of the husband with each of the
women not only did not preclude but seemed to nourish.

Most of the rows I experienced were not thought of as shocking
occurrences. Rows of that kind took place in the truly slummy
areas, with drunken fights between the menfolk or, worse, between
men and women or, worse of all between women alone. Such events
would really shock an ordinary working-class neighbourhood.

I remember too that in our neighbourhood we accepted suicides
as a moderately common occurrence. Every so often one heard that
So-and-so had 'done 'erself in', or 'done away with 'imself', or 'put
'er 'ead in the gas-oven', since the gas-oven was the most convenient
means of self-destruction. I do not know whether suicide took place
more often in the sort of groups I am speaking of than in middle-

class groups. It did not happen monthly or even every season, and not all attempts succeeded; but it happened sufficiently often to be part of the pattern of life. Among the working-classes it could not be concealed, of course, any more than a row could; everyone quickly knew about it. The fact I want to stress is that suicide was not felt to be simply a personal matter or one confined to the family concerned, but that it was felt to be bound up with the conditions of the common life. Sometimes the cause was that a girl had 'got 'erself into trouble' and for one reason or another could not go through with it; just as often it was that, for those who put their heads on a pillow inside the oven-door, life had become unendurable; they were ill and treatment seemed to be doing no good; they were out of work; or, whatever they did, the debts piled up. This was not long ago. The fact that suicide could be accepted – pitifully but with little suggestion of blame – as a part of the order of existence shows how hard and elemental that life could be.

Does this altogether explain, for example, the way many working-class men speak when no women are present? In part, perhaps; but one has to be careful of special pleading here. George Orwell, noting that working-class men use four-letter words for natural functions freely, says they are obscene but not immoral. But there are degrees and kinds of obscenity, and this sort of conversation is often obscene and nothing else, obscene for the sake of obscenity in a dull, repetitive, and brute way. And there are kinds of immorality; such men may use short and direct words about sex, which at first are a relief after the allusion of cabaret shows and the literature of sexual sophistication. But they use those words so indiscriminately and talk so preponderantly about sex as often to reveal a calloused sensibility. Listen to them speaking of their sexual adventures and plans; you are likely to feel smothered by the boring animality, the mongrel-dogs-rutting-in-alleyways quality. It is a quality which owes as much to an insensitivity in relations as to a freedom from hypocrisy. To each class its own forms of cruelty and dirt; that of working-class people is sometimes of a gratuitously debasing coarseness.

c. 'Putting Up with Things': 'Living and Letting Live'

I have spoken of a world and a life whose main lines are almost predictable, of work for a man which is probably not interesting, of years of 'making-do' for a woman, of the lack in most people of any feeling that some change can, or indeed ought to, be made in the general pattern of life.

By and large, seems to be the note that is struck, we are not asked to be the great doers in this world; our kind of life offers little of splendour or of calls for the more striking heroisms, and its tragedies are not of the dramatic or rhetorical kind. At least, that is the sort of view this world seems to invite us to take: to do its heavier work, with sights fixed at short distance.

When people feel that they cannot do much about the main elements in their situation, feel it not necessarily with despair or disappointment or resentment but simply as a fact of life, they adopt attitudes towards that situation which allow them to have a liveable life under its shadow, a life without a constant and pressing sense of the larger situation. The attitudes remove the main elements in the situation to the realm of natural laws, the given and raw, the almost implacable, material from which a living has to be carved. Such attitudes, at their least-adorned a fatalism or plain accepting, are generally below the tragic level; they have too much of the con-script's lack of choice about them. But in some of their forms they have dignity.

At the lowest is the acceptance of life as hard, with nothing to be done about it: put up with it and don't aggravate the situation: 'what is to be, will be'; 'if y' don't like it, y' mun lump it'; that's just the way things are'; 'it's no good kicking against the pricks'; 'what can't be mended must be made do with'; 'y've got to tek life as it cums – day in, day out'. In many of these is a note of dull fatalism; life is always like that for people like us. But the really flat ones are a minority among the phrases of roughly cognate type: in most the note is of a cheerful patience: 'y've got to tek life as it cums', yes; but also 'y've got to get on wi' it best way y' can'; 'grin and bear it'; 'ah well, least said, soonest mended'; 'oh, it'll all be the same in a hundred years' time'; 'all such things are sent to try us' (here, as in some others, the connexion with religion is evident); 'it isn't always dark at six'; 'we're short o' nowt we've got'; 'worse things 'appen at sea'; 'ah well, we live in 'opes'. It's all bound to be ups-and-downs, the rough with the smooth, round-abouts and swings: 'it's no good moaning'; 'mek the best of it . . . stick it . . . soldier on . . .'; 'don't meet trouble 'alf-way'. You may sort-of-hope for a windfall or a sudden, wonderful surprise, but not really; you've got to go on and 'mek yer own life'; 'keep yer end up'; 'life is what y' mek it'. 'Mek shift and fadge' and you'll be 'alright' – as private soldiers were when they knocked up something like a living space out of the most unpromising conditions.

This is not so much the cheerfulness of the stiff upper lip as of the unsuspecting, partly stoic, partly take-life-as-it-comes 'lower orders'. T. S. Eliot says somewhere that stoicism can be a kind of arrogance, a refusal to be humble before God: working-class stoicism is rather a self-defence, against being altogether humbled before men. There may be little you can do about life; there is at any rate something you can be. A working-class housewife, if she finds over a period that she has a shilling a week spare from house-keeping for emergencies, can say that she is 'quite happy'; and the adverb does not modify the adjective, but makes it absolute.

So to tolerance, to 'living and letting live'; a tolerance bred both from a charity, in that all are in the same lower situation together, and from the larger unidealism which that situation creates. The larger unexpectancy encourages a slowness to moral indignation: after all, it's no good creating problems; there are plenty as it is: 'anything for a quiet life'. The tolerance exists along with the conservatism and conformity already described; they clash only rarely. They co-exist, are drawn upon at different times and for different purposes, and people know instinctively which is relevant at any time. Far from contradicting, they thus mutually reinforce each other.

The stress on tolerance arises, then, chiefly from the unexpectant, unfanatic, unidealistic group sense, from the basic acceptance by most people of the larger terms of their life. Working-class people are generally suspicious of principles before practice (in the more articulate this occasionally becomes a thrusting brass-tacks 'realism' which is in fact a self-glorification, masking a disinclination to probe uncomfortably – 'let's get on with the job. All this theory gets you nowhere'). Most are likely to assume that you will lie rather than disappoint or hurt; you may thereby be going against a principle, but that is something outside, and people are here and now. You have to get along with them, to 'rub along' and 'mind yer own business' as you expect other people to mind theirs. Life is never perfect: avoid extremes; most things are 'alright up to a point', or 'alright if y' don't go too far'; and, after all, 'it all depends'. You may have views, but should never 'push them down people's throats'. Views never matter enough, but people do: you should not judge by rules but by facts, not by creed but by character. 'Y' can't change 'uman nature'; 'it teks all sorts to mek a world'; you should 'tek people as y' find 'em'; 'there's good and bad wherever y' go'; ''uman nature's the same wherever y' go', and 'a man's a man wherever y' go': 'everyone's got a right to live'.

All this supports the general lack of patriotism, the mistrust of the public or official things. The 'fear of freedom' may have tempted the middle-classes towards authoritarianism; it affects the working-classes differently. They still feel in their bones that the public and the generalized life is wrong. This rudimentary internationalism can co-exist with anti-Semitism or with strong feeling against Roman Catholicism (as representing Authoritarianism in its 'worst' form); but such intolerance comes out only occasionally, and the two worlds do not often meet.

We know that the pressure to conform expresses itself in an intricate network not of ideas but of prejudices which seek to impose a rigid propriety. They gain strength from the remains of the puritan-ism which once so strongly affected the working-classes, and which still rules fairly strictly a number of working-class lives. On most the puritanism, buttressing itself against the hard facts of working-class conditions, even now has some effect, lives to some degree among those in whom can be found the wider forms of tolerance. We may see this better by looking at attitudes towards drink and, more fully, sex.

On the one hand, drinking is accepted as part of the normal life, or at least of the normal man's life, like smoking. 'A man needs 'is pint'; it helps to make life worth while; if one can't have a bit of pleasure like that, then what is there to live for? It is 'natural' for a man to like his beer. Women seem to be drinking more easily now than they did a generation ago; even as late as my adolescence the 'gin-and-It' woman was regarded as a near-tart. But still, after the children have arrived, women's drinking is not usually considerable; the weekends are their big 'let-out'. Just how much beer-drinking a man may be allowed without incurring disapproval depends on his circumstances; there is a finely-graded scale of allowances. A widower might be expected to drink more than most, since he has not got a wife and comfortable home to go back to. A man and wife with no children can be allowed regular drinking, since they are not taking the bread from their children's mouths, and home without kids is not very inviting. A husband with a family should drink 'within reason', that is, should know when he has had enough, and should always 'provide'. There are occasions – festivals, celebrations, cup-ties, trips – when anyone might be expected to drink quite a lot. It is understandable that certain situations might 'drive anyone to drink'. On the whole, the emphasis is a double one: on the rightness of drinking in itself, and on the realization that, if it once 'gets hold', complete collapse – a near-literal home-breaking as the furniture is sold – may well follow.

It was clearly this latter side which gave such force to the anti-drink movement during the last century and in the first decade or so of this. It was easy to see how even a family which had had as good food as it wished and a few extras could be down to bread-and-scrape off an orange-box inside a month if the 'demon drink' took hold. Economically a working-class home has always been, and to a large extent remains, a raft on the sea of society. So the Temperance Movement was still going strong as late, at least, as the early thirties, when I signed the pledge twice at intervals of a year or so. I was between ten and twelve at the time, and signed with the rest of my Sunday school acquaintances; we felt in an obscure way that it affected our eligibility for places on the Whitsuntide 'treat'. I had a drunken uncle, the last of a line which stretched well back to the seventies, and had its counterpart in many of the families round us. We did not by then sing songs like, 'Please sell no more drink to my Father', or, 'Don't go out tonight, dear Father', or, 'Father, dear Father, come home with me now', or – my own favourite – 'My drink is water bright' (which went something like this: 'Merry Dick, you soon would know,/ If you lived in Jackson's Row/My drink is water bright,/My drink is water bright,/From the crystal spring'). We heard those only as amusement from our elders, who had been taught them as children: but we saw their point. We knew that too much drinking, even as little as three shillings a week more than a family could afford, meant quick poverty, 'tick' mounting until the final bust-up, clothing rapidly and obviously deteriorating, desperately worried mothers, lost jobs, rows of increasing force and frequency. 'Thank goodness, 'e's never been a drinker', housewives will still say regularly. There is little violent drunkenness nowadays, and much less drinking of all kinds, but drink is still regarded as the main pitfall for a working-class husband. Drink, then is 'alright', is 'natural', in moderation. Once the boundary, which varies with different kinds of family, is crossed, disaster may follow. On the other hand, the man who does not drink at all is a bit unusual – most working-class people would not ask for a majority of men like that, whatever the perils of drink.

A friend of mine from a nearby street was an only child and seemed to have no father; his mother was a tailoress, but always able to dress him well, and he had more pocket-money then the rest of us. He went to the pictures a couple of times a week, and could usually produce a penny for some chips. It was only in my teens that I discovered that his mother was a prostitute, operating in the city centre. She needed more money to bring up the boy than tailoring offered. (I think her husband had simply disappeared.) More, she was anxious that he should not 'suffer' because he had 'no father behind him', and the way of ensuring this which presented itself to her imagination was to provide him with the financial superiority which counts so much among boys. Much of what has been said already may go some way towards explaining why she thought so little of the sale of her body; my particular concern here is to point out that she was not ostracized, except by a few who talked of 'giving the street a bad name'. Most nodded at or talked to her as to anyone else, even though they would never have had recourse to prostitution, would indeed have been horrified at the thought for themselves. 'After all, she's got to live,' they used to say; they understood the pressure of the situation, and could see how some people were led to this solution. They did not 'turn against them' because of it: and although I heard from such people many a judgement on what they regarded in others as wanton and dirty behaviour, I do not remember hearing a moral judgement on this woman.

A few years later she was joined, on another 'beat' in the same area, by the younger daughter in a family of six children whose father had brought them up after his wife's death. They lived not far from the first woman, and often came in for adverse comment.

But it was inspired more by the fact that the father did not clothe or feed them as well as the neighbours thought possible, even in his difficult circumstances, than because one of the girls went out to prostitution.

Later, I served a spell as overnight dispatch-clerk to a long-distance transport firm, taking over from a youth who lived a couple of streets away from us. About four times a night the big lorries and their trailers pulled in from Newcastle, dropped some goods, and perhaps a road 'floozie', re-loaded, and headed for London. For the rest of the night-shift I was alone in the back streets of the city centre, except for the policemen, the night-watchmen and an occasional late prostitute. As I took over, my predecessor told me that he was sometimes visited, about half-past eleven, by a prostitute called Irene, who liked to have a cup of tea. She was a good sort and would occasionally 'give you a blow-through' in the furniture-van at the back, if she were not too tired. I met her only once, and she talked most of the time about the pain in her feet. She was almost completely unselfconscious about her occupation and might have been selling papers, so matter-of-fact and dull did she find it. I suppose my rock-climbing-undergraduate look put her off, for she made no offers and came back no more whilst I was there. Later, I used to see her looking into the windows of the posh corner-shops, when I passed through town occasionally at night. The poor girl must have had customers – young bloods from the better districts, visiting commercial travellers, students proving their man-hood, broken-down salesmen, young labourers with money and ale inside them, or those homeless labourers who move from town to town following the big jobs – but I never saw her with one. I remember she told me of a sister on the stage – 'she's luvly to look at'. There seemed to be a steady trickle of good-looking working-class girls into the choruses of the travelling revues.

I do not mean to suggest, in relating these incidents, that work-ing-class people are sexually more licentious than others: I think it doubtful whether they are. But sexual matters do seem nearer the surface, and sexual experience in the working-classes is probably more easily and earlier acquired than in other social groups. The nearness to the surface accompanies, as social workers sometimes point out, a great shyness about some aspects of sex – about dis-cussing it 'sensibly', about being seen naked, or even about undressing for the act of sex, or about sophistications in sexual behaviour. Even today few working-class parents seem to tell their children anything about sex. They know they will quickly pick it all up from the street-corner. But they are not deliberately leaving it aside because they know the street-gang will do the work for them; indeed, they are likely to be greatly upset if they find their children talking or acting 'dirty'. They leave it, I think, partly because they are not good teachers, are neither competent in nor fond of exposition, prefer knowledge to come incidentally, by means of apophthegm and proverb; and partly because of this shyness about bringing sex to the conscious and 'sensible' level. And this will apply as much to the man who, in a suitable context, will talk sex as freely as his mates, as to his perfectly 'clean-mouthed' wife.

But children after the age of ten, and especially boys, learn from the older ones in their groups and later at work. With boys the emphasis is, inevitably, on both the enjoyment of sexual experience and on its dreadful and exciting dangers; and particularly in the early stages, on the pleasures and dangers of masturbation. For many, masturbation soon gives place to some actual hetero-sexual experience. Obviously this is where a working-class boy's pattern in sexual life is likely to differ from that of, say, a public-schoolboy, living until he is eighteen largely in an all-boy community. From thirteen onwards working-class boys' talk, then, is very often of sex adventures, of how easy such and such a girl is to 'feel' or to 'get down' and so on. By eighteen those who wish it can have had a great deal of sexual experience. A group of bricklayers for whom I acted as labourer during a University vacation quickly elicited the information that I was virgin and thereafter regarded me, in a friendly way, as less than a man, as another kind of monk, dedicated to books rather than to religion. They all claimed to be 'getting it regular', though I am sure there was much exaggeration. The married men joined in the frequent sex talk as readily as the rest and regularly lamented their lost freedom, but in an expected kind of way.

How would one sum up the attitude of such men in general, to their irregular sexual experiences? I should perhaps add that there are, of course, many men to whom the foregoing does not apply. They have little sense of guilt or sin in connexion with their sex-life; they make much of sex, but not because underneath they feel lost and anonymous in the great urban mass. That would be to attribute the attitudes of other kinds of people to them. They are not indulging in the bravado of immorality about which much was heard in the behaviour of some groups during the twenties. Yet they do feel vaguely that 'scientific discovery' has made it all more legitimate as well as, with cheap contraceptives, easier. They are not happily amoral savages disporting in some slumland Marquesas Melville never knew. They take their sex-life easily, but do not rollick through it like citified versions of the 'apples be ripe' bucolics of T. F. Powys, or like contemporary versions of the great tuppers of the past. In some respects their attitude towards promiscuous sex activity does come from a long way back. But for them it is all rather scrabbily hole-and-corner. In most cases such activity does not seem to be continued after marriage, or to affect strongly the likelihood of a good marriage relationship.

My impression, though here I may be falling into a romantic error myself, is that more girls than boys escape altogether this bitty, promiscuous sexual experience. The names of the same girls who are willing crop up again and again; the easy ones are soon well known. Of course, the girls have much more to lose at the game; they are liable to 'get caught'.

To me the surprising thing is that so many girls are able to remain unaffected, to retain both an ignorance about the facts of sex and an air of inviolability towards its whole atmosphere that would not have been unbecoming in a mid-nineteenth-century young lady of the middle-classes. It is wonderful how, without evident prudishness or apparent struggle, many of them can walk through the howling valley of sex-approaches from the local lads and probably of sex-talk at work, and come through to the boy they are going to marry quite untouched mentally and physically. Their best light has been the implicit assurance that they would marry, that they were 'keeping themselves for one man', and this is not in a merely calculating sense.

My experience suggests, then, that most girls do not move from man to man, picking up fragmentary experience on the way, but that they begin courting early and go on steadily until an early marriage. Some still 'get into trouble' from fifteen onwards, but they are the exceptions. Many have had some sexual experience before marriage, but usually with the boy they eventually marry; they have not been promiscuous. Nor are they sheltered: from sixteen they are regarded as in most respects adult; they meet the boy they 'fall for' and start courting. They are probably almost completely ignorant of the practice of sex. They feel romantically towards the boy; he presses; it does not seem all that important to wait until marriage, and they yield. He will perhaps take precautions, but a proportion of the men will not, being unprepared or inexpert. If a baby is conceived, the marriage takes place sooner than was expected, but the girl is unlikely to feel that she has been caught. My impression is that most of the girls who lose their virginity before marriage lose it in this way – with boys they are genuinely fond of, when circumstances conspire – rather than from any deliberate passing from boy to boy 'for the fun of it'.

On the whole, once they are 'going steady', loyalty is assumed on each side, and there is little infidelity. The girls are not likely to regard themselves as wicked in anticipating the marriage. They are following a line which will quite soon land them with the attitudes and habits of their mothers, as 'decent' working-class housewives. Meanwhile, one may as well allow it: 'it 'urts nobody. It's natural, i'n't it?'

CHAPTER 4

THE 'REAL' WORLD OF PEOPLE

A. *The Personal and the Concrete*

Holding fast to a world so sharply divided into 'Us' and 'Them' is, from one aspect, part of a more important general characteristic of the outlook of most working-class people. To come to terms with the world of 'Them' involves, in the end, all kinds of political and social questions, and leads eventually beyond politics and social philosophy to metaphysics. The question of how we face 'Them' (whoever 'They' are) is, at last, the question of how we stand in relation to anything not visibly and intimately part of our local universe. The working-class splitting of the world into 'Us' and 'Them' is on this side a symptom of their difficulty in meeting abstract or general questions.

They have had little or no training in the handling of ideas or in analysis. Those who show a talent for such activities have, increasingly during the last forty years, been taken out of their class. More important than either of these reasons is the fact that most people, of whatever social class, are simply not, at any time, going to be interested in general ideas; and in the working-classes this majority – since they are not greatly tempted by other major interests, such as making money, or even by intellectual activities generated by their work – will stick to the tradition of their group; and that is a personal and local tradition.

As to politics, therefore, they have a limited realism which tells them that, as far as they can see, 'there's no future' in it for them. 'Politics never did anybody any good,' they will add; and there they are drawing upon more reputable assumptions, but applying them too widely. There are, of course, individual exceptions; and there are occasional increases in the intensity of political preoccupation among the majority. But in general most working-people are non-political and non-metaphysical in their outlook. The important things in life, so far as they can see, are other things. They may appear to have views on general matters – on religion, on politics, and so on – but these views usually prove to be a bundle of largely unexamined and orally-transmitted tags, enshrining generalizations, prejudices, and half-truths, and elevated by epigrammatic phrasing into the status of maxims. As I remarked earlier, these are often contradictory of each other; but they are not thought about, not intellectually considered. They have a hypnotic and final effect the sound of revealed truth, of the more unassailable cracker-mottoes:

'They're all talk – they've never done a day's work in their lives.'
'Of course, all politics are crooked.'
'Y' can't get a better made thing than one made in England.'
'Progress always goes on.'
'All Americans are boastful.'
'British is best when y'come to it.'
'England is the most important country in the world.'
'There's one law for the rich –.'
'There's now't to choose between 'em' (of political parties).

These, and a hundred similar apophthegms are repeated unquestioningly every day, as they have been for decades. Those which claim superiority for Britain are not 'patriotic', in any proper sense; they express an inherited assumption of national superiority. Though repeatedly told, especially during the last dozen years, about the change in England's international position, the majority of working-class people have no realization of it. Nor are they noticeably aware of the enormous changes in space and time relations which have taken place during the last twenty years. Their response to the constant demand on them to develop the 'double eye' has not been an adjustment towards, but a defence against, such a development. What can be adapted, translated into their own terms, is adapted and translated: what cannot be, is ignored and the empty space closed by a convenient maxim. Other classes have their own forms of escape: I do not mean to imply that the working-classes are alone with this problem, or alone in evading it.

They are assailed by a mass of abstractions; they are asked to respond to 'the needs of the state', and the 'needs of society', to study 'good citizenship', to have in mind the 'common good'. In most cases the appeals mean nothing, are so many words. They do not think such general calls, for duty, for sacrifice, for individual effort, are relevant to them. They themselves are the ground-base of society, they know; normally they go on living their own kind of life. When the larger world, society, the world of 'Them', needs the mass of the people, why then, they feel, they are quickly told where to go and what to do. For the rest, the local and concrete world is what can be understood, managed, trusted,

> Adjusted to the local needs of valleys
> Where everything can be touched or reached by walking,
> Their eyes have never looked into infinite space.

As the outer world becomes more and more streamlined, so the family and the neighbourhood come to be regarded, even more than formerly, as something that is real and recognizable. It would be difficult to overrate the centralization of modern life: it is easy to overrate the sense of anonymity which so far visits most individuals. Home is carved out under the shadow of the giant abstractions; inside the home one need be no more aware of those outer forces than is the badger under his mountain of earth. It is as much of a relief as ever it was, and perhaps even more of a relief, to come back to the local known group, to come across 'one of us'.

Other people may live a life of 'getting and spending', or a 'literary life', or 'the life of the spirit', or even 'the balanced life', if there is such a thing. If we want to capture something of the essence of working-class life in such a phrase, we must say that it is the 'dense and concrete life', a life whose main stress is on the intimate, the sensory, the detailed, and the personal. This would no doubt be true of working-class groups anywhere in the world. I remember a small and unprepossessing English private soldier who made friends with a splendid blooming opera star in Italy. He quickly had his feet under the family table every night, and developed a wide knowledge of and taste for the more genuinely native dishes. She was a working-class girl who happened to have been born with a good voice. He walked into her sprawling family as though he belonged there; which of course, he did, more than he belonged to the world of his own officers' mess. This suggests yet again the care with which we ought to approach an examination of the changes so far wrought in working-class attitudes by intense urbanization: the Italian family were still three-quarters peasant; the Englishman was in many respects a thoroughly urban figure.

The conversation which goes on connectedly and continually across the din of the machines, between girls on routine jobs in factories, is so local, so personal and so intimate that it makes the girls a close, embracing group. It is almost always elemental, sometimes rough, and often generous; its main themes are among the great themes of existence – marriage, children, relations with others, sex. Much the same is naturally true of men's working-groups. They are all doing what working-class people always do, wherever they find themselves and however unpromising their situation may appear; they are exercising their strong traditional urge to make life intensely human, to humanize it in spite of everything and so to make it, not simply bearable, but positively interesting. To some extent this is true of most people in any class, but is an attitude particularly encouraged by the nature of working-class life. Working-class people are only rarely interested in theories or movements. They do not usually think of their lives as leading to an improvement in status or to some financial goal. They are enormously interested in people: they have the novelist's fascination with individual behaviour, with relationships – though not so as to put them into a pattern, but for their own sake. 'Isn't she *queer*?'; 'Fancy saying a thing like that!'; 'What do you think she meant by that?' they say; even the simplest anecdote is told dramatically, with a wealth of rhetorical questions, supplementary illustrations, significant pauses, and alternations of pitch.

Yet working-class people have considerable sensitiveness in reaching conclusions on some things, in their own way. They constantly make rough-and-ready judgements on people, judgements not drawing upon concepts from an outside source, but based on the assumption that there are a few firm, important, desirable qualities; qualities embodied in phrases like, 'Ah tak a man as 'e is', and 'Y' know where yer 'ave 'im; 'e's not "say one thing and do another" '; qualities of friendliness and decent-heartedness, of directness and openness in dealing.

Within certain areas this power of intuitive judgement is well developed. Here, whether on individuals or on relationships, working-class people are still often acute, and pithy in their comment. They have developed the quality almost entirely 'in the field' rather than from reading: they have an acute eye for faces and ear for voices, an eye and ear which can sometimes be fresher and truer than those of a person who filters his perceptions through his reading and discussion. They are fond of 'weighing people up' by eye and ear: 'Ah don't like 'er,' they will say, 'she's got a false voice'; or, "'e's got eyes that look right through y',' meaning eyes that reduce you to a thing, that ignore the values of frankness and friendliness.

I deliberately qualified this claim for good intuitive judgement. In making it at all, one runs the risk of resurrecting once more the ghost of the noble savage, the simple unspoiled son of toil, fully equipped with finely discriminating organs (so much less stale and corrupt than the tired sophisticates who think). Working-class people can make quick impressionistic judgements of great skill in certain fields: outside them, or if they are deceptively approached under the correct flags, they can be as babies. One might give the title 'The Fall of the Innocents' to those activities in which working-class people, in particular, are duped, *simply because they have been approached along a line on which they are exposed* – that is, because they have been approached in a personal, friendly, and homely manner. We see this in a thousand advertisements aimed at them, in the editorial comment of some working-class papers and magazines, in the tone of the popular astrologers. The less-reputable clothing-clubs know they can go a long way if they lard each stage of the transactions with this strong personal quality; so do the door-to-door salesmen of bad bargains. And here the louder furniture stores are of unusual interest, especially because of an apparent paradox. At first glance these are surely the most hideously tasteless of all modern shops. Every known value in decoration has been discarded: there is no evident design or pattern; the colours fight with one another; anything new is thrown in simply because it is new. There is strip-lighting together with imitation chandelier lighting; plastics, wood and glass are all glued and stuck and blown together; notice after blazing notice winks, glows, or blushes luminously. Hardly a homely setting. Nor do the superficially elegant men who stand inside the doorway, and alternately tuck their hankies up their cuffs or adjust their ties, appear to belong to 'Us'. They are not meant to. With their neat ready-made clothing, shiny though cheap shoes, well-creamed hair and ready smiles they are meant (like the equally harassed but flashier motor-car salesmen) to represent an ethos. One buys the suggestion of education and elegance with the furniture.

If this were all, they would hardly succeed with working-class people; they would be likely to impress but also to 'freeze off'. But though they are obviously very smart and 'real educated', and though they insist on calling every young wife 'madam', they are also – it is their most effective quality – 'ever so nice and friendly'. In a sense, yes, almost all shopkeepers aim to be pleasant, may affect deference or mateyness: this is something more. This is a consistent and powerful use of the individual and domestic approach, and all the nicer because unexpected in so posh a gentleman. The proprietors realize that working-class people will be dazzled by the exuberance and glitter of their display, will be attracted and yet a little awed. The manner of their salesmen is usually, therefore, understandingly colloquial; not the 'now, ma' of the fairground salesman, but 'I know what it's like, madam,' or, 'I had a young couple just like you in only last week'; all in the tone of an understanding son who has done well and become cultured. It is not all as deliberate and conscious as I may have seemed to suggest; it is not altogether new or confined to this type of shop. But this type of shop – the huge, glossy affair aiming specifically at working-class customers – specializes in this approach. Those who direct them sense the working-class awe of and attraction towards metroland, and their accessibility by means of warm and friendly terms. The working-classes hold on to the personal because they can understand it; here, that part of the world outside which is after their money makes a pretty Trojan horse for them.

The general point is further illustrated by two institutions –professional sport and Royalty – which though they originate in the world outside, hold the interest of working-class people largely because they can be easily translated into personal and concrete terms.

At work, sport vies with sex as the staple of conversation. The popular Sunday newspapers are read as much for their full sports reports as for their accounts of the week's crimes. Sports conversations start from personalities, often spoken of by their Christian as well as by their surnames, as 'Jim Motson', 'Arthur Jones', and 'Will Thompson': technical details of play are discussed, often to the accompaniment of extraordinary feats of memory as to the history of matches many seasons back. The men talk about individuals whom they know, at least as figures on the field, in situations eliciting qualities they can respect and admire. Their attitude is not that suggested by such a phrase as 'a clean mind in a healthy body'. A passage like this, from a book of advice to young men, would be alien to their world, and not only because they are usually spectators rather than participants:

Regard your body as the engine – far more wonderful than any man-made machine – and you will find that you can derive endless pleasure from cleaning, fuelling, lubricating and testing it, as well as from actually racing it.

Working-class sports-lovers admire the qualities of the hunter and fighter and daredevil – the exhibition of strength and muscle, of speed and daring, of skill and cunning. The great boxers and foot-ballers and speedway riders naturally become heroes – very modified modern counterparts of the heroes of saga, who combined natural physical gifts with great application and cunning in the use of them.

I wonder whether this helps to explain the common distrust of the referee; at least, the distrust common at Rugby League matches. I do not mean simply the assumption, if things are going badly, that the referee is 'on their side'. I mean a deeply ingrained feeling that the referee is a sort of headmaster or Sunday school-ish corrector, running round in his neat shorts and blazer, nattering and blowing his whistle. This does not seem to be more than a vague and unconscious feeling; it does not usually produce any more active reaction than exasperated cries of 'Leave 'im alone, ref.', or 'Give 'im a chance, can't yer?'; but it is pervasive.

In those areas, in particular, where Rugby League is played, the home team is also an important element in the group life of the district. They are spoken of with genuine pride as 'our lads', and many of them may well be local boys – huge ex-miners or heavy steelworkers. I remember Hunslet Rugby team bringing the Cup home from Wembley years ago, coming down from the City Station into the heart of the district on top of a charabanc. They went from pub to pub in all the neighbourhood's main streets, with free drinks at every point, followed by crowds of lads prepared to risk staying out hours after their bedtime for the excitement of seeing their local champions.

Amid all the pressure of publicity which now surrounds the monarchy it is more than usually difficult to approach the true working-class attitudes to it. Working-class people are not, we know, particularly patriotic: they have streaks of insularity, of Francophobia and Americanophobia; but if put to the question they will soon say that working-class people are the same the world over. They remain confirmed anti-militarists; the memory of the old days, of brothers going into the army through lack of a job or to escape some trouble, and having to be bought out at great sacrifice, had only just begun to die when conscription came in; and for the seventeen years since then, there has usually been some member of the family in the Services.

How little, too, the aristocracy now counts in the folk-lore of the working-classes. It no longer has much power even to inspire ill-will, though with a few working-class women it still holds something of its snob-appeal. But on the whole working-class people, and in particular the men, simply do not include the 'upper crust' in their picture of life nowadays. Most of them will say, when they read of their doings – the conventional activities, rather than those of what remain of the 'bright young things', which still have some interest – that they ''ave no time for all that'.

What then, of the monarchy? Again, as an institution, it is scarcely thought of by the working-classes; they are not royalists by principle. Nor do most harbour resentment against it; they have little heat. They either ignore it or, if they are interested, the interest is for what can be translated into the personal. Since they are 'personalists' and dramatists, they are more interested in a few individual members of the Royal Family than in the less colourful figures of parliamentary government.

I am not thinking of the period, usually in adolescence, when some girls find a glamour in the Royal Family similar to that they find in film-stars; nor of the fervours of London crowds on special occasions. I am thinking chiefly of provincial working-class women over twenty-five. Their menfolk are either quite uninterested in Royalty or vaguely hostile, since it tends to suggest to them the world of special parades in the Services, of 'blanco and bullshit'. Working-class women, too, will with one part of themselves speak of the Royal Family in the way they might speak of any members of the aristocracy. Royal personages may have to do a lot of hand-shaking and the rest, but they are well-cared for; they have no money troubles like us; they don't have to struggle with the kids when they are tired out; they're 'waited on hand and foot'. This side will come out in reaction to the sillier Press-releases or column-ists' tales – that Princess A will darn all her husband's socks; or

Princess D will look after Baby Prince E herself. At this point, and it is always reached a number of times during any great Royal season, the reaction is plainly debunking: 'Y' bet she will.'

At the same time, they will often separate the Royal Family from its advisers, from the Government, from the rest of the aristocracy. It is this ability, to think of the members of the Royal Family as individuals, caught up in a big machine manipulated by 'Them', having 'a real family life' only with difficulty, which allows a great many women in the working-classes to feel well-disposed towards Royalty today, and to be as interested in their more 'homely' activities as are women of other classes. 'It's a rotten job,' people will say, 'they get pushed around as much as we do.' They then feel a lot of sympathy for all that is expected of the monarch, feel that she and her husband deserve all the goodwill they can get: 'She's a nice lass,' they will add. Other members of the Royal Family have their places, like figures in an interesting novelette – 'They say she's a mean thing'; 'They say 'e led 'er a dog's life'; 'She likes 'er bit of fun, she does.' They want, therefore, and their magazines provide them generously with, the fullest details of the home-life of the Royal Family; of what a poem about the Queen Mother, in the magazine *Silver Star*, called their 'warm and homely ways'.

B. *'Primary Religion'*

There are a few working-class areas in which a substantial proportion of people still attend church or chapel. And a multitude of small sects seem to flourish here more than elsewhere – in Gospel Halls of varying solidity, in converted shops on trolley-bus routes. Notably, there are the several forms of Spiritualism, which appear to attract, understandably, middle-aged widows. Often these sects include among their adherents some who also belong to church or to one of the larger nonconformist bodies.

So at least one member of most families in the extended sense of the word – perhaps an aunt or spinster cousin, if not a parent – is likely to be a regular attender at church or chapel. Church or chapel are still felt as in some sense a part of the life of the neighbourhood. People will still speak of 'our chapel', and many who do not normally attend will feel that an event there is a neighbourhood event, and so go to an anniversary service, or a bazaar, or a concert, or the start

D

of the Whitsuntide walk, or the Christmas pantomime. 'You can't see anything better at the Theatre Royal,' I've heard a hundred times about these last events.

For all that, my impression is that even this limited sense of belonging is weakening in most of the areas I know. Today, most working-class people go neither to church nor to chapel except on special family occasions, once the parental order to attend Sunday school has been withdrawn. In some places one of the recognized signs of becoming adult, together with going into long trousers for the boys or permission to use make-up for the girls, is this freedom to leave Sunday school and read the *News of the World* at home like Dad. Few among the working-classes seem to find their own way back to a church after adolescence. If old ties are cut, they are unlikely to be remade.

Though working-class adults do not as a rule attend any place of worship regularly, they are not consciously anti-clerical. Towards the parson their attitude is likely to be faintly cynical; he is in with the bosses. But it is usually a cheerful cynicism with no active hostility behind it. 'It's a good racket if you can get in on it,' they will say, 'good luck to 'em.' We're all rogues under the skin is the assumption, and opportunity's a fine thing: I'd probably do the same if I had the chance.

Yet they continue to be married and buried in church and chapel, to have children baptized there, and to send them to Sunday school. Are they simply band-waggoning, playing for safety? And when they pray in a tight corner, as they usually admit to doing, is that simply a panic measure or a strong upsurge of an always-latent superstition? Partly, no doubt; but not altogether. Along with other classes, but in their own ways, working-class people have been affected by ideas which seem to have disposed of the claims of religion. And their experience often seems to suggest that the professions of religion just would not work in 'real' life, and that they are often used to cover an inevitable jungle warfare. Yet, in coming to religious institutions at the important moments of life or in times of personal crisis they are not simply taking out a saving policy; they still believe underneath, in certain ways. At least, middle-aged people do, and here I am thinking chiefly of them.

They believe, first, in the purposiveness of life. Life has a meaning, must have a meaning. One does not bother much about defining it, or pursue abstract questions as to its nature or the implications which follow from such a conclusion; but clearly it is so. 'We're 'ere for a purpose,' they say, or, 'There must be some purpose or we wouldn't be 'ere'. And that there is a purpose presupposes that there must be a God. They hold to what G. K. Chesterton called 'the dumb certainties of existence', and Reinhold Niebuhr, 'primary religion'. Equally simply, they hold to what George Orwell called 'those things [like free-will and the existence of the individual] which we know to be so, though all the arguments are against them'.

Just as surely, they assume a life after death, what they usually call 'an after-life'. On this matter they have what Reinhold Niebuhr, again, calls 'the basic optimism of all vital and wholesome human life'. Look at the *In Memoriam* columns of local newspapers: how often an 'after-life' is mentioned, and how often it is regarded as a release from hard work 'here below', and the arrival at an easier happier existence; gone to 'a happy release', 'a blessed release', 'a better existence', they run, and add, 'gone before' or 'gone ahead'. They are usually selected from a printed card at the newspaper offices, and might appear to be no more than another example of commercialism providing for sentimentality, but the choice of phrases available on the card is decided by customers' demands, and they run on certain lines only and are not merely sentimentally felt, or accepted by habit.

Working-class mothers tend to see Heaven as a place for consolations and some reward. Punishment for sins is little thought of, since here below their kind have been the lackers. They have not always 'done right', but allowance will be made for their situation: they ask only – and they expect – 'fairness'.

Life in Heaven for such a mother is envisaged as a re-creation of the happier side of family life, with God as an extension of her own father (if he was 'a good dad'), and one much more able to straighten things out, not harassed by powers outside the family which he cannot control. Heaven will be, above all, the place for 'straightening out', and for comforting. Things will be easier there; there will be time to sit, to get a good rest. There will be a moderate and understanding 'jacket-straightening' for the 'bad 'uns' who led her such a dance. There will be a reunion with those who have gone before and have since been so much missed; with the lively-spirited young sister whom T.B., aggravated by the mill, took away; with the rickety bright son who went off at nineteen.

Hence the emphasis on a 'proper' funeral, a 'decent burial', 'putting 'im away splendid'; and the dislike of cremation as 'unnatural'. Heavy insurances cover the cost of a good burial for themselves, or of their black clothes for a relative's funeral. The more careful families begin a small insurance at birth. I still pay a penny a week burial insurance, which my mother began just after I was born: it will provide about fifteen pounds towards the cost of my funeral. Sometimes the insurances become a form of banking, and the death of a relative one of the periodic occasions for a general renewal of the wardrobe. Behind the 'decent' funeral is also the wish not to 'show y'selves up' before the neighbours, to do it proud on this important and public occasion. Behind it, too, is the assumption that neither the body nor those following it must go to the burial in the state of shabbiness which has been usual throughout life. It is, in no facetious sense, the biggest Whit-Sunday of them all. Like many an old working-class woman, my grandmother had a splendid laying-out gown and sheets ready against her death, and towards the end of her life she would remind us periodically where they were kept. But this particular feature was probably a direct relic of her rural background.

In the same way, the custom of laying on a good meal at a funeral, of 'burying 'im with 'am', is not simply an excuse for a good feed on the strength of the insurance policies. It is considered a suitable way of doing things, without for once pinching and scraping, on one of the rare occasions when the family gathers. We may be tempted, noticing how much the atmosphere lightens at tea and listening to the gossip which goes on for hours, to think that these are no more than gatherings for family gossip over a large meal. The gossip certainly takes place, as it does at a wedding, together with the large meal and the great number of people. But though the outward characteristics of a funeral gathering are in so many ways similar to those of a wedding, these similarities are the least important aspects.

Working-class people, when they insist on a church wedding or funeral, are drawing upon beliefs which, though rarely considered, are still in most cases firmly there. These beliefs, some of the basic Christian doctrines, they hold, but do not examine. Nor do they often think that they have much relevance to the day-to-day business of living. That is thought of as an altogether different matter, a hard and unidealistic matter; if you tried to 'live according to religion', well, you would soon find it was 'a mug's game'; would soon be 'done for'. They know that they and other people often do wrong, but by that they usually mean doing wrong towards other people; the sense of sin, of original sin, is on the whole alien to them. If one of their number is strikingly affected by the dogmas of religion, they are quick to say, 'Oh, 'e's got religious mania,' and to regard him as a harmless crank or near-lunatic. Sometimes he is, but not always, and they draw few distinctions here. They will allow much more readily for the religious person who tries with particular earnestness to body out his beliefs ethically. The Salvation Army is popularly regarded as an attraction to the slightly dotty; but, 'they do a lot of good' with their social aid schemes, and are respected for that: the *War Cry* still sells in the pubs.

In so far as they think of Christianity, they think of it as a system of ethics; their concern is with morals, not metaphysics. The verb in the commonly used phrase 'I don't believe in it' is usually doing duty for 'agree with' or 'hold with', since the point is almost always ethical. Yet they hold firmly to the view that Christianity is the best form of ethics. They will say, without sense of contradiction, that science has taken the place of religion, but that we ought all to try to 'live according to Christ's teaching'. In some ways they appear to accept everything about the universe that seems to come to them from 'the scientist'; but they will rightly refuse to accept the idea that he has no moral responsibility towards the application of what he discovers. I am not thinking of the fact that, in moments of fear – about the power of the hydrogen bomb, for instance – they, like many others, may wish to punish the scientists. I am thinking of the way in which, however scientific invention develops and whatever prestige and almost magical powers scientists may appear to possess, working-class people persist in assuming that there is a straightforward moral responsibility in both the act of engagement in, and the application of, such discoveries.

That sense of moral duties is what they chiefly understand, I have suggested, by Christianity. Christianity is morals; a phrase used above, 'Christ's teaching', is the one most commonly heard when the talk is in favour of religion. Christ was a person, giving the best example of how to live; one could not expect to be able to live like that today: still, the example is there. They like to speak of 'practical Christianity'.

The emphasis is always on what it is right for them to do, as far as they can, as people; people who do not see the point of 'all this dogma', but who must constantly get along with others, in groups; people who must learn how to co-operate, how to live on an exchange basis, how to give and take. The assumption behind the treatment of others is not so much that we are all children of God (though a form of that is there, in the background) as that we are all 'in the same boat together'. Like the barmaid Ida in Graham Greene's *Brighton Rock*, they do not think much about sin and grace, good and evil; but they are sure there is a difference between right and wrong. I think I see the limitations of such a position, but I cannot feel that it indicates as miserable a condition as Graham Greene finds; in the circumstances, they might have adopted several far less admirable attitudes.

Here, round the sense of religion as a guide to our duty towards others, as the repository of good rules for communal life, the old phrases cluster. Ask any half-dozen working-class people what they understand by religion, and very easily, but not meaninglessly, they will be likely to answer with one of these phrases:

'doing good',
'common decency',
'helping lame dogs',
'being kind',
'doing unto others as y'would be done unto',
'we're 'ere to 'elp one another',
''elping y'neighbour',
'learning to know right from wrong',
'decent living'.

This is the main reason for the steadiness with which children are enrolled for Sunday school. The subsidiary reasons are familiar: that parents like a quiet Sunday afternoon to themselves, sometimes extended by obliging the children to go for a good walk between the end of school and teatime; or that Mother has been cooking hard all morning and is tired; or that Father wants to doze after looking at the Sunday papers. But behind all these is the notion that Sunday school is a civilizing influence, that it helps the children to avoid 'getting into bad ways'.

It is a truism that the chapels owed much of their growth to this same ethical bent; that the churches were associated with privilege, with the upper classes, with ritual; that the chapels had ministers who were not Oxford-trained, and made wide use of lay preachers – themselves often men whose religion was a powerful down-to-earth moralizing. They were 'one of us', with what admirers called 'the gift of tongues', but doubters knew as 'the gift of the gab'. Neither the preachers nor the congregation had much time for ritual or for almost any 'form'; decoration had to be simple and forthright, like the order of service, and like the relationship laid down as proper between the minister and his flock. The heat of all this has long since died down, but many working-class people can today, on occasion, produce a flicker of the old fire. They enjoy indulging occasionally a suspicion that there is something sinister about the Roman Catholic church, a quality not unconnected, they feel, with 'all that incense swinging and candles and stuff'.

'A lot of praying doesn't do any good' (though some older people, women especially, still pray regularly, even though they attend no church): you can get as close to God on your own as do those who are 'always running after' the vicar or the minister: 'there's good in all sorts', and you do not need to go to chapel to be a Christian. 'I'm as good a Christian as you, though I don't go to church,' they say. With that often goes the implied reversal: 'You're as bad as I am, even though y' do go to church.' The regular church-goer, it is inferred, may be less virtuous than some of those who never attend. If he is very regular and something of a figure at church, he may well be a bit of a hypocrite – whereas the man who makes no pretensions, but does his best, is probably much nearer being a Christian. After all, doing your best to be an 'ordinary decent' person – that is what Christianity means, really.

Doing your best, but remembering the 'real world' outside, the world of work and debts. Life is making the best of things in this world, is 'rubbing along' as best you may; you may have 'Christ's teaching' somewhere at the back of your head: you may, when you think of it, admire it; but still, when it comes to the living of life itself, well 'you know . . .'. In any case, these 'deeper questions' do not seem to have made much difference to those who have had time, money, and inclination to pursue them.

Most people in the working-classes appear, therefore, not merely unfanatic but unidealistic; they have their principles, but are dis-inclined to reveal them in their pure state. For the most part their approach is empirical; they are confirmed pragmatists. It is an attitude derived not so much from a submission to the claims of expediency, as from a sense of the nearness of personal horizons, and of the folly of expecting too much, least of all from general professions. 'Ah like fair dealings' may seem an inadequate guide to the cosmos and can be self-righteous, but – said sincerely by a middle-aged man after a hard life – it can represent a considerable triumph over difficult circumstances.

c. *Illustrations from Popular Art* – Peg's Paper

This overriding interest in the close detail of the human condition is the first pointer to an understanding of working-class art. To begin with, working-class art is essentially a 'showing' (rather than an 'exploration'), a presentation of what is known already. It starts from the assumption that human life is fascinating in itself. It has to deal with recognizable human life, and has to begin with the photo-graphic, however fantastic it may become; it has to be underpinned by a few simple but firm moral rules.

Here is the source of the attraction, the closely, minutely domestic attraction, of *Thomson's Weekly News*. It is this, more than a vicarious snobbery, which makes radio serials with middle-class settings popular with working-class people, since these serials reflect daily the minutiae of everyday life. It is this which helps to ensure that the news-presen-tation of most popular newspapers belongs to the realms of imagina-tive or fictional writing of a low order. Those special favourites of working-class people, the Sunday gossip-with-sensation papers, the papers for the free day, assiduously collect from throughout the British Isles all the suitable material they can find, for the benefit of almost the whole of the adult working-class population. It is true that their interest, whether in news-reporting or in fiction, is often increased by the 'ooh-aah' element – a very 'ordinary' girl is knocked down by a man who proves to be a film-star; an attractive young widow proves to have disposed of two husbands with arsenic and popped them under the cellar-flagstones – and it is easy to think that most popular literature is of the 'ooh-aah' kind. One should think first of the photographically detailed aspect; the staple fare is not something which suggests an escape from ordinary life, but rather it assumes that ordinary life is intrinsically interesting. The emphasis is initially on the human and detailed, with or without the 'pepping-up' which crime or sex or splendour gives. De Rougemont speaks of millions (though he has in mind particularly the middle-classes) who 'breathe in ... a romantic atmosphere in the haze of which passion seems to be the supreme test'. As we shall see, there is much in working-class literature too which gives support to this view; but it is not the first thing to say about the more genuinely working-class publications which persist. For them passion is no more interesting than steady home-life.

Some B.B.C. programmes underline the point. Notice how popular the 'homely' programmes are, not simply such programmes as *Family Favourites* ('for Good Neighbours') nor simply the family serials and feature-programmes such as *Mrs Dale's Diary*, *The Archers*, *The Huggetts*, *The Davisons*, *The Grove Family*, *The Hargreaves*; but the really ordinary homely programmes, often composed, rather like the more old-fashioned papers, of a number of items linked only by the fact that they all deal with the ordinary lives of ordinary people. I have in mind programmes like Wilfred Pickles's *Have a Go* and Richard Dimbleby's *Down Your Way*. They have no particular shape; they do not set out to be 'art' or entertainment in the music-hall sense; they simply 'present the people to the people' and are enjoyed for that. So are the programmes which still make use of the music-hall 'comic's' tradition of handling working-class life, programmes like Norman Evans's *Over the Garden Wall* and Al Read's superb sketches. It is not necessary, for success, that the programmes should be a form of professional art; if it is really homely and ordinary it will be interesting and popular.

I have suggested that it is commonly thought that some magazines – for example, those predominantly read by working-class women and usually spoken of as '*Peg's Paper* and all that' – provide little other than undiluted fantasy and sensation. This is not true; in some ways the more genuinely working-class magazines are preferable to those in the newer style. They are in some ways crude, but often more than that; they still have a felt sense of the texture of life in the group they cater for. I shall refer to them as 'the older magazines' because they carry on the *Peg's Paper* tradition, and reflect the older forms of working-class life: in fact, most of them, under their present titles, are between ten and twenty years old.

Almost all are produced by the three large commercial organizations: Amalgamated Press, the Newnes Group, and Thomson and Leng. But the authors and illustrators seem to have a close knowledge of the lives and attitudes of their audience. One wonders whether the publishers take in much of their material piecemeal from outside, rather as the stocking-makers of Nottingham once did. Most of the material is conventional – that is, it mirrors the attitudes of the readers; but those attitudes are by no means as ridiculous as one might at first be tempted to think. In comparison with these papers, some of those more recently in the front are as a smart young son with a quick brain and a bundle of up-to-date opinions beside his sentimental, superstitious, and old-fashioned mother.

These older magazines can often be recognized by their paper, a roughly textured newsprint which tends to have a smell – strongly evocative to me now, because it is also that of the old boys' magazines and comics – of something slightly damp and fungoid. They can be recognized also by their inner lay-out, in which only a few kinds of type are likely to be used; by their covers, which are usually 'flat' and boldly coloured in a limited range – almost entirely of black with strong shades of blue, red, and yellow, with few intermediates. They usually sell at threepence each, and have such titles as *Secrets*, *Red Star Weekly*, *Lucky Star* (which now incorporates *Peg's Paper*), *The Miracle*, *The Oracle*, *Glamour*, *Red Letter* and *Silver Star*. They are apparently designed for adolescent girls and young married women in particular; thus, two in three of the readers of *Red Letter* are under thirty-five. There is some provision for older readers. The number of their readers varies between one-third and three-quarters of a million each, with most of them above the half-million. There will be much overlapping, but the total number of readers remains considerable, and they are almost entirely from the working-classes.

In composition they are all much alike. There are many advertisements, scattered throughout in penny packets, on the back cover and over large parts of the last couple of text-pages; there are usually no advertisements on the front cover pages and first text-pages. After the coloured cover, the inner cover page is generally given to some regular editorial feature; or the main serial, or the week's 'dramatic long complete novel', begins there. The advertisements, regularly recurring throughout the whole group of magazines, cover a narrow range of goods. Some cosmetics still use an aristocratic appeal, with photographs of titled ladies dressed for a ball. The same ailments appear so often in the advertisements for proprietary remedies that a hasty generalizer might conclude from them that the British working-classes are congenitally both constipated and 'nervy'. There are many announcements of cures for disabilities which are likely to make a girl a 'wallflower'. The 'scientists tell us' approach is there, but so still is its forerunner, the 'gypsy told me' approach. Thus, there are occasionally esoteric Indian remedies in this manner – 'Mrs Johnson learned this secret many years ago from her Indian nurse in Bombay. Since then, many thousands have had cause to be glad that they reposed confidence in her system.' For married women there are washing-powder advertisements, and those for headache powders or California Syrup of Figs for children. But, in general, the assumption is that the married women readers are young enough to want to keep up with the unmarried by the use of cosmetics and hair-shampoos. Mail-order firms advertise fancy wedge-shoes, nylon underwear for – I suppose – the young women, and corsets for the older. For all groups, but especially, it appears, for the youngish married women with little spare money, there are large advertisements (much the biggest in these magazines) inviting them to become agents for one of the great Clothing or General Credit Clubs which proliferate, chiefly from the Manchester area, and usually give their agents two shillings in the pound, a fat catalogue and free notepaper.

Stories make up the body of the text-pages, but interspersed are the regular and occasional features. There are no politics, no social questions, nothing about the arts. This is neither the world of the popular newspapers which still purport to be alive to events, nor that of those women's magazines which have an occasional flutter with 'culture'. There are beauty hints, often over the signature of a well-known film-star: and some very homely home hints; there is a half-page of advice from an 'aunt' or a nurse on personal problems – the kind of thing laughed at as 'Aunt Maggie's advice'; in fact, it is usually very sensible. I do not mean, though this is true, that there is never a breath which is not firmly moral. But the general run of the advice is practical and sound, and when a problem arises whose answer is beyond the competence of the journalist, the enquirer is told to go to a doctor or to one of the advisory associations. There is a fortune-teller's section, based on the stars or birthday dates.

The stories divide easily into the serials, the long complete story of the week, and the short stories (probably only one page in length). The long stories and the serials often have startling surprises, as a young man proves to be really wealthy or a girl finds she wins a beauty competition, even though she has always thought of herself as a plain Jane. This is particularly the case with the serials, which must be 'dramatic' and mount their accumulated series of suspended shocks as week follows week. So they tend to deal in what are called wild passions and in murder. There are handsome men on the loose, usually called Rafe. But much more interesting, because much more obviously feared, are the 'fascinating bitches', the Jezebels, as most advance trailers dub them. These are the women who set up in provincial towns and fail to report that they have a 'dreadful past' or that a 'dreadful secret' lies in their previous home a hundred miles away; or they get rid of pretty young girls by whom the man they are after is really attracted, by tipping them overboard from a rowing-boat, trussed in a cabin-trunk; or they convert an electric-kettle into a lethal weapon: 'She did not look evil – yet her presence was like a curse' – 'She was a woman fashioned by the Devil himself into the mould of the fairest of angels.'

The strong case against this kind of literature is well known, and I do not mean to take that case lightly. It applies, one should remember, to popular literature for all classes. When one has said that some of these stories supply the thrill of the wicked or evil, can one go farther? Can one distinguish them from the general run of this kind of popular writing? Denis de Rougemont points out that this type of story, especially when it is written for the middle-classes, usually manages to have things both ways, that though the villains never triumph in fact, they do triumph emotionally; that where, for instance, adulterous love is the subject, these stories imply an emotional betrayal. They 'hold the chains of love to be indefeasible and [imply] the superiority from a "spiritual" standpoint of mistress over wife'. 'Therefore', M. de Rougemont continues, 'the institution of marriage comes off rather badly, but that does not matter ... since the middle-class (especially on the Continent) is well aware that this institution is no longer grounded in morality or religion, but rests securely upon financial foundations.' M. de Rougemont also emphasizes the fascination of the love/death theme, of an adulterous love-relationship which can find some sort of resolution only in death.

There seems to me a difference between this and most of the

'thrilling' stories in these 'older' magazines. There seems to be little emotional betrayal of the explicit assumptions here; the thrill comes because the villain is striking – 'making passes at' – some things still felt underneath to be important, at a sense of the goodness of home and married life, above individual relations of passion. Thus there is no use of the love/death theme, since that would be to kill altogether the positive and actual home/marriage theme. The villain, inviting an adulterous relationship, seems to be found interesting less because he offers a vicarious enjoyment of a relationship which, though forbidden, is desired, as because he makes a shocking attack on what is felt to count greatly. He is a kind of bogy-man rather than a disguised hero. He does not usually triumph emotionally in the way he does in that more sophisticated literature which I take M. de Rougemont to be describing; this is, in fact, an extremely uncomplicated kind of literature.

These stories differ yet more obviously from many later versions of the sex-and-violence tale, from the kind of tale which is serialized in some of the Sunday papers. In those the author tries – while the rape or violence is being committed – to give a mild thrill and then laps the whole in hollow moral triteness. They are even further from the two-shilling sex-and-violence novelettes. They have no sexual excitement at all, and no description aiming to arouse it; and this, I think, is not only because women are not usually as responsive as men to that kind of stimulus, but because the stories belong to different worlds. These stories from the working-class women's magazines belong neither to the middle-class world, nor to that of the more modern Sunday papers, nor to that of the later novelettes, nor, even less, to an environment in which illicit relations can be spoken of as 'good fun', as 'smart' or 'progressive'. If a girl does lose her virginity here, or a wife commit adultery, you hear, 'And so that night I fell,' or 'I committed the great sin': and though a startled thrill is evident there, you feel that the sense of a fall and a sin is real also.

The strongest impression, after one has read a lot of these stories, is of their extraordinary fidelity to the detail of the readers' lives. The short stories take up as much space as the serial or long story, and they seem to be mainly faithful transcripts of minor incidents, amusing or worrying, from ordinary life. The serials may erupt into the startlingly posh world of what are still called 'the stately homes of England', or present a Rajah or a Sheik: but often the world is that the readers live in, with a considerable accuracy in its particulars. A fair proportion of the crime is of that world too – the distress when Mrs Thompson is suspected of shoplifting, and so on. I open *Silver Star*: on the inner front cover the complete long novel, *Letters of Shame*, begins:

As Stella Kaye unlatched the gate of number 15, the front door opened and her mother beckoned agitatedly.

'Whatever's made you so late?' she whispered. 'Did you remember the sausages? Oh, good girl!'

Stella looked at her mother's flushed face and best flowered apron. Visitors! Just when she was bursting to spring her news on them all! It would have to keep.

A typical copy of *Secrets* has as its week's verse, 'Mother's Night Out', about the weekly visit by Father and Mother to the pictures: 'It's Monday night and at No. 3, Mother and Dad are hurrying tea. In fact, poor Dad has scarcely done before Mother's urging, "Fred, come on!" '

A short story at the back of the *Oracle*, 'Hero's Homecoming', opens: 'Most of the women who dealt at the little general store on the corner of Roper's Road were rather tired of hearing about Mrs Bolsom's boy, but they couldn't very well tell her so because she was so obliging and so handy to run to at times of emergency.' A typical *Lucky Star* one-page story starts: 'Lilian West glanced at the clock on the kitchen wall. "My goodness," she thought. "How quickly I get through the housework these days!" ' It goes on to tell how, after deciding to leave her married children alone so as not to be thought a nuisance, she found fresh happiness in realizing how much she was still needed. 'Mary was an ordinary girl doing an ordinary job in a factory,' another story begins, and incidentally epitomizes the points of departure for almost all of them.

The illustrations help to create the same atmosphere. Some of the newer magazines specialize in photographic illustrations of the candid camera kind. The 'older' ones still use black-and-white drawings in an unsophisticated style. There exist, particularly in more modern publications, black-and-white line drawings which are very sophisticated: compared with them the cartoons still to be found in some provincial newspapers, drawn by a local man, belong to thirty years ago. So it is with most of the drawings here (the main illustration to the serial or the long complete novel is sometimes an exception); they are not smart in their manner, and their detail is almost entirely unromanticized. The girls are usually pretty (unless the burden is that even a plain girl can find a good husband), but they are pretty in an unglamorous way, in the way working-class girls are often very pretty. They wear blouses and jumpers with skirts, or their one dance-dress. The factory chimney can be seen sticking up in one corner and the street of houses with intermittent lamp-posts stretches behind; there are the buses and the bikes and the local dance-halls and the cinemas.

Such a nearness to the detail of the lives of readers might be simply the prelude to an excursion into a wish-fulfilment story about the surprising things that can happen to someone from that world. Sometimes this is so, and there is occasionally a stepping-up of the social level inside the stories, so that people can feel how nice it would be to be a member of the villa or good-class housing groups. But often what happens is what might happen to anyone, and the environment is that of most readers.

If we look more closely at the stories, we are reminded at once of the case against 'stock responses': every reaction has its fixed counter for presentation. I run through the account of a trial: the mouths are 'set', the faces 'tense with excitement'; tremors run down spines; the hero exhibits 'iron control' and faces his captors with a 'stony look'; his watching girl-friend is the victim of an 'agonized heart' as 'suspense thickens in the air'. But what does this indicate? That the writers use cliché, and that the audience seems to want cliché, that they are not exploring experience, realizing experience through language? That is true. But these are first, I repeat, statements; picture presentations of the known. A reader of them is hardly likely to tackle anything that could be called serious literature; but there are worse diets, especially today. If we regard them as faithful but dramatized presentations of a life whose form and values are known, we might find it more useful to ask what are the values they embody. There is no virtue in merely laughing at them: we need to appreciate first that they may in all their triteness speak for a solid and relevant way of life. So may the tritest of Christmas and Birthday card verses; that is why those cards are chosen with great care, usually for the 'luvliness' and 'rightness' of their verse. The world these stories present is a limited and simple one, based on a few accepted and long-held values. It is often a childish and garish world, and the springs of the emotions work in great gushings. But they do work; it is not a corrupt or a pretentious world. It uses boldly words which serious writers for more sophisticated audiences understandably find difficulty in using today, and which many other writers are too knowing to be caught using. It uses, as I noted in another connexion, words like 'sin', 'shame', 'guilt', 'evil', with every appearance of meaningfulness. It accepts completely, has as its main point of reference, the notion that marriage and a home, founded on love, fidelity, and cheerfulness, are the right purpose of a woman's life. If a girl 'sins' the suggestion is – and this reinforces what I said earlier about the ethical emphasis in working-class beliefs – not that the girl has 'sinned against herself', as another range of writers would put it, or that she has fallen short in some relationship other than the human and social, but that she has spoiled her chances of a decent home and family. One of the commoner endings to this kind of serial is for the girl either to find again the man responsible, and marry him, or to find another man who, though he knows all, is prepared to marry her and be a father to the child, loving them both. One can appreciate the force of the mistrust of 'the other woman', the Jezebel, the home-breaker, the woman who sets out to wreck an existing marriage or one just about to start. Even the man with a roving eye gets short shrift if he goes in for marriage-breaking; before that he comes under dispensations more indulgent than those accorded to women on the loose.

It is against this ground-pattern that the thrills throw their bold reliefs, and to which they are indissolubly bound. I do not think that the thrills tempt the readers to imitate them, or much to dream of them in a sickly way. They bear the same relation to their lives as the kite to the solid flat common from which it is flown. The ground-pattern of ordinary life weaves its strands in and out through the serials and the short stories, in all the magazines. It is the pattern of the main assumptions:

Don't spoil today because some friend has left you; you cannot say of ALL God has bereft you. Life is too brief for anger or for sorrow...

or :

Happiness is made up
Of a million tiny things
That often pass unnoticed...

In its outlook, this is still substantially the world of Mrs Henry Wood (*East Lynne; Danesbury House; Mrs Haliburton's Troubles*), of Florence L. Barclay (one million copies of *The Rosary* sold), of Marie Corelli (*The Sorrows of Satan* – a 'classic' to my aunts), of Silas K. Hocking (*Ivy; Her Benny; His Father*), of Annie S. Swan (*A Divided House*), of Ruth Lamb (*A Wilful Ward; Not Quite a Lady; Only a Girl Wife; Thoughtful Joe and How He Gained His Name*), and of a great number of others, often published by the Religious Tract Society and given as prizes in the upper classes of Sunday schools. It is being ousted now by the world of the newer kind of magazine. I wonder, incidentally, whether it is resisting longer in Scotland: a very plain but attractive threepenny weekly, *People's Friend*, is still published there; a similar magazine, the *Weekly Telegraph* from Sheffield, died only a few years ago, I believe. Some of the 'older' magazines are trying to preserve themselves by producing the glamour of the newer magazines, often linked to an inflated form of the older thrills. Tense and gripping new serials are announced on the placards, with large illustrations compounded of the old-style ordinariness and the new-style close-up.

But a few of the newer kind of magazines continue to increase their already phenomenal circulations. In many ways they embody the same attitudes as the 'older' magazines, though they aim at too large an audience to be able to identify themselves with one social class. They are considerably smarter in presentation and presumably can provide more specialized articles on home problems than the 'older' magazines. There are crudities in the 'older' magazines whose removal ought not to be regretted. I have not stressed these qualities because I have been concerned to show the better links with working-class life. But the smartness of the newer magazines often extends, it seems to me, to their attitudes, and the change is not always for the good. The smartness easily becomes a slickness; there is an emphasis on money-prestige (figures of salaries or winnings are given in brackets after the names of people in the news), much 'fascinated' attention is given to public personalities such as the gay wives of industrial magnates, or radio and film-stars; there is a kittenish domesticity and a manner predominantly arch or whimsical.

The 'glossies' are aiming, successfully, to attract the younger women who want to be smart and up to date, who do not like to seem old-fashioned. The 'older' magazines would perhaps like to catch up with the 'glossies', but that would be very costly; and there is still presumably a large enough audience for them to be profitably produced in much their old form. When that ceases to be the case they will, I suppose, either make really radical changes in the direction indicated by the 'glossies', or die.

CHAPTER 5

THE FULL RICH LIFE

There's but one and the same sense in everything for our class –
when you have earned for bread and taxes – live.

A. *The Immediate, the Present, the Cheerful: Fate and Luck*

From the concrete and personal to the immediate, the present, and
the cheerful. The stress on the need to 'keep cheerful' is derived, as
has been seen, from the assumption that life is bound to be materially
unrewarding and difficult. To qualify this attitude no farther would
be to leave it sounding too soft and weak: working-class people are
in many things sentimental, but their cheerfulness is fed chiefly by
their unsentimental qualities. They mistrust the leaders of the big
battalions, but usually with a humorous scepticism towards them and
their pretensions; after all, they say, 'we should know'. They are
cheerfully cagey towards both the leaders of the big battalions and
their big words; 'Ah'm not buying that,' they say – and yet do not
really 'hold it against Them'. They are often humorous towards the
world outside, and their humour is almost always debunking humour.
Their cheerfulness is founded as much on an unsentimental nonconformity as on an urge to 'cheer themselves up'. It helps them to cope,
and with a certain dignity. It can also make them, as the elevation of
a sense of humour into a primary virtue can make anyone, unrespon-
sive to much both in and outside their world. It helps to make them
sensible, reliable, unvolatile, unquixotic, and steady in a crisis;
and all those qualities can become faults, if they are not sufficiently
given the tension of their opposites.

There are many thrifty working-class people today, as there have
always been. But in general the immediate and present nature of
working-class life puts a premium on the taking of pleasures now,
discourages planning for some future goal, or in the light of some
ideal. 'Life is no bed of roses,' they assume; but 'tomorrow will take
care of itself': on this side the working-classes have been cheerful
existentialists for ages. Even of those who spend a more than usual
amount of time worrying about how things are going to 'pan out', it

is true to say that their life is one of the immediate present to a degree not often found among other classes.

Wives will still 'slip out' with their purses at 4.30 on many a day to get something for tea. There is little on the shelf and that is for special occasions. But this is not necessarily the living from hand to mouth which indicates poverty; it is not altogether indolence and forgetfulness: it is part of the climate of life; one moves generally from item to item. Wage-packets come in weekly and go out weekly. There are no stocks, shares, bonds, securities, property, trade assets. Someone left a few hundreds as a lump sum will still be called 'rich'. The little payment-books cluttered behind an ornament are marked by the week too, and are usually for 'paying-off'; e.g. for paying-off a debt already incurred – a clothing-check spent, last week's rent. Forms of saving or paying in advance are traditionally for specific purposes, as in the insurances against death or illness; or are usually for short-term if recurrent purposes, as with the payings-in for Christmas or holidays. A mistrust of a more general kind of saving is still quite common; you might 'get knocked down tomorrow', and then what would all the 'scratting and misery' of saving have done for you? And within that remark can be seen the real grounds for mistrust and for the resulting emphasis on making use of the money now. If people wasted nothing and lived with carefully calculated economy, they might be able to save a modest amount. They might, but it is not certain; and the discipline required would be more than most people would think worth while. It would mean a bare, oatmealy sort of life, for very little at the end; life 'wouldn't be worth living'.

This helps to explain two features in the spending of money which members of other classes find particularly difficult to appreciate. First, the way in which working-class people, once their immediate dues have been met, will spend much of the remainder on 'extravagances'. This will often happen even though there may be more money in the house than there has been for years, or than there well may be in a few months more. Second, of habits with money which exasperate or puzzle outsiders, is the order of priority into which working-class people will range the items between which they have to divide their income.

Thus, the replacement of necessary household equipment is likely to rank lower in the scale than it would among the middle-classes; sheets are often badly worn and much mended, and towels inadequate in number. This may not be due simply to a shortage of money; the shillings which bought a rather elaborate frame for a photograph on the dresser or a new ornament would have bought an extra pair of towels. And 'keeping a good table' usually means providing meals well-supplied with meat, especially for the man at the head of the house. This is still a common assumption, whether the husband is on heavy or light work. I know many working-class men who would be 'dashed' if they came home and found only one, not two, chops ready for them; or, if there were cold boiled ham, they would expect a quarter of a pound. 'Pleasure' – smoking and drinking, for example – is given a similarly high priority. Pleasures are a central part of life, not something perhaps to be allowed after a great number of other commitments have been met. The importance of each item in this rough financial pattern will vary from family to family; those who reverse the pattern itself are unusual.

Life goes on from day to day and from week to week: the seasons turn over, marked by the great festivals regarded as holidays or bean-feasts, and by an occasional special event – a wedding in the family, a charabanc trip, a funeral, a cup-tie. There is bound to be some planning; a twelve-week Christmas club for presents and extras, perhaps a club for Whitsuntide clothes paid in advance, and, after that, saving for a holiday in some cases. But in general the striking feature is the unplanned nature of life, the moment-to-moment meeting of troubles or taking of pleasure; schemes are mostly short-term.

Socially, also, each day and each week is almost unplanned. There is no diary, no book of engagements, and few letters are sent or received. If a member of the family is away, a weekly letter is some-what painfully put together on Sunday. Relatives or very close friends who have gone to live away are likely to be communicated with only by Christmas card, unless there is a special family event. But if they come back to live in the area the relationship will be taken up as though it had never been interrupted. And if one-time near neighbours meet by chance in town there will be a good gossip, one which seems just a continuation of its predecessors.

No dates are likely to be made for those few visitors who are on 'dropping-in' terms. A very frequent visitor may say on leaving that he might see them on Tuesday, but this is not regarded as an engage-ment to visit them, but rather as an indication that until then he will not be able to look in. The appearances of most other people who are on 'dropping-in' terms are likely to be as predictable as the planets.

All these things contribute to a view of life among working-class people which can from some angles look like a kind of hedonism, which finds life largely acceptable so long as the big worries (debt, drink, sickness) keep away, and so long as there is adequate scope for 'having a good time'. But it is a mild hedonism, one informed by a more deeply rooted sense – that the big and long-distance rewards are not for them. At a first hearing, 'why worry?' may seem to suggest a trivial attitude; but only those who expect to have to worry a lot would coin such a phrase and use it so frequently. And so with all the other phrases of this type – 'Always look on the bright side,' 'keep smiling,' 'a little of what y'fancy does y'good,' 'life i'n't worth living without a bit of fun,' 'make the most of each day,' 'we 'av'n't much money but we do see life.' Conversely, there is the dislike of meanness and tight-fistedness – 'Ah 'ate mean fowks,' and 'E's as mean as muck'.

Hence the cheerful man, the wit, the 'card', is still very highly regarded. He makes jokes at work and the time passes twice as quickly; he 'makes y' laugh'; he is 'right funny'. Or he sells you things on the market and you know he is a twister, but still you 'can't 'elp laughin'. He is the big, fat, round-faced, middle-aged man with a pint of ale in the cruder cartoons and picture postcards. He is the real working-class hero, the cheerful, not the romantic, hero. He is a man somewhere above forty, who has had a few knocks and knows how to take them, not a handsome young man. The working-classes have always loved a 'comic', as their biggest music-hall names indicate. They love the men who are 'fair Irish', full of a cock-eyed fun, and the women who are uninhibitedly and irrepressibly vulgar, like the late Nellie Wallace.

Some of even the cruder strains linger. I bought recently in the streets of Hull a twopenny broadsheet called *Billy's Weekly Liar* (*Twentieth Edition*), printed in a city on the other side of the country. It proved to be a relic of the same world as the comic postcards. A mock classified advertisement runs:

De-Luxe Kip-House
  A real home from home. Spring inferior bunks, extra large chambers (only need weekly emptying). Lively sheets and blankets . . .

and another:

WANTED: a man for our Research Laboratories for testing laxative. This is a sitting-down job, easy work and bonus on output . . .

and for a detergent:

All traces of dirt, stains, colour, buttons and clothes will vanish! The smell will amaze you, just like new-mown hay – after it has been through a horse.

The banner-motto for the whole paper is, 'Smile Dammit Smile!'

'Laugh and the world laughs with you'; Ella Wheeler Wilcox's lines have hung on the walls of unnumbered working-class living-rooms, not accepted in quite the tone she meant them to have, but speaking for a group of attitudes that is still strong.

Working-class people, as is well known, are fond of a gamble. Is this mainly a reaction from having to 'put up with things', from the realization that no gradual effort at change is likely to effect much, from the wish for sudden riches, for freedom from a dull job, for something for nothing? In those forms of gambling which require a certain amount of skill there is, too, as some writers have suggested, a pleasure in one of the few available outlets for self-expression. The man who has a 'system' for playing the 'pools' or horses is respected – and the results of his 'system' not always closely scrutinized. He is admired, rather in the way that a good footballer is, because he is 'making a science of it'. And behind all forms of gambling, whether or not they need skill, is the simple thrill of taking a chance, in which the emphasis is less on the worry of whether one will win than on the prior 'fun' – win or lose – of ''aving a go'. I stress this because I think it can easily be assumed that working-class people are more emotionally involved in their gambles than they are. There are hard cases, but by most the occasional gambles (though during the last two decades the 'pools' have ensured that these shall be at least weekly) seem to me not very seriously regarded. It is easy to think, from the statistics, that almost every working-class home is riddled weekly by neurotic desire to win on the 'pools'; that by Wednesday night the living-room table, strewn with paper, is the centre of feverish activity, and that the rest of the week is spent in indulging fantasies of what will be done with all the money; that Saturday temporarily plunges them to the depths, but that soon they are nourishing the next week's hope.

We should remember, first, the centuries-old belief in fate and destiny which has already been mentioned, that belief which survives in the reports of what the stars foretell, which are essential features of even the strikingly modern papers, in the fortune-tellers at the big city-fairs and the electric fortune-telling machines at the seaside, in the tea-leaves and palm-of-hand readers of which every district throws up a few, in Foulsham's *Dream Almanac*, in the widespread advertisements for four-leaved clover, for Joan the Wad, the Cornish Pixie, and for her consort Jack O'Lantern.

The belief in fate survives in *Old Moore's Almanac*, which claims a 'normal annual net sale of three millions' and dates itself '1699–1956'. The cabbalistic cover, announcing and exhibiting 'prophetic hieroglyphic engravings', looks little changed from the original issue, though now it includes an announcement of football pools forecasts. Inside are numerous closely printed predictions, by days and birthdays, and horoscopes, including those of famous men such as President Eisenhower.

In this part of experience the recurrent word, and it is very frequently used, is 'luck'. Luck is believed in and admired; you are born with it or you are not; it is as much a given quality as brains or a good eye. There are lucky incidents and features, of course, such as encounters with black cats or the possession of dark hair: and luck may go in cycles. But the basic assumption is that luck is something you are born with – 'better to be born lucky than rich', working-class people will say, of a man who has won a raffle, and 'of course, 'e's lucky', meaning that he is possessed of the quality. Even those who are not by birth 'lucky ones' will now and again have 'beginner's luck' or a stroke or 'run' of luck. Similar phrases are, of course, used in all parts of society, but not with the same frequency nor with quite the same meaning. To working-class people, luck figures as importantly and naturally as steady endeavour or brains or beauty; it is as much an attribute you have to accept. They are prepared to admire these other qualities, but give as much importance to the sheer chance of having luck with you. It may partly be explained in terms used before, by referring to the fact that in a life so materially limited one is led to hope for the sudden chance of fortune from heaven. But it is also rooted in a supernaturalism which has survived centuries, and is still enjoyed, not as a make-shift for the rewards which have not yet come, but because it makes life more interesting.

Hence the plethora of gambles and flutters. In the pockets and handbags of any group of working-class people there is likely to be a great variety of current tickets for lucky draws, workshop raffles, works' handicaps on big races, and club lotteries. Gambles can be organized around almost anything, and it is expected that almost everyone will take part. Allowances are usually made for the 'queer' person who has a moral objection, but it is an allowance inspired more by the general belief in 'toleration' than by understanding of the odd man's point of view. Naturally; since his case is not the whole case. When the organizers say to the person who objects, 'Well, why not 'ave a go, just for the fun of it,' or, 'Be a sport,' they are indicating an aspect just as important to them as to that to which objection is being taken. Of those they suspect of refusing to take part out of meanness, they will say, "E's no sport. 'E's afraid of losing 'is money.'

One advertisement by a pools firm, obviously aimed at the working-classes from its style of drawing and domestic interiors, shows a young man spurned by the girls as they ride off in others' cars. In pictures two and three he is seen, looking like a budding scholar who scorns delight and lives laborious days, filling in his 'pools' coupon at home and dispatching it. In block four, having won several thousands, he is flying round the corner in a snappy sports car with one of the girls from the first picture beside him, while the other young men trudge miserably past on the pavement. I would not deny that some of the 'pools'' potential customers would be likely to be affected by an approach of this type. But for many it all seems rather irrelevant. It is an advertisement wholly of an acquisitive society, a society which regards the cash-nexus as all important. Yet it is likely that the new features in gambling – its regularity, its centralization, the huge sums it offers, and its maintenance and extension by high-pressure publicity – will gradually bring about a changed attitude. I have no personal experience of the effect of a large win on the winners, nor of the neighbours' attitude to them. At present, for almost all the people I know, taking part is still a sort of throw, a gesture for luck. It would be 'nice' or 'a bit of alright' or 'luvly' if something turned up, and 'there's no 'arm in 'oping'. One could buy some things or do some things which otherwise could not be thought of, like having a really good holiday, or buying an electric washer, or setting up an unmarried daughter in a shop. One could taste a bit of the luxury one has always fancied. But one does not yearn anxiously each week for the chance to come up.

B. 'The Biggest Aspidistra in the World': Excursions into the 'Baroque'

The good life is not simply a matter of 'putting up with things', of 'making the best of it', but one with scope for having the 'bit extra' that really makes 'Life'. Most working-class people are not climbing; they do not quarrel with their general level; they only want the little more that allows a few frills. They learn the importance of this early. As I mentioned above, working-class children who earn some money are not usually expected to hand it over to help the family finances; it is more likely to be 'their little bit extra'. The extras for adults may be only occasional and quite small in apparent importance – fish-and-chips for supper in mid-week, for instance. But they add variety or colour or some gaiety to life; they are among the freely springing things in a life which is largely an imposed routine, the routine of clocking-in-and-out, or of the family's meals, washing, and repairs. Where the routine of work is rarely changed and is almost entirely imposed from outside, the attitude towards free and personal acts takes on a special complexion.

So, 'a little of what y' fancy does y' good'; 'when y' go out y' go out to enjoy y' self'; 'y' want a bit of real life'; 'y' like a reeight do'. In all these, still much used today, there is a note which has never been silent in English working-class life since the Wife of Bath, which sounds in Shakespeare's clowns, Mistress Quickly and Juliet's nurse, in Moll Flanders, and in the nineteenth-century music-halls. It has lost some of its old quality now, but more of its raucous and earthy flavour remains than is usually thought.

My own best illustration of the survival of this older spirit is a charwoman I knew in the late forties. She represented the rougher, the 'knees up, Mother Brown' type of woman. Her clothes looked as though they had been picked up individually from second-hand-clothing shops, and she wasn't very clean. Over a torn, old, and grubby blouse and skirt she had for the street an ex-army gas-cape; from that there stuck what might have been the head of one of the witches in *Macbeth*. She must have been in her middle forties, so that her face could not be called young; but it was not yet old or 'past everything'. It was well-lined but not haggard; it was scored with hard work, insufficient attention, and the lines which 'making shift', doggedness, fighting for your own, and an overriding bravado bring.

Her left eye had a violent cast and her lower lip a drop to the right, so that on the whole the bravado won. But it was a *farouche* bravado, even when she was in the easiest of spirits. Her hair was a dirty mouse colour, hanging in straggly locks from either side of an old felt hat which she wore rammed hard and unshapely to the head, held in place by a large pin with a piccaninny's head carved on the blunt end – a relic of a day at the sea, I suppose. Her shoes were split, sloppy, and entirely uncleaned; her lisle stockings hung in circles from the knees. Her voice was raucous and had been developed over the years by area and backyard 'callings' (the 'a' is pronounced as in 'shall') and 'bawlings-out'. She was not, as those who knew her only slightly thought, a widow: her husband had been in a mental home for about a dozen years, during which time she had looked after the family single-handed. Her effective married life had begun with three days' holiday at home, and had ended five or six years later, when 'They took 'im away'. So there she was at forty-odd with five of them to look after, or more accurately four, since the eldest son of eighteen was in the army. Then there was a fourteen-year-old girl who was 'bright' and had won a scholarship to the local grammar-school, a boy of ten who looked like resembling her, a girl of seven who had inherited several kinds of ill-health, and a girl of four, already pasty and with a continual cold.

They were all solidly ranged behind the mother and very cheerful, as she was. She had the spirits, and I say this with no intention of disparaging her, of a mongrel bitch. She fought hard and constantly for her children, but it never 'got 'er down', though she often exploded with temper among them. She was without subservience or deference, or a desire to win pity; she was careless of many things affecting her children and refused to worry or to take life earnestly. She asked those she worked for 'not to mention it to the Guardians', but did not cadge or respond to a gift in a way which might have suggested that further gifts would be gratefully received. If someone gave her a dress or an item of food she took it with a short word of thanks, and that was all. No doubt she often felt she could have done with some of the surplus money her employers seemed to have, but she obviously had no envy of their manner of life. The young middle-class housewives for whom she did the heavy work in a vigorous if careless-at-the-edges and knockabout fashion soon learned that any social pretensions or attempts at patronage would have been out of place. The truth was that she had a fuller life than some of those for whom she worked. Thus, if she had a day off, she thought nothing of moving with all available members of the family to the nearest seaside resort, which wasn't far, for a noisily enjoyable day, ending with fish-and-chips for all.

I may have romanticized her a little, and certainly she is not typical. But she has some of the working-class qualities I am now describing rather larger than life, as in a cartoon – their ability not to permit themselves to be altered, but to take or not to take, as they will and in their own way; their energy in insisting on a place for, and in enjoying, their traditional kinds of amusement and recreation, even when circumstances seem unusually daunting.

This is an attitude which requires of the things done for fun – of its decorative arts, of its songs, of its 'free' acts – a sprawling, highly-ornamental, rococo extravagance. It loves what might be called (without necessarily implying an historical link) the 'baroque', as Miss Lambert and Miss Marx have illustrated. It loves the cornucopia, all that is generous and sprawling, that suggests splendour and wealth by sheer abundance and lavishness of colour. It loves the East, because the East is exotic and elaborate. Perfumes should come from the Orient; chapels have for years preferred a bazaar to a sale-of-work (e.g. this recent poster: 'Hull and District Band of Hope and Temperance League – May Day Celebrations – Oriental Setting – May Queen: Miss Sheila Pugmire'). The cinemas sometimes follow the theatres in giving themselves names vaguely Eastern, and in general suggest a splendour which may be Eastern or European, but is never shy. The commissionaires of both look like Ruritanian generals; the moulded false-fronts of the *Plaza*, the *Palace*, the *Alhambra*, the *Regal*, the *Embassy*, and the *Rex* vie with one another all down the main road. The inflation of the popular magazine stories often touches the same chord; Eastern potentates are dearly loved.

I recall now and give sharper definition to an earlier point. Indoors, the basic furnishings of the home are surmounted by articles whose main charm is their high colour and suggestion of splendour. The older forms may often look almost grotesque, and the newer ones debased; but the tradition is unbroken. The wallpaper may have been ticketed at the shop, 'In the latest manner', but still has a bold pattern and colours. The older-style pots and decorated sea-shells are disappearing from the mantelpieces, and only a minority of the young couples will want a vivid clip-rug; but the replacements are just as vivid. It was not difficult to guess that working-class people would go back, as soon as they no longer had to buy utility furniture, to the highly-polished and elaborate stuff the neon-strip stores sell. Gone, we have already seen, is the lush aspidistra in its equally lush bowl which was fed on aspirins and weak tea when it flagged. But its successors in the window-space speak the same emotional language. And the flowers in the box outside are still those which best provide 'a bit o' colour'. Plastic gewgaws and teapots shaped like country cottages settle very easily with complicated lace-paper d'oyleys, complicated lace half-curtains, crocheted table-runners, fancy birthday and Christmas cards, coloured wicker shopping baskets, and 'fancies' (curiously constructed and coloured little cakes) for tea.

Many of the older working-class hobbies have a similar character. When an article is made, the interest is not in fittingness of colour combination or in unity of design, but in elaboration for elaboration's sake. Or rather, the more elaborate features both suggest abundance and, by being repeated several times in the one object, show a sure skill. There is usually little sense of the best possibilities of the material in itself, or regard for the purposes of the object. Think of the wild grotesqueries of fretwork, of the Houses of Parliament in matchsticks, of the duchess sets and tea-cosies and poker-work things exchanged as Christmas presents.

Outdoors, and especially in the more public parts of the cities, the cleaner lines of the twentieth century have made their impression, in the post-offices, the telephone kiosks, the bus stations. But in the working-class shopping and amusement areas the old idiom – in its modern style – persists; it persists for example, in the huge furniture stores, in the marzipan super-cinemas, and in the manner of window-dressing retained by the cheaper clothiers and outfitters. There is a working-class city centre as there is one for the middle-classes. They are geographically united, they overlap, they have concurrent lives; but they also have distinctive atmospheres. The centre belongs to all groups, and each take what it wants and so makes its own centre – favourite streets, popular shops (with 'Wooley's' – Woolworth's – a clear favourite with working-class people), tram stops, parts of the market, places of amusement, places for cups of tea.

In the working-class area itself, in those uneven cobbled streets to which until recently motor-cars seldom penetrated, the world is still that of fifty years ago. It is an untidy, messy, baroque, but on the whole drably baroque, world. The shop windows are an indiscriminate tangle of odds-and-bobs at coppers each; the counter and every spare stretch of upper space is festooned with cards full of proprietary medicines. The outer walls are a mass of small advertisements, in all colours. There are hundreds of them, in all stages of wear-and-tear, some piled a quarter of an inch thick on the bodies of their predecessors.

In those towns where they are still retained, the trams are obviously much more in place in the working-class areas than when they run up to the 'good residential' districts. Their improbable 'Emmett' shape, their extraordinary noisiness, which makes two or three together sound like a small fairground, the mass of tiny advertisements which surround their interiors, their wonderful double necklace of lights at night – all make them representative working-class vehicles, the gondolas of the people.

All this is the background to specific acts of baroque living. Most working-class pleasures tend to be mass-pleasures, over-crowded and sprawling. Everyone wants to have fun at the same time, since most buzzers blow within an hour of each other. Special occasions – a wedding, a trip to the pantomime, a visit to the fair, a charabanc outing – assume this, and assume also that a really special splendour and glitter must be displayed. Weddings are more often than not attempts for once to catch some of the splendour associated with the idea of upper-class life. The large cake is no doubt 'good', but the elaborate white dress and veil can only be poor imitations of a real thing which would cost a hundred guineas. The bridesmaids are all dressed alike, down to little arm-bands, long net gloves, and large hats; but the finish and the fit are not good. The drink flows freely and includes the richer varieties – port, especially.

The fairgrounds, like the furniture, have an intensely conscious modernity. The lovely stylized horses have almost gone, and so have the fantastic mechanical organs; each year bigger and louder relay-systems and more and more Coney Island-style coloured lights appear. But again the new materials are adapted to the old demands for a huge complication and exotic involution of colour, noise, and movement. The same demands are met in the large holiday camps; if you look closely at the interiors of the great public halls there, you may see the steel girders and bare corrugations of the roofs; but you will have to peer through a welter of artificial trees, imitation half-timbering, great dazzling chandeliers.

Most illuminating of all is the habit of the 'chara' trip. For the day-trip by 'chara' has been particularly taken up by working-class people, and made into one of their peculiar – that is, characteristic – kinds of pleasure-occasion. Some even take their week's holiday in this way, in successive outings. In its garishness and cheerfulness the 'chara' trip today still speaks the language of:

> Oh, I do like to be beside the seaside.

These buses, sometimes from a big town fleet, but often one of a couple owned by a local man, are the super-cinemas of the highways. They are, and particularly if they belong to a small firm specializing in day trips for working-class people, plushily over-upholstered, ostentatiously styled inside and out; they have lots of chrome bits, little flags on top, fine names and loud radios. Every day in summer the arterial roads out of the big towns are thick with them humming towards the sea, often filled, since this is a pleasure which particularly appeals to mothers who want a short break and lots of company, with middle-aged women, dressed in their best, out on a pub, club, or street excursion. Their hair has been in curlers the night before; they have eased themselves into the creaking corsets they do not wear every day, have put on flowered summer dresses and fancy shoes. One year, I remember, the fashion, except on really warm days, was for fur-lined bootees, the kind which show thick fur round the upper edges but are not so thickly lined throughout. They have gathered together all the bits-and-bobs of equipment which give a working-class woman, when she is dressed up, a somewhat cluttered and over-dressed air – things around the neck, a prized item of jewellery, such as a brooch or a cameo, pinned to the centre of the bodice, and a tightly-clutched handbag.

The 'charas' go rolling out and across the moors for the sea, past the road-houses which turn up their noses at coach-parties, to one the driver knows where there is coffee and biscuits or perhaps a full egg-and-bacon breakfast. Then on to a substantial lunch on arrival, and after that a fanning-out in groups. But rarely far from one another, because they know their part of the town and their bit of beach, where they feel at home. At Scarborough they leave the north side to the lower middle-classes who come for a week or two, and take rooms in the hundreds of little red villas. They leave the half-alive Edwardian elegance of the south end (it hasn't a beach anyway; the sea is a splendid frame for an esplanade and formal cliff-gardens) to middle-aged professionals, West Riding business-men who are doing quite well and have come in their Rovers. They walk down Westborough to the half-mile-long centre-piece around the harbour, where Jews up from Leeds for the season with van-loads of gaudy knick-knacks jostle for space with lavatorially-tiled fish-and-chip saloons ('Fish, chips, tea, bread and butter – 3/-: No Tea with own Eatables'). Here again the same clutter, the same extraordinary Bartholomew Fair of a mess, but even messier and more colourful than that they are used to in their own shopping-areas at home. They have a nice walk past the shops; perhaps a drink; a sit in a deck-chair eating an ice-cream or sucking mint-humbugs; a great deal of loud laughter – at Mrs Johnson insisting on a paddle with her dress tucked in her bloomers, at Mrs Henderson pretending she has 'got off' with the deck-chair attendant, or in the queue at the ladies' lavatory. Then there is the buying of presents for the family, a big meat-tea, and the journey home with a stop for drinks on the way. If the men are there, and certainly if it is a men's outing, there will probably be several stops and a crate or two of beer in the back for drinking on the move. Somewhere in the middle of the moors the men's parties all tumble out, with much horseplay and noisy jokes about bladder-capacity. The driver knows exactly what is expected of him as he steers his warm, fuggy, and singing community back to the town; for his part he gets a very large tip, collected during the run through the last few miles of town streets.

In all these acts one is "aving a go', a fling, making a splash. It is a short-lived splash, but a good one, because most of the rest of life is humdrum and regulated. One needs sometimes to make a gesture, even though finances do not reasonably permit it. A gesture like this, in sum, should have a suggestion of wealth and splendour about it – the charabancs are 'de-luxe coaches'; the pantomimes are fond of 'extravaganzas'; phrases like 'very fancy' and 'doing it in style' – that is, in the style in which posh folk are hazily assumed to pass their every day – strike the same note. I do not think this is so much what

M. de Rougemont calls 'a vague yearning after affluent surroundings and exotic adventures' as a thorough enjoyment of what really seem, temporarily, to be affluent surroundings and are all the more thoroughly enjoyed because they are known, without much yearning, to be temporary. It is less an expression of a desire for a heavily material and possession-laden life than an elementary, allegorical, and brief statement of a better, a fuller life. The properties are crude and physical, but they point towards an outlook much less material.

Some other classes have changed the outward expressions of their taste a great deal during the last fifty years, but on the whole working-class people have been little affected. They make nothing of Scandinavian simplicities; they are impressed by the ambassadorial air of the more formal, unfussy but good and solid, style in some present-day decoration – but think it a little cold and severe. Of all present-day middle-class styles the one nearest to their own ethos is that commonly represented in drawing-room dramas about upper-suburban life – flowery chintz and bits of shiny brass. They are nearest of all, though, to the prosperous nineteenth-century middle-class style; the richness showing well and undisguisedly in an abundance of odds-and-ends, in squiggles and carvings, in bold patterns; a *mélange* whose unifying principle is the sense of an elaborate and colourful sufficiency.

c. *Illustrations from Popular Art – Club-Singing*

Some features of songs and singing among the working-classes illustrate better than anything else both their contact with older traditions and their capacity for assimilating and modifying new material to their established interests. It is tempting to speak here of the great brass- and silver-bands, the district-bands and the works-bands, and of the annual festival and competitions. They have been active for more than a century. They find difficulty in maintaining themselves today, but still have about one hundred and fifty thousand players throughout the whole country, and there are more than two hundred bands in the north-west, mainly in Lancashire. Or one might speak of the splendid choral societies of the West Riding; even more, perhaps, of the one-hundred-years-old but still lively oratorio tradition of the chapels. For weeks before Christmas we used to be drafted out of Sunday school in my Primitive Methodist chapel to swell the chorus for that greatest of favourites, the *Messiah*.

E

As we walked through the streets to pass the stipulated hour between the end of Sunday school and going home for tea we noted that the bald brick front of the Wesleyans, three streets off, announced that they, too, were doing the *Messiah* again, and that the plain Methodists on the other side of the 'Moor' were trying *Judas Maccabaeus*, for a change. Each of them had engaged two or three professionals or semi-professionals for the principal parts, sometimes at considerable expense. There was much competition for the services of a trumpeter who was known throughout the city for his magnificent obbligatos. But the core of the entire performance was the choir, and that was made up of chapel members, led by rank upon rank, as it seemed to a little boy, of enormous-bosomed women and fierce old men; they roared into the 'Hallelujah Chorus' with a sureness and power which spoke of years of training in a tradition of full-bodied singing. I remember that once the Sunday school group at the back, always inclined to be restless, were convulsed because one old man, who must have been nearly eighty and sang like a patriarch inspired, was so carried away that he sang two 'Hallelujahs' too many, his voice roaring through the huge bare cube. His shame and distress were considerable. As the years passed, some of the children took up the tradition too. Even today, I should guess, you would find fifty people who could take up the 'Hallelujah Chorus' with you from any moderate-sized working-class crowd in Hunslet.

But popular secular music is more widely representative of working-class taste than the bands and the oratorio choirs, and will furnish the main illustrations here. I am not thinking of jazz and variants of it which have appeared in the last three decades. I am thinking rather at this point, though none of them is a pure repository of the elements I want to isolate, of the kind of thing printed in the song-books sold by some stationers and by Woolworth's (*McGlennon's Record Song-Book – 190th Edition; The Magazine of Song Hits – The Correct Lyrics of Thirty Songs; The Hit Parade; One Hundred Songs from Lawrence Wright*). They contain the words but not the music of anything from twenty to one hundred songs, all mixed together, the old and the new. 'Abide with Me' is likely to be followed by the latest lyric about England, then by 'Bird in a Gilded Cage', then by a new love-song or something about children from Charing Cross Road or America, such as 'I saw Mummy kissing Santa Claus'. I have in mind, too, some of the qualities displayed in 'Workers'

Playtime', and 'Works' Wonders', but not in the endless, tepid glu-
cose-and-water of some other radio musical programmes for workers,
which are not of the people, but of the world where things are done
for the people. In particular, I am thinking of the occasional singsongs and concerts in the pubs and clubs. But I shall confine myself to
the discussion of singing in the clubs, because enough has been written
elsewhere about cheerful group-singing in the public-houses and it is
difficult now to separate our true reactions from those the brewers'
advertisements seek to induce. In the working-men's clubs, customs
have not yet been exploited to support the profitable mythological
figure of the good-fellow-working-man-with-his-warm-common-
sense-and-honest-pint.

These clubs, independently controlled but each affiliated to the
Working Men's Club and Institute Union, were founded nearly a
hundred years ago to provide recreation, a place for talk and reading
and some education, for working-men. Their educational side is still
formally alive, though little more than that; they also operate some
provident schemes and maintain their own convalescent homes. They
are today the pub-cum-club for a very large number of working-
people. The working-man is far more of a clubman than is usually
realized. There are today well over three thousand separate working-
men's clubs, with a total membership of more than two million, of
whom about two hundred thousand are women. Membership costs
ten shillings a year, and control is vested in an elected committee,
with the day-to-day management in the hands of a full-time salaried
steward. Members are proud that their clubs are not run 'for the
benefit of the profiteers'.

A working-man goes to his club to drink, and usually gets his beer
a little more cheaply there than in a pub. But this is not the only
attraction; often he will pass the evening there and spend very little,
especially in mid-week. He will talk and play a game of darts or
billiards or cards or dominoes; he may take out a ticket in one of the
'draws'; he may have half a pint or a pint. Naturally, on weekend
nights he is likely to drink more, and about these nights there is a
pervading air of ''aving a good time', and the club will have arranged
a concert. At weekends, and especially for the Sunday concert, many
wives attend, usually as guests; they find the club 'very sociable'.

The majority of members seem to be family men; almost all on
the far side of twenty-five and most of them apparently somewhat

older. But I doubt whether this indicates that the clubs are losing their hold, that they appeal to a past generation. Rather it indicates that they appeal, have always appealed, to an older group, to those past the courting stage and the early years of marriage. Many young men are members and some are regulars; but from eighteen to the early twenties they will often be out after the girls or 'jazzing', and are likely to regard the club, even though they may drop in occasionally, as a bit old-fashioned. During the first few years of marriage, and especially before the children come or if the wife is working, the couple are likely to maintain the frequent picture-going which played such a large part in their courtship and is still invested with a suggestion of the really up-to-date pleasures available to modern youth with money in its pocket. By contrast, the club is likely to seem a little drab; many of those in the older districts are in poor buildings, and their interiors are not as frequently revivified as those of most pubs. By the time a couple has settled down to the harder facts of married life, the husband is likely to have become a more regular club-goer. The joint visits to the pictures may continue, but are less frequent; soon they are like most other couples of that age. They have taken over, with remarkably little change, the traditions suitable to their age within their community. Whatever the changes, there is still, for most, this steady settling after a few years of marriage; these years are sometimes extended today, but they are usually followed by the settling-down, which maintains its traditional character.

The weekend concerts vary in scope from quite simple affairs to those with 'bills' which suggest a variety-theatre. In manner they belong to an older environment; crooners (of certain types) appear nowadays, but in general the concerts have a flavour of the variety-hall-pierrot-show-concert-party era. There seems to be a great shadow-world of semi-professional entertainers, men and women who make a comfortable addition to their normal wages by regularly performing at club concerts, moving from club to club in the city as they become known and, if they are particularly good, building up a circuit in the industrial towns for thirty miles around. A typical bill might announce;

Freddy Eames (Sheffield)	*Baritone*
Bill Wilson (Doncaster)	*Piano*
Return Visit of the Popular	
Eileen Johnson (Leeds)	*Soubrette*

There are comedians and occasionally a ventriloquist, but the emphasis is on singing, both by individuals and by the company as a whole. Behind the paid stars of the concerts, and in special demand on 'Free-and-Easy' nights, are the individuals who can be relied on for a tune or a song, who are not paid but by custom are supplied with drinks, sometimes on the house, sometimes by members who 'send one up', or 'send one across'. Most clubs have among their number one or two known to have good voices and to be willing to 'oblige'. If they have no pianist among the members they always find someone who will play most of the night for a few shillings and drinks. Most of the time the music streams out without a break, one tune merging into another; the pianist plays by ear, and rarely falters for want of a tune of the right kind. Meanwhile the talk and laughter, the occasional shouts and the clinking of glasses go on, and the piano music is in the main a fitting background to it all. Occasionally someone will rise and move to the piano, probably urged on by his friends. There will be firm cries of 'Order please!'; the servers stop clattering; the company becomes still and looks towards the piano – and the singer delivers his contribution.

The manner of singing is traditional and has fixed characteristics. It is meant to embody intense personal feeling, but is much less egocentrically personal and soft-in-the-middle than the crooning styles; it aims to suggest a deeply-felt emotion (for the treachery of a loved one, for example), but the emotion has not the ingrown quality shown by the crooners. With the crooners, and particularly with the later exponents of special styles from America, one is in the world of the private nightmare; here, it is still assumed that deep emotions about personal experiences are something all experience and in a certain sense share. The manner of singing is therefore more open. On the other hand, it is not fully the public manner of the pantomime singer who has, at the end of Act 3, to 'give everything she's got' to 'Jealousy', with all the spotlights on her. Her manner is emotional, but the circumstances – the huge auditorium, the hundreds in tiers – call for a very broad brush, a simplification into boldly caricatured emotional strokes. Thus one arrives at the 'big-dipper' style of singing, the style used by working-class entertainers giving *individual* performances in the great public places. Here the voice takes enormous lifts and dips to fill out the lines of a lush emotional journey. Something of all this is in the club-and-pub style of singing, but

E*

reduced to scale and made more homely; the 'big-dipper' adapted for use in a moderately sized room. Each emotional phrase is pulled out and stretched; it is the verbal equivalent of rock-making, where the sweet and sticky mass is pulled to surprising lengths and pounded; there is a pause as each emotional phrase is completed, before the great rise to the next and over the top. The whole effect is increased by a nasal quality, though one slighter than that used by crooners. The most immediately recognizable characteristic is the 'er' extension to emotionally important words, which I take to be the result partly of the need to draw every ounce of sentiment from the swing of the rhythm, and partly of the wish to underline the pattern of the emotional statement. The result is something like this

> You are-er the only one-er for me-er,
> No one else-er can share a dream-er with me-er,
> (pause, with trills from the piano leading to
>   the next great sweep)
> Some folks-er may say-er . . .

And when the choruses come along, because the singing is what I have called 'open', the company are likely to join in less self-consciously than in most other forms of community singing today. However quickly the feeling may be dissipated afterwards, they have for the present a feeling of warm and shared humanity.

Similar considerations unconsciously guide the pianist. If he is going to be asked again, and get his pints on the piano top as often as he likes, he must know the exact idiom in which to play. This involves not only knowing the established songs and how to play them, but which of the new songs are catching on and, more important, how to play them so that, though their main lines are kept, they are transmuted into the received idiom. When this act of transmutation has been performed, the new and the old live together happily. The new has brought its individual contribution, but has been made part of the emotionally unified whole which contains songs from fifty years ago onwards. The pianist needs to know how to transmute every melody into a series of simple melodic intervals, into a pattern of strongly marked sentimental rhythms, how to linger on the long notes, how to weave in the little formal trills at the end of each section (as well as to provide the 'run-up' to the singer's next note), how to operate his loud and soft pedals, not in accordance with the demands of the score, but so as to keep up the ground-swell of emotion; he needs to iron out any subtleties and produce a broad strong beat. This seems to me, though I do not know enough about music to be certain, to have much in common with the beat of an old-fashioned waltz: metaphorically, it is the beat of 'a good weep', of a warm and pally feeling, of a heavy nostalgia. The manner has, I think, been modified to some degree, and in some places very considerably, by the jazz rhythms of the twenties; I doubt whether it has been much affected by later styles. At a casual hearing it might seem as though 'swing' has taken over, but this would be a misinterpretation. The emotional patterns bodied out by 'swing' are quite close to those of the older, waltz-derived, styles: in fact, 'swing' has been adapted and assimilated; a modern 'swing' song and an old-fashioned waltz tune live together with ease. The style often used in the more modern pubs is an exception; they seek to attract young couples by offering music 'in the modern manner'. But in many places the long-established style goes on with little change. Only a few months ago I heard a blind pianist, in a pub this time, in a West Riding mill-town. In his corner he played, literally for hours without a break, an accompaniment to the best-bar noises. At intervals his hand reached out to the spot where he knew they put his pint. He played songs which were sung seventy years ago and hit-tunes from the latest American musical, and there was no sense of a break in manner. No doubt he enjoyed playing, but one did not think of him as an individualist, as an individual performer; he was, rather, a participant – a respected and important participant – in a group activity. Far back behind the whole scene one could just see the outlines of the generations of folk-singing and folk-musicians who had gone before; and the otherwise silent blind man pouring out the music he knew was wanted gave, in spite of the modern-tinsel quality of much in the environment, something of a moving and archetypal quality to the whole experience.

The finest period in English urban popular song seems to have been between 1880 and 1910, when each great music-hall star had errand-boys and earls singing his or her characteristic songs. Many people not in the working-classes remember these songs now, but usually as something quaint. They tend to affect period-voices and feel that they are taking part in a nostalgic, comic, and interestingly archaic amusement.

But some of these songs are still sung in the clubs without sophisticated archness. They are obviously known to be old-fashioned, but that gives rise to the reflection that 'y' can't beat the old songs when it comes to a tune', which is true. It is also true, as of any period, that the few good songs are remembered from a host of indifferent ones. With them, all mixed together, are American songs from the same period (such as 'I'll take you home again, Kathleen' or Stephen Foster's 'Beautiful Dreamer'), songs from the First World War, songs from the twenties. An evening's playing will comprise a majority of songs dating from the last twenty years (put into the accepted idiom), but will include a substantial sprinkling of earlier tunes.

These earlier tunes divide fairly simply into two main groups – the seriously emotional, and the amused and mocking; the former seems to retain the stronger hold today. These are the songs which can still affect most of the hearers, and bring some of the women near to tears; sentimental ballads (their ages vary) such as : 'If You were the Only Girl in the World', 'Honeysuckle and the Bee', 'Silver Threads among the Gold', 'When Your Hair Has Turned to Silver', 'For Old Times' Sake', 'Dear Old Pals', 'Little Dolly Daydream', 'Bird in a Gilded Cage', 'Just a Song at Twilight', 'Lily of Laguna', 'Roses of Picardy', 'Danny Boy', 'No Rose in all The World', 'My Old Dutch', 'The Miner's Dream of Home', 'You Made Me Love You', and 'If Those Lips could only Speak':

> If those lips could only speak,
> If those eyes could only see,
> If those beautiful golden tresses
> Were there in reality.
>
> Could I only take your hand
> As I did when you took my name,
> But it's only a beautiful picture
> In a beautiful golden frame.

The cheeky, finger-to-the-nose and ain't-life-jolly song is the song of the working-classes when they are refusing to be down-hearted simply because they are working-class, when they are raucously confident. Here are the gay Lothario songs, like 'Hello, Hello, who's your Lady-friend?' ('It wasn't the girl I saw you with at Brighton . . .'), 'Who were You with Last Night?' ('Oh, oh, oh, I am surprised at you . . .'), 'Put Me Among the Girls' ('Do me a Favour, do . . .'), and 'Hold Your Hand Out, You Naughty Boy'. And the gay, rough and battered old types: 'Two Lovely Black Eyes', 'I'm One of the Ruins that Cromwell Knocked About a Bit', 'Where Did You Get That Hat?', 'My Old Man Said "Foller the Van" ', 'Any Old Iron', 'My Little Bottom Drawer', and 'Oh, Oh, Antonio'. Or the nonsense songs, which are simply excuses for a cheerful communal roar like 'Ta-Ra-Ra-Boom-De-Ay', 'Yes, We Have No Bananas', 'Felix', and 'Horsy, Keep Your Tail Up'. During the last twenty or thirty years there have been added to this group, 'I've Got Sixpence', 'Roll Out The Barrel', 'The Lambeth Walk', 'Run, Rabbit, Run' (from the Second World War), 'Mairzy Doats' and the 'Bunch of Coconuts' song.

Thus working-class groups still sing some of the songs their grandparents sang. They do not sing any from before then; the oldest works in the canon date from the heyday of the great urban music centres. They would not be happy singing 'My Bonnie Lies Over the Ocean', or 'Johnny's so Long at the Fair' and they leave 'Little Brown Jug' and 'There is a Tavern in the Town' to the Scouts and students. I remember the chill which fell over a bar, as though two police-spies had suddenly given themselves away, when an acquaintance of mine, after buying a drink for the man who had just 'rendered' 'Broken-hearted Clown', invited him to lead us all in 'Clementine'.

As the years have passed, some songs have been lost, but a score of old ones remain in the repertoire. The exact distribution of old to new songs varies. In some places you will hear no more than that they 'like an old one now and again'; at others the old songs may constitute a quarter of the evening's singing. But though new songs are almost everywhere in the majority, each one, if it is to be taken up, must meet certain general requirements of melody and sentiment. The two go together, but I should guess that the suitability of melody, of tune, is the harder to find: hundreds of songs appear with the most unexceptionable lyrics, but they catch on only if the tune is catchy. If these two demands are met, the versification can be – perhaps should be – of the utmost simplicity.

Songs which do not meet the requirements are not likely to be taken up, no matter how much Tin Pan Alley plugs them. Sometimes a huge effort at publicity and distribution ensures that a song which would otherwise be altogether ignored does raise a little interest for a week or two; but when the pressure is relaxed, and in the circumstances of the industry it cannot be long maintained, it drops out of sight. Great public events – a war, a coronation – set the writers feverishly trying to produce a song which will connect; the song-books of the war-years are full of utterly forgotten chest-beating patriotic songs whose composers were seeking another 'There'll Always Be An England'. Less important public events are made the occasions for jolly or stirring songs or for additions to the line of nonsense songs. Unearth the paper song-books of the last ten years and you will find entombed there cheerful little songs about National Service and zebra crossings. They arrived still-born; they had neither the melody nor the large generalized sentiments which make for success.

In America they produce songs with titles such as 'They needed a Song-bird in Heaven, so God Took Caruso Away', and 'There's a New Star in Heaven Tonight' (on the death of Rudolph Valentino). I do not know how they fared in the United States, but here they seemed to have little success with working-class people. I should guess that this was not simply due to a lack of the right kind of melody, but also to their lack of sufficiently generalized emotion. Their form of emotional expression is not unusual; 'Sonny Boy', an American song but one very popular over here, introduces the idea of the angels taking away the little boy because they are lonely. But 'Sonny Boy' is not a particular boy; he is a symbolic boy, one in the line which includes the lad who many years ago pleaded, 'Please, Mr Conductor, Don't Put Me Off the Train' and the child who lately cried, 'How Much is that Doggie in the Window?' (at least, English people have insisted on taking it as a child's request, though the full verse suggests that an American adult heading West for California is speaking).

At the time of writing 'How Much is that Doggie in the Window?' and 'Oh, my Papa' (adapted from a Swiss operetta and played as a peculiarly plangent trumpet solo) are the latest songs to gain complete entry into the canon. They join survivals from the last twenty or thirty years such as, 'Shepherd of the Hills', 'Underneath the Arches', 'Home on the Range', 'We'll Meet Again', 'Broken-hearted Clown',

'I'm Dreaming of a White Christmas', 'Jealousy', 'When You Played the Organ and I Sang the Rosary', 'My Sister and I', 'Love's Last Word is Spoken, Chéri' (the tune and sentiments are so congenial that there is no difficulty of nationality here), 'Music, Maestro, Please', 'Dinner for One, please James' (again, with these last two, tune and sentiment triumph over differences of social class), 'Souvenirs', 'Auf Wiedersehen', 'Wish Me Luck as You Wave Me Good-bye', 'Cheating Heart' (one contemporary singer's recording of this won immense popularity because, I think, it combined the crude elements of the 'big dipper' and intimate crooner manners), and 'Paper Doll'. I first heard 'Paper Doll' sung in the 'red-hot' fashion by an American star crooner, and it seemed quite unsuitable for transplantation to Northern England; but two or three years later a local amateur sang it whilst I was in a Hull pub, and it had been beautifully translated. 'I'd rather have a paper doll to call my own/Than just a good-for-nothing real life gal' was delivered in the American version with immense speed and attack, and the final 'gal' was a powerful sock of a drawl. In Yorkshire the whole thing was taken at half the speed, the rhythms pulled out to the usual up-and-down pattern, and 'gal' transmuted into the standard Northern English moan-ending on 'er'.

'I'm sending a letter to Santa Claus', sometimes sung by Gracie Fields, is especially worth hearing as an example of the kind of song which makes its niche soon and retains it. The melody is as much in keeping with the tradition as is the theme; and in clubs the pianist's delivery abounds in the favourite trills and 'runs-up' between each of the sentiments.

It is clear that these songs work within a firm and restricted group of conventions. We may leave aside the more obvious conventions of apparatus and properties, since they are well known. More important are the clichés in melodic movements, such as those which announce that we are approaching the intensely sad part in a song of lost love: or the half-dozen notes, played in a certain way between two lines of the lyric, which indicate at once, even if you have entered the club only at that moment, that this is a song about childhood.

Yet these qualities illustrate more than the imaginative poverty of the mechanical song-writers; they illustrate a characteristic of their audience similar to that discussed in connexion with the stories from

Secrets and *Glamour*. These are strictly conventional songs; their aim is to present to the hearer as directly as possible a known pattern of emotions; they are not so much creations in their own right as structures of conventional signs for the emotional fields they open. The metaphors are not meant to be imbued with complex suggestion; they are part of a fixed and objective currency; very small change, in a few broad denominations, but recognizable in their own territory. They have not the subtlety and maturity in attitudes we may find in some Elizabethan songs. But even if that earlier peasant audience was capable of a fine response, is it not also worthy of remark that working-class audiences today, after nearly one hundred years of hard and often ugly urban life, should hold as strongly as they do to themes which, though very simply apprehended, are by no means unadmirable? 'After the Ball is Over' is a melodramatic song; it is not even a people's song as the ballads were, but a commercial song taken over by the people; but they have taken it on their own terms, and so it is not for them as poor a thing as it might have been.

The themes are also conventional, and their roots are love, home, and friendship. Love, first, as warm and personal, as a compensation for the lack of this world's goods, as going on 'just the same' in spite of troubles, 'true love' as better than money or many lovers (e.g. 'Bird in a Gilded Cage'). There is a strong interest in treacherous love, love lost through jealousy, the lonely individual left by a faithless lover ('Broken-hearted Clown', 'Love's Last Word is Spoken, Chéri', 'Jealousy', and the near-'classical', 'On with the Motley', from *I Pagliacci*). Of the force of home as a theme ('I'll take you home again, Kathleen', 'Home' – 'And though fortune may forsake me/Sweet dreams will ever take me ... Home') I need probably say no more. Interlinked with it is the figure of the mother ('Silver Threads among the Gold', 'She's an Old-Fashioned Mother', 'That Old-fashioned Mother of Mine', 'She's My Mother Dear') either sitting at home and typifying all for which home stands, or dead and looking down affectionately on her still-loved ones. So one branches out to boys abroad or otherwise away from home, orphans, children in sentimental situations ('My Sister and I', 'I'm Sending a Letter to Santa Claus').

Friendship embraces neighbourliness, loyalty, growing old with comrades, and implies that these, like love, are better than money or fame. 'Comrades', a Boer War favourite, is still sometimes sung:

> Comrades, comrades, ever since we were boys,
> Sharing each other's sorrows, sharing each other's joys,
> Comrades when manhood was dawning,
> Faithful whate'er might betide,
> When danger threatened my darling old
> Comrade was there by my side.

With it go 'For Old Time's Sake', 'Dear Old Pals', and (for a wife as both wife and comrade) 'My Old Dutch'. From the theme of friendship as better than riches it is an easy step to that of the necessity for being happy and cheerful, even though poor, as in the comparatively recent, 'Spread a little Happiness as you go by'. So enter all the songs of the second main type, the cheeky and nonsensical songs.

But the majority are the sentimental, and especially the sad and nostalgic. 'Strange how potent cheap music is,' said Amanda to Elyot in Noël Coward's *Private Lives*, and indeed it is so, and that not only to working-class people. But some of the melodies are lovely, and if they are not too distorted in the singing can move a listener in much the same way as the arias from the lusher Italian operas. Like these operas, the songs have limited and bold emotional equipment, without subtleties; but the springs of the heart are working. It is not enough simply to dismiss them as, to quote Cecil Sharp, 'noxious weeds – the debased street music of the vulgar'. They are vulgar, it is true, but not usually tinselly. They deal only with large emotional situations; they tend to be open-hearted and big-bosomed. The moral attitudes behind them are not mean or calculating or 'wide'; they still just touch hands with an older and more handsome culture. They are not cynical or neurotic; they often indulge their emotions, but are not ashamed of showing emotion, and do not seek to be sophisticatedly smart. I suppose this may be one reason why so many of the older songs are still clung to; they come from a period when it was easier to release the emotions.

It is this unity of emotional expression which permits a great freedom in moving between different types of song. Thus religious – or what are thought to be religious – songs, are popular, and a singer will pass from a song about love to a religious song and so to what would be called a 'classical' song, with no sense of incongruity in her or the company; the emotional atmosphere gives an all-embracing unity. We might call this the 'Gracie Fields switch', since Miss Fields is its most notable exponent; she can move successfully from a back-yard comic-song to a 'classical' or 'classical religious' song such as: 'The Lost Chord' ('Seated one day at the organ/I was weary and ill-at-ease . . .'), or 'Bless This House' (which has the Home/God tie – 'Bless this house, O Lord, we pray/Make it safe by night and day . . . Bless the hearth ablazing there/With smoke ascending like a prayer'); and so to 'The Holy City', or 'Ave Maria', or 'The Lord's Prayer'. In the latter category come also 'Oh, for the Wings of a Dove' (of which a recording made by a boy soprano used to be very popular), 'All Through the Night', 'The Old Rugged Cross', and the hymn which more than any other belongs to the working-classes, 'Abide with Me': it is sung at football matches and other large public occasions, and many a working-class mother asks only for that at her funeral. My mother did so, and my grandmother some years later; for both of them it had an enormous weight of suggestion, of God as Father, of Heaven as Home, and of the long day of work which had been their lives, drawing to a close.

This is the sort of music which a relative of mine calls, 'Music which meks yer want to give all yer money away' (admirable working-class wit – she has never had any money to spare). But she would also include in the group 'Danny Boy', the few melodies of Tchaikovsky which have reached her, and perhaps even such a song (a secular song but one delivered with a great weight of quasi-religious feeling) as 'Now is the Hour'. The religious songs do give something of a feeling that the others cannot give, a vague but strong sense of being uplifted, of the holy. But this is only an addition to the main general feeling which they share with all the other successful sentimental songs, the songs which bring tears to the eyes; the same kind of emotion floods through them all. It is not difficult to understand why the films' aerial massed strings and huge angelic choirs, singing in the vaulted upper regions 'I'll Walk Beside You', 'You'll Never Walk Alone', 'I Believe', 'My Friend', or 'I'm Walking Behind', are so easily accepted; or why the echo-chamber has become so popular – since it suggests both something out of this world and the intimacy of that singing in the bath which makes us all feel that we have fine voices. Similarly, it is obvious why 'close harmony', with its suggestion of unity and friendship, is widely popular, and why the more glutinous modern styles of singing are easy successors to what I called earlier emotional 'rock-pulling'. The older tradition of singing is undoubtedly being weakened: but at present it still is more than the remnant of an older manner, is still to some degree remaking itself, still actively taking from the new songs what it wants.

But in what way can working-class people be said to accept, to 'believe in', songs of this kind? I may well have suggested too large an emotional surrender, too full and direct a belief in what the songs say, groups united by the tears standing in every eye.

That would be far too simple a view. In one sense it is true to say that the songs are taken seriously, if by that is meant that they are not being deliberately 'guyed', or enjoyed as quaintly out of date. 'If Those Lips could only Speak,' a very good song, is enjoyed much in the way, I imagine, that our grandparents enjoyed it; there is probably some added nostalgia in that it speaks for a time when love and home could more easily be allowed their proper emotional scope. It suggests underneath something of the feeling that is prompted by a fine old man or woman, of whom it will be said, 'Ah, it's a pity there's not more like 'em today.'

On the other hand, the belief, the taking seriously, is not an unqualified matter. It subsists with an awareness that songs like this, whether new or old, are 'very sentimental'; and that awareness expresses itself in the strain of debunking songs about sentimentality. In one kind of comic song working-class people deliberately overdo the emotion they usually accept. 'There was I, waiting at the church' is one example, and 'I never cried so much in all my life' is another. Other songs of this type spend most of their length describing, with all the usual emotional movements, the home and wife who have been left behind – and the last line reveals that the husband left voluntarily and wouldn't dream of going back. But the limits of this are intuitively defined: I once heard a young man deliver his own mocking version of a popular sentimental song, and not only fail to make the company laugh, but raise in them the strong, though unexpressed, sense that he had been guilty of a lapse of taste. He had, in fact, been cheap rather than vulgar; he had not so much laughed affectionately at the emotions as destroyed them.

'A feeling heart' can often be soft and sentimental, but is not to be derided. Most of these songs express, in their melodies, in their verses, in the manner in which they must be sung, the 'feeling heart'. They touch old chords; they suggest values which people still like to cherish. Life outside, life on Monday morning, can be a dour affair. Meanwhile, these sentiments are right, people feel, 'when y' get down to it'. The songs warm and encourage at the time, and no doubt their sentiments remain somewhere in the memory through all the unsentimental ordinariness of the working-week.

PART TWO

YIELDING PLACE TO NEW

CHAPTER 6

UNBENDING THE SPRINGS OF ACTION

By this means, a kind of virtuous materialism may ultimately be established in the world, which would not corrupt, but enervate the soul, and noiselessly unbend its springs of action.

DE TOCQUEVILLE

A. *Introductory*

Up to this point I have been chiefly concerned with the way in which some older elements persist in working-class life. And the most remarkable feature seems to be the extent to which, in view of all the appeals now made to working-class people from other areas, older attitudes do manage to survive, whether for good or ill. I need only recall once more the great success of Mr Wilfred Pickles. His manner is too 'blokeish', too evidently 'all pals together', 'rough diamonds but hearts of gold', for my taste. He seems to me to indulge the northern working-class, by echoing their own view that no one can beat them at salty repartee and an unaffected four-square wisdom. But a large part of his success comes from the fact that his programme, 'Have a Go', provides a forum in which they can express and applaud the values they still admire. These have, again, a simple and limited range, but in spite of the pretentiousness which such a programme can tend to encourage, they are not meaningless to the people who applaud them. 'Straight-dealing', 'good neighbourliness', 'looking on the bright side', 'openness', 'lending a helping hand', 'not being stuck-up or a getter-on', 'loyalty'; all these are a good deal more healthy than the commercial values – pride, ambition, outdoing your acquaintances, show for its own sake, conspicuous consumption – which working-class people are consistently invited to adopt nowadays. And their persistence is not merely formal and in the head.

I turn now to some features of contemporary life which seem to encourage working-class people to adopt different attitudes or to modify the old. To concentrate on the probable effects of certain developments in publications and entertainments is, of course, to isolate only one segment in a vastly complicated interplay of social, political, and economic changes. All are helping to alter attitudes, and some of them undoubtedly for the better. I shall be especially concerned with regrettable aspects of change, since these seem the more evident and important in the field I am examining.

Yet throughout it will be necessary to remember, and I shall try to recall when relevant, the evidence of this first part. For what have been called the 'older' attitudes and those now to be discussed can be found at the same time in the same people. Changes in attitudes work their way very slowly through many aspects of social life. They are incorporated into existing attitudes and often seem, at first, to be only freshly presented forms of those 'older' attitudes. Individuals can therefore inhabit more than one 'mental climate' without conscious strain. Though the nature of the 'older' order may be more immediately evident in middle-aged people, the newer appeals obviously touch them also. Conversely, a young man who seems at first almost completely typical of the second half of this century will reveal attitudes which recall his great-grandfather. It follows that the success of the more powerful contemporary approaches is partly decided by the extent to which they can identify themselves with 'older' attitudes.

Before examining in detail some relevant features in modern life, it may be helpful to select a few elements in the 'mental climate' and to enquire how far they can link themselves, or appear to link themselves, to long-established and often worthy assumptions. What relationships may there be between the older 'tolerance' and contemporary forms of the idea of 'freedom', between the older group-sense and modern democratic egalitarianism and between (paradoxical though it may seem at first) the older sense of the need to live in the present with the newer 'progressivism'? In what ways may 'tolerance' help the activities of the newer entertainers? By what means may scepticism and nonconformity be made tarnished ghosts of themselves? Can the idea of "aving a good time while y'can' because life is hard open the way to a soft mass-hedonism? Can the sense of the group be turned into an arrogant and slick conformity? Can a greater consciousness of these traditional virtues be developed into a destroying self-flattery? The enquiry, it will be seen, is mainly concerned with what may be called invitations to self-indulgence. Some attention will also be given to the trend towards a sort of cynicism. Related to the cynicism can be a sense of loss, though this affects only a small minority. But the minority is an important one, and I shall therefore speak separately of the sense of loss, particularly as it affects 'the uprooted'.

In some respects the three closely related ideas of freedom, equality, and progress still nourish the assumptions of a majority of people, whether they are of the working-classes or not, in ways which would have been more compatible with mid-nineteenth-century intellectual opinion than they are with our own. What is the nature of the appeal made by, for example, the idea of progress, to working-class people today? Whatever the situation in other classes, there is much in working-class experience, especially during the last half-century, to ensure that progress should still seem an undeniably valid notion. Progress as an assumption connects easily with the traditional hope-fulness and pragmatism of working-class people. More specifically, the effects of social, political, and material progress became evident to the working-classes later than to the middle-classes. It was in the latter half of the last century and the opening years of this century that the effects of these changes first came home forcefully to the bosoms of working-class people, in the extension of the franchise, the possibilities of much greater material comforts than had been known before, the effect of the Education Acts, and in much else. Succeeding decades have seen genuine and important improvements in the standard of life of working-class people. My grandmother and mother would have had much less worrying lives had they brought up their families during the mid-twentieth century. All their lives they needed, quite simply, many more of some essential goods and services than they had. As I think of them it seems to me that to call the working-class attitude towards progress only a form of materialism, as some writers do, is often to underrate it. They wanted these goods and services not out of a greed for possession, a desire to lay their hands on the glittering products of a technical society, but because the lack of them made it very difficult to live what they called a 'decent' life, because without them life was a hard and constant fight simply to 'keep your head above water' spiritually as well as economically. Thus, with a better place to wash in and better equipment, it would have been possible to keep the family as clean as they felt 'proper'. We no longer hear about the sheer stink of a working-class crowd. A real progress was clearly possible and was a worthwhile aim.

Thus the idea of progress is still behind much of the formal common speech of working-class people. But popular publicists push the idea beyond any reasonable limits. For a number of obvious reasons, popular publicists have always found and presumably always will find the notion of progress a congenial one. The pressures of a complex and crowded commercial life today cause it to be extended until it becomes a limitless 'progressivism' of things.

'Time marches on . . .' says the thrilled and eager voice of the film commentator, and the roll of drums and lifting blare of trumpets indicate the goodness of that fact in itself. 'Let the great world run for ever down the ringing grooves of change' cries the advertising copy-writer at his most inspirational, finding Tennyson's metaphor the best expression of the mood he wishes most often to invoke. The leader-writers of the popular Press make great play with horizons, new dawns, broad highways, forward movements (marchings and floods), and forward-lookers.

An age is most affected, it has been said, not by the ideas of an original thinker but by what it gathers from his ideas after they have been through such a simplifying and distorting sieve. I remember meeting this observation for the first time in an essay about the influence of the ideas of Machiavelli on Elizabethan England. It is perhaps more widely applicable today, when the popular audience is many times greater than the intellectual audience and is ceaselessly supplied with information of a kind. Yet it is important to remember that, in so far as ideas affect working-class people, they do not usually affect them as ideas, are not intellectually received and scrutinized. This is true even at a time when everyone is expected to have 'views'. The ideas seem to be adopted rather as received tags ('they say it's all relative nowadays'; 'they say it's all a matter of your glands'), and are held on to when they seem comforting in much the same way as the older tags ('Ah well, it's all a matter of luck'; 'Well, what is to be, will be').

The ideas which the popular publicist uses most will be those which help to keep his audience receptive to his approaches. Each of the three ideas discussed in this chapter has contributed largely, in its legitimate aspects, to the bringing about of those improvements in the lot of working-people which were so badly needed. The improvements were desired and hoped for, I have suggested, for more than material reasons. It is the irony of the present situation that those ideas, misused, are now tempting a physically and materially emancipated working-class to have a largely material outlook.

The temptations, especially as they appear in mass-publications, are towards a gratification of the self and towards what may be called a 'hedonistic-group-individualism'. I do not mean to imply that such tendencies are altogether new. These forces would not have their success were it not that we are all inclined to prefer the easy to the hard road, and the levelling half-reason which justifies weakness to the hard fact which shocks and insults before it braces.

Nevertheless, contemporary society has developed with particular skill the techniques of mutual indulgence and satisfied 'ordinariness'. As traditional sanctions were removed or, in popular belief, proved irrelevant, so the popularizers with their great new machines for persuasion occupied the open country left. They found their customers among all classes. This cannot be over-emphasized; a passage by Julien Benda makes the necessary cautionary point:

We speak of the bad taste of our 'democratic' society. We mean by that a society whose tastes have become those of the people or at least such as we usually expect of the people (namely, indifference to intellectual values, religion of emotion). We intend by that neither to curse nor to flatter any particular political regime. We would willingly say with a woman of the 18th century, 'I call "people" all those who think commonly and basely: the court is full of them.'

It may well be, however, that working-class people are in some ways more open to the worst effects of the popularizers' assault than are some other groups. Those who today, after the considerable sifting carried out by the educational system, perform the mass of work which is not intrinsically interesting and which makes only small critical and intellectual demands, are politically and economically freer than ever before. They have more money to spend than ever before; there are plenty of people more able than ever before to provide for them at the level of the lowest common denominator of response. In many parts of life mass-production has brought good; culturally, the mass-produced bad makes it harder for the good to be recognized. 'Brute necessities', the more pressing hardships of working life, have been greatly lessened. Working-people are more free, but they also have the freedom of a vast Vanity Fair of shouting indulgences. It is hard to find a way through such a crowd, especially as the entertainers are adept at discouraging the subversive thought that outside there may be other, quieter regions.

Yet in many important ways these tendencies are meeting resistance. In the private areas of life, people can still draw to a large extent upon older promptings, and that ability affects also their response to the myriad voices from outside. I have quoted freely, in the chapters that follow, from earlier expressions of alarm similar to mine, some of them over a hundred years old. The comfort they give can easily be exaggerated, and it would be a dangerous mistake to assume from them that all these external forces have no internal effect and that therefore my main argument is undermined. But these older admonitions caution us not to see ruin too quickly; and in part they give encouragement, are a reminder that, because people in all classes persist in living the larger part of their lives with little immediate reference to the debilitating forces outside, the process of debilitation is much slower than it might have been.

B. *Tolerance and Freedom*

Since therefore it is unavoidable to the greatest part of men, if not all, to have several *opinions*, without certain and indubitable proof of their truths; . . . it would methinks become all men to maintain peace and the common offices of humanity and friendship, in the diversity of opinions. . . . We should do well to commiserate our mutual ignorance, and endeavour to remove it in all the gentle and fair ways of information; and not instantly treat others ill, as obstinate and perverse, because they will not renounce their own, and receive our opinions.

JOHN LOCKE

Toleration is not the *opposite* of intolerance, but is the *counterfeit* of it. Both are despotisms. The one assumes to itself the right of withholding liberty of conscience, and the other of granting it.

TOM PAINE

It will be useful first to recall that group of attitudes which includes an unidealistic tolerance, a pragmatism, a taking-life-as-it-comes, a goodwill-humanism, a dislike of objecting on principle (rather than for clear and recognizably 'human' reasons). There are some things no decent person would do, it is assumed, and they are fairly easily known. If judgement seems to be invited on much more, then the suspicion of 'moral talk' (which can obviously have a healthy feature) comes into play, and there is a switching-over to an appropriate, blurring counter – 'y've got to live and let live'; almost anything is 'alright in its place'; 'it doesn't matter what y' believe so long as yer 'eart's in the right place', and 'it wouldn't do for us all to think alike'.

The argument here is that the concept of an almost unlimited inner freedom, as it has been conveyed to the working-classes through increasingly shallow channels, has flowed into and absorbed the older notion of tolerance, and taken it much farther than it had gone before. I am not speaking of the sense of social freedom which working-class people have today, of that sense which is illustrated by the lack any longer of a serious feeling that the aristocracy counts for much, and by the refusal of working-class girls to go into domestic service, even though conditions there may sometimes be better than in factories. I am not speaking of the justified feeling of increased political and economic freedom, though all these are related to what I have in mind. I am thinking rather of the manner in which the concept of freedom has been transmitted, of the muddled but nevertheless strong assumption that old sanctions have been finally removed, that 'science' has altogether removed the claims of religion, that psychology has justified the utmost 'broadmindedness'.

The popularizers reinforce, with a flattering mushiness, the old phrase that 'after all, it's only 'uman' with the suggestion that 'scientists tell us' that 'inhibitions are wrong'. It was always a comfort to think that nature free is also naturally good; now we know. This becomes very soon the idea of freedom as a justification. It is always freedom from, never freedom for; freedom as a good in itself, not merely as the ground for the effort to live by other standards. One can easily see how this may spread in a class which has never before felt so free; one can understand the force of the resistance which is encountered the moment it is suggested that freedom is not an absolute, not 'being', but only the 'ground of being'. It is in the interest of the organs of mass entertainment that this attitude should be maintained.

Thus the concept of freedom may widen until it becomes the freedom not to 'be' anything at all, and certainly hardly to object to anything at all. A man is free not to choose, but if he uses his freedom to choose so as to be unlike the majority, he is likely to be called 'narrow-minded', 'bigoted', 'dogmatic', 'intolerant', 'a busy-body', 'undemocratic'. No one is so much disliked as he who persists in 'drawing comparisons'; he spoils the party-spirit. The popular Press – though it makes a speciality of safe or pseudo-controversy – hates genuine controversy, since that alienates, divides, and separates the mass-audience, the buyers.

There can arise, then, not the assertion of a freedom to be non-political; nor simply its use, in disappointment and puzzlement, to 'contract out' of the shouting and generalities which assail everyone today; but a deep refusal to be committed outside the small known-area of life. 'Anything goes' is related to 'live and let live', but carries the matter a good deal farther; the open mind has become a yawning chasm. Tolerance becomes not so much a charitable allowance for human frailty and the difficulties of ordinary lives, as a weakness, a ceaseless leaking-away of the will-to-decide on matters outside the immediate touchable orbit. Listen to people bringing out today the old apophthegms about tolerance; with them will come some new ones whose inspiration is not so much a charity as a refusal to admit that anyone can be judged for anything, and that includes ourselves. 'Everyone's entitled to his own opinion' may indicate strength or weakness; but when, as today, it is constantly surrounded by appeals for the 'open mind' and for 'broadmindedness' – open for its own sake and broad enough not to cause any unpleasantness by requiring disagreement with anyone – one knows where the emphasis lies. The tolerance of men who have some strength and are prepared, if necessary, to use it, is a meaningful tolerance; the tolerance of those whose muscles are flabby and spirits unwilling is simply a 'don't-hit-me' masquerading as mature agreement. Genuine tolerance is a product of vigour, belief, a sense of the difficulty of truth, and a respect for others; the new tolerance is weak and unwilling, a fear and resentment of challenge.

In this condition people will accept almost anything without objecting. Think of some later developments in sensational publications. Sometimes people are mildly shocked by them: 'Oh, they'll do anything nowadays' they say, with a slightly embarrassed smile. The phrase is not a condemnation, but an allowance and an accepting; it is one of the phrases which indicate a paralysis of the moral will which is settling upon many people, in deference to their assumption that freedom must never be attacked. Behind it stand: 'After all, it does no real 'arm', 'Wouldn't you do the same in 'is place?', 'A man's got to live', 'Well, it brings in the money, dun't it?', 'Well, it gives yer a laugh at any rate', and 'What do yer expect? – they've got their living to earn'. 'Anything's alright provided it's not over-done' becomes 'It's alright if y've got the time and the inclination'; 'It doesn't matter what y' believe so long as yer 'eart's in the right place' is partnered by the much more extensively suggestive 'It ain't what y' do, it's the way that y' do it'. The tolerant phrases have been joined by others in similar dress; the new depreciate the old, and together they become the ritual uniforms of a shared unwilling-ness to admit that freedom can have its punishments. Anything goes and there is no scale.

c. 'Everybody's Doing It Now' or 'The Gang's All Here': The Group Sense and Democratic Egalitarianism

We saw how the strong sense of the group among working-class people can express itself as a demand for conformity. The group is warm and friendly; it does a great deal to make life more pleasant and manageable. But it has sharp methods with those who, from within it, begin to deride its values.

I suggest that this sense of the importance and the predominant rightness of the group is being linked to, and increasingly made to subserve, a callow democratic egalitarianism, which is itself the necessary ground for the activities of the really popular publicists. There is, it is true, a powerful pressure, notably from advertising copy-writers, to sell to all classes the ramified forms of individualism by which their kind of commerce must live, in the stress on the virtue of 'going one better', 'getting on', 'being wideawake', out-doing all others. But I can see little evidence that there they have so far had any considerable success with working-class people. Some-times an advertising copy-writer will get his lines crossed and produce copy designed to reach the body of the working-classes (rather than the minority who are much affected by these assump-tions), though appealing to assumptions more characteristic of other classes. But on the whole the accuracy of the advertisers' aim is formidable. They have by now had plenty of practice and yearly gain in sureness.

To point to this phenomenon today is not to discover, as though it were something new in human nature, that we all sometimes, and some of us much of the time, like to feel that we are going the way the world is going, that our actions are supported by a general consent. Nor is it to forget the respectable ancestry of the idea of equality in Western Europe. But that common desire, reinforced by a galloping egalitarianism, has during the past sixty or seventy years been more and more played upon to move and persuade, in magazines and newspapers specifically designed to attract a literate working-class.

From then on has developed, with increasing elaboration, all the well-known cant of 'the common man'; a grotesque and dangerous flattery, since he is conceived as the most common or commonplace man. 'Rely on the people'; all are equal, all have a vote; all are 'as good as one another'; 'the voice of the people is the voice of God' (to recall an old-fashioned form); therefore in all things, says the publicist, your attitudes are as good as anyone else's: but since you share the opinions of the great majority, you are more right than the odd outsiders. The popular papers, always identifying themselves with 'the people', conduct polls on this matter and questionnaires on that matter among their readers, and so elevate the counting of heads into a substitute for judgement.

Behind all this an important radical principle is being appealed to, one always central to working-class people. One can hear behind 'Ah'm as good as you', the assertion of an independence of spirit which holds fast to this fundamental equality, which will not tolerate false professions of superiority, and which is strengthened today by a suspicion that at bottom, in spite of 'all the talk about democracy', 'ordinary people' do not matter, 'do not count'. But, from giving a proper sense of self-respect, 'Ah'm as good as you' can turn into the surly 'Yer no better than me', which is the harsh ass-cry of the philistine in his straw, who will tolerate no suggestion of a challenge or awkward example. It can become a cocksure refusal to recognize any sort of differentiation, whether of brains or of character. One of its forms is illustrated in the newer kinds of competition in some popular publications, where the process of arriving at a correct answer can only be one of pure luck. Any advantage gained by brains or effort has been precluded; and in the more advanced forms of competition everyone gets a prize of sorts. Everyone wins; the 'competitors' pay sufficient on their entry forms to cover the cost of the prize they are given, but no one feels bettered by anyone else.

Whatever is, is right – if the people believe it. 'The little man' is made to seem big because everything is scaled down to his measure; his responses, the limits of his vision, are the recognized limits. Thus, if a writer fails to appeal at once and on the usual first inadequate reading, then he is at fault, and never the reader. The idea of literature as direct communication is paramount; there is no intermediate link. The writer does not stand before his experience and try to recreate it in a form of words, with which – rather than with the writer himself directly – the reader must seek an understanding according to its complexity. Complex – that is, searching or taxing – literature must therefore be discounted; good writing cannot be popular today, and popular writing cannot genuinely explore experience.

'It is you, the ordinary people, and not the members of the Cabinet, who decide this country's fate'; one can see the truth there, but constant inflation makes it equivalent to a lie. In strip-cartoons, in magazine short stories, in the intimate gossip-columns, the hero is the little man; 'Just Joe', as a song title has it. He is the little man who is not brave or beautiful or talented, yet who is loved, not in spite of but because of this. 'I love you . . .', says the girl in the final paragraph, revealing to the overwhelmed young man that all the time he had the sixty-four dollar answer but did not know it, '. . . because you are ordinary.' I found three post-O. Henry quick-twist tales in two successively-read women's magazines, each having the happy revelation in the last paragraph that he or she, far from being 'clever' or 'high-brow', was just a decent ordinary person after all. On Sundays, in particular, journalists with suitably democratic names make their columns ring with straight pride in speaking for the common sense of the ordinary man, which is better than all the subtlety of the intellectuals who 'have notions'. We are encouraging a sense, not of the dignity of each person but of a new aristocracy, the monstrous regiment of the most flat-faced.

Something of the success of the radio 'soap-operas', with working-class women as with others, is due to the consummateness of their attention to this kind of attitude, to their remarkably sustained presentation of the perfectly ordinary and unremarkable. In the strip-cartoons, watch the 'little man' worrying for days on end about his daughter's chances in the school cookery-competition. Here the initial criterion is the exact reverse of Keats's 'load every rift with ore'; to succeed, not to startle or puzzle or otherwise put off, the cartoonists must carry out a daily exercise in spinning out the unimportant and insignificant.

In cartoons the little man is no longer likely to deflate the boss's pretensions by pointing out something truly silly about him, or by scratching an ear and then quietly doing the job that has cost the big men so much trouble and fuss; that could be comic art, and so in the end serious. Now he beats the boss for silly reasons, or asserts that he is better simply because he is a little man. And his successes are always intolerably small successes; but he wins through in the end, as little men's values always do in this 'great big shaggy old world of ours'. Democratic egalitarianism, paradoxically, requires the continuance of the 'Them' and 'Us' idea in some of its poorer forms.

More and more the weekly magazines invite their readers to write their papers for them in the form of contributed snippets. It may be cheaper, and certainly the customers like it. The anecdotes have to be funny or odd – 'she woo'd and won him with Yorkshire pudding' – but still 'it might have happened to you'. They encourage at once both the pally feeling that we are all little men together, but that still 'we do see life'.

As is often pointed out, popular journalists describing some important figure shy away from suggesting differences between him and 'ordinary folk'. The impulse behind this is a good one. People want to feel that to those who are engaged in organizing their lives 'human things' do matter. This attitude is probably healthier than that which prefers major public figures to be remote and godlike. As usual the problem is one of degree, of how an attitude which can be valuable when it is in a working relationship with others which qualify it, becomes a weakness when it is emphasized in isolation. In America, a former President of Harvard says, the only innate differences of ability which will be recognized are in sport. In England, matters are not yet quite so far gone; though it is assumed that one should not make much of intellectual ability. Every rich girl is a poor little rich girl underneath, really wanting nothing more than a home like the rest of us. Every tycoon, general, or major politician, of our Party, is at bottom ordinary and 'homely', fond of his pipe, of his chair at the fireside, and of his visit to a football match, when he 'mingles with the rest of us'. In Dewey's words:

We praise even our most successful men, not for their ruthless and self-centred energy in getting ahead, but because of their love of flowers, children, and dogs, or their kindness to aged relatives.

For officially high-ranking, but anonymous or colourless figures, not even irrelevant grounds for praise need be sought. All senior civil servants are tea-drinking 'buzz-fuzzes', hidebound and lazy. We recall Auden's counter-balancing lines about those who work on:

... problems no smiling/Can dismiss; ... /[unseen by] the weak,/ The inattentive, seeking/Someone to blame; ...

'Highbrow-hating', in anger bred by fear of an implied criticism is not strong among working-class people. But much of the glorification of 'the common man' clearly provides good ground for an extension into highbrow-hunting, and many of the popular journalists try to introduce that sport to their working-class customers. Whilst writing this section, I picked up the current copy of a popular paper and found a columnist describing a chance meeting with some 'bearded arty-arty boys'. My impression is that this kind of attack has not so far had much success. Working-class people are on the whole just not interested in artists or intellectuals; they know of their existence, but regard them as oddities rarely seen within their orbit, like snail-eating Frenchmen. Meanwhile, some journalists, those who have a dislike of whatever is intellectual or serious, continue to use their columns to discharge their dislike and fear. The publication of the British Council report is made a yearly excuse for a tirade on the waste of good public money on highbrow exercises by flabby young men. A case of homosexuality is used as the jumping-off ground for an attack on the debased world of Bohemia. Modern art will only be mentioned if someone has given an excuse for trouncing the odd. The Arts Council is a 'fiddle' by a lot of 'cissies' who despise the amusements of the plain Englishman; and the B.B.C. is little better. Any University Extension lecturer is a stodgy 'do-gooder' and his students spotty-faced and thin-blooded. Anyone who in any way suggests that there may be some things to have doubts about in our present forms of recreation or our mass public assumptions is a spoilsport and crank.

Hence the aggressive 'plain man', the embattled low-brow, tone of many columnists and leader-writers; the inverted snobbery of those film critics who insist that they are 'simple and ordinary men-in-the-street', who seek only to be amused and leave more intellectual 'pretensions to others'; or the lowbrow snobbery of some of the more popular question-answerers in those numerous wireless programmes of the brains-trust type. In these programmes the democratic lust for widespread and fragmentary opinion unites with a slight residual awe for knowledgeable people and also with a slight resentment of them. The latter has some satisfaction in hearing the experts fall out; at such times there arise from the programme what Mr Gilbert Harding has described as 'the elemental odours of the bull-ring and of the bear-pit'.

It seems to me that one can detect a development in this process of levelling-down even among the popular columnists themselves. Until a few years ago the columnists, much as they affected the hearty plain-man style, were usually men with more widely-ranging minds than most of their readers. But latterly some have appeared whose subject-matter – and often style, too – reflects only the petty. In comparison with them, Cassandra of the *Daily Mirror* is full of life, culture, and intelligence; behind his writing is the assumption that, though we cannot all be quick-thinking, energetic, and able to pursue an interest in many subjects (and are, of course, none the worse for that), nevertheless such qualities are worth while and make very interesting reading. With some of the newer journalists, there is the flat assumption that the lowest level of response and interest only is *de rigueur*. These are the men who speak of 'the views of established authors' and 'the classics' as though of a strange world, the men who provide syndicated ordinariness for the millions. These are the back-scratchers for 'the common man', the cheer-leaders of the 'damned compact majority', who smooth over faulty argument and blunt thought by hearty evasion and calls to ridicule. They must, by deriding any kind of authority wherever they find it, appeal to and calm any submerged sense of inferiority and disquiet. If major examples do not come along often enough, there is usually some headmaster or headmistress in Warrington or Derby or Yeovil whose decision about school-clothing or speech-day pronouncements about 'the younger generation' can be given a national castigation in the interests of the free and right-thinking parent.

Let us – like the good Home Service types we are—be cosy together. For that I take to be the mark of our Home Programme, the cosiness of plain easy folk. Not for us the constant glitter, the determined high spirits, of the Light Programme; not for us the aesthetic values, the fastidious accents of the Third Programme. Between the raucous lowbrows and the lisping highbrows is a fine gap, meant for the middle or broadbrows; and you and I, in our homely fashion, fill that gap nicely. We can be cosy together in it. We can talk about bilberry pie. And I take this – under whatever local name the fruit may be known – to be the best pie in the world.

This is middle-class or 'middle-brow' writing, but too illuminating to omit. The tone is naturally somewhat different among writers for the working-classes. There is to be seen behind this passage, as behind similar ones directed to working-class people, an appeal – in the call to all right-thinking and balanced men – to a valuable and still powerful ideal, the ideal of the whole man who can be serious without solemnity and cheerful without cheapness, who pays his dues to his household's and his country's gods, and stands foursquare in integrity and sound sense. But the appeal has in many cases run to seed, has become, in fact, a kind of patronage, sometimes a concealed contempt, of the reader; and a *ducdame* – a cry 'to call fools into a circle'.

Again and again, popular writers must assure their readers, and often themselves, of their 'complete sincerity'. They insist that 'you cannot deceive ordinary folk', and that you must 'believe in yourself as a writer'. But elsewhere the same people are likely to refer to the 'infidelity of public support', and admit that 'the multitude follows the band'.

All qualities which, for good or ill (and in the passage above Dewey mentions only the ill), make the extraordinary man extraordinary, must go by default or be reduced to a manageable oddity. All professors are absent-minded or ineffective; all scientists are weird and bespectacled: they have to be made into mythical figures so that they may be brought within the recognizable world. Indeed, oddity or idiosyncrasy is one of the few admitted forms of individuality or exceptionableness. The man who by and large shares our views but has striking individual quirks does duty for him who has a real exceptionableness rooted in character. So, though the popular columnist must speak for us he should also make us aware of himself as prickly, or at any rate, as personal; that is why so many go in for what almost amounts to undue exposure of the personality. To working-class people and to a great many others the typically out-spoken member in a radio quiz-team represents both the old-style 'card' and this modern allegorical figure, the 'idiosyncratic hero'. The attitude gains strength from the excessive admiration for 'free-dom' in a society which seems more and more unfree. We will pay handsomely that man who gives some release to our sense of in-feriority and disillusion by expressing himself violently in print on what we all hate. The more idiosyncratic a man's statements of his views are (but with no question of the value of those views), the surer we may be that he – and therefore, vicariously, ourselves – are free to 'speak our minds'. Here pre-eminently, 'it ain't what you do, it's the way that you do it'; 'it ain't what you say, it's the way that you say it.'

How inadequate for a political democracy is this kind of ostrich act. It undervalues enemies and induces a blindness to some of the dangerous realities of the search for power. In some countries, where other factors assist the growth of a leader-cult, this very reduction of the great has come in as a reinforcement. The man-of-power pursues his plans in realms unimagined by the ordinary man; the ordinary man meanwhile happily stares at picture postcards of the man-of-power smiling understandingly at an aged peasant-woman, or dandling a steel-worker's fat baby, or laughing at a popular variety-turn.

On the other hand, this attitude encourages a disregard for what-ever worthwhile qualities may have contributed to the arrival at a socially beneficial position. It depreciates the value of a fine applica-tion of intellectual gifts, the courage to take unsentimental and unpopular decisions, a disciplining of the self. The word 'discipline', for example, is almost unusable in popular writing, except in a derogatory sense; it suggests 'pushing people around', the Armed Services, 'being got at', and is rejected out-of-hand. The people who have trained themselves to exercise these qualities can be assumed not to feel the want of public admiration, and one does not regret the lack of that. One can regret the softening effect of this view on those who hold it.

These are peculiarly dangerous comforts of unreason, and pecu-liarly those of a democracy. As in so many things a working-man here seems to be in different situations in his private and in his public life. At work, in the world he really knows, he can still recognize the worth and the admirable qualities of 'a good boss', and does not usually mean by that an indulgent boss, but one who ''as 'is 'ead screwed on t'right way', and whose yea is yea and nay is nay. In his local area, he can still recognize and admire 'a good man', a reliable or devoted or independent spirit. Outside, the great sea of undifferentiated porridge awaits him, where all the crucial characteristics, the dangerous troughs as well as the guiding features, have been obliterated. All he needs to float across, it is suggested, is 'a heart in the right place', a sense of humour which prevents him from being a spoilsport and prompts a laugh at anything odd, and that sense of 'how far to go' which is indispensable to the decent and reasonable man. A song the Scouts are said to have sung has a specialist bias, but its tone is closely related to that of the popular columnists:

> He'll look without dread at the snags on ahead,
> Wine, Women and Highbrows too;
> He won't run aground but will work his way round;
> With a smile, . . .

Oh, wonderful second line ! – the stiff upper lip and a ready cheerfulness outstaring the aesthetic Gorgon.

By all these means the fact of being able to 'rejoice in concurring with the common opinion', being able to feel one of the main herd, is made the excuse for gross insensitivity; that insensitivity feeds on its own pride, the 'hubris' of the 'ordinary chap'. More, working-class people may be the readier to accept this kind of appeal precisely because, though they traditionally like to feel members of a group and are ready to assume the virtue of agreement with the group, there is much in the public world which puzzles them. When you are taking part in some mass-activity, no matter how mechanical the activity may be, there is something warming in the feeling that you are with everyone else. I have heard people give, as their reason for listening to a popular wireless programme, not the fact that it is amusing, but that it 'gives you something to talk about' with everyone else at work. The advertisers sense this when they ask, 'When they are talking about the big match on T.V., will you have to remain silent?' There is more than keeping up with the Jones's in that; there is being one of a group. Lonely people, listening to the wireless booming out the voices of a thousand workers on holiday singing 'If you were the only girl in the world', can derive some comfort from the fact that every wireless in the street is linking the neighbours in a sort of communion. There can be added pleasure in the warm dark super-cinemas, from the fact that the 'you' who is cajoled, invited to laugh, flattered, is not simply the individual 'you', but a great composite 'you' of the unexceptional ordinary folk; minnows in a heated pool. The same kind of thing may sometimes be seen in an undiscriminating looking-in, night after night, at T.V. Everything and almost anything is acceptable because, as important as the intrinsic interest of any programme itself, is the sense that you are one in the big group watching the world (the world of events and personages) unroll before you. These tendencies, I think, may assist the emergence of a cultural group almost as large as the sum of all other groups. But it would be a group only in the sense that its members shared a passivity. For the majority of them work would be dull and ambition out of place. But nightly, dead from the eyes downwards, they would be able to link on to the Great Mother. They might spend their days fixing a dozen screws on each of a hundred T.V. sets, but their nights could be passed sitting in front of one. The eyes would register but not connect to the nerves, the heart, and the brain; they would connect to a sense of shared pleasure, of pleasure in simply sharing the unifying object, not in the object itself.

D. *Living in the Present and 'Progressivism'*

When the taste for physical gratifications among such a people has grown more rapidly than their education and their experience of free institutions, the time will come when men are carried away, and lose all self-restraint, at the sight of the new possessions they are about to lay hold upon.

DE TOCQUEVILLE

Aristocratic nations are naturally too apt to narrow the scope of human perfectibility; democratic nations to expand it beyond compass.

DE TOCQUEVILLE

It is not difficult to see that a sense of the need to live in the present and for the present, that the putting of a high value on the need to "'ave a good time', may subserve the wider self-gratification to which people are so much called today. Here my contention is that most people are subjected to a sustained and ever-increasing bombardment of invitations to assume that whatever is, is right, so long as it is widely accepted and can be classed as entertaining. This, and the older sense that it is important to 'enjoy y'self while y' can', are connected. To these a third element attaches itself, that of 'progressivism'. 'Progressivism' assists living for the present by disowning the past; but the present is enjoyed only because, and so long as, it is the present, the latest and not the out-of-date past; so, as each new 'present' comes along, the others are discarded. 'Progressivism' holds out an infinite perspective of increasingly 'good times' – technicolor T.V., all-smelling, all touching, all-tasting T.V. 'Progressivism' usually starts as a 'progressivism' of things, but cannot stay there; it ineluctably spreads beyond things, by dubious analogies.

I noted earlier that, like the concept of unlimited freedom, the notion of unlimited progress survives with the popular publicist, very little affected by the events of the last half-century; on this side he is far from modern, is still of the environment of the 1851 Exhibition. To be progressive, 'forward-looking', 'as modern as tomorrow', is still one of the desirable ends-in-themselves. The last-quoted phrase is from American advertising, and prompts the reminder that the acceptance of 'progressivism', as of much else discussed here, is effected as much by American films as by our own publicists. To me, the most striking feature in working-class attitudes to America is not a suspicion, though there is often that, nor a resentment at 'bossiness', but a large readiness to accept. This arises mainly from the conviction that in most things the Americans can 'show us a thing or two' about being up to date. In so far as to be up to date is felt to be important, America is the leader; and to be up to date is being made to seem very important.

This particular pattern of assumptions is reinforced, among working-class people in particular, by the fact that they are substantially without a sense of the past. Their education is unlikely to have left them with any historical panorama or with any idea of a continuing tradition. This may be more true of older people than of younger; much has been done to improve this field of teaching during the last twenty years. I am not making an incidental attack on the efforts of teachers; but their time is limited, and with many children (their background being such as I have described and their intellectual aptitudes limited) the teachers' best efforts tend to 'go in at one ear and out at the other'. Therefore a great many people, though they may possess a considerable amount of disconnected information, have little idea of an historical or ideological pattern or process.

Their minds rarely go back beyond the times of their own grand-parents; before that is a darkness out of which one or two items emerge, not usually in a proper order or with a supporting back-ground – Guy Fawkes and the Gunpowder Plot, the French Revolution, Wolfe at Quebec, King Alfred and the cakes. With little intellectual or cultural furniture, with little training in the testing of opposing views against reason and existing judgements, judge-ments are usually made according to the promptings of those group-apophthegms which come first to mind. The outlook of the group will decide whether those apophthegms are of a kind which help or hinder a decent way of life.

Similarly, there can be little real sense of the future. The future as a matter of families passing from generation to generation stops short at grandchildren or perhaps great-grandchildren; after that, there is another darkness, probably shot through with suggestions of skyscrapers, neon-lighting, and space-ships. Such a mind is, I think, particularly accessible to the temptation to live in a constant present. If the temptation succeeds, a condition may be induced in which time has been lost: yet time dominates, because the present is for ever changing, but changing meaninglessly, like the clicking-over of lantern-slides with no informing pattern. Each innovation is assumed to be better than its predecessors, simply because it comes after them: any change is a change for the better so long as it is in chronological succession. A paragraph by Newman remarkably forecasts the condition to which many who nightly now watch the latest and greatest and most up-to-the-minute grand cinematic spectacle are being disposed:

They see visions of great cities and wild regions; they are in the marts of commerce, or amid the islands of the South; they gaze on Pompey's pillar or on the Andes; and nothing which meets them carries them forward or backward, to any idea beyond itself. Nothing has a drift or a relation; nothing has a history or a promise. Everything stands by itself, and comes and goes in its turn, like the shifting scenes of a show, which leaves the spectator where he was.

Since the world is assumed to be one of incessant change, in which the future automatically supersedes and is preferable to all in the past, the past becomes laughable and odd. To be 'old-fashioned' is to be condemned. There are exceptions here: certain old-fashioned things, which speak of older values, are quaint and nice. 'Old-fashioned mothers' had a hold on the really important things and are regularly sung about. With them are associated various accepted properties, such as willow-pattern pottery. Humbugs are the better for being old-fashioned, and the herbalists still do a good business in old-fashioned country remedies. 'Me dad was 'ard – but 'e always 'ated a lie,' working-class people will say; or 'Me mother always said – "right's right and wrong's wrong", and y' can't do better than that when all's done and said.' The use of such phrases indicates, I think, a valuable resistance to the shallower aspects of modernism.

But by many, and especially by younger people, almost everything old-fashioned is increasingly coming to appear stuffy and probably laughable. This is something more than the looking to the future, the impatience with the slowness and backwardness of older people, which are characteristic of energetic young people at any time. All periods before our own were unknowing, old, and prudish, it is assumed; they were slow, dull and are now 'corny'. 'It's old-fashioned' and 'It's not in the fashion' are used equally to condemn dress, behaviour, styles of dancing, moral attitudes (e.g. 'outworn beliefs', 'outmoded creeds'). 'To be in the fashion', to 'have the latest' is therefore to have the best. 'It's new – it's different': therefore it must be better: and the future will be even better still.

To this is related the glorification of youth. If the newest is best, then the young are more fortunate than the old; youth is modern, up to date, heading for the even more modern future. The journalists address themselves particularly to the 'younger generation . . . which is fast-moving . . . vital . . . keen to get on . . . looking ahead . . . vigorous . . . independent . . .' – and which provides a valuable potential market for years to come.

Some advertisers of goods which adolescents can already buy make the same kind of appeal, using a growing minor mythology imported from America, but modified for British tastes. This is the mythology of the teenage 'gang' fond of jive and boogie-woogie but still healthy and open-faced, informally dressed in crew-neck sweaters and slacks, full of gaiety and drive, the reverse of everything dusty and drab.

This kind of shiny barbarism is having some success here, and where that success is with working-class people it probably gains strength from an ability to hook on to the older and more solid,

'yer only young once. Enjoy yerself while y' can'. The new callow-
ness attaches itself to the older and more sober pragmatism, and
debases it too. Surrounded by a great quantity of material goods
designed to serve and amuse and yearly increasing in number and
ingenuity, but with little sense that these are the end-products, and
in many cases the more trivial products, of centuries of slowly-
acquired knowledge and skill: surrounded, in fact, by more available
things than any previous generation, people are almost inevitably
inclined to take up these things just as they appear and use them in
the manner of the child in the fairy-tale, who found toys hanging
from the trees and lollipops by the roadside. The great weight of
persuasion is in favour of the cultivation of that habit, and after all,
'why not?'

By all these means the band-wagon mentality can be induced.
It cocks a snook at whoever is not on the wagon, but has itself
abrogated personal responsibility for choice. So the wagon, loaded
with its barbarians in wonderland, moves irresistibly forward: not
forward to anywhere, but simply forward for forwardness's sake.
Somewhere out in front are the scientists ('it's new – it's scientific')
handling the controls. 'Democratic nations care but little for what
has been, but they are haunted by visions of what will be,' said de
Tocqueville; 'Copywriters should emphasize the more pleasant side
of their proposals; they should always try to please their readers,'
writes the specialist on advertising; 'There's a good time coming,'
sings the crowd on the wagon.

Fortunately the success of 'progressivism' is still much qualified.
The persistent if subdued mistrust of science has been strengthened
by the latest revelations of its power to harm. Sometimes the objection is to what is thought of as a mismanagement of some particular
aspect of progress, or of its excessive speed. Here, the underlying
acceptance of 'progressivism' may be unaffected. The view is rather
that it is very good to keep on going on, but that 'They' should take
care not to get us into a speed wobble.

But just as often, at present, one hears phrases which indicate a
deeper mistrust of 'progressivism', a mistrust of the values of 'progressivism'; 'things look flashier, but they're not always as well-
made as they used to be,' people say, and more important, ' . . . all
these inventions ! But where do they all *get* you?'

E. *Indifferentism: 'Personalization' and 'Fragmentation'*

If tolerance is good, if to share the views of the group is good, if to 'enjoy life while yer can' is good; if, in addition, all men are free and equal, and life is constantly changing and progressing, then there must eventually follow a loss of a sense of order, of value, and of limits. If that is good which is the latest in the endless line and which meets the wishes of the greatest number, then quantity becomes quality and we arrive at a world of monstrous and swirling undifferentiation. This kind of undifferentiation can lead, as Matthew Arnold pointed out a century ago, to 'indifferentism', to an endless flux of the undistinguished and the valueless, to a world in which every kind of activity is finally made meaningless by being reduced to a counting of heads.

It seems to me a reaction from this, a drawing-back from the emptiness which is threatened, that encourages the present fondness for 'sincerity' as an end in itself. There comes to mind the extensive older charity of the working-classes and its relation to their mistrust of abstractions ('It doesn't matter what y' do so long as yer 'eart's in the right place'). Nowadays this attitude is expressed more and more, precisely because it does give some sort of measure in a world where measure is otherwise very difficult to find. 'Well, at any rate, 'e meant well, and that's all that matters' may become a cover for the lack of any confidence in the ability to reach a moral decision. Sincerity is clearly not enough: but it has to do where there seems to be nothing else.

Thence flow wider evasions, an increasing use of phrases like, 'After all, it's only natural', and 'Well, it does no one any harm', and 'It does y' good anyway, they say'. Or the evasions in language which make 'orthodoxy' or 'authority' automatically pejorative; and make gambling on the pools 'investments'; a history of the social importance of ideas could be traced in word-changes like these. Everything is 'a matter of taste', and 'one man's meat is another man's poison'. Usually there is a rider indicating the existence of an undefined but generally agreed outer boundary, 'Mind you, I don't hold with . . .'; and from that comes some sort of assurance that after all there is an order somewhere. If this were carried forward, to meet a testing problem in ordinary life, the shock would be great; but in day-to-day personal life earlier sanctions still to a great extent prevail.

F

Yet no division like this can be healthy or more than temporary in the long run.

The situation is made worse by the fact that there is a sense in which, although no authority is felt to be justifiable, authority can be increasingly leaned upon. The use of phrases like, 'They ought to do something about it', 'They ought to get us out of it', 'They ought to do this about the Health Service and that about the schools', may occur more easily against the background described in this chapter. We can soon put ourselves into a position in which we lie back with our mouths open, whilst we are fed by pipe-line, and as of right, from a bottomless cornucopia manipulated by the anonymous 'Them'. One would be happier if the dislike of authority were more often an active dislike, implying a wish to stand on one's own feet. But it can frequently be a sullen shaking-away of the idea of authority co-existing with an assumption that nevertheless something or somebody outside should provide. The joint effect of these two attitudes will be to increase the peculiar deadness and unresponsiveness of many people towards calls upon them from outside their personal and domestic lives. We are moving towards a world of what Alex Comfort has called 'irresponsible obedients'; it would be better if more were 'responsible disobedients'.

So the claims of conformity increase. 'Only connect,' said E. M. Forster, thinking of the conflict between the claims of the inner and the outer life. 'Only conform,' whispers the prevailing wind today. Nothing much matters anyway, but the majority are probably right, and you ought to go along with them. You need only believe what the rest believe; to do otherwise is a sort of sin against the laws of life. If there are no values anyway, no ground for deviating, the only duty is to keep to the middle of the crowded road. 'Ten million people – or thirteen million readers or listeners – can't be wrong.'

So the noiseless 'unbending of the springs of action' continues and increases. So there must eventually disappear the sense of tension in living, and with it any real taste for its challenges. The power of real enjoyment, even of the pleasures which are so multitudinously offered, must decline also. 'Having a good time' may be made to seem so important as to override almost all other claims; yet when it has been allowed to do so, having a good time becomes largely a matter of routine. The strongest argument against modern mass entertainments is not that they debase taste – debasement can be alive and active – but that they over-excite it, eventually dull it, and finally kill it; that they 'enervate' rather than 'corrupt', in de Tocqueville's phrase. They kill it at the nerve, and yet so bemuse and persuade their audience that the audience is almost entirely unable to look up and say, 'But in fact this cake is made of sawdust.' We have not reached this stage yet, but these are the lines on which we are moving.

The over-exciting and eventual killing of response can best be illustrated by isolating two main characteristics of popular writing, 'personalization' and 'fragmentation'. Both exist in the older- as in the newer-style publications; but the differences, the vastly increased skill in presentation and manipulation, are striking.

If I suspect the intensely personal interest in the popular Press today, I am not suddenly discovering with disgust that almost everyone is interested in, and has always been interested in, 'a good human tale'. Even the phrase 'I do enjoy a good murder' is at least a hundred years old; and the great range of 'low' literature in the last century abounded in accounts of murders, executions, and murderers' last confessions. 'There's nothing beats a stunning good murder, after all', said one of the running patterers who hawked news-ballads and broadsheets. But I am pointing to an over-use of the personal element so strong that it needs another phrase to describe it, one without the favourable connotations of such phrases as 'interested in the personal and the intimate' or 'fond of a good story'. One of the more ugly contemporary noun-verbs, such as 'to personalize', seems to be needed.

The quite unusual degree of 'personalization' in the newspapers designed particularly for working-class people is derived, one can see immediately, not only from the common human interest in the detail of other people's lives, but also from the peculiarly strong working-class attachment to the concrete, the emotionally bold and understandable, the local and particular. Here working-class people have always been able to respond, and often with wisdom and understanding. The early popular papers knew this, and began that process, which is today in so advanced a state, of extending the personal note beyond its reasonable limits. It has perhaps been extended not simply in response to the inner dynamic in the life of newspapers which makes it necessary for them constantly to be going one better than their neighbours, but also because the wish for the personal among readers is reinforced by contemporary conditions. I have suggested earlier that working-people cannot fail to be aware today, to a degree hardly known before, of the larger and public aspects of social life. They are aware of an area of life in which they undoubtedly have a part but which they often find difficult to comprehend. They naturally try to understand that outside life better by relating it to the personal and local life in which they know and act and suffer and admire. In such circumstances the desire for an assurance that the values of the local and personal do count, that some sentiments which all can understand and appreciate as 'decent' are common to all, grows stronger. They are glad when a voice from that huge outer world uses their accents. Many politicians know this; most of the journalists who write features about the Royal Family know this. The proprietors of some holiday-camps know this; their camps are vast and garishly splendid, but the cheer-leaders set out to link everyone in 'pally' groups, and the w.c.s are marked 'lads' and 'lasses'. The promoters of football pools know this; they issue invitations to join their 'gang', 'circle', or 'group'. The wireless-variety and T.V.-cabaret stars of programmes specializing in a fake intimacy know this. The radio 'disc-jockeys' and the producers of radio programmes with 'resident teams' know this. Advertising broadcasters know this; they announce themselves as speaking from 'Your neighbourly station, Radio —' and run programmes with such titles as 'Neighbour's Choice' and 'Friendly Fun'. I remember a consumptive mill-girl in a busy York-shire sanatorium who was much moved when a 'disc-jockey' played her favourite song, 'A Tune for You'; his signed photograph was on her locker thereafter. What a phoney sense of belonging all this is, this which is offered by the public pals of this publicly gregarious age; it would be better to feel anonymous; one might then be moved to some useful action to improve matters.

Yet it would be wrong not to appreciate the strength of this desire. The questions people are asking are good question – 'How does this connect with human life and its problems, as we know them?' The pressures of commercial publication and the collapse of almost all sanctions except that of freedom ('giving the public what the public wants') have ensured that the readiness to give answers in the terms people want is carried to a point at which such answers are given where they are not relevant, where it is dangerous to think them relevant. You do not learn more about Mr Shepilov by knowing that he draws doodles of horses at the conference table; you only escape the real problems. As the 'personalizing' technique becomes yearly more machine-tooled, so a good instinct is pulled out of shape, and used for over-simplifications, soft deceptions, and perilous distortions. We sink further into a dream of an unconscionably intimate world in which not only may a cat look at a king but a king is really a cat underneath, and all the great power-figures Honest Joes at heart. A world so complex that even those who are immersed in the business of tending its more important machines can only hope to understand a little of it, is daily reduced to a local and spuriously manageable 'ooh-aah', when the paper drops on the mat.

There are strange movements in countries on the edge of the Iron Curtain; a colony is becoming restive; America has issued a new statement about the use of the H-bomb. These will only win an important place if they can be 'personalized' in a way that the story about a curious parson at Halifax can be. If not, they must take their chance of a secondary position, leaving the front and main headings to;

> They baited me, says widower
> She climbed mountains in evening dress
> Mary won't be there on THE DAY
> Crazy Vicar told them all
> His cat attended the conference
> Three priests guard the poor-box
> He goes to work on roller-skates
> I suffered it all.

In case that does not seem personal enough, there is an increasingly popular 'no-nonsense', 'cut the cackle' and 'let's face it' approach;

> These chaps ought to pack it up
> Nark it, chums
> Pipe down on these stupid by-laws
> Turn it in, Mr Thompson
> Husbands, don't be so daft
> You've had it, folks.

This is what its defenders call 'cheeky' and 'gay' journalism. Usually its gaiety and cheek are on the level of the boy who makes

F*

faces, for his pals' amusement, at a policeman's back, and from a safe
distance.

The corollary of successful 'personalization' is constant and considerable simplification. The reader must feel intimately one with the
dream that is being presented to him, and he will not feel this if he
has to make an effort to think about the weight of a word, or puzzle
over a nuance, or follow even a moderately involved sentence-struc-
ture. Since these qualities are the results of trying to express the
complexity of a subject, it follows that the personal dramas daily
unfolded in the simplest language are also emotionally and intellectually conceived in the simplest manner. But the 'average reader'
(who, for the publicist after mass sales, must be a hypothetical figure
compounded of three or four key-responses at their most simplified)
need never feel out of things.

The magazines go beyond the stories to the 'short short stories' or
the 'one-minute stories', of which the most striking quality is not
their brevity but the skill with which they have been designed to slide
down. Since nothing must impede the flow, there is nothing a reader
can ever get a grip on, nothing real about the world they are supposed
to create. Read twenty or thirty of them in succession; you will not
only be surfeited with the fraudulent twist-endings, but weighed down
with a sense of having lived in a slick and hollow puppet-world.

Thus the popular Press has to become ever more bitty in its
presentation of what is to be read, and thus what is to be read is
gradually ousted by what is only to be seen. The 'strips' spread like
a rash, from the bottom corner of the back page through all the inner
pages, take over a page of their own, and still crop up here and there
elsewhere. There has to be some verbal guidance to the action, but
descriptive comment is kept to a minimum: the aim is to ensure that
all necessary background information is contained in the dialogue
which bubbles out of the characters' mouths. No doubt the reasons
for this are the same as those which prompt the popular novelist to
avoid general description and get on to dialogue quickly. In dialogue
people speak to us; in descriptions we have to come to terms, alone,
with the words on the page.

At the lowest level all this is illustrated in the sales here of the
American or American-type serial-books of comics, where for page
after page big-thighed and big-bosomed girls from Mars step out of

their space-machines, and gangsters' molls scream away in high-powered sedans. Anyone who sees something of Servicemen's reading, of the popularity of American and English comics (with the cruder English boys' comics serving their turn where the supply of hotter material runs out), knows something of all this. The process continues, for a substantial number of adolescents especially; a passive visual taking-on of bad mass-art geared to a very low mental age.

It can be said, with some justice, that this is an age of 'opinionation', that though few people take the trouble thoroughly to understand any problem, a great many assume that their opinions on almost every general issue will have weight, and that most issues are, or should be, simply explainable even to a poorly-developed or to a lazy mind. We must, above all, keep up to date; with what Mr Khrushchev said yesterday, and what Tito did today. Tolstoy's Levin knew the type, but he is more common nowadays – 'why, oh why, does the partition of Poland interest him? . . . there was nothing to be said. It was interesting simply from the fact that it had "appeared".' But 'opinionation' is not to any considerable extent a weakness of working-class people; perhaps their lack of interest in general questions impedes its development. The pattern of their interests and the forces of the times cause them to be invited, however, to the enjoyment of 'fragmentation', to the 'dolly-mixtures' pleasures of a constant diet of odd snippets, of unrelated scrappy facts, each with its sugary little kernel of 'human interest'. Or they take up those wireless programmes (they seem to have increased in number since the war) which, though they may contain some odd bits of information by the way, have their main appeal from the fact that they proceed by short spurts, by the clash and rattle of personalities exhibiting themselves successively in short spasms. Most of them are variants of the knowing-personality-deploying and argument-for-its-own-sake ('well, at least it was *stimulating*') games.

To judge by all this, our wind for reading is not increasing, but is being kept at the two- or three-syllabled word and seven-word-sentence level. The process is not new; most of the fragmentary magazines are between forty and sixty years old. Each magazine develops its own style: this one is predominantly the family paper, this the competitions paper; this has a special interest in the 'odd' in history, geography, and anthropology; this is particularly visual. All have in common the assumption that their readers are short-winded. All premasticate their material so that it shall neither bore nor tax anyone, shall not prompt any effort at correlation or comparison. They must be capable of being read in a very easy gear, or more, in a free-wheeling sort of way. There must be no connected sequences of any length; everything is interesting, as interesting as the next thing, if only it is short, unconnected, and pepped-up. The rain of undifferentiated anecdotes pours down: a hen is born at Bolton (Lancs.) with two heads, a politician commits suicide, a mother in Edmonton (Alberta, Can.) has her third set of triplets, what odd habits lemmings have, a cyclist in Sunderland is lifted clean off the road by a freak wind. One doesn't read such papers; one 'looks at' them.

The advertising copy-writers continue and develop the manner:

You can only hope to keep your reader's attention for a minute at a time. Make sure he gets what you want him to get in that minute. Design your layout so that all its elements help to make his eye move down the path you determine, with no awkward bumps on the way. Keep to small groups of letters and words. He can't take in more than five or six at a glance. Any longer unit will displease your reader. And then you've lost him.

However, if a word of more than three syllables has to be used, the journalists usually provide an asterisk leading to a 'pally' explanation – 'that means – to us, fellers'.

'Short, unconnected, and pepped-up'; the third quality follows from the first two. In a permanent diet of hors d'œuvres each new item must contain at least the tang and tastiness of its predecessors. This search for a 'pepping-up' has today gone much farther than ever before. *Sweeney Todd* and *Maria Marten* had body in their sensationalism, had something to be sensational about, and they held their popularity for years. Today new sensations by the dozen have to be found daily. So there has to be a continuous straining, a vast amount of sleight-of-hand to pass off what is really thin tack as strong and meaty stuff, an endless inflation and distortion of angle so that the tiny shall appear immense; mice are photographed from below and their huge shadows passed off as genuine horrors. This kind of thing is farther away from *Maria Marten* than that melodrama is from *Macbeth*.

When those who earn their livings by making the kinds of appeal described throughout this section find themselves under attack, their defensive procedure is an illuminating confirmation of the analysis given earlier of the assumptions underlying their efforts. They lay about them in a fury of self-justification, using just those approaches (whether they actually meet the case against them is not much considered) which they know will tell upon their audience. They accuse their accusers of being 'reactionary' and 'repressive'; they have implied that freedom alone is not enough. They further accuse their opponents of 'snobbery'; they have perhaps implied that all men are not naturally good. Whenever useful, they mention their opponent's age, 'seventy-two-year-old Mr B.' or 'sixty-five-year-old Mr C.'; democracy is youthful and forward-looking; clearly these are old fogies. They counter-accuse their accusers of being 'holier than thou', of smugness, of 'hypocrisy'. The reasoning seems to be as follows: (1) The only value is freedom; (2) Therefore to have an open mind is the only firm line required; but (3) These people have suggested that some uses of freedom may be wrong; they have taken a moral line; and therefore, (4) They must be hypocrites; they are hiding something; they want freedom for themselves, but not for others. This is the other side of the coin which has 'sincerity' on its face. If you accept total freedom, but do not advocate any 'line' of your own, you may come in for praise because your muddling through indicates that you are 'sincere, anyway'. Suggest a rule and you will attract the full weight of opprobrium for the greatest sin in the new catalogue, 'hypocrisy'. All this the defenders dress up in the familiar manner, with the frank man-to-man tone (after all, our best defence is that *you* read us, and the great British public just would not read anything vicious or corrupting). The final card is a variant on the 't'aint what you do, it's the way that you do it' approach. In a world of limitless freedom, what we do does not matter, so long as we do it with style. Above all, we will not be boring. 'We do our best not to be dull about anything'; we try never to be 'pompous', always to be 'lively'. Laudable aims, were it not for the pressures on mass-publications already outlined, and the relegation of more important principles. In the circumstances, these aims become the justification for getting a laugh, pepping things up, at any cost. 'Anything for a laugh'; no matter if the story is distorted, or if words and emotions have become simply things which are played and tickled with: at least we did not bore; you cannot accuse us of dullness. And in the end success pardons all.

I have compiled, from the frequency with which they appear in the editorials of popular newspapers, a list of epithets indicating the virtues and vices in the new canon. For the vices:

pharisaical; timid; dull; equivocal; snobbish; canting; mealy-mouthed; conventional; hypocritical; ponderous; pompous; humbugging; official; and, of course, boring.

These are the fourteen Deadly Sins of the old gang; and how alike they all are. For the virtues:

new; different; unorthodox; frank; cheeky; outspoken; wide-awake; live; vigorous; zestful; vivid; gay; lusty; enterprising; ebullient; crusading; 'urchin grin'; candid; audacious; youthful; sincere.

Here the basis seems to be the adolescent-against-the-teachers code, a schoolboy's callow bluntness.

CHAPTER 7

INVITATIONS TO A CANDY-FLOSS WORLD: THE NEWER MASS ART

For a multitude of causes, unknown to former times, are now acting with a combined force to blunt the discriminating powers of the mind, and unfitting it for all voluntary exertion to reduce it to a state of almost savage torpor.

WORDSWORTH

Plenty of people will try to give the masses, as they call them, an intellectual food prepared and adapted in the way they think proper.

ARNOLD

Ah – the day I read a book!
. . .
. . .
Someday – Ah'm gonna do it again.
A song by MR 'SCHNOZZLE' DURANTE

Yes, we shall set them to work, but in their leisure hours we shall make their life a child's game. . . . Oh, we shall allow them even sin, they are weak and helpless, and they will love us like children because we allow them to sin. We shall tell them that every sin will be expiated, if it is done with our permission, that we allow them to sin because we love them . . . and they will have no secrets from us. . . . The most powerful secrets of their conscience, all they will bring to us, and we shall have an answer for all. And they will be glad to believe our answer, for it will save them from the great anxiety and terrible agony they endure at present in making a free decision for themselves.

DOSTOYEVSKY

A. *The Producers*

I attribute my success to giving the people what the people want. I am not a snob.

A POPULAR MUSICIAN

When we consider the extraordinary skilfulness of the modern literature of entertainment we tend to make two errors of emphasis. We associate it too much with only a few dozen names, the usual popular parallels with the couple of dozen serious (for want of a better word) contemporary writers whose names most frequently recur in the weekly reviews. And we often simply assume that the attitude of these writers towards their work is wholly commercial and cynical.

The greatly successful popular writers, the literary Department Stores, are formidable and fascinating figures. One can picture the secretaries and stenographers, the tape-recorders, the 'ghosts' on the periphery, the syndicated articles, the 'no reproduction in whole or in part', the complex and efficient dream-words factory in a large old house somewhere in the warm South, from which the latest fantasy or piece of clever flattery by the Master goes out to the weeklies, the American market, and the farther Dominions.

But such people, however mechanized their organizations, could not be responsible for the vast *bulk* of popular literature. Roughly eighteen thousand books a year are published in England, and of these novels of entertainment form a large part. And what of the paper-backs which pour from publishing-houses few have ever heard of, which make ragged and gaudy the windows of the stationers, the new magazine-shops, and the station bookstalls? These are the books by writers who, probably working under several names, produce anything from four to a dozen titles a year, and are often paid at piece-rates, by the thousand words. The market seems to be highly competitive, and those who succeed – that is, make a good living without necessarily becoming nationally-known figures – need to have an acute sense of what the public wants. Thus, one of them says that two of his rules-of-thumb are never to put in any 'boring description' (I should guess that it is assumed that any description of more than a couple of lines will be boring), and to make sure to get dialogue on the first page. For those who can supply what is wanted, a handsome living can be provided; and one which carries with it almost complete anonymity:

Among democratic nations, a writer may flatter himself that he will obtain at a cheap rate a meagre reputation and a large fortune. For this purpose he need not be admired; it is enough that he is liked. The ever-increasing crowd of readers, and their continual craving for something new, ensure the sale of books which nobody much esteems.

Nobody much esteems them, but 'esteems' is a verb of value; whereas to be liked, as De Tocqueville indicates, is the test.

These writers are competent, and no doubt in much of the tactics of their writing they aim consciously to give the public what the public wants. But to think of them as consciously compounding in just the right proportions all the various ingredients which go to make their success is, apart from much else, intellectually to over-estimate most of them. If we read a number of cheap romances we will find it hard to sustain a belief that the world they present has been deliberately conceived from outside. Writing like this, maintained so consistently, and so unerring in its sense of what the reader wants, can hardly be constructed intellectually; and certainly not by minds of the calibre usually revealed in these works. They are, rather, produced by people who possess some qualities in greater measure than their readers, but are of the same ethos. 'Every culture lives inside its own dream'; they share the common dream of their culture. They can publish in great quantity and over year after year, without the phases which in a serious writer mark developments in his experience and consequent changes in his manner of expression, because they write semi-automatically. This also applies to many popular journalists. Biographical literature about popular journalism always stresses the importance of 'an instinctive sense of your audience', a belief in yourself', and a 'complete sincerity'. But to talk of 'sincerity' helps no more than to talk of 'utter cynicism'. Clearly a man may not be altogether a conscious manipulator but still have an eye on the main chance. At the conscious level, a reading of popular literature makes plain, one may find a hard-boiled cynicism or a burning sense of a mission to serve 'the people', to be their voice. More often, one finds a logically untenable but obviously bearable mixture of both. Thus, the dust-jacket 'blurb' for A. P. Ryan's *Lord Northcliffe*, describes Northcliffe as 'a strange mixture of zest and cunning, sincerity and cynical stunting'.

Nor is there necessarily insincerity in the performances of the more popular singers. Miss Betty Driver's motto is, 'We all have a song in our hearts.' No doubt Miss Vera Lynn has a sound idea of the elements she must stress to acquire her characteristic effect – the simplified but forceful emotional pattern, the complicated alternations of emphasis, the extraordinary control of vowel-sounds which allows them to carry the feeling required. These are what her listeners want, so that the songs shall call up their special kind of imaginary world. But it is also, I should guess, Miss Lynn's imaginary world, one she naturally inhabits at the actual moment of singing. Her 'blurb'-writers are probably not far off the mark when they speak of 'the ringing sincerity of her famous voice': she sings, as someone has said, in the way a factory-girl hears herself singing in her head.

There is a similar truth behind the easy exaggeration of this passage:

I was once present at the script conference of an *Old Mother Riley* film: Let me gravely assure those ready to sneer at the cynical commercialism of this successful series that the conference room bounced with creative euphoria. Tears of helpless laughter shook the gathered business-men as they decided how often Old Mother Riley was to fall downstairs, or into the water.

Presumably most writers of fantasy for people of any class share the fantasy worlds of their readers. They become the writers rather than the readers because they can body those fantasies into stories and characters, and because they have a fluency in language. Not the attitude to language of the creative writer, trying to mould words into a shape which will bear the peculiar quality of his experience; but a fluency, a 'gift of the gab', and a facility with thousands of stock phrases which will set the figures moving on the highly conventionalized stage of their readers' imaginations. They put into words and intensify the daydreams of their readers, often with considerable technical skill. Their relation to their readers, we have seen, is more direct than that of the creative writer. They do not create an object-in-itself; they act as picture-makers for what is behind the readers' daydreams but what cannot have a local habitation and a name because of imaginative inability. I remember a girl in the provinces who had written nearly a dozen books before she was twenty-one. She had begun at fifteen, and after that, 'they just poured out, you know'. Another authoress had produced hundreds of paper-backed gangster-thrillers. She lived quietly with her husband in an outer London suburb. When she was asked how she set about her writing she replied, 'I just go broody at the typewriter.' She added that her ambition was to write 'a serious, spiritual work that will last – one with a stiff back'.

There is a temptation among some social critics to see in all this popular literature, especially in its more advanced contemporary forms, some sort of plot by 'the authorities', a clever way of keeping the working-classes quietly doped. But many of those who are doing their very competent best – 'sincerely' and so on – in this field are themselves of working-class origin, products of the scholarship system, quick-witted and energetic boys who have 'got on' because they have that 'gift of the gab', and know their people as one only knows those among whom one grew up. If there is a plot, it is a remarkably cunning one: 'They' have tempted without difficulty some of the brighter minds in the working-classes to lead a kind of weakening of their own class – partly for money, partly for the best of inadequately examined reasons. These young men always insist, in their memoirs, that they 'really belong to the people – share their laughter and tears – are ordinary like them – always imagine that they are simply writing a letter home'.

The unconscious irony of this is hard to bear, especially when one thinks of the huge commercial organizations for which it is meant to serve as a genuine justification. More, the tone has usually something of a winning quality, in a kind of eagerness behind the clichés – until one remembers the unsentimental and unflattering manner of those from the working-classes who pre-eminently spoke for and to the aspirations of working-class people fifty years ago.

B. *The Process Illustrated: (i) Weekly Family Magazines*

[They] took the bone out of the mouth of the educationists and of the earnest citizens who believed that a literate democracy would be sober in its taste.

A. P. RYAN

I have argued that the process whereby popular journals go farther and farther in their efforts to capture and hold their public, to win them at whatever cost, is a result both of commercial pressures and of the ethos which the readers and writers alike share. The competition is keen enough to ensure that popular papers, magazines, and paperbacks can rarely settle to one style. A few still survive with little change, but for most editors and publishers the struggle to remain out in front with the first half-dozen of their kind is never relaxed. One magazine will snatch a short lead for a month as some smart man discovers yet another novel angle on the old appeals; but its editors will be harried by the knowledge that if they are not ready to replace it with yet another angle, their rivals will adopt it and themselves go one farther. So the distressing dance continues, and the public are introduced to newer and stranger subtleties: we get now a good deal more than 'the Press we deserve'. For the process must feed upon itself. Thus, it seems to me evident that most of our popular journals have become a good deal worse during the last fifteen or twenty years than they were during the fifty years before;

that they have disregarded or implicitly undermined worthwhile attitudes more boldly and effectively in this last twenty years of their seventy-odd years' life than they did in their first fifty years. No doubt six years of war chiefly helped to accelerate the process. When the war ended, all popular journals knew, too, that soon the artificial truce would end. The more ambitious ones had used their patrols well and made their dispositions for a particularly intense fight – for the distribution of almost the whole of the British reading-public among a few big powers. The period of National Service gives an opportunity to continue the general process: young men, bored but unable, except in rare cases, to take up any connected or developing activities of their own, provide a tempting field for sales now and for the formation of habits which will decide their future reading.

Many ways of illustrating this change suggests themselves. One might, for instance, carry out a comparative analysis of the whole style and manner of the one-hundred-years-old *News of the World* and one of the more modern Sunday papers. The *News of the World* is itself the only publication I know which has managed to retain a pre-eminent position with all classes (it is read by one in two of all adults in the country) by persisting in being substantially what it has been. There are a few changes, chiefly in styles of photography and drawing, but on the whole the old recipe still holds, and by now has acquired a sort of supporting 'period' attraction for many people. Or one could compare the two styles in sexy-papers – the raw-sexy and the best-of-both-worlds sexy. In the latter, more common today, the sex-dope is provided, but always with a quick preliminary glance over the left shoulder at 'morality' – 'They should not have printed this story (given in full, with photographs). We know all decent citizens will object as we do to the habits of some newspapers: The *Sunday* — has decided that, in the interests of the great body of respectable citizens, it must expose this evil in our midst. The first of three illustrated and unexpurgated accounts of this abominable vice racket begins next week. Order your copy now.' The pseudo-moral Janus glance tends to be used in papers not specially appealing to the working-classes. But the habit inevitably spreads, especially in some of the more modern popular Sunday papers, and in those which seem insecure, and so tend to be more responsive to new styles and manners.

Again, one might mention the changes of policy in some of the illustrated weeklies during the last few years, though these are not sufficiently particular favourites of the working-classes to claim special attention. Changes of manner seem to have occurred frequently, with now a decrease in the social concern unless a somewhat sensational article could be written about a 'social evil', and now an attempt to get back to a manner nearer to that which, apparently, was originally intended.

Equally illuminating is the course followed by some daily newspapers, especially during the last ten years. A similar process can be seen in the way newer and glossier women's magazines are capturing the working-class audience from the un-glossy magazines discussed earlier. They have particular success, I suggested, with younger working-class women who feel smarter and want, understandably, to remain smarter than their mothers. Too often this means presenting a vision of life for the working-classes just as 'nice' as that of the middle-classes: 'You can do wonders with a bit of cretonne'; 'How I glamorize my bedroom by the Honorable . . .'; 'A new way of arranging Birthday Cards'; 'When she isn't filming — lives in a spacious but modest apartment in Kensington. About the house, she wears an old towel – doesn't possess a pinny'. The more old-fashioned papers try to catch up by introducing illustrated biographies of the more notorious film-actresses.

The nature of these changes is shown even more vividly in the developments in 'cheesecake' presentation, in pin-up photography, in England during the last fifteen years. Pin-ups used to be, and still are, standard decoration for servicemen's billets and the cabs of lorries; but now, whether we will or no, we are all assaulted by them. They are the most striking visual feature of mid-twentieth-century mass-art; we are a democracy whose working-people are exchanging their birthright for a mass of pin-ups. The older ones were fairly simple, a comparatively 'straight' photograph of a girl's legs, or of her body in a bathing-costume; some may still be seen in the older kind of newspaper and magazine. Nowadays such photographs would be considered too 'corny' for most to print; we have already arrived at technicolor 'cheesecake' in 3D. Any photographer specializing in the pin-up business knows that he must produce photographs sailing as nearly as possible to the laws of indecency and carrying a powerful charge of that sort of suggestion which it is difficult to bring within the orbit of any regulations, simply because it does not depend primarily on the amount of body exposed, but makes its point by suggestion, by the turn of a leg or the bend of a shoulder, or by the juxtaposition of the model and some otherwise unexceptionable object. The photographer lies on his back and photographs upwards, or cranes across the girl's left shoulder; she climbs up ladders or peeps round bedroom doors or holds a candle with a coy look. A pose 'has something' because it shows the cleft between the breasts much more deeply than usual; a costume, photographed so, makes very suggestive use of the division in the backside. Each week the readers must be given something 'better' than last, and 'better' than rival publications are offering; the cunning angle-shot, for instance, which emphasizes the little bump of the nipples under opaque material, or the free use of nearly transparent nylon which allows the dark shading of the nipples' aureoles to show (nylon has been a great help to the cover-girl photographers – 'You can do wonders with a bit of nylon').

By now it must be one of the more wearing minor professions, this competition to supply the dozen-or-so really special large-size pin-ups which the new-style papers want each week; wearing for the photographer who follows his hunch through a dozen shots in search of a pose that will make the front-page; wearing for the scores of models and 'curvaceous' chorus-girls who earn extra money and some publicity by weekly spending chilly hours in improbable postures. Sometimes a male pin-up for the ladies is produced, but the more successful magazines are not likely to be so biologically behind-the-times. And all the photographs have to be supplied with captions, sickeningly arch and banal in their punning and alliteration: 'Curvaceous Cutie' or 'Sauce for the Sailors' or 'Bikini Bombshell' or 'Atomic Armful'. The caption-writers must be in danger of developing a nervous alliterative tic.

Thus we move towards the purely pin-up magazines, such as the new group of small picture-monthlies, which sell at about one shilling and are crammed with chorus-girls, film-actresses, and models. They are introduced with the usual would-be-witty rubrics and surrounded by all the ballyhoo of show-business. The 'cheesecake' is a little more advanced than most newspapers would feel prepared to print at present, and especially well-photographed on glossy paper. In between there are usually a few adolescent 'amusing tales' and a simple ghost-story or two.

Any of the changes I have mentioned could be examined in more detail. But it seems on the whole more useful to discuss some developments in weekly family magazines, so as to illustrate the pressures which are being put on the older magazines by those in the newer style, and some of the ways in which they respond to those pressures. A few of the older magazines have not yet radically altered, but scarcely one has been able to avoid making some changes towards the newer forms, e.g. in the use of pin-ups or 'strips', or in reducing the number of more properly domestic features in favour of those which domesticate the world of famous public personalities or improperly inflate the domestic doings of private individuals. Most magazines have during the last few years undergone some form of face-lift. One, perhaps, still aims to be a decent family magazine but has had to seek new manners of colonization and so sets out to be the most cosily and whimsically 'homely' of all the cheaper magazines. Another, perhaps, still strongly hopes to attract people with mildly enquiring minds, but has decided that it can now do this only by addressing itself not to working-class but to lower middle- or middle-class people.

Most of the magazines of this kind are extremely fragmentary in their approach. Little tablets of curious information are scattered throughout, each with its black, eye-appealing title:

Paid £400 for his ice-cream cornet
Caterpillar in pop popped off
Looked at lovely ladies – lost his overcoat.

This is bittiness run riot. Yet far behind there sometimes lies, and especially when magazines such as these treat of oddities from history, geography, literature, and the sciences, the remnant of a healthier quality. Though these features often cater for a meaningless curiosity, they have their origin in an enthusiasm for knowledge. One cannot laugh at what may have been the beginning of a genuine intellectual curiosity, however clumsily it expressed itself. For the newly-educated working-classes at the turn of the century this kind of thing could indicate a respect for, a fascination with, all the world of interesting information now open. At its best such an attitude can be a pure love. When it predominantly expresses itself in the sort of feature shown above it encourages, rather, a niggling curiosity which is likely to get in the way of real knowledge. Mr A. P. Ryan, discussing changes in one of the older family magazines, notes a development similar to the one I am describing:

The significance of this primitive – . . . is that so large a part deals, even in a gossipy way, with serious subjects and people. The breaking away from the old culture was a gradual process . . .

Most of the jokes in the older family magazines carry on the tradition still found in the picture-postcards; basic figures are the Scotsman who is mean about money, the fat mother-in-law, the amusingly drunk man, and the courting couple who linger far too long in the front-room and are separated by a crushing witticism from father in his pyjamas. On the whole these magazines are on the side of the fathers; they appear to envisage as their main audience the thirty-years-old-and-upward working-class family man and his wife. They often make special provision for the men who enter numerous newspaper competitions every week. But they naturally include features for other members of the family also.

In general, the print and format are much as they have been for decades. There is usually a page of letters to the editor; about pets in council-houses, should children have their hair permanently waved?, 'young thugs' (all this psychology is nonsense, they should be whipped). There is often a complete page of illustrated jokes, little black-and-white boxes with two or three lines of print under. The style of illustration, here and in the short stories, is in most cases as homely and old-fashioned as an aspidistra. The short stories are very plain little stories about plain people, like those in the older women's magazines. There are the usual crowds of advertisements and the popular '2-inch Bargain Spaces', that is, large blocks of illustrated 'Bargains by Post' – musical instruments, government surplus blankets and binoculars, curious gadgets for the home. The more usual advertisements maintain their traditional form: jewellers offer 'the ring of your dreams'; there are corsets by mail-order or needle-loom carpeting direct from the mill; dozens of proprietary medicines make their claims; books from not-very-well-known publishing-houses – on home-doctoring, the march of history, every child's encyclopaedia – claim to be remarkably cheap and remarkably comprehensive; the clothing-clubs make their call to people wanting 'a friendly and interesting' spare-time money-making occupation. With it all goes much homely advice, most of it sensible.

But most of these magazines are acutely aware of the dangers of becoming stodgy and qualifying for dismissal as altogether 'corny'. So increasingly they tend to introduce the newer manners, but still so far along with, rather than instead of, the old. The amount of 'cheesecake' is often increased, and sometimes there is a pin-up girl on the cover. With the old-style 'strips' there are now some in the new manner, about crime in fast cars and adventures in space-ships, each with a ravishing blonde floozie as well as a lantern-jawed detective or space-pilot; and each in the new style of drawing, a style derived from the American 'strips' and differing from the older English ones as a slick milk-bar differs from an unimproved fish-and-chips shop.

There is, of course, up-to-the-minute film and radio gossip, and the latest T.V. news. Above all, there is often now a sensational serial story or biographical feature. The forces of the time ensure that such a serial cannot be planned to run for much more than a month, so every three or four weeks the magazines themselves and the news-agents' side-hoardings announce that yet another thrilling, tense, and 'dramatically passionate' story is about to be unfolded. But in these stories the only real sophistication is usually in the visual presentation and even that is only partly sophisticated. They claim to be stirring, but are as milk-and-water compared with what one may find in almost any sex-and-crime novelette. Nevertheless, they aim to attract in a modern manner. Each poster and each instalment is likely to be illustrated by 'genuine photographs from life'. Yet at bottom most of these magazines remain what they have always been in spirit, and their audience, though it may hanker after neon-lighted sins, remains unsophisticated and provincial. The poster announces, say, a daring new serial on *Life with my Desert Lover*; and from it allures a pleasantly English-looking chorus-girl from Scunthorpe, tricked out unconvincingly in silky pants and brassière, with a few beads. Even were one to ignore the face, the pose of her body speaks of what the patrons of the City Palace of Varieties, Leeds, would recognize as 'real sexy' rather than of the smouldering instinctive sexuality of an Arabian girl of pleasure. There probably follows a few weeks later a story with a title like *Law of the Pagan*, illustrated by the picture of a beautiful girl trapped by a savage band. 'Throw me to your hounds . . . murder me,' she is likely to cry from her poster, 'I shall not give in to you.' Homely savagery; she will have the face and the attractively-waved auburn hair of the girl who smiles from the four-penny patterns for knitting jumpers. It is clear that the moment she is released she will hide that not-altogether-nice bathing costume masquerading as a wild animal's pelt beneath the cable-stitch cardigan she made for twelve-and-six and the rather fashionable skirt she got half-price at the C & A sale.

It seems doubtful whether most of the older magazines will be able to retain even this homely note in their daring. Some recent ventures, in subject and presentation, suggest that it is now being rapidly ousted, as a result of the pace set by those older weeklies which have more wholeheartedly adopted the newer manners and by some of the newcomers. Magazines of this kind constantly claim to be 'modern' and 'forward-looking', and do put rather a special emphasis on attracting young people. They have a higher proportion than the older-style magazines of advertisements for techniques to make young men tough or to increase height; several of their features – about the oddities of courtship and the curiosities of early married life, and so on – are clearly aimed at readers under thirty. But on the whole such papers obviously aim still to appeal to the whole family. Most of them include features on women's and men's dress, the usual 'pools' guides, competitions for people of differing interests, the typical family advertisements, and a nurse or older sister who answers readers' problems as sensibly as do her colleagues in the older kind of women's magazines.

These newcomers are, in fact, *family* magazines, with readerships that are both large and varied. It is a mistake to think of them as 'young men's leggy papers'. Such a publication is likely to be read nowadays by one in four or five of the total adult population, to be similarly distributed through the classes as is a typical family magazine of the older kind, but to have two or three times the number of readers. More important, such a new-style publication will be likely to have the same proportions of readers in each age-range as does a family publication in the old style; and its proportions of women readers at all ages are likely to be as high as are those of the older magazine – that is, to be not significantly less than the men. These newer family magazines are making the older ones fight for existence all along the line because they are their direct competitors and successors. That we do not always recognize this is probably partly due to our disinclination to admit that the true succession has been taken over by these dubiously dressed newcomers.

Matthew Arnold noted that popular publications always have a good share of 'generous instincts', and in this reflect the character of their readers. These popular journals in the modern style habitually combine their sensationalism with an easy radicalism; their general overt tone is socially (but vaguely)progressive and, of course, moral. There is sometimes a small religious section, or a small ethical prose-poem of the sort always to be found in the older magazines. But such things seem to me to disguise the more important but less overt tendencies; even the currently popular attacks on 'gimmicks' can be 'gimmicks' themselves. The overt morality is in accordance with working-class attitudes; but if it is good for a laugh to deny that morality implicitly, then it is likely to be denied. The only firm quality is the quixotic, that of people who are what used to be described as 'anyway for a rotten apple'. There is a parallel in the use of moral elements by some advertisers.

In the body of its text a magazine in the newer style is superficially like the old; it is made up of bits-and-bobs of information: short articles on figures in history, Teddy boys, curiosities from many lands: and the captions appear much as they have always done. But a closer examination shows that in moving towards the newer styles these magazines are moving into a narrower world. The old-fashioned magazines sought the curious and the startling; in the newer style the emphasis is much more on the simply startling, in crime, in sexual matters, and in the supernatural. How strong, incidentally, the old interest in the supernatural remains, no matter what the changes in its presentation. Current events are likely to be treated only if some slightly sexual or apparently startling angle can be given to them. There have to be a great many pictures, especially the pin-up photographs. The emphasis, then, is more on the startling than on the curious; or rather, the assumptions behind this world are so narrowed that it seems as though only that which is startling – preferably in one of the three ways named above – will arouse curiosity. As a result, even those inevitable items which are not in themselves startling have to be 'pepped up', even more than some newspapers would think reasonable at present:

She likes to sing – in her scanties
Thousands of men fight for one woman
The butler who beat the Duchess
She loves it – hot.

Of course, popular papers have always been under the stress of trying to be bright and interesting. But during the last half-century their world has become increasingly competitive. And during the last thirty years the radio has taken away their opportunities of presenting the news when it is brand-new. The serious papers report what we briefly know already, and comment upon it or provide more background; the more popular papers move in the direction of startling substitutes. A comparison of the layout of a magazine in the older stype with one in the newer style makes my general point even more forcefully. The newer ones are nothing if not smart and 'snappy'. They tend to use, and in the manner of advertisement artists, a far wider range of type than do magazines in the older style; their cartoons and jokes (which are often very funny, when they forget the narrow run of husband-and-wife bickerings) are in the new sophisticated style. They often pay particular attention to article-headings, which are not from standard types but are specially drawn in a bold and arresting manner. They are altogether slicker, in their appearance and in their treatment of the old basic material, than the magazines from which they have evolved; they are truly modern, mid-century magazines.

Yet they seem to me only technically an improvement on the older style of magazines; they have more skill in discovering new ways of enjoying the old pleasures and in the apparent daring with which they present them. To the older type of paper they are rather like the latest synthetic cocktail to a glass of not-very-strong beer. Comparing the two kinds of journal, one is forced to conclude that the newer forms are less wholesome even than the older. I have suggested that on the whole their interest is not so much in the widely curious as in the narrowly startling and sexually-sensational. What is worse, this sex-interest is largely 'in the head' and eye, a removed, vicarious thing. It thinks of itself as a smart and sophisticated interest, but is really bloodless and reduced to a very narrow range of responses; slickness disguising emotional thinness is no improvement on the older kind of family magazine. The apologists for the modern kind of magazine are usually pert and even morally self-congratulatory about the old-fashioned stuff they have displaced; they have no grounds to be.

C. *The Process Illustrated: (ii) Commercial Popular Songs*

Popular songs do not so plainly show the effect of modern commercial organization as does popular reading. Perhaps this is because the production of popular songs does not offer scope for commercial activity on so large a scale. There has been centralization, as everyone who has heard of 'Tin Pan Alley' knows, so that today almost the whole activity of song production and distribution is controlled from London. There is practically no writing of songs by members of the working-classes for their local groups. The crude urban poets who sold their own broadsheets in the streets of the large cities had disappeared by the end of Edward VII's reign, or soon after. This was written on the death of Edward VII:

> The will of God we must obey
> Dreadful – our King taken away
> Greatest friend of the nation
> Mighty monarch and protector.
> . . .
> Greatest sorrow England ever had
> When death took away our dear Dad;
> . . .
> His mighty work for the nation,
> Strengthening peace and securing union,
> Always at it since on the throne
> Has saved our country more than one billion.

Not many had so much charm: Arthur Morrison remarks that 'last dying confessions' of murderers almost always had the same burden:

> Take warning by my dreadful fate,
> The truth I can't deny
> This dreadful crime that I are done
> I are condemned to die.

But the words of the verses could not be more crudely banal than those used in what may be a vestige of the same tradition. I mean the custom, still alive among working-class children and adolescents, of putting words about the latest murder to an existing popular tune. The murders by Dr Buck Ruxton produced:

> Red stains on the carpet
> Red stains on the stairs . . .
> (to the tune of 'Red Sails in the Sunset')

and:

> When you grow too cold to steam
> I'll have you to dismember . . .
> (to the tune of 'When I Grow Too Old to Dream').

Adults still sometimes invent jokes on such themes: the Christie trial in 1953 produced a crop about 'cupboard love'; 'seven women at home and not one to make a cup of tea', was another, and a fair example of the usual level.

The singers who wrote their own songs or worked with their own song-writer for years have almost entirely gone. But still working-class people insist, and the commercial houses meet this demand, on being able to identify favourite songs with favourite singers; this is Vera Lynn's, this Frankie Laine's, this Gracie Fields's song.

Contemporary lyric-writers know working-class song-forms and much of the idiom; probably some of them still belong to the people and send in their songs from the provinces. But though the songs still illustrate much in working-class life, they seem to me to do so in a more generalized way than would have been the case fifty years ago. The newer songs tell us something of working-class attitudes, but those attitudes are here insufficiently relieved by a sense of the intimate human qualifications which real closeness brings.

In discussing changes in song I have a personal difficulty, that many of the older songs recall my own childhood and adolescence and I find myself tempted to claim, with little thought, that they are much better than most songs of the last twenty years. Obviously I was putting into the earlier songs my own unordered emotions (as young people are into those of today). To some extent the same problem arises in a discussion of reading, but it seems harder to stand outside the songs than the books and magazines. The songs seem to get more deeply under the emotional skin than the stories. Or the problem may be chiefly that I lack, in dealing with songs, the critical equipment I am accustomed to use on the printed word.

This proviso is necessary and indicates the elusive and difficult nature of any discussion of the lines of change in popular song. I shall therefore restrict myself to a few features in which some change seems evident, and in which it seems possible to reduce sufficiently the effect of more subjective responses. I am not concerned with the formal features of urban popular song from a hundred years ago to the present, with the high degree of stylization, the simple emotional patterns, the circumscribed use of language and the stanzaic crudities. Nor shall I be implying that all the songs of forty or fifty years ago were strong and healthy in idiom and manner, or forgetting that we remember the best songs from a large number of weak ones.

I remarked earlier that bad songs may be transmuted and very banal verses infused with decent emotion, either by a private individual singing 'in his head' or by a public singer in touch with his audience. This is as true of some contemporary songs as it was of 'Bird in a Gilded Cage'. And there are some contemporary popular singers whose performances are as entertaining and admirable, in their very different ways, as those of the stars of fifty years ago. Yet there are certain developments in public manners of singing which seem particularly related to the centralizing tendencies of modern society.

The strain of 'cheering-up' songs is an old one, and one with an admirable aspect. Behind songs of this kind is the assumption that life is bound to be hard, but that one must not be downhearted ('Are we downhearted? No!'). One has to keep one's end up like everybody else: 'We're all in it together.' Songs of this kind are still written today, and some of them are delightfully catchy. But often the tone of their delivery suggests that the cheering up and the group-sense with which it is associated are being made self-congratulatory. They are being changed to: 'What's it matter so long as you keep cheerful,' or, 'It's foolish, but it's fun.' There was a character called Mona Lott in 'Itma' whose catch-line was, 'It's bein' so cheerful as keeps me goin'', delivered in a graveyard voice. For the generalized character the manner of delivery of these songs suggests the catch-line would be, 'It's being so ordinary as keeps me cheerful', delivered in a voice of light-headed self-satisfaction. Real dissatisfaction, with oneself or the outer conditions of one's life, would seem not merely out-of-date but slightly subversive, as though one should wander through a holiday-camp at the height of the season with Kafka in the pocket, a drawn look and an occasional hollow laugh.

Written illustration is of little use when the manner of delivery is being discussed, but the sort of change I mean may be noted by comparing the usual style of public delivery of such a song as:

> If you're tired and weary
> Just carry on,

which still has something of the old patient putting-up with things, without the pretence that there is really nothing to put up with since we can all be cheerful together; by comparing that with the usual sagging poverty in the delivery of some of those more recent songs which invite us simply to 'dream' or to 'wish' when in trouble.

A worse example of the exploitation of the link between 'neighbourliness' and cheerfulness is the vapidly heartless, 'aren't we comics?' air of some commercial bands flogging themselves to be funny with such a song as, 'Why Does Everybody Call Me Big Head', the last two words being delivered with a heavy, flat beat. Marie Lloyd and her contemporaries sang for working-class people laughing at themselves, at their own oddities and their troubles. In the newer style the melodies usually have their vigour syncopated out of existence in favour of a drumming mass-call which suggests an increasing reliance on the group-appeal simply as an escape from personality and choice. The fibre of personal oddity and positive group-sense are both missing. 'Why worry' can be either a near-stoical cheerfulness before circumstance or an evasive assertion that nothing is ever worth worrying about (so long as you are with the gang) posturing as gaiety: everything depends on the tone. The cheerful 'card' of these songs, like the 'Honest Joe' of the Press, is today more often than not a hollow little man clinging to a mask.

One does not meet often enough the mood and rhythm of delivery associated with songs like 'Any Old Iron' and 'My Old Man said "Foller the Van"'. Nor does one find often enough the moderately ironic attitude to love which was common two or three decades ago in such songs as, 'Why Did She Fall for the Leader of the Band?', 'Ain't She Sweet?', or 'That's My Weakness Now', or even in, 'I can't give you anything but love, Baby', where the words ('Diamond bracelets Woolworth doesn't sell, baby') and the over-exaggeration of the wail introduced an element of self-mockery. This kind of song does still appear, and there have been a few attractive recent examples: for instance, the 'Dummy Song', which rejects a girl-friend, with great vitality, in favour of an amenable dummy made out of domestic odds-and-ends, 'the leg off the table', and so on. And a similar spirit is still strongly alive in a few of the more truly working-class radio-variety programmes. But my impression is that the better examples usually come from America now. An example is 'They call me the Rock of Gibraltar', which is usually delivered with great 'punch'.

The mocking and debunking songs had their vitality from both belonging to a class and being able to laugh, within certain limits, at the life of that class. Such a combination is not easily achieved under contemporary conditions of production and presentation.

In the styles of singing just described the sense of being part of a group was predominant. There seems to be a similar development in the public performance of more personal styles. The change is from what I called earlier the 'big-dipper' or 'modified big-dipper' style to an extremely 'internal' style. This is the claustrophobically personal manner of some successful men crooners today and, at its most intimately and appallingly exposed, of women crooners with the late-night broadcasting bands. These are manners which naturally have much in common with the 'big-dipper' manner but, like many other contemporary entertainments, these are the same yet not the same, the same but gone 'soft in the middle'. In the older manner the singing was both personal and public or communal. The personal emotions were whole-heartedly accepted and also felt to be common to all. In the later manners there is a huge, public effect and the use of echo-chambers makes this more impressive than the effect which can be gained in a large variety-hall; and there is an enforced intimacy like a close-up on an immense screen. The singer is reaching millions but pretends that he is reaching only 'you', and this is a deterioration from the communally-felt personal emotion of the 'big-dipper' manner. The would-be personal is many times larger than life and has lost its sanction in the group. I think that this may be the equivalent in song of the increasing 'personalization' in popular newspapers.

In the root-attitudes themselves there is no marked change. There does seem to be a difference in what might be called the attitude-to-the-attitudes. The old appeals – to the plain man, friendliness, cheerfulness, home, love, and the rest – are still to be found, but now in an increasingly self-conscious form. Thus modified they also are becoming, like the manners of singing, 'soft-in-the-middle'; they are becoming a romantic sentimentality towards the self. My interest lies, therefore, less in the assumptions themselves than in the way in which the assumptions are now felt. Again, one can know this fully only from hearing the songs sung, since so much depends on tone, on emphasis and repetition. But more particular reference will be possible here than was possible in the discussion of styles of singing.

The emphasis on the virtues of the ordinary man, as more 'real', more shrewd and honest than others is being developed, here as elsewhere, into a form of snobbery. All men are equally good, but plain folks are better than others, to adapt a phrase of George Orwell's. The really important thing, it is suggested, is to be friendly, to be 'one of us'. This is neighbourliness spilling over into an undefined weak communalism, acquiring its communalism only from a general agreement that all shall be proud to be weak together; 'friendliness' as of peas finding pride in being so like other peas, or of hens talking of the 'nice' spirit of the battery. So one is invited to sing, 'Come in, Neighbour!', or, 'Ain't it grand to have good neighbours?', (the old word must still be used since it carries valuable overtones). Home therefore becomes more important than ever, becomes a soft but back-slapping retreat, with a large mat at the door saying a bright 'welcome' to all good types. No doubt some enterprising salesman will soon produce a doormat inscribed 'pals only' or 'Cum in, lads and lasses', since to be a pal seems the only condition of entry to the houses celebrated in a hundred songs of this type.

The logical next stage in this sequence of linked attitudes – be ordinary; be 'pally'; be cheerful, but all in an un-vital kind of way – is the provision of escape-hatch attitudes for the moments when the cold water of life breaks in; when one is in danger of realizing that, in spite of having all the right group-tickets, somehow one has not 'made out', is less as a person than one perhaps ought to be, and is, but now in a disturbing sense, little. It may be inevitable and valuable for all of us sometimes to feel like this. But if the song-writers are listened to the feeling will not last long, and eventually the habit of it may be altogether lost. The sedative is provided in two connected forms. First, though it may sometimes seem as though one is doing nothing with one's life, one can at least ('you're free, aren't you?') pretend and dream and go on making wishes. Second, if one sometimes has the beginnings of a feeling of inadequacy, one may stifle it by remembering that love conquers and excuses and makes up for all.

One may doubt whether there is anything worth bothering about in the world outside; one may be 'cagey' about the calls to one kind of belief or another; one may find oneself often unable to cope with that outside world. But there is always love, as a warm burrow, as a remover of worry; love borne on an ingratiating treacle of melody.

'Snug as a bug in a rug,' people used to say; now the songs speak of 'little nests'; and their tone has enormous undertones of submerged self-pity.

Further, if there are no values outside the present and local, if 'religion is out-of-date', then for those whose sense of life is essentially personal, love may perhaps be inflated to fill the gap, may be not merely linked with religion (as in the older songs) but made a substitute for religion. Love can be the end of everything, and after the coming-together in love, there will be no more than a vague sense of uplift-going-on, of dawns perennially rising, of great chords sounding some sort of affirmative gesture towards the universe – as in the classic ending on a close-up clinch of the romantic films, the massed choir in an 'O altitudo', and the 'I'll love you for ever' from the hero and heroine. 'For ever' – against time and worry and depression, Love; Love for its own sake, like that of a pair of budgerigars in their shiny cage. It is no accident that one of the more common metaphors in this type of song is that of 'love-birds'. Love is eternal, and will outlast not only the ordinary accidents of life but the stars themselves. From there it is an easy step to the adoption of quasi-religious language for the praise of human love.

It is true that this kind of assertion in love-poetry has a long history – the Elizabethan sonneteers, for example, employed these and many other related conceits. But reminders of this kind do not really help much; we have to keep our points of comparison and development much more close and relevant.

We saw earlier how easy it is in working-class singing to move, without sense of incongruity, from domestic love and friendship to God's love and Heaven. So the ground was prepared for this extension. But we must realize that there is an extension; from home-family-love-neighbourliness to Our-Father-in-Heaven, where the values associated with Our-Father-in-Heaven are felt to be similar to those of a loving home, so that there is no sense of incongruity in passing from one to the other; from that to the point at which the assumption is that love has replaced religion, that, in particular, the 'we two only' or 'just the two of us' idea of love can be given all the trappings of religious feeling – for itself and in itself; there is nothing outside. Then follow quickly all the celestial choirs roaring out against a hollow background suggestive of infinite height and space; the melodies inflated into the vaguely Handelian by massed strings, bells chiming in the background, and the voice of the soloist riding a well-defined beam in the accepted style. For the love-song sung in the religious manner the two main styles seem to be the 'elevated celestial' or 'Sweetheart of the Universe' for women, which suggests an angelic but yet intensely feminine spirit: and for men what might be called the 'strangulato', a peculiarly thick form of singing from far back in the throat, suggesting a strong, almost muscle-bound or passion-bound man, tight-gripped by a near-divine emotion.

Since the last war there has been a revival of what might seem at first glance explicitly religious songs. But these do not indicate a withdrawal from the extreme position described in the preceding paragraph, where religion had been replaced by a love-affair. They are a further extension of that tendency. In the whole manner of their presentation it is clear that God has come in again as a partner in the biggest love-affair of all. These songs are therefore even further in spirit from those earlier songs, in which to sing about religion was to express a sense of the values of home and neighbourliness. They are disguised love-songs, love-songs enjoying a special 'uplift' from the assumption of a close 'nesting' or 'love-bird' relationship to God.

If all this were a close guide to the way working-class people, and others, actually live and respond today, then matters would have reached a depressing state. The tendencies are regrettable and will no doubt increasingly make their effect. But people do not have to sing or listen to these songs, and many do not: and those who do, often make the songs better than they really are. The situation of popular song helps to illuminate that of the more advanced modern publication. It prompts a further reminder that, though the publications reach more people more consistently than do the songs, people often read them in their own way. So that even there they are less affected than the extent of their purchases would seem to indicate.

D. *The Results*

How may one summarize the probable effects of the more widely read publications, the popular daily and Sunday papers, and the cheap magazines? Are there likely to be any pervasive results from a constant and largely unrelieved diet of this kind of reading?

There may be, first, a disconnecting effect in reading-matter which is almost entirely sensational and fantasy-producing, no matter how trivial its sensations may often be, reading cut off from any serious suggestion of responsibility and commitment. On the evidence of the developments discussed above, sensation and fantasy are increasing their hold, but in thin and debilitated forms. Compare the old broadsheets on executions or even the *Police News*; these new things are smarter, less immediately shocking, but at bottom no less indefatigably wedded to the same appeals. Sensationalism has learned to wear a white collar, and is full of persuasive and smooth social 'ploys'; it has all 'gone to the head', and is as much without a belly-laugh as it is without bowels of compassion. There are recurrent cries against our 'sex-sodden papers'; they attribute more life to these papers than they have. 'Sodden' suggests some weight, some body; but these have not body enough to be sodden in anything. Everything has gone vicarious: this is puff-pastry literature, with nothing inside the pastry, the ceaseless exploitation of a hollow brightness. Nothing can be delivered straight, not even the weather forecast; 'It will rain' has to be 'You'll need a mac, today, chum'. Even the sensationalism is often only apparent. Thus a headline such as that given earlier (and it is typical of many), 'Thousands of men fight for one woman', proves to be simply a note about the swarming of bees. This kind of thing is 'What the Butler Saw' with no cards in the machine; but the sales-talk is wonderful:

For our sense of wonder is not aroused by enormous, sensational things – though that is what a dulled sensibility requires to provoke it to a sort of *ersatz* experience of wonder.

Examine a group of modern pin-ups: at first they look extremely suggestive and in some ways they are. And yet they are strangely ersatz, the sex has been machined out of them; at least, all has gone except a strange kind of sex. They inhabit regions so stylized, so pasteurized, that the real physical quality has left them. But they have an unreal and remote perfection in their own kind of 'sexiness'. Everything has been stripped to a limited range of visual suggestions – can one imagine a musky body-smell, un-artificially disordered hair, an uneven texture to the skin, hair on the arms and legs, beads of perspiration on the upper-lip, on one of these neatly-packaged creatures? Put them alongside a Degas dancer and the unreality comes out strikingly. Are such things likely to increase sexual immorality among young people? I find it hard to imagine much connexion between them and heterosexual activity. They may encourage masturbation: in their symbolic way they may promote that kind of sealed-off sexual response.

The same ersatz quality is often apparent in that 'large outspokenness' of which the popular Press is so proud. Much of it is a sort of shadow-boxing and stylish punch-pulling, a harmless muscle-flexing under arc lights. Now and again there is a genuine attack, but usually on something small and safe. More often the enemies are either men of straw, bogus Aunt Sallies such as 'conventional people'; or if the attacks are on real people – as on an Archbishop, to praise by implication the unhypocritical 'little man' – they usually prove on examination to be a few safe feints. There are a few exceptions, but in general these papers neither shock with their 'shocking' revelations, nor hurt with their 'straight attacks'.

The objection to simplification and 'fragmentation' rests on somewhat similar grounds. Such an objection is not based on an unspoken regret that, though we are now a literate people, not everyone reads, say, T. S. Eliot. The objection that can be made is much narrower and more specific. After all, there might reasonably have been an improvement in the general standard of reading, in its quality, over the last fifty years; a great deal has been done to try to ensure it. And certain developments do suggest that such an improvement has taken place. But when we look at the increase, proportionately, in the hold which the simplified and fragmentary publications have come to exercise during the same period, and at their failure to be one whit better than the publications of half a century ago, it becomes very doubtful whether we can claim that there has been any general improvement in the quality of reading. It seems, rather, as though a very large number of people are being held down at an appallingly low level in their reading. By now the massive publications provide worse fare than almost any individual reader requires; but that is according to their nature, as mass-publications. The stores which seek small profits and quick returns obtain their huge clientèle by producing, for example, shirts more cheaply than anyone else; but they restrict the number of styles to those most popular: if we like those styles, we may well buy from them a shirt in other ways good. The massive popular Press must restrict itself to the appeals and attitudes which are most popular; and in these much less tangible matters there are not the compensations of shirt-buying. We come together in our self-indulgences; and since here the norms are hard to discover and hold, we do not always recognize them as indulgences.

Thus few people have more than one speed in reading. There is a more than adequate supply of material designed to be read at top speed, and that speed is useless for most worthwhile reading. Equally, the crude high-lighting of, for instance, character-description in popular fiction makes readers less likely to be willing to tolerate the qualifications, the apparent uncertainty of outline, the nuances, the lack of bold and simple strokes, which any character-analysis of subtlety involves. This is not to regret that they are unwilling to tease out the situation of Strether in Henry James's *The Ambassadors*; the 'ordinary' is complex too; there are no simple people. Short-winded sentences, with scarcely a subordinate clause in qualification, the epithets flat and tagging dumbly each to its noun; the lack of any texture or sense of depth: to use writing like this to describe character is like building a house from spent matchsticks.

Unfortunately it is not possible to quote an actual example from a modern popular publication, but they may be very easily found. They will usually prove to be in some ways more skilfully written than most of the stories in the old-style magazines, and often to have more life, or more of a callow kind of life. Some of the objections to them would apply also to the stories in the old-style publications. But this newer writing has often a cheap gum-chewing pert glibness and a streamlining which mark it at once as mid-twentieth-century popular writing. To me, its worst feature is the brash confidence with which it presents, and assumes as universally valid, an outlook such as I have just described. This is roughly the manner of writing:

There were only two of us from Longton's Mill at the Kosy Holiday Kamp – unless you count Mabel Arkwright. But we don't, usually. Apart from poor old Mabel's spotty face, there's her owlishness – always got her head in some book and peering like mad.

Anyway, June and I knew we were in for a smashing time the moment we set eyes on the place . . . three dance-halls, two sun-bathing parades, lots of milk bars – just the job!

And then, sure enough, up rolled a real eyeful! One great big hunk of luscious manhood! Marlon Brando and Humph. Bogart in one.

So we were all set for a real good time – when along comes this Dorothy Temple. Ginger hair she called auburn, and a soft sort of 'let me be the pretty soothing wife' look.

So we knew it was going to be a fight to the finish . . .

... Was her face red? That fixed her alright. Last we saw of her she was off for a good walk, with Mabel and a book.

Pardon me? Oh, – what happened to Marlon-Brando-and-Humph.-Bogart? Well, excuse me just now. . . .

The quotation from *East Lynne* which follows is in certain ways less alive than much of this modern writing; it relies too easily on a sort of oratory. But the particular comparison I am anxious to make is between what I can only call – at the risk of sounding portentous – the moral tone, the differences in the approach to life and to relationships which lie between each passage:

Tears were streaming down the face of Mrs Hare. It was a bright morning after the snowstorm, so bright that the sky was blue and the sun was shining, but the snow lay deeply upon the ground. Mrs Hare sat in her chair, enjoying the brightness, and Mr Carlyle stood near her. The tears of joy and of grief mingled: of grief at hearing that she should at last have to part with Barbara; of joy that she was going to one so entirely worthy of her as was Mr Carlyle.

'Archibald, she has had a happy home here: You will render yours as much so?' 'To the very utmost of my power.' 'You will ever be kind to her, ever cherish her?' 'With my whole heart and strength. Dear Mrs Hare, I thought you knew me too well to doubt me.'

'Doubt you! I do not doubt you: I trust you implicitly, Archibald. Had the whole world laid themselves at Barbara's feet, I should have prayed that she might choose you.'

As evidence of the richness of texture which a very good writer will give to an apparently simple description of character, here is George Eliot describing a Church of England village parson, one of a type with which she had little sympathy:

On the other hand, I must plead, for I have an affectionate partiality towards the Rector's memory, that he was not vindictive – and some philanthropists have been so: that he was not intolerant – and there is a rumour that some zealous theologians have not been altogether free from the blemish; that although he would probably have declined to give his body to be burned in any public cause, and was far from bestowing all his goods to feed the poor, he had that charity which has sometimes been lacking to very illustrious virtue – he was tender to other men's failings, and unwilling to impute evil. He was one of those men, and they are not the commonest, of whom we can know the best only by following them away from the market-place, entering with them into their own homes, hearing the voice with which they speak to the young and aged about their own hearth-stone, and witnessing their thoughtful care for the everyday wants of everyday companions, who take all their kindness as a matter of course, and not as a subject for panegyric.

We read, with the new material, by reaching a region where nothing real ever happens, a twilight of half-responses automatically given. 'Meaningless and niggling' curiosity is more and more appealed to. But less and less is there a sense of the fibre of life. And this, for the readers, is perhaps the worst effect of all. It is not possible that people could positively, could actively enjoy this; there is nothing for them to be engaged with, to be positively reacting to. Since nothing is demanded of the reader, nothing can be given by the reader. We are in a pallid half-light of the emotions where nothing shocks or startles or sets on edge, and nothing challenges, or gives joy or evokes sorrow; neither splendour nor misery: only the constant trickle of tinned milk-and-water which staves off the pangs of a positive hunger and denies the satisfactions of a solidly-filling meal.

As I have indicated, this is an almost entirely unrelieved diet for a great number of people; they see practically no other reading. The mass-publications must try to ensure that their customers want no other reading, must constantly try to tighten their grip, or their great structures would be in danger of collapsing. Popular reading is now highly centralized; a very large body of people choose between only a small number of publications. This is a very small and crowded country; today almost everyone can be supplied at almost the same time with the same object. The price paid for this in popular reading is that a small group of imaginatively narrow and lamed publications are able to impose a considerable uniformity. These publications must aim to hold their readers at a level of passive acceptance, at which they never really ask a question, but happily take what is provided and think of no change. There must be no significant disturbing of assumptions, nothing more than a light titillation. The popular Press, for all its purported 'progressiveness' and 'independence', is one of the greatest conserving forces in public life today: its nature requires it to promote both conservatism and conformity.

That these things have not so far had a more obviously harmful effect on the quality of people's lives is due to that capacity – one of the chief refrains of this essay – to live easily in compartments, to separate the life of home from the life outside, 'real' life from the life of entertainment. Working-class people have traditionally, or at least for several generations, regarded art as escape, as something enjoyed but not assumed to have much connexion with the matter of daily life. Art is marginal, 'fun': 'It teks y'mind *off* things'; 'It teks yer *out* of y'self'; 'It meks a *break*, and a bit of a change' (the italics are mine). Whilst they are enjoying it, people may submit themselves, may identify themselves; but at the back of their minds they know it is not 'real'; 'real' life goes on elsewhere. Art may 'tek yer *out* of yerself'; but the form of that phrase indicates that there is, inside, a 'real' you for which art is not expected to speak; except to reflect, by conventional means, certain agreed assumptions. Art is for you to *use*. Hence the very common habit among women of testing a novelette by looking at the opening page to make sure it gets off to a good start with plenty of dialogue, and then looking at the final page to make sure it ends happily; they do not read to be disturbed or left with questions hanging.

Yet even this explanation makes the happy ending appear too much of an indulgence. For working-class people the happy ending, as I tried to show earlier, is often a happy ending in the kind of life they have around them, in home and family; but in that life when things have 'worked out', when the clouds have blown away. They know life is not really like that; they do not expect life ever to be like that in some hazy future. But they say it is 'nice to think of' a life like that; and this attitude seems to me near at times to being a kind of vision, a glimpse of another order.

It is commonly assumed, therefore, that working-class people are more deeply affected by their reading than they are: that, for instance, they uncritically adopt Christian names from their novelettes or films. It is true that if a name is not too outlandish it may find a foothold. Then the force of conformity, rather than the power of the novelette in which it appears, may help it to acquire great popularity very quickly. The Registrar of Tottenham has reported that at one time one girl baby in five was called 'Doreen'. But most working-class wives, though they may read story after story in the magazines, will laugh at the odd neighbour who is so affected by them as to call her child 'Dawn' or 'April'. In large part they laugh because she has carried the stories into real life, and that is a little comic, or even slightly simple.

This general attitude, in co-operation with 'tolerance', helps to explain also why working-class people are unwilling to object to even the most extreme developments in their publications. A grey-haired mother thumbing through one of the more startlingly visual weekly magazine/newspapers may seem a bizarre figure, though she is common enough. But, of course, she looks only at the parts which interest her: as to the pin-ups, well, she 'tolerates' them, she 'doesn't mind them – they put them in for the lads, y'know'. Similarly, people can remain little affected by the more advanced approaches of the advertisers; they take them in an oblique way.

All this may be a useful sterilizer against infection, but can be a dangerous one, especially today. In the new atmosphere, art is not only a temporary escape, or 'fun'; it is also, working-class people feel, a commercial racket, a money-making game at bottom. It becomes harder than ever even to conceive that a writer may work, not for money, but for much less calculating reasons. 'A good book is the precious life-blood of a master spirit', said Milton. If the work of a good contemporary writer is brought to the notice of most adults, they will not only find it difficult to follow his approach to life, but will readily and firmly assume that he is, like the rest, though in some strange and unamusing way they have not quite got the hang of, 'on the make', 'just writing for the money'.

The mass of talented commercial writers ensures that most people are kept at a level in reading at which they can respond only to the crudely imprecise, the expected, the primary, the highly coloured; and towards that, as towards almost all art, most people have a cheerful cynicism. They read nothing but the most popular writing; why should they, if writing is what they take it to be? Why should they work on their reading? All the family read one of the modern weekly magazine/newspapers (and probably insist that they 'only take it for the jokes'); father has an older kind of family magazine; mother has one of the older women's magazines and one of the new glossy ones; the daughter has yet another glossy magazine; the boys look at a popular paper each day, at a gangster paper-back each week, and at the two or three Sunday papers which all the family see. Purely on this evidence, the situation looks dreadful: sensation, fragmentation, over-simplification, unreality; 'never a real or a good thing read', to paraphrase D. H. Lawrence. The surprising thing is how much family life goes on in its own way, how little it is so far affected in its rhythms and values by the endless rain of confetti-literature now falling upon it.

Yet it all has the effect of increasing that division of the world in two which I have already stressed. People know they are 'being got at', but limit the results upon themselves by relegating most of the persuasions to the world of 'Them'. 'Oh, They'll put anything [or 'say anything'] in the papers nowadays', they remark; or 'Still, it's only a book.' They buy the papers by the million, and the editors, at election time, try to persuade them to vote as the papers would like. The customers, unless they take one of the more narrowly-committed popular papers, vote with little reference to the persuasions of the papers, but bear them no ill-will and continue to buy them. They assume that a great deal they read in the papers is phoney, that 'it's your money – or your vote – that they're after'. They find the papers easy to read, and amusing for those things they are prepared to give attention to. They know the newspaper-firms are 'not in it for the good of their 'ealth', but, 'good luck to 'em': meanwhile, the readers get the amusement they want.

To recall finally the main arguments of this and the preceding chapter, since one largely illustrates the other. The process of softening-up by the most general appeals continues and widens: the new manners include a variety of 'democratic' tones of voice and are decided by the urge for gaiety and slickness at all costs; the main assumptions are over-weening egalitarianism, freedom, tolerance, progress, hedonism, and the cult of youth. Liberty equals licence to provide what will best increase sales; tolerance is equated with the lack of any standards other than those which are so trite and vague as to be almost wholly incantatory and of little practical use; any defence of any value is an instance of authoritarianism and hypocrisy.

Examples can be found in any of the more popular daily newspapers; this fictitious article is faithful to the general substance and spirit of them all:

IT BEATS ME

Here we go again, chums!

Who is it *this time*?

Only the 60-year-old bachelor Archprelate of Pontyholoth (side-photograph of the Archprelate in his gaiters, caught in an unguarded moment, so that he looks remarkably like a variety comedian's version of a bumbling bishop).

He was talking the other day to the League of Christian Women (average age 62) about THE WAY WE SPEND OUR SPARE TIME.

Well ... well ...

Do *you* like a spot of T.V. after a hard day's work?

... You shouldn't – not according to the bachelor Archprelate.

... 'Too many people,' he said, 'take all their recreations passively nowadays. This can do them no good.'

Do *you* like a mild flutter on the pools every week?

... Sorry, pal, you shouldn't – not according to the 60-year-old Archprelate.

... 'It may be,' he said, 'that we should think much more about the freedom we allow to such organizations in our national life.'

BLIMEY, THAT SURE IS FIGHTING TALK

Who would have thought that a Christian leader in 1956 could forget the first essentials of democracy?

We may be a bit simple, but we always understood that Christian leaders should inspire us with the virtue of TOLERANCE.

Perhaps we got it wrong, because we also thought that Christian leaders were on the side of FREEDOM and EQUALITY.

But maybe these ideas are only alright for the Archprelate and his pals.

Anyway, I hope that someone in the poor old worried League of Christian Women got up and reminded him of those ideas.

... and that someone whispered a short word or two about the dangers of REACTION – and of HUMBUG – and of HYPOCRISY – and of SMUGNESS, for our Christian leaders.

.. and that someone else suggested that the Archprelate could do with meeting *ordinary folk* a bit more and with getting a better understanding of their *good sense*.

If they didn't –

IT BEATS ME

We all need to remember, every day and more and more, that in the last resort there is no such person as 'the common man'. If we do not, we may in the end have allowed individual decision to slip away in our dutiful democratic identification of ourselves with a hypothetical figure whose main value is to those who will mislead us. We need to hold fast to the basic facts about the nature of popular

G

publications – that they are now the products of large-scale commercial organizations, that they belong not to the history of the Press properly speaking, nor to affairs, nor to politics, but to entertainment; that their handling of 'opinion' is a largely irrational manipulation for the purposes of entertainment, that when one of these papers says, 'We give the facts . . . astounding . . .', this is not so much a statement of their attitude as an entertainer's patter, of the same order as, ' There's nothing up my sleeve.'

Writing in the latter part of the last century, William Morris regretted the lack of a popular art and looked forward to its revival:

Popular art has no chance of a healthy life or, indeed, of a life at all, till we are on the way to fill up this terrible gap between riches and poverty.

If that gap were closed there might be an end, he continued, to:

that fatal division of men into the cultivated and degraded classes which competitive commerce has bred and fosters.

The gap between riches and poverty has not been closed to an extent or in a manner which would have satisfied Morris. But much has been done to narrow the gap; the activities of competitive commerce can do much less than formerly to keep it open. Has the gap between the 'cultivated' and the 'degraded' classes lessened? Are we even a little nearer a popular art of the kind William Morris would have recognized?

We are moving towards a mass-art; millions each week and each day see the same paper and see few other publications. To become a mass-art it has to grip and hold down the level of taste, and is doing so with great effectiveness. Competitive commerce has changed horses and rides now as the champion of those hitherto 'degraded' classes, because now those classes, if all their contributory sixpences are added together, are worth riding for. And the new champions of the working-classes must keep them together, united at the level of their more indulgent instincts. Inhibited now from ensuring the 'degradation' of the masses economically, the logical processes of competitive commerce, favoured from without by the whole climate of the time and from within assisted by the lack of direction, the doubts and uncertainty before their freedom of working-people themselves (and maintained as much by ex-working-class writers as by others), are ensuring that working-people are culturally robbed. Since these processes can never rest, the holding down, the constant pressure not to look outwards and upwards, becomes a positive thing, becomes a new and stronger form of subjection; this subjection promises to be stronger than the old because the chains of cultural subordination are both easier to wear and harder to strike away than those of economic subordination. 'We are betrayed by what is false within,' by our common weaknesses and by the ability of these popular journals to have things both ways, to express our habitual moral assumptions but in such a way that they weaken the moral code they evoke; to say the right things for the wrong reasons.

I have spoken chiefly about developments in those popular publications which make a special appeal to working-class readers. It is worth remarking, for emphasis, that the trend is clear not only in the more advanced modern publications but in some of those – newspapers, in particular – which began by trying to be serious as well as popular, and are still not wholly committed to the new styles. The accounts by some of the journalists who have worked on these papers, of the constant pressure to be 'bright' at the expense of the more sober qualities, merely confirm what observation over the years suggests.

More important, the general argument applies just as strongly, though the historical background is somewhat different, to publications which aim to attract the large body of lower middle- to middle-class readers. Working-class and middle-class people often share the same publications; and class-divisions become less clear as circulations increase. And those popular papers – as distinct from what are usually known as the 'quality' papers – which do aim more specifically at a middle-class audience are affected by similar cultural trends to those affecting the popular papers aimed chiefly at working-people. The popular middle-class papers are as trivial and as trivializing as those for the working-classes. For myself I find the dailies aimed particularly at middle-class people more unpleasant than those for working-class people. They tend to have an intellectual smugness, a spiritual chauvinism and snobbery, and a cocktail-party polish which makes their atmosphere quite peculiarly stifling.

CHAPTER 8

THE NEWER MASS ART: SEX
IN SHINY PACKETS

A. *The Juke-Box Boys*

This regular, increasing, and almost entirely unvaried diet of sensation without commitment is surely likely to help render its consumers less capable of responding openly and responsibly to life, is likely to induce an underlying sense of purposelessness in existence outside the limited range of a few immediate appetites. Souls which may have had little opportunity to open will be kept hard-gripped, turned in upon themselves, looking out 'with odd dark eyes like windows' upon a world which is largely a phantasmagoria of passing shows and vicarious stimulations. That this is not today the position of many working-class people is due mainly to the capacity of the human spirit to resist; to resist from a sense, even though it is not usually defined, that there are other things which matter and which are to be obeyed.

But it may be useful to look now at some of those points in English life at which the cultural process described in the last two chapters is having its strongest effect. We should see there the condition which might already have been reached were it not for the resistances I have repeatedly stressed. One such illustration is to be found in the reading of young men on National Service. For two years many of them are, on the whole, bored; they are marking time until they go back to their jobs; they are adolescent and have money to spare. They are cut off from the unconsciously felt but important steadying effect of home, of the web of family relationships; perhaps also from the sense, at their place of work, of being part of an organization which has a tradition in its own kind of skill. They are as a result open to the effects of the reading, both fragmentary and sensational, so freely provided for them. The only bound books read by a great many, my own experience strongly suggests, are likely to be those written by the most popular crime novelists. Otherwise, they read comics, gangster novelettes, science and crime magazines, the newer-style magazines or magazine/newspapers, and the picture-dailies. Luckily, National Service lasts only two years; after that, they go home and back to work, still readers of these publications, but soon also men with commitments, with more demands on their time and money, probably with a good chance of picking up older, neighbourhood rhythms, with a good chance of escaping from the worst effects of what can be a glassily hermaphrodite existence ('life like a permanent wank [masturbation] inside you', as a soldier once described it to me), and one not connected to any meaningful sense of personal aim. I know there are exceptions and that much is being done to improve matters; but, given the background described in the preceding chapters, this is for many the predominant atmosphere during the period of National Service.

Perhaps even more symptomatic of the general trend is the reading of juke-box boys, of those who spend their evening listening in harshly lighted milk-bars to the 'nickelodeons'. There are, of course, others who read the books and magazines now to be discussed – some married men and women, perhaps in particular those who are finding married life a somewhat jaded affair, 'dirty old men', some schoolchildren – but one may reasonably take those who, night after night, visit these bars as typical or characteristic readers of these most developed new-style popular journals.

Like the cafés I described in an earlier chapter, the milk-bars indicate at once, in the nastiness of their modernistic knick-knacks, their glaring showiness, an aesthetic breakdown so complete that, in comparison with them, the layout of the living-rooms in some of the poor homes from which the customers come seems to speak of a tradition as balanced and civilized as an eighteenth-century townhouse. I am not thinking of those milk-bars which are really quick-service cafés where one may have a meal more quickly than in a café with table-service. I have in mind rather the kind of milk-bar – there is one in almost every northern town with more than, say, fifteen thousand inhabitants – which has become the regular evening rendezvous of some of the young men. Girls go to some, but most of the customers are boys aged between fifteen and twenty, with drape-suits, picture ties, and an American slouch. Most of them cannot afford a succession of milk-shakes, and make cups of tea serve for an hour or two whilst – and this is their main reason for coming – they put copper after copper into the mechanical record-player. About a

dozen records are available at any time; a numbered button is pressed
for the one wanted, which is selected from a key to titles. The records
seem to be changed about once a fortnight by the hiring firm; almost
all are American; almost all are 'vocals' and the styles of singing much
advanced beyond what is normally heard on the Light Programme
of the B.B.C. Some of the tunes are catchy; all have been doctored
for presentation so that they have the kind of beat which is currently
popular; much use is made of the 'hollow-cosmos' effect which
echo-chamber recording gives. They are delivered with great pre-
cision and competence, and the 'nickelodeon' is allowed to blare out
so that the noise would be sufficient to fill a good-sized ballroom,
rather than a converted shop in the main street. The young men
waggle one shoulder or stare, as desperately as Humphrey Bogart,
across the tubular chairs.

Compared even with the pub around the corner, this is all a
peculiarly thin and pallid form of dissipation, a sort of spiritual dry-
rot amid the odour of boiled milk. Many of the customers – their
clothes, their hair-styles, their facial expressions all indicate – are
living to a large extent in a myth-world compounded of a few simple
elements which they take to be those of American life.

They form a depressing group and one by no means typical of
working-class people; perhaps most of them are rather less intelligent
than the average, and are therefore even more exposed than others to
the debilitating mass-trends of the day. They have no aim, no
ambition, no protection, no belief. They are the modern equivalents
of Samuel Butler's mid-nineteenth-century ploughboys, and in as
unhappy a position as theirs:

The row of stolid, dull, vacant plough-boys, ungainly in build,
uncomely in face, lifeless, apathetic, a race a good deal more like the
pre-Revolution French peasant as described by Carlyle than is pleasant
to reflect upon – a race now supplanted . . .

For some of them even the rough sex-life of many of their contemporaries is not yet possible; it requires more management of
their own personalities and more meeting with other personalities
than they can compass.

From their education at school they have taken little which connects with the realities of life as they experience it after fifteen. Most
of them have jobs which require no personal outgoing, which are not
intrinsically interesting, which encourage no sense of personal value,

of being a maker. The job is to be done day by day, and after that the rest is amusement, is pleasure; there is time to spare and some money in the pocket. They are ground between the millstones of technocracy and democracy; society gives them an almost limitless freedom of the sensations, but makes few demands on them – the use of their hands and of a fraction of their brains for forty hours a week. For the rest they are open to the entertainers and their efficient mass-equipment. The youth clubs, the young people's institutes, the sports clubs, cannot attract them as they attract many in their generation; and the commercial people ensure, by the inevitable processes of development in commercial entertainment, that their peculiar grip is retained and strengthened. The responsibilities of marriage may gradually change them. Meanwhile, they have no responsibilities, and little sense of responsibilities, to themselves or to others. They are in one dreadful sense the new workers; if, by extrapolation simply from a reading of newer working-class entertainment literature, one were to attempt to imagine the ideal readers for that literature, these would be the people. It is true, as I have said, that they are not typical. But these are the figures some important contemporary forces are tending to create, the directionless and tamed helots of a machine-minding class. If they seem to consist so far chiefly of those of poorer intelligence or from homes subject to special strains, that is probably due to the strength of a moral fibre which most cultural providers for working-class people are helping to de-nature. The hedonistic but passive barbarian who rides in a fifty-horse-power bus for threepence, to see a five-million-dollar film for one-and-eightpence, is not simply a social oddity; he is a portent.

B. *The 'Spicy' Magazines*

What are such men likely to read, apart from picture-dailies, the more sensational Sunday papers and newspaper/magazines? The public library has no appeal, nor even perhaps those stationers' four-penny libraries whose main function is to hold a large stock of the kinds of fiction – 'Crime' or 'Tec' or 'Mystery', 'Westerns', and 'Romance' or 'Love', as the shelves are usually headed – of which the public libraries never have enough copies. One needs to look rather at those 'magazine shops' of which there is always one in every large working-class shopping-area. Their window-space is littered and over-hung with paper-backs in varying stages of disintegration, since they operate a system of exchanges – an expensive one, usually, since paper-backs originally costing two shillings change hands at sixpence a time. Here, too, there is a rough division of material into three themes – Crime, Science Fiction, and Sex novelettes.

I noted from one window on one day the following characteristics of the main groups; the magazines were not displayed in their sections, of course, but in the usual profuse disorder:

A. *Crime*. The prevailing note here, since most are from America and have been published since the American outcry against magazines which seemed to glorify crime, is that 'Crime Doesn't Pay'. They are likely to have sub-titles such as , 'Published in the cause of the Reduction of Crime'. Whatever the formal professions, the interest and excitement remain all with the gangster, or the detectives are temperamentally gangsters who chance to be on the side of the law. Titles run on these lines:

Super Detective	F.B.I. Crime Cases
H.Q. Police Stories	Thrilling Police Cases
True Detective	Secret Detective Stories
Crime Unlimited	Top-Flight Detective Tales
Smashing Police Stories	Candid Camera Detective
Hot-Spot Police Tales	

The format is almost always the same; flat paper, crude print, vivid glossy cover: obviously there is much 'ghosting' and interchange of material.

B. *Science*. Here the titles ring the changes on, 'Science', 'Space Science' and 'Spaceways', with adjectival support from, 'Startling', 'Weird', 'Future', 'Astounding', 'Fantastic', 'Super', 'Thrilling', and 'Authentic'.

Again, the same flat paper with glossy covers. This is the sort of science fiction which preceded, and presumably goes on unaffected by, the elevation of some writing on similar themes into a subject for serious discussion in the literary weeklies. The manner and situations are alike extremely limited. In most stories there is a nubile girl, dressed in what a costume-designer for a second-class touring revue might be expected to consider a 'futuristic' outfit. This usually means a very short and pleated white skirt, and an abbreviated top incorporating some sort of modernistic motif. This is 'sex stuff' with zip-fasteners instead of the old-fashioned blouses and skirts; vicarious fornication (with no details) on a spaceship moving between Mars and Venus.

Of the third group, the sex-novelettes, I shall say more, separately. These three groups cover almost the whole non-periodical stock of my specimen shop and the others of its kind. The old 'Westerns' and 'Boxing', which would have been major groups twenty years ago, exist only on the fringes today.

These magazines appear to have a particular appeal, I have suggested, for adolescents of below the average intelligence and for others who, for one reason or other, have not developed or do not feel themselves adequate. The advertisements are predominantly compensatory. This may be a convenient place at which to digress briefly about compensatory advertising of the more elementary kind, which constantly appears both in the type of magazine now being discussed and in a much wider range of periodicals.

At their simplest such advertisements appeal to a sense of physical inferiority, they urge the reader to learn how to stop smoking and so acquire a clearer eye and brain, a steadier and firmer hand grip; 'Be Tall', they urge, 'Build Your Physique', 'Why Be Scraggy?', 'Glowing Vitality for *You*', '*They* took my course...' says an extremely muscular advertiser, 'and look at the difference in *Them*! *You* send for details and I'll give *You* a husky body.'

From there it is a short step to the nerve-advertisements, and the inferiority-complex advertisements:

Do you suffer from nervousness, inferiority-feeling, lack of confidence, stammering, failure of necessary poise, hesitation and humility? – all these indicate a fundamental maladjustment arising from a SUBCONSCIOUS FAILURE OF NERVE-ORIENTATION

Learn to generate POSITIVE instead of NEGATIVE Drives! Create for yourself a DOMINANT and ASSERTIVE personality!

or to some things which seem even more powerful:

IT SEEMS INCREDIBLE

How far have YOU tapped your own immense forces of potential development?

DO YOU WISH TO? [A modernistic drawing is likely to appear here of a male figure with rays of vital force streaming from him.]

Then free them and control them—from the day you master this amazing system.

USE to the full your own ASTONISHING HIDDEN DYNAMIC! This volume can REDIRECT YOUR LIFE.

Often the same organization makes both the basic appeals (are you simply nerve-ridden?) and those more positive, where the sense of inadequacy is not so strongly stressed, but still it is assumed that you would like to win more friends and influence more people. You may discover how to do so by paying, say, £2 for a book on 'The secret of successful personality-selling'. New ones, making even bigger and better claims and with yet more dynamic titles and similarly large prices, come out at frequent intervals:

Is life giving YOU the rewards you want and deserve? Do you want to go on living fruitlessly and purposelessly . . . nagged by timidity and fear?

If not, here is the solution you seek.

From it you will win money, power, fame, and the esteem of all your acquaintance [a strange echo of the close of Freud's twenty-third Introductory Lecture, on the artist as a self-rewarding phantast – 'He has won – through this phantasy – what before he could win only in phantasy: honour, power and the love of women.' Stranger still, how such a would-be resounding final chord sounds a thin egocentric echo to Bacon on 'the farthest end of knowledge': 'for the glory of the Creator, and the relief of man's estate'].

To return to the magazines themselves: there are a number of 'spicy', 'off-the-shoulder' periodicals, or sex-and-bittiness weeklies and monthlies, whose bark is in an illuminating way much worse than their bite. They can be bought from almost any newsagent, not only from the 'magazine shops', and some of them have considerable sales. I have not been able to find figures of their distributions by class, but know them to be popular among working-class and lower middle-class young men.

They are, first, repositories of jokes, many of them illustrated and with the emphasis on very obvious, limited, and only moderately exceptionable sexual innuendoes. Each of them usually has a cross-word, a page on sport, fortune-telling-by-the-stars, and short-short stories. The stories might be expected, from the layout and drawings, to be sexy, but prove to be as domestically whimsical as those in a modern women's home magazine. The narrator is a young man who is either not long married or, to judge from the mildness of his whistles after the girls, won't be long before he settles down with a decent lass.

Nowadays there is sometimes a film-serial, with décolleté photographic illustrations. For the rest, there are a great many drawings of various sizes, with jokes underneath. Most of these magazines aim to be very smart and modern, although in general their layout is hardly slicker than that of some family magazines. They establish their claim to modernity and sophistication largely by using artists in the newer style. Their pages have not, therefore, the quieter domestic lines of the older magazine artists, but rather those of the Englishmen who have learned from the Americans, notably from Varga. There have to be photographic pin-ups, and in the absence of a considerable use of colour photography and some of the more expensive devices which help their rivals, most of these magazines seem to try to ensure that their photographs shall be as daring as possible and that the models really shall appear to be coming right out of the page at the reader.

They are all consciously sexy-naughty, aware that they are being daring, having a bit of a fling, at least in their illustrations. But obviously one can feel like that only by assuming the existence of values which one is flouting. There is little that is ingrown or overheated about these magazines; they belong to the same world as the older women's magazines, after all. The strongest objection is not to their sexiness but, as so often with the newer kinds of magazine, to their triviality: they get the thrill of naughtiness so easily and on such slight and spurious evidence.

There exists a number of more narrowly working-class magazines which, partly because of their local and specific character, differ strikingly from the group I have just described. None of them seem to have long lives, but new magazines in the same tradition appear almost as soon as police action has led to the closing of their predecessors. Usually, they appear monthly and sell for sixpence. I shall describe the character of some which circulate mainly in the north, but there are local magazines of a similar type in the south. The more successful northern magazines may be bought, to my knowledge, from Manchester to Hull and from Middlesbrough to Nottingham. At least one reached a sale of more than one hundred thousand copies of each issue, which suggests a readership of not less than one-third of a million. This particular magazine was certainly read predominantly by members of the urban working-classes in the north-east.

The composition of each issue of a magazine of this type is very simple. There is usually a small sports item, something on films, an odd short-short story (meant to look sexy, but really pure froth), and a few advertisements (for lucky charms and the like). The rest of the space is generally devoted to jokes, printed plain in double columns, and to drawings, either illustrating the jokes or in their own right, because they are suggestive. There are not many photographs of models, perhaps – this is a guess – because they would be too expensive. Instead, these magazines tend to use for their more important illustrations, for those which take the place of the photographic pin-ups in the more elaborate magazines, drawings which seem to have been executed originally in heavily-shaded pencilling and then photographed. The final effect is roughly similar to that of the usual photographic pin-ups. Photographed drawings have this further advantage, I imagine; that the artist, who usually works in the Varga idiom, can let himself go on what he regards as suitable parts of the girls' bodies so as to produce a picture even more boldly suggestive than the normal photographic pin-up. One such magazine used to make a particular feature of accentuating the nipples as they protruded underneath a dress. Similarly, the breasts can be very boldly shaped and divided.

In general, these magazines belong to the world of the dirtier picture-postcards; they have a similar vulgarity and a similarly circumscribed view of the possible situations for humour – backsides, 'jerries', knickers, 'belly buttons', breasts (and now 'falsies', the most popular new feature in all the sex-joke magazines). They may be a little cruder than the postcards. When I say this, I am not thinking of such features as the outstanding nipples and the implausibly swelling thighs. The crudest element in all these magazines is usually the drawing of the girls' faces, especially in the larger studies; they are of a quality I have not seen in the postcards. They have a large-mouthed and brassy vulgarity of expression. I do not think I am speaking here of something which a more generous spirit would recognize as 'rough but earthy gusto, the Chaucerian touch'. This is a pseudo-sophisticated and knowing urban coarseness which it would be a romantic folly to mistake for anything else. These magazines hold their readers, I should guess, by the peculiar suggestiveness of their photographed drawings, and by a certain recognizable quality in the faces and properties shown in them. I open one issue at a double-page drawing of a girl in shorts, with a hugely plunging neckline to her blouse, club-riding on a sports bicycle as so many girls from the northern towns do at weekends. She has unmistakably the face of the one in most large groups of working-class girls who blatantly 'knows what it's for'. In this very restricted sense, in a limited realism of expression, these magazines belong to the working-classes in a way that the nationally distributed 'spicy' magazines – and the popular modern magazine/newspapers for that matter – do not.

c. *Sex-and-violence Novels*

I would emphasize the symbolical fact that we have stopped making formal declarations of love at the very time we have allowed wars to begin without any declaration either. We are returning to the age of abduction and rape, though minus the ritual that has surrounded such violence in Polynesia.

DE ROUGEMONT

The 'blood-and-guts' sex-novelettes can be bought not only from the 'magazine shops' but from some railway-bookstalls. They are usually in a corner, all together, lying beneath the cards of aspirin and the styptic pencils. There are the dailies and weeklies, the welter of little 'hobbies' and 'handicrafts' magazines, the Penguins and the Pelicans; and then the sex-novelettes – they all make a picture of some of the stresses inside our culture. The regular presence of the sex-books indicates, I suppose, that railway-reading can be a release-valve for people who would 'not be seen going into' one of the 'magazine-shops', and would hardly take this kind of book into the house. But boundaries move so quickly that within the last five or six years many ordinary stations have begun to stock this sort of paper-back; they are ceasing to be even slightly furtive reading.

These novelettes do not stand alone as social portents. They are one element, in my view the most striking, in a general trend. Related elements are those sex-and-violence serials which some of the more sophisticated papers run. Such papers began, I think, by selectively serializing the latest marathon sex-and-history novels from America. But perhaps the supply of these was inadequate, or perhaps they required too much editing or were too expensive.

Whatever the cause, it was not long before serials on the established pattern were being specially written – as far as possible with one item of sexual excitement and one suggestive drawing in each instalment. If an instalment would not easily lend itself to a suitable illustration, the heroine (so often a twentieth-century Moll Flanders trained in bourgeois preservative-ethics by the middle-aged heroine of a radio soap-opera) could always be shown facing the future starkly as she left her bed in the morning. Again, one might trace the development in the detective as a character from those in the early Edgar Wallace stories to those in the most popular of the stiff-backed gangster novels today. The later detective is often a low-fronted tough, distinguishable from the crooks he opposes chiefly in that he happens to oppose them, and in that he displays, at suitable moments, the fashionable streak of soft sentiment: his manners, his brutality, his sexual code, his general attitude to experience, are all those of an exhibitionist delinquent.

To appreciate more closely the exact quality of the later paper-backed novelettes of sex-adventure (they usually call themselves simply 'gangster-fiction'), one should compare them with an earlier type. When I was adolescent we used to be offered, if we wanted a 'spicy' book, novels by writers with indubitably French names – such as Pierre Laforgue, to invent one in the usual style. From the number of books attributed to each author and the likenesses between them, it seems probable that much 'ghosting' went on. Perhaps the publishers held a few names as garages hold their 'trade' number-plates, and affixed them to scripts which conformed to pattern. These stories had, and still have – I bought some a few weeks ago, dated 1947 – 'flat' paper, uncertain print, and a coloured picture on the cover. On the cover, as throughout, the atmosphere is more Edwardian than mid-century. The authors' names establish the tone, which is that of a mild naughtiness popularly associated with the idea of 'la Gay Paree'. The cover-ladies affect immutably the fashions of thirty or forty years ago; they peep through titles such as *Stolen Joys*, *Dangerous Bliss*, and *Passionate Nights*. They are the soft and wilting victims on ottomans of dark handsome men (with names like Raoul) in dressing-gowns. It is all very much a nursemaid-naughtiness, the sex of the boudoir, soft as a house-trained cat: it makes much of wisps of lace and mouths in a moue, and dissolves into dots at the slightest sign of potential impropriety.

Since the mid-thirties this group has been almost entirely ousted by a new style in sex-novels spreading from America. They may well have been inspired by the appearance of books such as *The Postman Always Rings Twice* (1934), by James M. Cain; and there are similarities in the work of Mickey Spillane, a more recent American writer. But their roots spread more widely and deeply than that.

In their paper, in their style of printing, and in the fact that they have glossy covers, these newer novelettes are like the old; they sell at one-and-sixpence or two shillings, as the others do now. Thereafter, the differences are considerable. The new-style stories are recognizable, first, by their terse, periodic titles. Almost every one is a complete phrase or sentence, as in these imitations:

Sweetie, Take it Hot   The Lady Takes a Dive
Broads [Girls] Don't Like Lead
Don't Tempt Me, Hotsy   Baby, Here's Your Corpse
Death-Cab for Cutie   Aim Low, Angel
Miss Fandown Takes the Drop
Sugar, Rods [Guns] Don't Talk Back
The Killer Wore Nylon (like the pin-up photographers, these authors are fond of nylon)
Sweetheart, Curves Can Kill
No Talk from Tombstones
Lady, it's Cold Down There.

The authors are usually American or pseudo-American, after the manner of the American shirt-shops in the Charing Cross Road. Most of them have 'tough' names, with forenames in the style of Hank, Al, Babe, Brad, and Butch. Two authors charged with writing books of this kind explained in court that their pen-names had been provided by their publishers. Various firms, mostly in London, publish the books; they seem either to buy the rights from America or to make use of English authors.

In comparison with the cover-girls here, those of Pierre Laforgue are homely. These are the lush but 'gone wrong' descendants of those Varga girls who decorated servicemen's billets from Kirkwall to Kuala Lumpur. Their blouses sag permanently where the last attempt at rape was beaten off; they hold not a cigarette but a smoking 'rod'; they have hanging lower lips and weals; they 'go in and out in the right places', and not by half-measures; they have 'got what it takes', which means huge thighs, prominent nipples, and 'straining breasts'.

Their authors' favourite descriptive epithet for them is 'sexational': one hesitates to think what they would do to a Pierre Laforgue lady.

They would undoubtedly be violent, because these are novels of violent sex, in which sex seems to be regarded as thrilling only when it is sadistic. There must be violence all the time: between the men, prolonged arm-twistings, razor-slashings, long-drawn-out beatings with rubber tubes: 'He had a wound in his cheek that looked like a mouth that wouldn't stop bleeding.' When man meets woman the air is heavy with violence, with drug-inspired moans, with embraces ending in bloody bites on both sides (the usual number seems to be two violent sexual contacts in each novel, as well as a few single-sex beatings-up); tongues get fiercely to work and finger-nails claw: 'all the time her hips kept going like they had a dynamo inside there . . . she'd pull away, then she'd purr like a pussy when I snatched her back again.'

There has been a literature of sexual adventure for centuries; one thinks of Nashe's *Unfortunate Traveller*, in one of its aspects, or of Defoe's *Moll Flanders*. There has been a literature of violence: there has been, on a small and esoteric scale, a literature of sadism and masochism. But this new form is rather different. This is not produced for a small and perverse set such as made their own use of the works of the Marquis de Sade. It has a wider appeal at its own level. It differs from the sex and violence of Nashe and Defoe in its ingrown quality: it is violent and sexual, but all in a claustrophobic and shut-in way.

Further, and here it contrasts strikingly with the writing of such as Pierre Laforgue, it exists in a world in which moral values have become irrelevant. The Laforgue books have often titles like, *Should He Forgive?*, *Shameful Payment*, *Fallen Beauty*, *Sullied Madonna*, *Bought Kisses*, and *Retribution*. Such titles would be almost impossible for these later works, since 'forgiveness', 'shame', 'retribution', and 'to be sullied', 'to fall', or 'to pay' are concepts outside their moral orbit. In a list of fifty-five works by one author I found only one title which had a moral reference. In one novel from the Laforgue school a handsome young man, making up to an unattached girl who is stranded for the night in his house, writes a poem. It proves to be a piece of feeble Georgian verse. But neither the men nor the women in the later works ever heard of poetry, except perhaps when they were scaring the life out of their teachers for a few unprofitable

years at school; and their authors would as soon have them mention
poetry as they would have them take a youth club for a camping
holiday. If a Laforgue man and woman came together, with an
attraction on each side, one has something after this fashion:

His breast was throbbing against her as he tightened his embrace.
Her eyes were like liquid flames. At that moment she was intensely
feminine.

'You are all mine, my darling. How I love you,' he murmured.

She gave a low cry of blissful ecstasy, followed by a long sigh of
utter happiness, and pressed him hotly to her. Her warm arms em-
braced him yet more closely. There was no hesitation, no shame and
no regret in her soul as she led him silently towards the bedroom. . . .

Cliché-ridden and soggy romanticizing: but this is how later
couples are likely to come together, when they own to an attraction:

So she was no more than a little girl, huh? So I was just a heel and
a lowdown jerk? So what!

All at once her body was pressing firm and yet trembling against
me under that scanty dress. I could feel every line and curve of her.
How hard can a girl press up to a guy, brother? Why do a dame's
tears taste so good?

I started to open her dress fiercely, but I was all thumbs with excitement. She showed me how, in between a mixture of whimpers and
passionate gasps. And then . . . we met, like a pair of savage animals.

If a couple come together without love in a Laforgue novel (she
has to do so for the money, or is for some other reason in his power),
there is usually a vague pointing towards the exciting horrors ahead:

'I have to go . . . I have to go . . .', she repeated endlessly to herself.
Her mind was a turmoil as the words echoed through it. 'Tonight
. . . at 10 . . . in the Regal [an hotel]. *And then* . . .'

'And then' no doubt she will have to submit to the embraces of
an unscrupulous theatrical manager. But that is the end of a chapter,
and when we meet her again, six months are likely to have passed
and her husband will be about to come home to find her apparently
faithless. If a Laforgue type of novel decides to go further it will
produce, before the dots take over, an undressing scene ending like
this: 'she lifted the last veil of modesty'. The later novels do not want
to end there, but if they did they would have to use different phrases.
If there is nothing toward which you can feel naughty, then a phrase

like 'veil of modesty' is without meaning; 'there ain't no such thing' as modesty. So, when a new-style man and woman come together without love they do so as physical enemies:

I guess she knew just what was happening to me as she lay there rubbing her knees together, like a cat against a trouser-leg.

'Are you going to ask me nicely,' she said, in a kinda soft purring voice, 'an' say you're sorry for the scrap we had?'

Gee, bud, some dames don't know the rules. . . .

'Listen,' I said, 'the way I treat dames there's no place for "sorry" – or for "please".'

She grinned and lay back some more, with her breasts still heaving after the scrap. I could feel the blood beginning to beat in my head.

'Honey-baby,' I said, 'you got it coming right to you. And no fancy-talk by way of prelims either.'

She didn't budge as I leaned over and tore off her dress in one. Then her négligée – that split like a burst sheath. I guess she thought passive resistance would beat me, so she went all stiff.

But now it was my turn to see plenty – and this time her eyes had a kinda excited fear in them. But she still wasn't for moving, and that made things sorta difficult at first. So I whipped my belt off and strapped her arms to the bedhead. Then I kissed her, hard; she bit back at me till the blood spurted from my lips.

By this time I sure was wild. And she – she was moaning and frantic with passion. 'Cut me free – tear me,' she moaned, I tore her alright – all strapped up, just like that.

It will be seen that the style is debased Hemingway, the word-bound tough-ox or hairy urban-ape, who gets along with a clipped minimal vocabulary. 'Kinda' is used much, to preserve the tough, corner-of-the-mouth quality at moments when the author wishes to use phrases too literary or 'soft' for the male narrator. 'She said, in a soft purring voice' or, 'her eyes had an excited fear in them' would probably be felt to be unusable without this modification. Or the hairy ape can express the full excitement or horror of his experiences only by reductive inversion: 'she wasn't exactly overdressed, that baby'; or, 'after the boys had done with him, he didn't exactly look pretty'.

Underneath, yet coming out occasionally, is the streak of senti-mentality to be found in many contemporary tough heroes, in fiction at all levels. Here the standard attitude-linking phrase is, 'I may be lousy (rough/rugged/a heel) . . . but I ain't quite that kind of guy.'

Thus, a male narrator may slug and fornicate his way through fifteen chapters. He is probably searching for his lady-friend, since many of the narrators spend their time looking for their kidnapped loves. He finds her, and mercilessly beats up her captors. But she by then is dead – shot through the stomach whilst being used as a naked shield by her gaolers. Or perhaps she is alive but reveals that all the time she has loved some mousy jerk down-town. The narrator takes that – there's some things a guy don't kick against, brother. He is on his beam-ends now, without money and with no prospect of work in that area; he is once again disconnected, on the loose. At this moment there often appears what must be the modern equivalent of the stray mongrel which gave comfort to so many wanderers in Victorian melodrama. In these stories there is usually a half-wit gangsters' stooge, or a 'floozie', who has been an unwilling appendage to the kidnappers' establishment and is now released – and lost – after the carnage. The story is then likely to end in this manner:

Never know when I'm well out of the dirt, that's me. I tried to go tough on her, but I found I kinda couldn't [this, too, must be the equivalent of the melodramatic villain's secret tear at the voice of the little orphan]. I could tell I was going to make another loony proposition.
'O.K. . . . O.K. . . .' I said. 'So there's room in the car . . . so two can live as cheaply as one . . . for a few days, anyways. . . .
'. . . alright. Think nothing of it. Put it down to the way I happen to be built, that's all.'

So they both climb aboard the car, and head for the next state. My impression, which I am unable to illustrate in the text (my examples have had to be invented), is that the more popular of these writers are much more powerful as writers than their predecessors. This may seem puzzling at first, but I think the explanation is related to that lack of moral reference already noticed. There is, of course, a certain amount of ostensible moral reference; 'crooks' are defeated in the end, and so on. But it is no part of the texture of the writing, is in fact implicitly denied by that. The Laforgue writers really belong to the same world as the writers for the older women's magazines; or, like the authors in the 'spicy' weeklies, they are naughtily disobeying the edicts of that world just as the writers in the women's magazines are obediently upholding them. But both recognize the edicts. The thrill, such as it is, comes from appearing to flout the edicts. Just as the women's-magazine writers have simply to point to the stock moral situations by using the stock moral clichés, so the Laforgue writers have simply to point to the stock immoral situations by using the stock clichés of immorality. It is all no more than a mild excitement-of-situation derived from the relation of these situations to an agreed code. Therefore the writing can be, and almost always is, perfectly flat, a mere pressing-down of the known keys to produce the required moral/immoral play of relations.

But the aim of the later writers is to make their readers feel the flesh and bone of violence. They cannot invoke the stock and formal thrills of anti-code behaviour, since there is no code: they must directly stir their readers' senses. They are, therefore, oddly enough and in a very limited way, much more in the situation of the truly creative writer towards his material than are writers of the Laforgue type, or the writers of love-stories in the women's magazines, or the writers of naughty stories in the 'spicy' magazines. The gangster writers have to ensure that the physical thrill is actually communicated:

Suddenly Fatsy brought his knee hard up into Herb's groin. Herb's face came down sharp and Fatsy met it with his ham-like fist. The knuckles splintered the bone and made blood and flesh squelch like a burst pomegranate. Herb fell back to the tiled floor, retching teeth. He was bubbiing gently as he lay there, so Fatsy gave him one in the belly with his steel-shod shoe. Then – just for luck – Fatsy ground his foot straight on to the squelchy mess that useter be Herb's face.

The writing at places such as this has often a kind of power; it strums on the nerves of the readers. But it is a narrow power; when it moves away from the situations which excite it falls into banality. One author has explained how much he enjoys 'living through' the fights and sex-encounters he writes about, in terms which suggest that the 'living through' is a very intimate matter. The statement seems to throw light on the limited but undeniable power of novels such as these; on, to name only one example, the monstrously effective passages in one novel where the narrator has sexual combat with a fat, dirty, and sweating nymphomaniac.

The possible power, as well as the narrowness and the banality, of this kind of writing may be seen from a comparison of a typical gangster-fiction novel with William Faulkner's *Sanctuary*. *Sanctuary* was published in 1931, and some features of it may well have been taken as models by the first writers in the new style. An extract from *Sanctuary* is given here, immediately after a longer imitation of gangster-fiction writing, one typical of the crucial scenes in many of these novels:

And all the time old Liz squatted near the fire, like a moulting old parrot. Her eyes were nearly lost in circles of puffy fat with red rings round them. Her cheeks were cracked in lines where some white powder had stuck on and gone dirty. Her stockings were rolled down to her knees, and her knees were white like uncooked pastry. She wore an old purple lace dress, tight and bulgy round her sack-like body. Her hands were like hams going blue and bad.

'Time we fixed up Molony,' said Lefty at last.

He tossed away the butt of his cigarette and went over to where Molony was fastened to the centre-post. Molony had pretty well recovered from that smack on the carotid artery when he'd gone black and dropped. By now his face was just yellow and strained with panic, and his eyes stuck out like a strangled rabbit's.

'You can't do this to me, Lefty,' he said.

Lefty went up to Molony and carefully showed him the knife; then let him see it placed against his stomach. Then Lefty pressed gently but firmly like a butcher going into steak. He was still grinning straight into Molony's eyes when Molony let out one rattling scream and sagged. Lefty sniggered then, pulled out the knife and wiped it very carefully. 'Now for the dame,' he said.

The girl felt herself retching with horror as the waves of panic and pain succeeded each other. Between whiles Butch had been slapping her hard across the eyes with his open hand, and every so often he'd made as though to drive his knee into her groin.

By now her dress was torn down to her stomach and her négligée ripped and soiled. As her almost naked breasts rose and fell, Lefty, from near the stove, watched out of the corner of his eyes and every so often spat deliberately into the embers. After a while the red waves of pain began to overwhelm her, but just before she went under she saw Lefty get up with a new and horrible look in his eyes. . . . She began giving little agonized gurgling sounds and her legs twitched in spasms.

In a similarly crucial scene in *Sanctuary*, Temple is taken by Popeye to Miss Reba's brothel to be concealed:

She drank beer, breathing thickly into the tankard, the other hand, ringed with yellow diamonds as large as gravel, lost among the lush billows of her breast. . . .

Almost as soon as they entered the house she began to tell Temple about her asthma, toiling up the stairs in front of them, planting her feet heavily in worsted bedroom slippers, a wooden rosary in one hand and the tankard in the other. She had just returned from church, in a black silk gown and a hat savagely flowered; the lower half of the tankard was still frosted with inner chill. She moved heavily from big thigh to thigh, the two dogs moiling underfoot, talking steadily back across her shoulder in a harsh, expiring, maternal voice.

'Popeye knew better than to bring you anywhere else but to my house. I been after him for, how many years I been after you to get you a girl, honey? What I say, a young fellow can't no more live without a girl than . . .' Panting, she fell to cursing the dogs under her feet, stopping to shove them aside. 'Get back down there,' she said, shaking the rosary at them. They snarled at her in vicious falsetto, baring their teeth, and she leaned against the wall in a thin aroma of beer, her hand to her breast, her mouth open, her eyes fixed in a glare of sad terror of all breathing as she sought breath, the tankard a squat soft gleam like dull silver lifted in the gloom.

The narrow stairwell turned back upon itself in a succession of niggard reaches. The light, falling though a thickly-curtained door at the front and through a shuttered window at the rear of each stage, had a weary quality, a spent quality; defunctive, exhausted – a protracted weariness like a vitiated backwater beyond sunlight and the vivid noises of sunlight and day. There was a defunctive odour of irregular food, vaguely alcoholic, and Temple even in her ignorance seemed to be surrounded by a ghostly promiscuity of intimate garments, of discreet whispers of flesh stale and oft-assailed and impregnable beyond each silent door which they passed. Behind her, about hers and Miss Reba's feet, the two dogs scrabbled in nappy gleams, their claws clicking on the metal strips which bound the carpet to the stairs.

Gangster-fiction writing is in large measure dead, full of trite simile, weak imitation of tough American talk, and flatly photographic description. It moves in jerky, short-winded periods which match the thinness and one-sidedness of the imaginative presentation. Yet it undoubtedly has in parts a kind of life. When it is describing the thrill of inflicting pain, it sometimes moves closely along the nerve. It moves then with a crude force as it creates the sadistic situation; the images cease to be clichés and catch the nerve-thrill. It turns directly on to its object and immerses itself in the detail of pain. At such moments it has the life of a cruel cartoon, and presents a similarly two-dimensional and lop-sided picture of experience.

Sanctuary is admittedly an early pot-boiler; yet one can see in it the marks of a serious and disinterested creative writer. A gifted, varied, and complex perception is at work, picking up sights, smells, noises, and weaving them together in a scene of some complexity – the squalid and grotesque and withal pathetic atmosphere of the place; the dreadful, garish, and yet near-comic figure of Miss Reba; the terror of the girl held by the man, led up the stairs of that place, encompassed by the bizarre maternal quality of the old bawd. Faulkner is seeing, smelling, hearing, responding round and through the experience.

And his language stretches and strains to meet the demands of the emotional situation; words and images become alive as they explore its nature. Rhythms and periods evolve and become complex, as they seek to suggest its complexity. So, to change the metaphor, the prose acquires a stronger texture, more 'body', than that of gangster-fiction. The Faulkner passage has had to discover this texture so as to convey the sense of a larger pattern. He sees beyond the rape. The horror is real, and the more real because there is, implicit in the passage, a sense of a saner world outside, of sunlight and sanity. That sense gives a moral perspective to the whole passage. We see the horror as it is, without intermediate moral comment, but we see it for what it is only because of this larger sense, embracing and surrounding it all the time, of an order without.

With the gangster-fiction writing we are not aware of a larger pattern. We are in and of this world of the fierce alleyway-assault, the stale disordered bed, the closed killer-car, the riverside warehouse knifing. We thrill to those in themselves; there is no way out, nothing else; there is no horizon and no sky. The world, consciousness, man's ends, are this – this constricted and overheated horror.

Reliable figures of sales are not easy to obtain, but enough information is available for a fairly true estimate. The publishers make big claims. Of one book, they say that more than half a million copies have been sold. Since this is predominantly literature for passing from hand to hand, privately or through the magazine-shops, the total number of readers of this one book is not likely to be less than two million. A different firm of publishers claims to have sold more than three hundred thousand copies of another book. More than fifty titles have been produced in about six years by one author (or by several authors writing under the same name), and sales of nearly ten million are claimed for them. Of another author's books more than six million copies are said to have been sold in three years. Yet another author is reputed to have sold about one hundred thousand copies of each of his books, and to produce a new issue every five weeks – a total of one million new copies by one author in each year. And there are many such authors and publishers.

I began by thinking mainly of the juke-box boys, taking them as lay-figures in this discussion of the lower levels of reading among urban adolescents. To them can be added, I suggested, some married people and a large number of conscript servicemen who, more than the other groups, pass the books from hand to hand. At one trial which involved the publishers of some of these books it was claimed that there was an increasing demand for them from the Forces. Whether the demand is increasing I am not able to say, but my experience certainly indicates that a large demand already exists among servicemen. There are, of course, other readers of all ages: but these three groups seem likely to form the majority of readers for this kind of novelette.

It would be easy to try to relate the reading of these books to active delinquency but, so far as I know, no one has proved that such a relationship exists. And it seems to me, when I try to appreciate the nature of the power this writing has, that the effect on a reader is likely to be much more inward, to be more a matter of fantasies than of action. This kind of literature, in fact, seems to be the most advanced form so far produced of that more general group of writings which provide sensation-without-commitment.

Yet there is a striking difference between this kind of publication and those I described as 'ersatz' in their sensationalism. This sensationalism is blatantly and crudely real. I wonder whether the almost subterranean appearance of this kind of writing is in part due to an unconscious desire among many readers for a sensationalism less artificial than that found in the more widely and publicly disseminated productions. From this aspect these novels might be related to those local 'dirty' magazines whose peculiarly 'real' qualities I discussed above. The two types of production may be, though this is not their most important feature, answering an unconscious reaction from the artificiality of so much mass-sensationalism.

More importantly, it seems probable that the cheap sex-fiction has developed in the way illustrated partly because our great cities have become more crowded, and because a sense of direction has become harder to find in them. May there not be parallels between this kind of development in popular reading and some other more general social developments which are causing concern today? It is all one city from this point of view; the 'Spike' of these stories is the slower-witted half-brother of Kafka's 'K'. This is the popular literature of an empty megalopolitan world. It is related, in its submerged sense of a great hollow where some purpose might be, to elements in Ernest Hemingway. *A Farewell to Arms* closes with Henry leaving the hospital where Catherine has died:

> 'You can't come in now,' one of the nurses said.
> 'Yes, I can,' I said.
> 'You can't come in yet.'
> 'You get out,' I said, 'the other one too.'
> But after I had got them out and shut the door and turned off the light it wasn't any good. It was like saying goodbye to a statue. After a while I went out and left the hospital and walked back to the hotel in the rain.

A typical gangster-novelette is likely also to close with the narrator leaving the dead body of his love behind:

> When I saw Fan was dead and cold, I just turned away. Spikey was saying something over and over, but I only knew there was a great hollow inside of me. I left the joint and started walking. I walked a mighty long way in the cold night. In the end, Spikey overtook me. 'Come on, pal,' he said, 'there's a gang of us going on to Mike's place. The girls'll be glad to see you.' I didn't answer. Maybe I didn't really hear. I only knew I wanted to go on walking, walking alone in the night.

In both books that final emptiness, though it is in each case specifically related to a death, symbolizes also a much wider and more pervasive emptiness. Indeed, the girls can only mean so much because they have seemed the only meaningful things in a whole dis-illusioning world. The parallels of tone are in most cases striking. I ought to add, perhaps, that the efforts made by each type of passage are not so much alike as this comparison suggests. The effects are decided by all that has gone before in each novel. The similarities are illuminating here; but Hemingway's world, I need hardly say, is much more mature than that of the gangster-novelette authors.

In the world of ganster-fiction there can be no happy endings, nor any endings which are really beginnings, attempts to restart life by staying in the same spot and doing what you can to build the city. You either end in the flat emptiness just illustrated, or induce the temporary impression of a new start by getting into a fast machine and roaring away down a concrete highway (the characters are usually rootless, without homes or permanent work). The tyres scud on the surface, the demands of the city are left behind; the demands on the personality are – you continue to hope – left with it; you are heading West, to a world where there may still be the childhood dream. Not that you really think so, but you go on – progressivism translated into an endless and hopeless tail-chasing evasion of the personality. This is the usual manner:

So we quit that city and headed down the turnpike for the next. I was dead sick of that joint and the countryside sure looked good to me with the sun on it. I let the old Chev. full out and she roared down the concrete at a steady eighty. I kept on like that for I don't know how many hours – biting off the miles – heading for I don't know what. . . .

Running away from megalopolis; but in megalopolis's own product, the life-consuming machine. He'll be back; there is another town ahead, just the same as the others. After that, another escape; and so on, till sudden death puts an end to it. There comes to mind the ending, a century and a half ago, of *Sense and Sensibility*:

Between Barton and Delaford there was that constant communication which strong family affection would naturally dictate; and among the merits and the happiness of Elinor and Marianne let it not be ranked as the least considerable, that though sisters, and living almost within sight of each other, they could live without disagreement between themselves or producing coolness between their husbands.

CHAPTER 9

UNBENT SPRINGS: A NOTE ON A
SCEPTICISM WITHOUT TENSION

I perceive we have destroyed those independent beings who were able to cope with tyranny single-handed: . . . the poor man retains the prejudices of his forefathers without their faith, and their ignorance without their virtues; he has adopted the doctrine of self-interest as the rule of his actions. . . .

DE TOCQUEVILLE

A. *Scepticism to Cynicism*

I use the word 'cynicism' as a rough label for a group of attitudes more positive than those described in the two preceding chapters. These 'cynical' attitudes are not chiefly an accepting; they have something of active self-protection about them. I have referred to them incidentally more than once, but they require fuller attention, especially because they are frequently attacked by certain kinds of speaker – presidents of religious assemblies, headmasters on speech-days – in terms which seem often to suggest a failure to understand much of their nature. We are all familiar with reports of meetings at which the 'couldn't care less attitude of the modern generation' has been deplored. Is this attitude really typical of working-class people today? If so, in what forms and why?

I think there is a sense in which this spirit can be said to affect many working-class people, though it is not peculiar to them. It probably flourishes in the same climate as breeds indulgence. To recapitulate the relevant connecting-points from a previous chapter: democratic egalitarianism can encourage a suspicion of all authority and responsibility; the notion of unmodified progress can encourage a band-wagon mentality. But the band-wagon seems sometimes to be heading only towards more complex dangers. One remains on the wagon but in a divided mood. There is still progress, but one believes and yet does not believe in it. There is still freedom, but a sense of unlimited freedom for its own sake can have a way of going bad on people. 'Anything goes' may sound gay, but can be a verbal posture inspired by fear. Indifferentism is likely to follow, with its own kind of tyranny. If all are of equal value, nothing is of

225

much worth. There is in the end an emptiness and a purposelessness indicated by such phrases as, 'what's the use?', and 'who cares?'; nothing seems to 'add up'.

Yet behind the modern forms of this apparent cynicism one may also see something of that earlier noncomformity, of scepticism towards public and 'boss-class' assertions of good intent. On this healthier side the currently popular, 'I'm not buying that' is linked to the traditional spirit of 'I do not conform' (though this exact phrase was never typical of the working-classes). The contemporary cynical mockery connects with the older debunking and comic art. The refusal to accept any publicly offered values is related to the old pragmatic and unidealistic root. The refusal to admit any exceptionableness is a distortion of the older refusal to bow down before pomposity and officialdom. Thus Pip and Joe, at the beginning of *Great Expectations* – to choose one example from hundreds – automatically hope that King George's men will not catch the prisoners escaped from the hulks.

In its newer uses, 'I'm not buying that' can often be a flat refusal ever to 'buy' anything. The earlier 'I do not conform' was often a positive assertion that official standards would not be accepted, because they ran counter to other standards, held by individuals and believed to be higher. The new attitude is frequently a refusal to consider any values, because all values are suspect. 'I dissent' becomes 'It's all boloney', a mockery of all principles and a willingness to destroy them. Cheerful debunking becomes an acid refusal to believe in anything. Anti-authoritarianism becomes not merely a nonconformity nourished by a sense of the value of personal and individual life, but a refusal to accept at all the idea of authority: 'I'm not going to be used like a dog' becomes 'I'm not going to be bossed around by anyone'; and there, as elsewhere, the tone is as important as the words.

I am not suggesting, therefore, that such attitudes are new. Indeed, many of the phrases used here are centuries old. Even, 'I'm aboard, Jack, pull up the ladder', has been in use in a variety of forms for at least half a century; and 'wide', used in much the same way as in 'wide boy' today, dates from 1887.

I am suggesting that the use of such attitudes appears to have been extended latterly, as a saving armour against a world which is in much suspected, in spite of its obvious improvements; an armour behind which most of the wearers are puzzled before they are self-indulgent. Where domestic or personal roots are weak or have been forcibly broken, these attitudes can quickly lead to an extensive moral 'spivvery'.

It seems to me that these attitudes are at present still employed mainly for contact with the world outside, with those who are not 'Us'. We are back with the double view, once again strengthened. The failure to 'connect' increases; at a time when so much is expected of each man as a citizen, the springs with which he might irrigate that part of life are infected at the source. 'The mass man,' says Ortega y Gasset, 'is simply without morality.' Yet that is only generally true of the 'mass man' as a mass man, as the 'common man'; it is untrue of him as an individual, living a life which has some recognizable meaning to him. And he continues to wish for connections between the two kinds of life. Thus, spontaneous and strong applause greets the member of a B.B.C. team who contributes to a discussion on 'our present difficulties' (after the political and economic members have spoken) his conviction that what we really need is 'a change of heart'. He has touched the submerged wish for rules of conduct which are 'straighforward', which are associated with the thought of religion and which apply to public as firmly as to private life.

But very frequently, as we all know, one meets the assumption that in public 'anything goes' (sometimes reinforced by something of a desire to 'get yer own back'); the assumption which makes people ready to cheat in outside matters where in local matters they are normally honest; the tradition of 'seeing y' pals alright', which usually means cheating those outside, for whom you work, so as to show loyalty towards the group you know personally. You will not fiddle from your mate, but you will flog anything you safely can from the 'firm' or the Services. You will not twist a neighbour, but a middle-class customer is fair game. I remember a young working-class wife being offered by the British Legion the cost of a house-removal. The man who carried out the move for her with a horse and cart suggested that they should double the charge, claim on the Legion, and split the difference. This was done, and for all I know the man may have regularly employed the trick. I should guess that most of his customers could have been as easily persuaded, and were otherwise as honest, as the one I knew. The public, the 'outside', eye was being used; 'the Legion' was as anonymous as the old Board of Guardians, and you naturally got what you could from them. It would have seemed 'soft' not to do so and, by refusing, you might have embarrassed the flesh-and-blood man who stood before you and seemed so helpful. It would seem a bit silly to strike attitudes about such things; everyone does them every day; and other promptings could be muffled by the use of such phrases as 'a *quiet* fiddle' or 'a *gentle* fiddle'.

At any period this, too, will be among the attitudes of working-class people. After all, they feel, this kind of thing is done to them, who have so little to sell or exchange, most of the time. But it appears to be strengthened now by a suspicion that there is no principle to be trusted outside, that one would be a fool to think there were.

Further, the apparent cynicism is in part a saving inhibition, a defence against constant assault. In the age of the public-address systems, the 'common man' (especially during the long wars, but increasingly now in peace also) is for ever hearing the multitudinous tones of exhortation and invocation: the 'this won't hurt a bit' encourager, the plummily explanatory tone of the master-official; all the voices which constantly over-coax, over-sell, over-'kid': 'Do *you* suffer from — ?', 'Why *you* should eat —'; 'Conqueror or Conquered, ... which are *you*?', 'Have *you* got — ?', '*You*'ll be amazed', '*You* too can have —', 'There's a — for *you*', 'Did *you* know that — ?', 'What would *you* have done?' If the 'common man' did not find a defence against all this, he would be as harassed as a solitary bell-boy in a Grand Hotel. He is not much deceived; he has some awareness of his own difficulties in judging and coping; he has a much more sensitive awareness of the fact that he is being 'got at', being worked on'. He has suspected 'fancy talk' for generations. He can 'see through' most appeals, and is on constant watch against being 'taken in'.

Today he is so bespattered by the ceaseless exoteric voices, is invited so frequently to feel this, this, and this, to react to this, to do that, to believe this – that in recoil he often decides to feel none of these things, neither the glories nor the horrors. He goes dead to it all. He develops a strong patina of resistance, a thick and solid skin for not taking notice. When the voices, especially those of the Press, really have something important to speak to him about, he gives them the old smile and continues to read the funny bits. They have cried 'wolf' too often. The B.B.C. News Service is trusted, with the qualifying suspicion that it is the voice of officialdom in the last resort, and the qualifying conviction that it is dull anyway. To the papers, the response is a mild and easy cynicism:

'Oh, y' read all kinds of things in the papers.'
'It's all lies in the papers.'
'The papers are full of lies.'
'It's all propaganda in the papers.'

When I was a boy the older generation of working-class people used often to say, as evidence of the truth of some fact, 'Oh, but it was in the papers.' That phrase seems to me now almost entirely unused. One goes on reading the papers, even the political parts, so long as they are made human and personal. At the back of the mind, in matters inviting any form of genuine belief, there sounds an echo from a bottomless unbelief. It is interesting to read details of the lives of film stars, and particularly of their private lives; but if one is expected really to believe that So-and-so is happily married, well, one smiles again – and goes on reading. I listened to several groups of working-class people talking about Captain Carlsen and the *Flying Enterprise*, at the time when every organ of publicity was making the most of it. They were one and all utterly unaffected by the massed shouts that here was individual heroism of a high order. They did not express reasonable doubts about the nature of the act; they simply, and as it were automatically, assumed that it was phoney, that commerce was at the back of it somewhere, and that the papers were involved in the trick. There was no heat; just the usual killing assumption. Working-class people tend to take the pleasures offered from outside, whilst inwardly having little respect for the environment providing those pleasures; they readily take amusement from that environment, but 'aren't such chumps' as to believe in it. In view of the situation described in the two preceding chapters, this is not only an understandable but, in origin, a healthy reaction.

In the world of work, in the bosses' world, it is generally assumed that cash rules, that everyone is out for gain. The working-classes are at ground-level in the economic jungle; they may not see the higher deceptions or the higher sacrifices, but they see the individualism of a cash-democracy at work in a thousand small ways. If they are intermediaries between the boss and the customers, they are often expected to learn the relevant ways of fiddling in their trade. 'Fiddling', twisting, seem the normal characteristics of the process of 'getting on' as they see it practised. One sad sight is a hired crafts-man with a boss who acts only as executive and indulges in the usual amount of twisting. The craftsman may carry out his part of the contract honestly, but in conversation – to show that he knows the world he is in – he makes a brave show as a cynic and 'fiddler' in small things. He sees a gulf between publicly professed morality and the reality. If he is moving towards middle-age he remembers the thirties and the way men were often discharged, so long only as the bosses' ship could be kept afloat. He feels fairly sure that in the end the cash-nexus wins – 'money talks'. The defining phrases roll out:

'It's all a money-making racket.'
'It's all money – money – money.'
'Everyone's out for number one.'
'It's a money-making concern.'
'Everyone's out for himself in the long run.'
'Everybody's on the make.'
'It all comes back to money/economics in the end.'
'They're all on the fiddle.'
'Y' never get owt for nowt.'
'There's a catch in it somewhere.'

Amid all this, 'Honesty is the best policy' comes to seem as out of date as the poker-work in which it was traced over the brass-bedstead. Unless you are a fool you 'scrimshank' where you can:

'It's a living, i'nt it?'
'Y' may as well fiddle. They'll all fiddle yer anyway.'
'Why should I worry?'
'Never mind [if something goes wrong], I ain't paid to think.'
'They'll see y' carry the can alright.'

Hearing these phrases day after day from a group of workmen we might easily conclude that their cynicism was complete. But such speech is in part formal or symbolic; it indicates that they know a hawk from a handsaw, that they have no illusions about the true nature of industry.

So it is with their attitudes towards the more public or official areas of life. Of the cheerful cynicism towards the clergy – 'nice work if y' can get it'; 'wonderful what 'y can get paid for nowadays' – I wrote in an earlier chapter. Much the same is true, though here it has a sharper edge, of attitudes towards politics and politicians. It is generally assumed that politicians are:

'All twisters/crooks.'
'Only out for their own ends.'
'Feathering their own nests.'
'Looking after number one.'
'All talk.'

''E's a real politician alright,' they say, meaning that he is 'all talk and no do', and that 'such as 'im never really do owt for people like us'. Again, many of these are very old cries, and natural to working-people; but they are used very frequently today, and used now with the flat assurance that it is the same all over, and in all parts of life.

In times of war it has never been easy to persuade the body of working-people to feel enmity towards the other side; 'They' seem too obviously at the back of it: it would be foolish to expect the 'ordinary man' to respond like Rupert Brooke, when he is drafted into the Services. He goes in because he has to, because 'They'll always get yer in the end'; 'They' hold all the aces. Today the almost universal assumption, whether in time of war or of peacetime National Service, is that the whole thing is suspect, that 'I' am only in it because 'I' was not as quick as the other guy to think of a 'fiddle'. Here more than ever can be seen the complicated interweaving of reasonable and dignified attitudes with the wider newer forms. The whole business is so involved, so anonymous, that people say, 'Ah'm just living through it till I get home – and after that, "Damn you, Jack"; shut the door and leave the Missus, the kids and me alone'; or, 'Ah'm fighting, not for me country, but for me family'; or, 'Why am I in it? – oh, Ah was daft enough to let them catch me'; or, 'Me? – Ah'm just a mug. Ah let them get me'; or, 'Ah can't do anything. Ah'd be a mug to try – only bring trouble on meself.' 'We're all in it together,' meaning that we are all caught. The Services are held together not mainly by discipline nor by *esprit de corps*, nor by the enlightenment which Current Affairs talks bring,

H

but by the interlocking multitude of little cells of personal relationships which men create for themselves inside the huge impersonal structure. These personal relationships, more than anything else, can make decently bearable the boredom I described in the preceding chapter.

Eventually, nothing in this big world can move the 'common man' as a 'common man'. He is infinitely cagey; he puts up so powerful a silent resistance that it can threaten to become a spiritual death, a creeping paralysis of the moral will. We hear much of the gullibility of working-class people, and have seen that there is plenty of evidence for its existence. But this disillusionment presents as great a danger now, and one which (this cannot be said too often) they share with other classes. Outside the personal life they will believe almost nothing consciously; the springs of assent have nearly dried up. Or worse, they will believe in the reducing and destroying things but not in assertions of positive worth: if you assume that most things are a 'sell', it is easy to accept every bad charge, hard to accede to a call for praise and admiration. Some of the more powerful influences in modern society are tending to produce a generation expert at destroying by explaining-away, insulated from thinking that there is ever likely to be a cause for genuine enthusiasm or a freely good act, automatically suspicious of anything not in itself disillusioned or patently self-seeking; the catch-phrase is the brittle and negative, 'so what?'

The situation is made worse by the fact that the reading of very many people, after they have left school, presents them with a picture of a world in which, though their own moral rules in local or parochial affairs are usually assumed, there is little conception of more general actions or principles. What a narrow, what a selective view of modern life, and of the lights by which men live, is presented by many popular papers. For all their readers know, the world of thought or artistic expression, of individual self-sacrifice, of disciplined submission to a purpose, might hardly exist. How many have heard of Albert Schweitzer, except on the rare occasions when some item concerning him has had a brief 'news value'? It is easier to undervalue much in human experience when one's reading is so selectively produced.

As a reinforcement there is, behind, the disinclination to strike attitudes, to take oneself too seriously, the slowness to moral indignation, and in addition, the 'Leave me alone. Ah'm as good as you' cry of the disappointed decent man. The situation is worse outside than in local communities, but even outside is saved from having its fullest effect by the ability of people often to act, when it 'comes to it', in accordance with an old tag or aphorism. In the end, there are some things one just does not do, though one would not be prepared to justify them in argument. This seems a poor substitute for a positive sense of things one does not, or of things one does, or should do. At its fullest it appears in the form of a statement from the dock by a man accused of murder three or four years ago: 'Oh no, I'm not particularly moral – but I'm not a murderer.' There are some things one does not do, like committing murder: but the first clause in that statement, 'I'm not particularly moral,' is not so much an admission of faultiness, as an assertion that one belongs with the great big illusionless majority; one is not odd. Unextended, as it is for most people at present, this network of attitudes allows them to go on, very puzzled, but for most of the time with some sense that in important matters and when the need arises they 'know the difference between right and wrong'.

All these attitudes can feed upon themselves, and so spread a nerve-killing effect over other areas. They can become another kind of self-indulgence, a contracting-out. There is then a loss of moral tension, a sort of release in accepting a world with little larger meaning, and living in accordance with its lack of internal demands. 'All right,' says one of Thurber's husbands, with some satisfaction in knowing at last where he stands, 'so you're disenchanted – so I'm disenchanted – so we're all disenchanted.' Everything is tainted, including me; everyone is out for what he can get; so one can dismiss all the big words. If you try to 'live by principle' you are foolish; 'y' can't be Christian today or y'll be crushed down': the phrase 'high ideals' is commonly used derisively. Ideals may be a sign of lack of self-seeking, but they are unworkable; they do not square with hard facts. If anyone else seems to be trying to 'live by principle' he may be a fool or a prig; look for the clay feet. If he is clearly not a fool and does not sound like a prig, but if he will insist that some things are more worth while than others, then he is probably a hypocrite – simply because there can be no justification for such attitudes. They must be a form of 'line-shooting' which we have not 'cottoned-on to' yet. All this will make it harder for the unusual person who is in something – his rules of conduct, the books he reads, the music he likes – unusual, to be left quietly alone as one who is 'alright, but a bit odd'. The 'Orlick' spirit and the 'Sweeney' spirit ('That's all the facts when you come to brass tacks') can co-operate with contemporary disillusionment and doubt to produce a great emptiness, a hole which is guarded as jealously as though it were a towering principle. This could become the common situation if change were to continue in the way just described. At present the more usual attitude is a not-unattractive, because a limited, and often amusedly borne, 'disenchantment'.

B. *Some Allegorical Figures*

Can I now bring into sharper focus this picture of unexceptional but on the whole decent men much beset and equipped with an uninspiring and disconcerting cover of clichés and attitudes? Is it possible to do this by calling up a person who in this at least is typical of many, is of his time? The type of conscript soldier discussed above will not serve, for his condition is often partly temporary; nor will a rootless minor technician, trained by a technical institute to serve a technocratic age; some of his attitudes are in part the product of a special form of not-belonging to any traditional social order. I choose rather a small craftsman or skilled worker, a plumber or a house-painter, or a man who comes to maintain one of the household machines; one of those who exasperate middle-class housewives by their disinclination to be particularly interested in the job they have come to do, a man who gets on with his work but shows no enthusiasm – and probably leaves a mess when he goes.

Perhaps, in all this, such a man is making a response to his situation of more maturity than is always realized. He knows his job and can do it without much strain; it requires no special skill other than that long established by practice. After a time he can hardly be interested in what he does; the same dozen or so jobs recur too often for that. He moves each day from house to house, according to a list passed to him in the morning by the girl in the shop. He would grin if you spoke to him of 'service to the community': 'ay, but it dun't add up to much' he would be likely to say. He is engaged by a small firm on a fixed wage, which varies only a little in accordance with a bonus system. The business is run, perhaps, by two men, who employ him, two other craftsmen and a girl, who looks after the shop. He knows they 'fiddle' a bit: he knows they get more out of the business than he does, and with little risk: he knows they worry a lot and seem no happier than he is. For himself, he would not want a life so worried, even for the sake of the extra money; nor would he like the responsibility. He wants to earn enough to be able to buy the extra things he really enjoys. He could earn more, as some of his mates do, by working himself 'to death' on private and untaxed work at nights and weekends. But 'What do they get out of it?' he asks, 'there's no fun in a life like that.' He is without ambition, but also without a keen eye for small gain; he bears his specially energetic mates no real ill-will. He does not respond to calls aimed at the 'getter-on', and suspects most other calls.

There are, of course, indolent and scrimshanking men, who do a bad job out of a near-vicious laziness, who take a revenge in that and in leaving as much mess as possible. But he is neither lazy nor stupid by nature. In some ways he is intelligent; had he been born into the middle-classes he would, with his natural ability, have made an at least adequate self-employed shopkeeper or professional man. He is not sour, and still has some craftsman's pride in turning out what he calls 'a reasonable job'. The adjective is a modifier, to indicate a job which is not a little masterpiece of his craft (he does that on repairs at home or as a hobby), but a job which is not botched. He does not scrimshank because 'y' may as well do a reasonable job while yer about it'.

He sees no need and would not wish to kowtow to the customers, though some of his fellows do that, and get cups of tea and tips on the side. He does not rush, but works at what he calls a 'steady' pace; and the adjective is again a modifier. He will not deliberately 'go slow', but why, he thinks, should he 'work his guts out' for a woman with more conveniences than his own wife, or for the bosses' profit?

In the eyes of the lady of the house – as she rushes around cleaning, with a dozen things under way at once, and all of them her responsibility, her property, her interest – he is bound to appear to be working at half-speed; but no one moves as quickly as a house-proud wife. She is tempted to call him shiftless and unco-operative, if not surly. He on his side may well regard her with a slightly ironic eye. He has to come to terms, to highly qualified terms, with the possibilities of his working-life. He does not ask a great deal, and he gives fair if unenthusiastic service. He has much of the nonconformity and independence of his grandfather, with the modifications which the twentieth century encourages. At home he is not greatly different from his grandfather in many important matters. William Morris described, in 1879, a similar situation much more eloquently than I can. My point is that, though the conditions of working-people have much improved since Morris wrote, there are important features in contemporary society which encourage working-people to retain these attitudes almost undiminished:

It is quite true, and very sad to say, that if anyone nowadays wants a piece of ordinary work done by gardener, carpenter, mason, dyer, weaver, smith, what you will, he will be a lucky rarity if he gets it well done. He will, on the contrary, meet on every side with evasion of plain duties, and disregard of other men's rights; yet I cannot see how the 'British Working Man' is to be made to bear the whole burden of this blame, or indeed the chief part of it. I doubt if it be possible for a whole mass of men to do work to which they are driven, and in which there is no hope, and no pleasure, without trying to shirk it – at any rate, shirked it has always been under such circumstances. On the other hand, I know that there are some men so right-minded, that they will, in despite irksomeness and hopelessness, drive right through their work. Such men are the salt of the earth.

The apparent cynicism of a man such as the one I have described is much less than that of a second typical figure, the spiv or near-spiv, as he can be met in all classes. But in some ways their attitudes are similarly informed. The spiv is a more positive figure, a sort of inverted 'go-getter', a 'casher-in' on disorder. For those who occur among working-class people, the favourite phrases are:

'I'm in the know.'
'I'm knowing/wideawake/wide/a wide boy.'
'I wasn't born yesterday.'
'I know my way around.'
'I'm no Joe.'
'No flies on Charlie.'
'I'm a wise guy.'
'I'm clever/a clever sod/no fool.'
'I know how to look after number one.'

'You don't catch me on that.'

'It's a mug's game.'

'Not *me*.'

'Since when . . . ?'

It may be that this attitude is stronger among those under thirty than among older people, since most older people have memories of the thirties and the war, of sacrifice and co-operation and neighbourliness: the later forties and the fifties have not given such scope for the rediscovery of these virtues.

Naturally, other classes have their own forms, for I am doing no more than touch on a matter which affects all levels of society, in a complexity of ways. One of the more sophisticated middle-class variants of 'I'm a wise guy' is 'I'm a realist, old chap!' Then there is a middle-class equivalent of the 'cheerful card', the man who is in on all rackets, 'everybody's pal' if it comes to a 'fiddle', the 'good fellow' who is 'on the inside': and so on right up to the owners of 'the accosting profile' in Auden's poem, 'Watch any Day' – the enormously assured, with the little, nervous give-away gestures. They all share features of a culture from the man who makes what he can by selling shoddy lino at working-class doors through a host of congenital canvassers and 'promoters' up to the really big speculators.

There is the highly-finished and painful social dance-routine of some people who live, at whatever level, on publicly selling their personalities. At night, off duty, they tend to frequent predominantly male bars, and present an appearance compounded of the metallically-cynical and the little-boy-lost. A lower middle-class example comes to mind. In clothing such a man often leans to a sporting, mixed with a gentleman-about-town, effect, a suggestion of a gallant Artillery captain in mufti, or of a character from a short story by Somerset Maugham. He tries to engage the barmaid in sophisticated conversation, offers her a gin-and-It, or port-and-lemon, and tries to forget the hunt for commission-sales by day. In general appearance he aims to be brisk and well-shaved, with a neat moustache in a dark thin pencil line: in manner he is all 'how to win friends and influence people', at least during the day. His ready smile does not quite reach the eyes. In bar-room company he carries on conversation in spurts of part-sentences, punctuated by hearty echoing laughs, sprayed round the company to draw them all in. There is a certain amount of slapping of his own thighs and others' shoulders, for emphasis. A great deal is done with nods, winks, innuendoes, the technical jargon of the bar and minor commercial world. When the mask slips, one realizes why he dislikes a stillness, either in his environment or in himself; underneath the eyes plead, and the braced lips are unhappy.

The doggy communion of the bars is often the nearest which people such as this are able to approach to a sense of a group. It can help to reassure barrow-boys, door-to-door salesmen, and the more prosperous ones with a fine brilliantine bloom on their ears, a faint smell of perfume, and an air suggesting complicated dealings in fancy-goods. Looked at casually, in all their young-men-on-the-spree apparent splendour, they may seem the direct descendants of the Edwardian mashers; they are, but times have changed; the ground has become hollow under their feet. A bar-room provides relief, because there they no longer have to go through the bourgeois motions; they can react into the only other attitude they know, the 'widely' cynical.

It would be extraordinarily illuminating, and extraordinarily difficult, to trace the links between all this and some attitudes among more intellectual people during the last three decades; the connexions between the 'I couldn't care less' of the rankers, the 'anything goes' of bright young things, and some prevalent intellectual positions. Thus it seems to me that there is sometimes, in this last milieu, a particular enjoyment in the game of disconnected 'knowingness', in blowing the froth off each other's intellectual small beer, in the Swedish drill, for its own sake, of a well-informed mind, in some of the forms in which acute intellectual curiosity operates from a non-attached base. There is sometimes a fear of emotion disguising itself as a rejection of sentimentality, an extreme suspicion of any talk about 'ends and values', a tendency to evade such challenges by the device of oblique and clever 'cracks'. There is often a shrugging-away of authority, not simply of authority in others, but of the authority which is at times required from us – as may be seen in some schoolmasters with their senior forms or evening-classes, some adult education tutors, some young dons in seminars. Riddled by a fuzzy form of egalitarianism, ridden with doubt and self-doubt, believing nothing and able to honour almost no one; in such circumstances we stand on nothing and so can stand for nothing. We are tempted to make the 'all pals together' spirit take the place of such authority as our position asks us at least to aim to evoke.

'The teachers have read Lytton Strachey, and the children's teeth are set on edge,' said T. S. Eliot. So are the teeth of the teachers. These attitudes can therefore be an expression of a kind of honesty and dignity. But there can also be an astringent pleasure in the condition. 'Intellectual sadism' has its rewards, critical assertion is much less open to attack than creative absorption; there is some amusement and some safety in calling continually, 'Your lie is showing/Your creed is creased.'

There are a great number of parallels and variant forms of all this in the literature of the time, and at all levels; for example, in Hemingway, Maugham, Huxley, Waugh, P. H. Newby (see the central character in *Mariner Dances*), Henry Green (see, for instance, *Back*), Peter Cheyney, Hank Janson, and more recently in the whole presentation of Jim Dixon, in Kingsley Amis's *Lucky Jim*. These writers are lumped together without any common disparaging implication; they differ in the degree of disinterestedness, which can be gauged only from an actual reading. But all are illuminating the same destructive element.

In giving my illustrations I have deliberately moved some way from working-class people: it is necessary, finally, to try to suggest more precisely the nature of their cynicism. It seems to me that the majority of working-class people are less affected by cynicism as 'cashing-in' than by cynicism as emptiness. Yet that, as I have said, provides further ground for the spread of self-indulgence. Most working-class people have been affected by the developments I have tried to outline, have been to some degree 'disenchanted' and find themselves now 'mocked by unmeaning'. In almost everyone the shyness about belief has some effect. The refusal to 'give out' for fear of being diddled means the acceptance eventually of a flat, tough, and tasteless world.

Meanwhile, home is an important refuge; local life can go on, not as yet much affected; a craft can be a private stay: in their public aspects many working-class people are set back, and withdraw into a hurt but also sometimes an indulgent cynicism. It is difficult, by its nature, to find more than a very brief expression of the main attitudes from within the working-class themselves. But this from an ex-minor-public-school boy down on his luck speaks for much in the experience of working-class people of his generation as well as for those of his own class:

It's all very well for the moralists to talk ... but ... from school right into a bloody war that wasn't my making. Frightened to death half the time, so bored the other half that there was nothing to do but go to bed with a pretty girl. Then back to civvy street, peddling these blank machines and walking ten miles a day for fat old women to shut their doors in my face.

CHAPTER 10

UNBENT SPRINGS: A NOTE ON THE UPROOTED AND THE ANXIOUS

Do, please, write a story of how a young man, the son of a serf, who has been a shop boy, a chorister, pupil of a secondary school, and a university graduate, who has been brought up to respect rank and to kiss the priest's hand, to bow to other people's ideas, to be thankful for each morsel of bread, who has been thrashed many a time, who has had to walk about tutoring without goloshes, who has fought, tormented animals, has been fond of dining at the house of well-to-do relations, and played the hypocrite both to God and man without any need but merely out of consciousness of his own insignificance – describe how that young man squeezes the slave out of himself, drop by drop, and how, awakening one fine morning, he feels running in his veins no longer the blood of a slave but genuine human blood.

TCHEKOV

'But remember his education, the age in which he grew up,' observed Arkady. 'Education?' broke in Bazarov. 'Every man must educate himself, just as I've done, for instance. . . . And as for the age, why should I depend on it? Let it rather depend on me. No, my dear fellow, that's all shallowness, want of backbone!'

TURGENEV

A. *Scholarship Boy*

For my part I am very sorry for him. It is an uneasy lot at best, to be what we call highly taught and yet not to enjoy: to be present at this great spectacle of life and never to be liberated from a small hungry shivering self.

GEORGE ELIOT

This is a difficult chapter to write, though one that should be written. As in other chapters, I shall be isolating a group of related trends: but the consequent dangers of over-emphasis are here especially acute. The three immediately preceding chapters have discussed attitudes which could from one point of view appear to represent a kind of poise. But the people most affected by the attitudes now to be examined – the 'anxious and the uprooted' – are to be recognized primarily by their lack of poise, by their uncertainty. About the self-indulgences which seem to satisfy many in their class they tend to be unhappily superior: they are much affected by the cynicism which affects almost everyone, but this is likely to increase their lack of purpose rather than tempt them to 'cash in' or to react into further indulgence.

In part they have a sense of loss which affects some in all groups. With them the sense of loss is increased precisely because they are emotionally uprooted from their class, often under the stimulus of a stronger critical intelligence or imagination, qualities which can lead them into an unusual self-consciousness before their own situation (and make it easy for a sympathizer to dramatize their '*Angst*'). Involved with this may be a physical uprooting from their class through the medium of the scholarship system. A great many seem to me to be affected in this way, though only a very small proportion badly; at one boundary the group includes psychotics; at the other, people leading apparently normal lives but never without an underlying sense of some unease.

It will be convenient to speak first of the nature of the uprooting which some scholarship boys experience. I have in mind those who, for a number of years, perhaps for a very long time, have a sense of no longer really belonging to any group. We all know that many do find a poise in their new situations. There are 'declassed' experts and specialists who go into their own spheres after the long scholarship climb has led them to a Ph.D. There are brilliant individuals who become fine administrators and officials, and find themselves thoroughly at home. There are some, not necessarily so gifted, who reach a kind of poise which is yet not a passivity nor even a failure in awareness, who are at ease in their new group without any ostentatious adoption of the protective colouring of that group, and who have an easy relationship with their working-class relatives, based not on a form of patronage but on a just respect. Almost every working-class boy who goes through the process of further education by scholarships finds himself chafing against his environment during adolescence. He is at the friction-point of two cultures; the test of his real education lies in his ability, by about the age of twenty-five, to smile at his father with his whole face and to respect his flighty young sister and his slower brother. I shall be concerned with those for whom the uprooting is particularly troublesome, not because I under-estimate the gains which this kind of selection gives, nor because I wish to stress the more depressing features in contemporary life, but because the difficulties of some people illuminate much in the wider discussion of cultural change. Like transplanted stock, they react to a widespread drought earlier than those who have been left in their original soil.

I am sometimes inclined to think that the problem of self-adjustment is, in general, especially difficult for those working-class boys who are only moderately endowed, who have talent sufficient to separate them from the majority of their working-class contemporaries, but not to go much farther. I am not implying a correlation between intelligence and lack of unease; intellectual people have their own troubles: but this kind of anxiety often seems most to afflict those in the working-classes who have been pulled one stage away from their original culture and yet have not the intellectual equipment which would then cause them to move on to join the 'declassed' professionals and experts. In one sense, it is true, no one is ever 'declassed'; and it is interesting to see how this occasionally obtrudes (particularly today, when ex-working-class boys move in all the managing areas of society) – in the touch of insecurity, which often appears as an undue concern to establish 'presence' in an otherwise quite professorial professor, in the intermittent rough homeliness of an important executive and committee-man, in the tendency to vertigo which betrays a lurking sense of uncertainty in a successful journalist.

But I am chiefly concerned with those who are self-conscious and yet not self-aware in any full sense, who are as a result uncertain, dissatisfied, and gnawed by self-doubt. Sometimes they lack will, though they have intelligence, and 'it takes will to cross this waste'. More often perhaps, though they have as much will as the majority, they have not sufficient to resolve the complex tensions which their uprooting, the peculiar problems of their particular domestic settings, and the uncertainties common to the time create.

As childhood gives way to adolescence and that to manhood, this kind of boy tends to be progressively cut off from the ordinary life of his group. He is marked out early: and here I am thinking not so much of his teachers in the 'elementary' school as of fellow-members of his family. "E's got brains', or 'E's bright', he hears constantly; and in part the tone is one of pride and admiration. He is in a way cut off by his parents as much as by his talent which urges him to break away from his group. Yet on their side this is not altogether from admiration: "E's got brains', yes, and he is expected to follow the trail that opens. But there can also be a limiting quality in the tone with which the phrase is used; character counts more. Still, he has brains – a mark of pride and almost a brand; he is heading for a different world, a different sort of job.

He has to be more and more alone, if he is going to 'get on'. He will have, probably unconsciously, to oppose the ethos of the hearth, the intense gregariousness of the working-class family group. Since everything centres upon the living-room, there is unlikely to be a room of his own; the bedrooms are cold and inhospitable, and to warm them or the front room, if there is one, would not only be expensive, but would require an imaginative leap – out of the tradition – which most families are not capable of making. There is a corner of the living-room table. On the other side Mother is ironing, the wireless is on, someone is singing a snatch of song or Father says intermittently whatever comes into his head. The boy has to cut himself off mentally, so as to do his homework, as well as he can. In summer, matters can be easier; bedrooms are warm enough to work in: but only a few boys, in my experience, take advantage of this. For the boy is himself (until he reaches, say, the upper forms) very much of *both* the worlds of home and school. He is enormously obedient to the dictates of the world of school, but emotionally still strongly wants to continue as part of the family circle.

So the first big step is taken in the progress towards membership of a different sort of group or to isolation when such a boy has to resist the central domestic quality of working-class life. This is true, perhaps particularly true, if he belongs to a happy home, because the happy homes are often the more gregarious. Quite early the stress on solitariness, the encouragement towards strong self-concern, is felt; and this can make it more difficult for him to belong to another group later.

At his 'elementary' school, from as early as the age of eight, he is likely to be in some degree set apart, though this may not happen if his school is in the area which each year provides a couple of dozen boys from 'the scholarship form' for the grammar-schools. But probably he is in an area predominantly working-class and his school takes up only a few scholarships a year. The situation is altering as the number of scholarships increases, but in any case human adjustments do not come as abruptly as administrative changes.

He is similarly likely to be separated from the boys' groups outside the home, is no longer a full member of the gang which clusters round the lamp-posts in the evenings; there is homework to be done. But these are the male groups among which others in his generation grow up, and his detachment from them is emotionally linked with one more aspect of his home situation – that he now tends to be closer to the women of the house than to the men. This is true, even if his father is not the kind who dismisses books and reading as 'a woman's game'. The boy spends a large part of his time at the physical centre of the home, where the women's spirit rules, quietly getting on with his work whilst his mother gets on with her jobs – the father not yet back from work or out for a drink with his mates. The man and the boy's brothers are outside, in the world of men; the boy sits in the women's world. Perhaps this partly explains why many authors from the working-classes, when they write about their childhood, give the women in it so tender and central a place. There is bound to be occasional friction, of course – when they wonder whether the boy is 'getting above himself', or when he feels a strong reluctance to break off and do one of the odd jobs a boy is expected to do. But predominantly the atmosphere is likely to be intimate, gentle, and attractive. With one ear he hears the women discussing their worries and ailments and hopes, and he tells them at intervals about his school and the work and what the master said. He usually receives boundless uncomprehending sympathy: he knows they do not understand, but still he tells them; he would like to link the two environments.

This description simplifies and over-stresses the break; in each individual case there will be many qualifications. But in presenting the isolation in its most emphatic form the description epitomizes what is very frequently found. For such a boy is between two worlds of school and home; and they meet at few points. Once at the grammar-school, he quickly learns to make use of a pair of different accents, perhaps even two different apparent characters and differing standards of value. Think of his reading-material, for example: at home he sees strewn around, and reads regularly himself, magazines which are never mentioned at school, which seem not to belong to the world to which the school introduces him; at school he hears about and reads books never mentioned at home. When he brings those books into the house they do not take their place with other books which the family are reading, for often there are none or almost none; his books look, rather, like strange tools.

He will perhaps, especially today, escape the worst immediate difficulties of his new environment, the stigma of cheaper clothes, of not being able to afford to go on school-holiday trips, of parents who turn up for the grammar-school play looking shamefully working-class. But as a grammar-school boy, he is likely to be anxious to do well, to be accepted, or even to catch the eye as he caught the eye, because of his brains, at the 'elementary' school. For brains are the currency by which he has bought his way, and increasingly brains seem to be the currency that tells. He tends to make his schoolmasters over-important, since they are the cashiers in the new world of brain-currency. In his home-world his father is still his father; in the other world of school his father can have little place: he tends to make a father-figure of his form-master.

Consequently, even though his family may push him very little, he will probably push himself harder than he should. He begins to see life, for as far as he can envisage it, as a series of hurdle-jumps, the hurdles of scholarships which are won by learning how to amass and manipulate the new currency. He tends to over-stress the importance of examinations, of the piling-up of knowledge and of received opinions. He discovers a technique of apparent learning, of the acquiring of facts rather than of the handling and use of facts. He learns how to receive a purely literate education, one using only a small part of the personality and challenging only a limited area of his being. He begins to see life as a ladder, as a permanent examination with some praise and some further exhortation at each stage. He becomes an expert imbiber and doler-out; his competence will vary, but will rarely be accompanied by genuine enthusiasms. He rarely feels the reality of knowledge, of other men's thoughts and imaginings, on his own pulses; he rarely discovers an author for himself and on his own. In this half of his life he can respond only if there is a direct connexion with the system of training. He has something of the blinkered pony about him; sometimes he is trained by those who have been through the same regimen, who are hardly unblinkered themselves, and who praise him in the degree to which he takes comfortably to their blinkers. Though there is a powerful, unidealistic, unwarmed realism about his attitude at bottom, that is his chief form of initiative; of other forms – the freely ranging mind, the bold flying of mental kites, the courage to reject some 'lines' even though they are officially as important as all the rest – of these he probably has little, and his training does not often encourage them. This is not a new problem; Herbert Spencer spoke of it fifty years ago: but it still exists:

The established systems of education, whatever their matter may be, are fundamentally vicious in their manner. They encourage *submissive receptivity* instead of *independent activity*.

There is too little stress on action, on personal will and decision; too much goes on in the head, with the rather-better-than-normal intellectual machine which has brought him to his grammar-school. and because so often the 'good' boy, the boy who does well, is the one who with his conscientious passivity meets the main demands of his new environment, he gradually loses spontaneity so as to acquire examination-passing reliability. He can snap his fingers at no one and nothing; he seems set to make an adequate, reliable, and unjoyous kind of clerk. He has been too long 'afraid of all that has to be obeyed'. Hazlitt, writing at the beginning of the nineteenth century, made a wider and more impassioned judgement on trends in his society; but it has some relevance here and now:

Men do not become what by nature they are meant to be, but what society makes them. The generous feelings, and high propensities of the soul are, as it were, shrunk up, seared, violently wrenched, and amputated, to fit us for our intercourse with the world, something in the manner that beggars maim and mutilate their children, to make them fit for their future situation in life.

Such a scholarship boy has lost some of the resilience and some of the vitality of his cousins who are still knocking about the streets. In an earlier generation, as one of the quicker-witted persons born into the working-classes, he would in all probability have had those wits developed in the jungle of the slums, where wit had to ally itself to energy and initiative. He plays little on the streets; he does not run around delivering newspapers; his sexual growth is perhaps delayed. He loses something of the gamin's resilience and carelessness, of his readiness to take a chance, of his perkiness and boldness, and he does not acquire the unconscious confidence of many a public-school-trained child of the middle-classes. He has been trained like a circus-horse, for scholarship winning.

As a result, when he comes to the end of the series of set-pieces, when he is at last put out to raise his eyes to a world of tangible and unaccommodating things, of elusive and disconcerting human beings, he finds himself with little inner momentum. The driving-belt hangs loosely, disconnected from the only machine it has so far served, the examination-passing machine. He finds difficulty in choosing a direction in a world where there is no longer a master to please, a toffee-apple at the end of each stage, a certificate, a place in the upper half of the assessable world. He is unhappy in a society which presents largely a picture of disorder, which is huge and sprawling, not limited, ordered, and centrally heated; in which the toffee-apples are not accurately given to those who work hardest nor even to the most intelligent: but in which disturbing imponderables like 'character', 'pure luck', 'ability to mix', and 'boldness' have a way of tipping the scales.

His condition is made worse because the whole trend of his previous training has made him care too much for marked and ticketed success. This world, too, cares much for recognizable success, but does not distribute it along the lines on which he has been trained to win. He would be happier if he cared less, if he could blow the gaff for himself on the world's success values. But they too closely resemble the values of school; to reject them he would have first to escape the inner prison in which the school's tabulated rules for success have immured him.

He does not wish to accept the world's criterion – get on at any price (though he has an acute sense of the importance of money). But he has been equipped for hurdle-jumping; so he merely dreams of getting-on, but somehow not in the world's way. He has neither the comforts of simply accepting the big world's values, nor the recompense of feeling firmly critical towards them.

He has moved away from his 'lower' origins, and may move farther. If so, he is likely to be nagged underneath by a sense of how far he has come, by the fear and shame of a possible falling-back. And this increases his inability to leave himself alone. Sometimes the kind of job he gets only increases this slightly dizzy sense of still being on the ladder; unhappy on it, but also proud and, in the

nature of his condition, usually incapable of jumping-off, of pulling-
out of that particular race:

Pale, shabby, tightly strung, he had advanced from post to post in
his insurance office with the bearing of a man about to be discharged.
. . . Brains had only meant that he must work harder in the elementary
school than those born free of them. At night he could still hear the
malicious chorus telling him that he was a favourite of the master. . . .
Brains, like a fierce heat, had turned the world to a desert round him,
and across the sands in the occasional mirage he saw the stupid crowds,
playing, laughing, and without thought enjoying the tenderness, the
compassion, the companionship of love.

That is over-dramatized, not applicable to all or even to most –
but in some way affecting many. It affects also that larger group,
to which I now turn, of those who in some ways ask questions of
themselves about their society, who are because of this, even though
they may never have been to grammar-schools, 'between two
worlds, one dead, the other powerless to be born'. They are the
'private faces in public places' among the working-classes; they are
Koestler's 'thoughtful corporals'; they are among those, though not
the whole of those, who take up many kinds of self-improvement.
They may be performing any kind of work, from manual labour
to teaching; but my own experience suggests that they are to be
found frequently among minor clerks and similarly black-coated
workers, and among elementary school-teachers, especially in the
big cities. Often their earnestness for improvement shows itself as an
urge to act like some people in the middle classes; but this is not a
political betrayal: it is much nearer to a mistaken idealism.

This kind of person, and we have seen that this is his first great
loss, belongs now to no class, usually not even to what is called,
loosely enough, the 'classless intelligentsia'. He cannot face squarely
his own working-class, for that, since the intuitive links have gone,
would require a greater command in facing himself than he is capable
of. Sometimes he is ashamed of his origins; he has learned to 'turn up
his nose', to be a bit superior about much in working-class manners.
He is often not at ease about his own physical appearance which
speaks too clearly of his birth; he feels uncertain or angry inside when
he realizes that that, and a hundred habits of speech and manners,
can 'give him away' daily. He tends to visit his own sense of

inadequacy upon the group which fathered him; and he provides himself with a mantle of defensive attitudes. Thus he may exhibit an unconvincing pride in his own gaucheness at practical things – 'brain-workers' are never 'good with their hands'. Underneath he knows that his compensatory claim to possess finer weapons, to be able to handle 'book-knowledge', is insecurely based. He tries to read all the good books, but they do not give him that power of speech and command over experience which he seeks. He is as gauche there as with the craftsman's tools.

He cannot go back; with one part of himself he does not want to go back to a homeliness which was often narrow: with another part he longs for the membership he has lost, 'he pines for some Nameless Eden where he never was'. The nostalgia is the stronger and the more ambiguous because he is really 'in quest of his own absconded self yet scared to find it'. He both wants to go back and yet thinks he has gone beyond his class, feels himself weighted with knowledge of his own and their situation, which hereafter forbids him the simpler pleasures of his father and mother. And this is only one of his temptations to self-dramatization.

If he tries to be 'pally' with working-class people, to show that he is one of them, they 'smell it a mile off'. They are less at ease with him than with some in other classes. With them they can establish and are prepared to honour, seriously or as a kind of rather ironical game, a formal relationship; they 'know where they are with them'. But they can immediately detect the uncertainty in his attitudes, that he belongs neither to them nor to one of the groups with which they are used to performing a hierarchical play of relations; the odd man out is still the odd man out.

He has left his class, at least in spirit, by being in certain ways unusual; and he is still unusual in another class, too tense and over-wound. Sometimes the working-classes and the middle-classes can laugh together. He rarely laughs; he smiles constrainedly with the corner of his mouth. He is usually ill at ease with the middle-classes because with one side of himself he does not want them to accept him; he mistrusts or even a little despises them. He is divided as in so many other ways. With one part of himself he admires much he finds in them: a play of intelligence, a breadth of outlook, a kind of style. He would like to be a citizen of that well-polished, prosperous, cool, book-lined and magazine-discussing world of the

successful intelligent middle-class which he glimpses through doorways or feels awkward among on short visits, aware of his grubby
finger-nails. With another part of himself he develops an asperity
towards that world: he turns up his nose at its self-satisfactions, its
earnest social concern, its intelligent coffee-parties, its suave sons at
Oxford, and its Mrs Miniver'ish or Mrs Ramsey'ish cultural pretensions. He is rather over-ready to notice anything which can be
regarded as pretentious or fanciful, anything which allows him to
say that these people do not know what life really is like. He wavers
between scorn and longing. He is Charles Tansley in Virginia
Woolf's *To the Lighthouse*, but is probably without such good brains.
Virginia Woolf often returned to him, with not so deep an understanding as one might have hoped; she gives very much the cultured
middle-class spectator's view:

... a self-taught working-man, and we all know how distressing
they are, how egotistic, insistent, raw, striking, and ultimately
nauseating.

and again:

I'm reminded all the time of some callow board-school boy, full
of wits and powers, but so self-conscious and egotistical that he loses
his head, becomes extravagant, mannered, uproarious, ill at ease, makes
kindly people feel sorry for him and stern ones merely annoyed: and
one hopes he will grow out of it.

He has not the compensations of a craftsman; he has not, usually,
the consolations of religious belief, and so neither the sense of community with others this may give nor the rule it may help to establish
within himself. He has not the driving-force of a money-maker –
of a grocer out for gain, a commercial entrepreneur, or an unabashed
seller of his own personality. He is earnest for self-improvement, but
not with the energy and eagerness of his uncle of forty years ago, of
the Mr Lewishams who swotted at the Polytechnic and read Shaw
and Wells. There is little excitement and adventure about his search
for improvement and knowledge; his texts are the early Aldous
Huxley and perhaps Kafka. He is sad and also solitary; he finds it
difficult to establish contact even with others in his condition: 'With
dulling voice each calls across a colder water.' He is hemmed in
because in the last resort he is scared of finding what he seeks; his
training and his experience are likely to have made him afraid of

decision and commitment. Of him may be said what Toynbee said of the 'creative genius':

> He will have put himself out of gear with his field of action, and in losing the power of action he will lose the will to live.

But he is not a 'creative genius'. He is clever enough to take himself out of his class mentally, but not equipped, mentally or emotionally, to surmount all the problems that follow. He is denied even the 'consolations of philosophy', of acquiring such comfort as there is, in part at least, from assessing his situation. Even if he achieves some degree of culture, he finds it difficult to carry it easily, as easily as those who have not had to strain so much to get it, who have not known like him the long process of exploitation of 'brains':

> You are gifted from above with that which ordinary people have not got: you have talent ... talent places you apart. ... You have only one defect. Your false position, your sorrow, and your catarrh of the bowels are all due to it. That is your extraordinary lack of education. Pray forgive me, but *veritas magis amicitiae*. ... You see, life has its conventions. In order to feel at ease among intelligent people, in order not to be a stranger among them, and not to be overwhelmed by them, you must be to a certain degree educated. ... Talent brought you into that circle, you belong to it, but ... you are drawn away, and you waver between cultured people and the lodgers, *vis-à-vis*.

Though he is not of the 'creative minority', he is just as surely not of the 'uncreative majority'; he is of the uncreative but self-doubting and self-driving minority. He has great aspirations, but not quite the equipment nor the staying-power to realize them. He would be happier if he were able to perceive his own limits, if he learned not to over-estimate his possibilities, if he resigned himself, not so much to 'being the fool you are', as to being the moderately equipped person he is. But his background, his ethos, and probably his natural qualities make such self-realization difficult; he therefore remains harassed by 'the discrepancy between his lofty pretensions and his lowly acts'.

B. *The Place of Culture: A Nostalgia for Ideals*

> . . . For we are all divorced from life;
> We are all cripples, more or less.
> (The little clerk in Dostoyevsky's *Notes from Underground*)

It will be clear that the intellectual and cultural aids now to be discussed appeal to more than 'scholarship boys' of the kind I have just described. Presumably they are designed to reach as many as possible of those people who, for whatever reasons and with whatever background, feel in some ways lacking and hope that training of this sort can make good their deficiency. There are many people who seek culture and intellectual training without expecting more from them than they can properly give, and who can connect their search with the actuality of social and personal life. But such people may be better mentioned in the next chapter.

The range of mental compensations is wide and various, and I do not think I can avoid moving in this section between details from various cultural levels. But in the uncertainties and aspirations I am describing the various kinds of people I refer to do seem to merge. At the most elementary level there are advertisements not far removed from those of a rather vague psychological kind I illustrated earlier. At the other extreme there are appeals to those who seek to be in the forefront of cultural matters. In between there are, for example, advertisements which seem to have scarcely any connexion with the desire for culture but make a direct and practical appeal to the urge to succeed at work. Yet the tone of their announcements seems to suggest that they will attract not so much purposive and practical as vaguely dissatisfied readers:

They used to be on the same bench, but routine work wasn't good enought for Bill. WHAT ABOUT YOU?
Are you a SURE HIT like Bill Watson or a FLOP like Jim Simpson? [Here are likely to be contrasting photographs of one cheerful and one anxious young man.]
Bill set about equipping himself through the . . . system.
He's Chief Mill-Overseer now and *Going Places Fast.*

The next example is of a more direct kind:

Readers get Books-for-Nothing.
We are among the Largest Providers of Up-to-the-Minute Correspondence Training.

[The use of capital letters in these advertisements often recalls the fairground-hawkers.]

These valuable books are MUSTS for YOU. In them you will find clear accounts of all our courses, whether Technical, Administrative or Supervisory. JUST NAME YOUR FAVOURITE COURSE.

From these one moves naturally towards more general mental aids, to the many advertisements offering the secret of fluent expression, of speaking like a 'Dominant and cultured individual'. 'The Modern Encyclopedia of Ideas will make you a Master of Language':

Those who have developed their gift of speech carry weight and the fruits of real success are theirs.

When a contribution by you is demanded [presumably this does not necessarily indicate that most of the people at whom this advertisement is directed are much called upon to make speeches], you will display decisive and unhesitating fluency.

All this costs only thirty shillings. Or:

Are you TONGUE-TIED?
Do you wish to be SILVER-TONGUED in SPEECH?
Life's richest rewards may still be YOURS, even though you were not fortunate enough to go to a University.

WORDS – WORDS – WORDS

Prosperity and Regard depend on your COMMAND of LANGUAGE no matter in which walk of life you decide to act.

Then there are various elementary versions of Roget's *Thesaurus*, sometimes presented in a visually simplified way, perhaps after the manner of a horoscope or of some of those 'What to do in the garden each week of the year' diagrams; so that if you want a few synonyms for 'beautiful' you make two or three small manual adjustments and the required words appear. The *Universal Vocabulary Diagrammatic Outfit* will:

Make your life anew . . . a magic key which will give you entry to a fuller and more positive existence, leaving behind the dull routine of your life today.

YOU can persuade . . . assert . . . dominate . . . and all with unsuspected and unheard-of beauty and fluency.

Advancement – Fame – and the Social Status for which you yearn can be yours TODAY.

You will be thrilled and gain assurance and uplift from its ease. The SECRET OF MASTERFUL WRITING AND SPEECH is at your FINGERTIPS.

For those who aspire more generally to culture or even to the status of the artist there are numerous schools for writing. 'Have you a hunch that YOU could be a writer? If so – post this form':

Do your friends say 'You ought to write a novel' when you tell them an anecdote?

Do they say how much they love getting your letters?

Numerous people like this never acquire the know-how and so their talents never bring them the fame and the fortune which they rightly deserve.

Then there are portmanteau guides to an over-all culture:

Music – Art – Literature

Here is the fullest outline yet issued of the glorious perspective of Culture.

THIS CHANCE WILL NOT OCCUR AGAIN

Numerous celebrated people acknowledge gratefully its assistance.

Each example is accompanied by a clear and helpful account of its artistic characteristics.

With this book you will have the entry of all the world's greatest works of art.

With this guide you too can make powerful and illuminating comments when the talk turns to THINGS OF THE MIND.

Six guineas for three volumes is a likely price, but that may include a free copy of a book such as, 'A Guide to the Telling Phrase and Happy Metaphor . . . indispensable for anyone who wishes to express himself fluently and interestingly'.

One may be tempted, noticing this kind of thing only occasionally, to assume that it affects no more than a minute fraction of the population. But if one regularly notes such advertisements it becomes clear – as they follow one another, several in each issue of many magazines, and some taking a full page – that their audience is greater than most of us think. On the advertisements page of a typical 'quality' weekly for the week in which I am writing there are eleven advertisements. Three of them are not relevant: two are borderline cases (one for the self-teaching of a foreign language by means of phrase-books, and one an official announcement on the need for a certain type of specialist teacher): the remaining six are of the kind I am describing – for postal training in a system which claims to make any career open to the student, for a fine command of English, for profitable creative writing, and so on. Distinguishing by the amount of space each type of advertisement takes, the result is that, from four full columns, one is not relevant, three-quarters of a column are borderline, two-and-a-quarter columns are on our theme. A current 'quality' monthly has eight front advertisement pages. Advertisements of this type take up the equivalent of two of them, or a quarter of the space – with the aids to creative writing or to verbal skill more in evidence, as compared with those for technical or similarly vocational courses, than they are in the 'quality' weekly.

I have no statistical evidence as to the extent of the appeal of such advertisements. Certainly they must be expensive to insert and would presumably not be used so intensively unless a fair number of people responded to them. For the students, too, these courses are usually quite expensive and seem to me likely, in most cases, to be less effective than public adult education. But it seems unlikely that public adult education can ever attract many of these students. No doubt some of them answer the advertisements in the knowledge that they will have to work hard to come within sight of the tempting goals indicated. For a majority, the tone of the announcements often suggests, the 'call to study' or to 'culture' will be only allegorical. There seems to be offered an almost magically quick method of removing an unformulated feeling of insufficiency. The advertisements of this kind in the 'quality' weeklies and monthlies are obviously not directed exclusively to people from the working- or lower middle-classes But working- and lower middle-class readers are among their intended audience, and surveys suggest that they succeed in reaching a substantial number of readers of this kind; and similar advertisements appear regularly in the more specifically working-class magazine.

The demand for aids of the kind I have just illustrated is only one way in which a wish for entry into the cultured life can express itself. One might discuss the same situation more widely by reference to some current tendencies in reading. I have in mind a reading of cultural publications which is from one aspect improper, which is inspired by too strong and too vague an expectation. It is my impression that this kind of interest in serious publications is more common than is generally thought. There is often a continuous line from elementary promptings to learn 'dynamic speech and writing' to some forms of membership of the 'minor intelligentsia', from an obsessive and often rather bizarre interest in some panacea for the world's ills (by means of a system) to a condition of formidably dense 'opinionation'.

For some people the late *John O'London's Weekly* obviously met a strongly felt need, one stronger, I think, than it could have legitimately claimed to meet. Others are proud of reading J. B. Priestley and writers such as him, because they are 'serious writers with a message'. Others have learned that Mr Priestley is a 'middlebrow' and only mention him in tones of deprecation. They tend to read bitterly ironic or anguished literature – Waugh, Huxley, Kafka, and Greene. They own the Penguin selection from Eliot, as well as some other Penguins and Pelicans; they used to take *Penguin New Writing* and now subscribe to *Encounter*. They know a little, but often only from reviews and short articles, about Frazer and Marx; they probably own a copy of the Pelican edition of Freud's *Psychopathology of Everyday Life*. They sometimes listen to talks on the Third Programme with titles like, 'The Cult of Evil in Contemporary Literature'.

Some have a precarious tenancy in several near-intellectual worlds. If so, they are likely to believe in 'freedom' and to be 'anti-authoritarian'; they will have heard of the National Council for Civil Liberties and will read the *New Statesman and Nation*. They will know the anti-Munnings arguments for modern art, particularly for Picasso. They will know the arguments about the debasing effect of the popular Press and the corruption of advertisements. They will find some pleasure in that kind of analysis, a pleasure which can easily become a sort of masochistic nihilism. Yet they will be more disconcerted when meeting 'reactionary' opposition than they should be, because they will then be meeting externally problems still not resolved in their own personalities. They will still like, but be ashamed of, some pleasures which they know in their conscious and cultured part to be improper. They will feel that they share something of the 'waste land', of the '*Angst*', of the intellectuals; but will really be in a waste land of their own. In any case, they will over-estimate the satisfactions of intellectuals.

A very few acquire a bright finish and practise 'opinionation' which,

as I have said, is a slightly more intellectual form of 'fragmentation'.
In 'opinionation' they can enjoy the crackle of mainly borrowed
ideas, can try to have at call a view on anything – on the H-Bomb,
on 'woman's place', on modern art, on British agriculture, on capital
punishment, on 'the population problem'. Their training helps them
to take on, to assimilate without absorbing, a great number of such
items, to 'have views' at second, third, and fourth hand; it encourages
the rabbit's-eye view. We are familiar with the way in which this
can become a mental promiscuity; and the situation of those who
long for this kind of expertise, but have a poor background and
inadequate training in handling ideas or response to imaginative
work, is particularly unfortunate. They grip hold of a number of
badly understood ideas, but on the whole feel astray. They read the
reviews more easily than the books which are being reviewed, and
in the end take them as a fairly regular substitute. They wander in
the immensely crowded, startling, and often delusive world of ideas
like children in their first Fairground House of Thrills – reluctant to
leave, anxious to see and understand and respond to all, badly wanting
to have a really enjoyable time but, underneath, frightened.

They have, in some degree, lost the hold on one kind of life, and
failed to reach the one to which they aspire. The loss is greater than
the gain. The homes of some of those who achieve even an apparent
poise tell as much as anything else. They have usually lost the cluttered
homeliness of their origins; they are not going to be chintzy. The
result is often an eye-on-the-teacher style of furnishing like their
favourite styles in literature; rooms whose pattern is decided by the
needs of the tenants to be culturally *persona grata*, not to fall into any
working-class 'stuffiness' or middle-class 'cosiness'; intensely self-
conscious rooms whose outward effects are more important than
their liveableness. They are committing an error which they have
noted in the bourgeoisie and the respectable working-classes, who
make their glossy ornaments and the patterned side of the curtains
face the street rather than inside. Each room echoes a thousand others
among those who sought cultural graduation at the same time, and so
most of them have an anonymous public air, similar to that of unrelieved utility furniture. So much is designed for effect, for culturally
keeping up with the Koestlers. There is little healthy untidiness,
natural idiosyncrasy, straight choice of what is personally liked. There
is no plain vulgarity unless certain identified vulgarities have become

fashionable. Few things are chosen because someone in the house really likes them, in the way that makes their Aunt say of the 'loud' vase she got for Christmas, 'Ee, i'nt it luv'ly.' 'Never a good or a real thing said' by the room, because the room is not yet a part of the actuality of life. The room indicates, rather, a division of experience and, more important, it expresses a kind of wish.

The foregoing is deliberately a selective account, meant to bring into focus a situation which, though it affects only a small minority, illuminates some wider aspects of this essay. Since many of the details – of reading and other habits – have been drawn from my own history, I have been strongly aware of a tension between the wish to define my own follies and the wish to justify them. Perhaps on the whole the former has predominated. As a result it probably seems in parts rather harsh, and might appear too much to imply that people such as these are slightly ridiculous, if not dishonest:

She knew the type so well – the aspirations, the mental dishonesty, the familiarity with the outside of books.

There is some truth there, but it is too hard, too unyielding; it would be truer to say, 'How pathetic,' were it not that the moment it is uttered the unjustifiable patronizing is plain. People such as this are often over-intense, it is true. Their urge for culture has sometimes a grim and humourless air – but not one as grim as popular publicists, when they mock at self-improvement, try to make out. Yet how much the attitude commands respect; that at a time when it is so easy to be led into arrogant low-browism, some retain an idealistic love for 'things of the mind'. Behind even the more unhappy expressions of the attitude there often lies an idealism, or better, a nostalgia for ideals. People such as this lean so intensely towards culture precisely because they over-value it, even see it sometimes as a substitute for the religious belief which they cannot quite face as a serious possibility. Religion is suspect; even more, 'class' and money are suspect. Culture is a sign of disinterested goodness, of brains and imagination used to give liberty and poise. Behind the often strange forms of striving is a wish for the assumed freedom, for the power and command over himself, of the 'really cultured' man. This may be a delusion, since it expects more from culture than culture can give; but it is a worthy delusion.

These people are as much affected by their time, in this, as are some people who can give their insecurities a more presentable dress. It is easy to lay too much at the door of this 'strange disease of modern life', and that phrase is a hundred years old, anyway: but in part these are Matthew Arnold's 'aliens', one hundred years later and with an even colder wind blowing:

But in each class there are born a certain number of natures with a curiosity about their best self, with a bent for seeing things as they are, for disentangling themselves from machinery, for simply concerning themselves with reason and the will of God, and doing their best to make these prevail; – for the pursuit, in a word, of perfection ... and this bent always tends to take them out of their class, and to make their distinguishing characteristic ... their *humanity*. They have, in general, a rough time of it in their lives.

Arnold's undefined afflatus never did sound altogether convincing; but there is an important truth in the passage, and it has some force even now. Some of this century's 'aliens' joined the Communist Party or the Peace Pledge Union or the Left Book Club or the Commonwealth movement or the Social Credit Party in the thirties. They often had a purposiveness then which is harder to find in the fifties, but the urge remains. They 'want to do something about things' but feel frustrated – by the variety and magnitude of the problems they discern crouched all round them; by a sense that, though they appear to be expected to be knowledgeable about so much, to have views on so many things like good democratic citizens, there is really nothing they can effectively do to solve any of the problems. 'Save his own soul he has no star' was applied by Hardy to Jude the Obscure; but the light of the soul in today's Judes is a flickering and insecure one, since they are made insecure by doubts about their own adequacy to reach firm decisions. They are made insecure by the multitude of contradictory voices, each well-informed, sure, and persuasive; the voices which say, 'Ah, but it all depends ...', or 'These are only statistics, and you can't trust statistics', or, 'This is only emotive language'. They are intimidated by the extreme difficulty of deciding just what is morally the right thing to do. Worst of all, their confidence is undermined by a lurking fear of the meaninglessness of those basic questions in themselves (is this good? is this right?), which yet they find themselves unable to cease from asking. The last clear sign-posts begin to disappear into the mists of an endless relativity:

does anyone ever really act from principle? or do they merely *seem* to?; are they, in fact, 'pulling another fast one'?; are they foolishly deceiving themselves?; are they simply in need of a tonic? 'The best lack all conviction'; we would be in the presence of the tragedy of the well-intentioned, were it not that the nature of the situation disallows tragic attitudes – which in any case the actors would suspect – and rarely allows them to achieve the strength for tragedy. Usually they remain in regions where 'everything is below the level of tragedy except the passionate egoism of the sufferer'.

They are left with a deadly unwinged honesty, often unrelieved by a saving irony towards the self. But still it is a kind of honesty; its most common face has the uncertainty of that of a boy in strange company. It is indecisive; it expects no cause for enthusiasm, yet regrets this fact. Behind the shyness there is often an undefiant moral courage. It is hidden because these people have learned that if it is expressed it is likely to be mocked. The search for some sort of belief, however disguised, and its constant rebuttal, can leave them for years emotionally inhibited. Or their longing for a belief is often disguised as yet another form of apparent cynicism, not exactly that common to large numbers in the working-classes, but related to it, and with a deeper hold. Here it is strengthened by the load of inadequately possessed knowledge. If they had absorbed the knowledge, perhaps it would not have had so weakening an effect. Just enough about the social sciences, about anthropology, about sociology, about social psychology, has been acquired to supply a destructive reference on most occasions. 'What about the Polynesians?' has now succeeded the political 'What about the Russians?' as the key-question. They take up the game of finding clay feet, but without the pertness of more intellectually confident debunkers: they are inwardly depressed by their constant suspicion that everything and everyone has been found out. They are the poor little rich boys of a world over-supplied with popularized and disconnected information, and much less able to find meaningful groupings for its information. Yet there can be a kind of pleasure in feeling like a cross between Mr Kingsley Martin and Tiresias; and one can in a way enjoy taking the lid off with Graham Greene.

Because this apparent cynicism is really a nostalgia for belief there is a peculiar interest, not unmixed with envy, in observing other men going through the contortions and strains of finding belief. Mingled with that is the endless suspicion of deception; these others are perhaps hypocritical: at any rate there is a resentment that for oneself there seems no possibility of such positive and affirmative action, 'There are only the various envies,/All of them sad'.

A few find an adequate public face – 'I have no illusions. I do not seek to "sell" anyone anything. I know better than to moan in public.' For most, some feature of the face is illuminating – a crinkled fore-head, eyebrows drawn together, a 'shaded eye'; most of all, the mouth, with the lower half only prevented from slackening unhappily by the tightened upper. The upper half provides a front to disguise the deeper discontents, gives a suggestion of a loss-cutting quasi-stoicism. This is the most common expression and one, like most of the others, slightly self-pitying and self-indulgent. Under the pressure of all this living inside oneself, preying over these kinds of doubt, it is easy to see oneself as a version of the dissident Byronic hero. From the Renaissance, from Robinson Crusoe, from Rousseau, various forms of romantic individualism proceed – and in part this is yet one more form of them, but one often gone to seed in self-regard. These dissatisfied romantics, though beset by the sense of a need to make the voyage, rarely set out because there is rarely enough conviction even that the journey is really necessary: they more often become 'the malcontented who might have been'.

Beneath their apparent cynicism and self-pity is a deep sense of being lost, without purpose and with the will sapped. It sometimes seems to me that the situation is most difficult during their twenties, when the most strenuous search for cultural and intellectual satisfac-tions which are rarely gained takes place. There is usually a change after the first few years of marriage. But at first, and for a year or two, they have a trapped look, as though they have, by marrying, been guilty of a bourgeois weakness and, worse, allowed themselves to be caught, to betray their freedom. The climate of the time, as they apprehend it, almost spoils them for undertaking marriage without considerable emotional difficulty. This does not mean only meeting the inevitable complications in the first stages of living with someone else. But they have to learn that one can admit one's deepest emotions, need neither disown them nor wear them on the shoulder like chips; they have to come to the point of realizing that there is nothing stuffy about trying to be a good husband and father, that one may be as much in the truth there as one will ever be in any area of life.

For most, especially during early manhood, there is the sense of a bruised consciousness; they 'sit in darkness and the shadow of death . . . fast bound in misery and iron'. Their roots have been taken up for scrutiny too often; they have become intellectual and spiritual waifs and strays. The questioning continues, and with it the fear of finding answers:

> We would rather be ruined than changed.
> We would rather die in our dread
> Than climb the Cross of the moment
> And see our illusions die.

The submerged idealism and the pervasive indecisiveness ensure that they will not 'cash in': fundamentally, they care; they want to do the right thing. They are in many ways small and pitiful and indulgent; yet the self-consciousness, with all its ramifications, has its attractiveness and its merits. Many of them have resisted some of the worst drugs; they stand for something. And as society comes nearer to the danger of reducing the larger part of the population to a condition of obediently receptive passivity, their eyes glued to television sets, pin-ups, and cinema screens, these few, because they are asking important questions, have a special value. Fundamentally, their questions affect us all today since they are to do with the importance of roots, of unconscious roots, to all of us as individuals; they are to do with those major social developments of our time towards centralization and a kind of classlessness; and they are to do with the relationship between cultural and intellectual matters and the beliefs by which men try to shape their lives. People such as this are therefore among the more sensitive, though now bruised, tentacles of society. The main body on the whole ignores them; but the symptoms they show refer in some degree to all. Bishop Wilson's conclusion of a hundred years ago is just as true today:

The number of those who need to be awakened is far greater than that of those who need comfort.

CHAPTER 11

CONCLUSION

Reflecting upon the magnitude of the general evil, I should be oppressed with
a dishonourable melancholy, had I not a deep impression of certain inherent
and indestructible qualities of the human mind.

WORDSWORTH

... One would have said beyond a doubt
That was the very end of the bout,
But that the creature would not die.

EDWIN MUIR

A. *Resilience*

I have said little about the valuable social changes of the last fifty
years, and much about the cultural dangers which are accompanying
them. Obviously, no one could fail to be glad that most working-
people are in almost all respects better off, have better living conditions, better health, a larger share of consumer goods, fuller educational opportunities, and so on. What I have illustrated, unless my
diagnosis is wrong, is that the accompanying cultural changes are
not always an improvement but in some of the more important
instances are a worsening.

Nor have I referred much to the influence of the 'earnest minority'
among working-class people, since my chief concern has been with
attitudes among the majority. Yet I do not mean to under-estimate
the effect the 'earnest minority' has, or to imply that this minority is
not so likely to be found today. And since the minority has had and
may continue to have (though this is by no means certain) an influence on their group out of all proportion to their numbers, it is
important that something should be said more directly about them.
I have in mind people such as those who take up voluntary trade-
union activity, and those who seek adult education through, for
instance, the classes run by the Workers' Educational Association.
One of the plain advantages in our present situation is that those
working-class people who have this kind of interest are today able
much more fully than formerly to develop and exercise it.

In the last century people such as this actively and often at great sacrifice supported Trade Unionism when it had its way to make, they worked for Labour representation in Parliament, they were connected with the Co-operative Movement and were the pillars of local chapels. They were men of the type who at Leeds in the sixties called a conference of the Leeds Working Men's Parliamentary Reform Association to consider the formation of a national body to conduct a crusade for reform in the industrial areas. They worked for Hyndman's S.D.F. in the eighties, and for the I.L.P. in the nineties. They helped to set up the Labour Representation Committee at the turn of the century and so assisted the birth of the Labour Party. Their leaders, through the decades, were men such as Tom Mann, Ben Tillett, Keir Hardie, and George Lansbury. Many of them are today doing valuable work in political and trade-union affairs, and in the numerous new forms of relationship between employees and management.

During the mid- and late-nineteenth century their reading was likely to be wide, solid, and inspiring. They read volume after volume of Morris and Ruskin. They read Henry George's *Progress and Poverty* (1881) and Blatchford's *Merrie England* (1894). Over a million copies of *Merrie England* were sold, most of them at one penny each; and sixty thousand copies of *Progress and Poverty* were sold within four years. They subscribed to Blatchford's *Clarion* in the nineties, and helped to run Clarion Cycling and Clarion Cinderella clubs. Some of them, with many others whose interests were not so strictly political, joined Mutual Improvement Societies and Mechanics' Institutes, and attended University Extension lecture-courses or others of the various forms of further education. They bought the volumes in Morley's Universal Library and other cheap series. They were to be found among the thirteen thousand purchasers of the first two volumes of Macaulay's *History*, and the twenty-six thousand purchasers of the third volume. Later, they read Shaw and were among those who bought a total of two million copies of Wells's *Outline of History*, and who read the *Science of Life* and *Work, Wealth and Happiness of Mankind*. From 1929 onwards they bought the one-shilling copies of Watt's Thinker's Library. They were some of those for whom the organization of Services' Education during the last war had real meaning and use. They make good use of the public libraries and often listen with genuine interest and discrimination to the Third Programme. They are in the habit today of buying copies of Pelicans, and help to make possible the one-hundred-thousand issues of ten titles by one author which Penguin Books produce. They have helped to increase the sales of 'quality' newspapers and journals, and have contributed to the post-war expansion in further and part-time education organized by the voluntary bodies, the universities, and the Local Education Authorities.

In England and Wales there are now about one hundred and fifty thousand people who take part in the liberal, non-vocational study of the humanities which is organized by voluntary bodies and. university extra-mural departments – that is, approximately one in two hundred adults. The Workers' Educational Association has about ninety thousand students, of whom the largest single group (16,000), other than that comprising people on 'home duties and nursing', is that of manual workers. The total is not large, but has been substantially increased since before the war; almost certainly it can be further increased if money is available. But it is not likely to increase in any striking degree. The more radical problems, in particular as they affect the W.E.A., might almost be deduced from the preceding chapters of this essay. They are: to increase the proportion of students undertaking the more sustained and searching tutorial courses, and to increase the proportion of working-class students. The personal and social needs for self-acquired education seem by no means obvious and pressing today. The productions of the popular publicists are much more powerfully offered now than they were when liberal adult education for working-class people began just over fifty years ago. The difficulty now lies less in the material lack of working-people than in their being over-provided with one kind of material. The economic barriers to knowledge have been largely removed, but there is still a struggle – to ignore the myriad voices of the trivial and synthetic sirens. The W.E.A. has a duty always to be thinking of proper ways of approaching working-class students who may be almost entirely without previous training. But at the centre of its work it must offer a kind of discipline to its students, one which is sharply opposed to the trivialization, the fragmentation, and the opinionation encouraged by popular providers. The possibility of speaking to the condition of the much larger numbers of people who are not intellectually inclined is not within the province of the W.E.A. as it is at present organized.

We saw how popular publicists try to encourage most working-class people to underrate the 'earnest minority' because their very existence, their turning away from the common fare and their search for a more nourishing food, is an implicit judgement on the publicists themselves. The enquiring and serious working-class student is easy game for them; people who insist on getting knowledge against the odds, whether the odds are material or less tangible, can soon appear stodgy and over-earnest. For my part, it seems difficult to overstress the importance to a society of people such as this, who are prepared to address themselves to study, usually after a day's work and often in unpropitious conditions, inspired by a sense, however disguised it may sometimes seem, of the power and virtue of knowledge.

It is a special pity, therefore, that there is little regular periodical provision of the kind of discussion such people require. I mean that we need more journals which would not be popular in any of the ways I have described, but would be intelligent and searching, and yet would start from the sort of background their readers have. This is a particularly complex matter, and I raise it only because it bears directly on much that has been discussed in previous chapters. For the 'earnest minority' who seek culture and intellectual background often go now to journals which have the faults of the world of popular publications in other, if more subtle, forms (misuse of the idea of 'freedom', 'opinionation' in place of 'fragmentation', a kind of cynicism showing as a 'knowingness'), or to journals which satisfy a fashionable 'culture-vulture' wish which is the cultural equivalent of the interest in dress catered for by the more elegant fashion-magazines, or to journals whose tone is too oblique for any but a small part of their audience. A proportion of 'prestige' reading of serious journals is neither avoidable nor automatically to be deplored: it can be one stage towards a discriminating reading. But when there is a great deal of it, as I think there is today, it seems likely that some need is not being met, that an important opportunity is being mis-used. I wonder how far this lack is the result of a failure to under-stand the situation of the intellectual minority among ordinary people; how far many of those engaged in the dissemination of ideas realize the urgent and worthwhile needs of this minority who look to them for help. To attempt to solve this problem can lead to a lot of mistaken postures; it is not easy to find a decent platform without becoming occasionally priggish and portentous. But the present situation offers few grounds for satisfaction.

At the risk of sounding, myself, like a superior distributor of praise and blame, I should add that members of the 'saving remnant', in so far as they engage directly in social activity as part of the 'working-class movement', do not often seem sufficiently prepared to reconsider their aims. I have recalled their work for social reform and have stressed that it was inspired not primarily by a search for material goods but by a sense of the need for higher satisfactions by working-people, satisfactions which would more easily be obtained once material improvements had been made. The greatest need now is for this minority to reassess the position, to realize that the ideas for which their predecessors worked are in danger of being lost, that material improvements can be used so as to incline the body of working-people to accept a mean form of materialism as a social philosophy. If the active minority continue to allow themselves too exclusively to think of immediate political and economic objectives, the pass will be sold, culturally, behind their backs. This is a harder problem in some ways than even that which confronted their predecessors. It is harder to realize imaginatively the dangers of spiritual deterioration. Those dangers are harder to combat, like adversaries in the air, with no corporeal shapes to inspire courage and decision. These things are enjoyed by the very people whom one believes to be adversely affected by them. It is easier for a few to improve the material conditions of many than for a few to waken a great many from the hypnosis of immature emotional satisfactions. People in this situation have somehow to be taught to help themselves.

The 'earnest minority' is very important, but it would be a mistake to allow the discussion of their situation to close a book chiefly concerned with attitudes among a majority. I have already suggested that the maturity which most people may acquire does not necessarily have to be nourished by further education and does not necessarily express itself in political activity. It is important to recall, also, the resilience of the newer approaches which is to be found in most people, a resilience of their own kind which expresses itself, as always, in personal and concrete terms. It is necessary to stress the strength with which much that is valuable in the 'older' attitudes is held on to, and with which much that is new and may seem, at first glance, merely injurious, is assimilated and adapted.

There is, after all, an inherent danger of exaggeration in essays of this kind. There is a danger of gradually becoming remote from our everyday sense of the endless variety and complexity of human nature. In this particular instance, as I noted at the very beginning, there is a danger of failing sufficiently to allow for the mitigations of older influences, of ignoring the less admirable aspects of the 'older' attitudes and the more admirable of the new. As we study popular publications we insensibly tend to give them, so great is their mere bulk, a larger prominence in the whole pattern of people's experience than, in fact, they have. In the areas in which they have their most intensive effect, that effect can be harmful: over some wider aspects of experience, they may have some adverse effect too; but there the effect is quite slowly felt, is checked and neutralized again and again by other forces. People are not living lives which are imaginatively as poor as a mere reading of their literature would suggest. We know this, simply from day-to-day experience. Most contemporary popular entertainment encourages an effete attitude to life, but still much of life has little direct connexion with it. There are wars and fears of war; there is the world of work, of the relations, the loyalties and tensions there; there are the duties of home and the management of money; there are neighbourhood ties and demands; there are ill-ness and fatigue and birth and death; there is all the world of local recreation. That is why I tried much earlier to describe the quality of ordinary working-class life, so that the closer analysis of publications might be set into a landscape of solid earth and rock and water.

Among working-class people, then, how much of a decent local, personal, and communal way of life remains? It remains in speech, in forms of culture (the Working-Men's Clubs, the styles of singing, the brass bands, the older types of magazine, the close group-games like darts and dominoes), and in attitudes as they are expressed in everyday life. Marriage and the home retain their importance more strongly than we are often inclined to think. The notion of tolerance is fre-quently stretched beyond the point of any discrimination, but still works valuably in many ways, as a strong charity rather than as a weakness. The stress on the personal is often misused, but can still give an admirable tension and one especially necessary when life tends to become more public and uniform. Scepticism and non-conformity may often be pulled out of shape until they become a kind of cynicism, but yet they have valuable forms, notably in the enormous ability of people silently to ignore, only to appear to be affected, to let things 'slide off their backs'. Similar qualities help them to sense and often to reject the denial of life in the apparently well-intentioned as much as in the clearly self-interested; to sense, even in matters in which they are largely at sea, a lack of the kind of vitality they trust and admire. With that is the ability to absorb where they wish, and for the rest to carry on, unimplicated underneath, still to keep a hold on a valuable ethical rudder – so that almost all the new material has yet to be presented in what at least seems to be a moral appeal. And there is the ability to keep on 'putting up with things', not simply from a passivity but because that is where one starts from, from the expectation that one will have to put up with a lot; and the maintenance of the traditional corollary of this, to put up with things cheerfully. Again, the cheerfulness is often undermined, is made a self-conscious shadow of itself, but still in some ways it has energy. The power to throw up comedians such as Norman Wisdom is one illustration of this. So is the exercise of cheerful debunking; it can be heard particularly in response to appeals which go too far ahead of contemporary taste; for example, in the laughter which is caused by the script or by the tones of voice used in some short advertising films and some cinema news-reels. All these attitudes are founded on a strong self-respect which is, in most cases, only another way of describing the still considerable moral resources of working-class people. In sum, these resources enable them to ignore much and to make much else better than it really is, to continue putting their own kind of vision into what may not really deserve it, as they have been used to doing for decades in commercial songs and stories. As a result, working-class people are a good deal less affected than they might well be. The question, of course, is how long this stock of moral capital will last, and whether it is being sufficiently renewed. But we have to be careful not to underrate its effect at present.

The preceding paragraph may seem unduly optimistic if we look only at many younger people. Then we remember how much working-class people resume their older attitudes after the years of exceptional freedom in adolescence, courtship, and the early years of marriage; how much, though some new manners are carried into their mature years by each generation, is sloughed away of the more trivial invitations to change. I was tempted to believe at one time, hearing the phrase so often from my middle-aged aunts, that every working-class woman said, somewhere between forty and fifty,

'Ah cum to think more like me mother every day.' There was self-flattery in the thought, and it was sometimes used to excuse stupidity and a refusal to think for oneself. But it indicated the strength which the old attitudes always have; and on balance, the more clamant voices from outside being as they are, it works for good.

How much, in spite of all the canned entertainment and packeted provision, the urge to express oneself personally and freely by mending and making persists. How strongly 'odd-jobbery', 'doing things about the house', survives, even where the husband is not particularly a 'good 'un' in his other habits. In part he is expected to see to such things because there is not the money for or the habit of calling in a local craftsman, a joiner or plumber or painter. But also this kind of activity is still felt to be a proper part of home life; Dad may not be the sort who will take a hand with making a rug or toys for the children; but he is likely to see to the taps or fix an extra shelf in the kitchen or change the boy's bicycle chain. In winter, particularly, many a good husband seems to be always pottering on odd jobs during the evenings.

From there it is an easy step to real 'handymanship', and to the hobbies proper. The counters of working-class paper-shops, towards the weekend, are crowded with a great variety of what the trade calls the 'hobbies' Press', such periodicals as *Angler's News*, *Cage Birds* and *Bird Fancy*, *Smallholder*, *Popular Gardening*, *Practical Mechanics*, *The Woodworker*, and *Cycling*. There are in all about two hundred and fifty periodicals devoted to sports, hobbies, and entertainments. There are two on the breeding of pet fish, seven on domestic pets and cage-birds, one on bell-ringing, ten on aspects of fishing, several cycling papers and dog papers, and almost two dozen on general aspects of hobbies and handicrafts. A substantial number of them make a special appeal to working-class readers, or to them along with lower middle-class readers. In these activities, as is sometimes pointed out, working-class men still exercise personal choice, act freely and voluntarily. Their regular jobs are often undemanding and undiscriminating, but here, by their integrity and devotion to a craft, however curious some of the crafts may seem, they can be specialists.

There may be mentioned here, too, the persistence of the desire to grow things, in window-boxes and on patches of sour soil in back-yards, which are often well-tended; and on allotments – behind hoardings in the main street or on the edge of the permanent way, or on strips of three hundred square yards let at a nominal rent under the provisions of the 1922 Allotment Act ('Every citizen who is able and willing to cultivate an allotment garden is legally entitled to be provided with one'). I have already remarked that working-class people, when they have been moved to a new housing estate, often make little of their large private piece of garden; they are used to small pockets of dirty land stuck away under the mass of urban building, and find themselves out-faced at first by a virgin piece bigger even than an allotment, and bounded by piece after piece of equal rawness and bareness. It is true that the urge to cultivate plants never affected more than a minority; and the interest in allotments, like that in fishing, seems now to be declining a little. Yet there are still one and a half million worked allotments in the country.

On the other hand the interest in breeding animals and birds not only survives but in some branches is increasing. Whippet and greyhound breeding seems almost dead except in a few mining areas or for commercial purposes; canary-breeding is not increasing, but there is a growing interest in some other forms of cage-bird breeding, notably of budgerigars. The Hulton Survey suggests that bird-fancying is more popular with working-class people than with any others. There are about half a million pigeon fanciers in Great Britain, organized in about one thousand Homing Clubs. The clubs usually have their headquarters in a local pub; each member pays an annual subscription of about one pound a year, and a shilling for each bird he brings to the racing point. These are the men whose birds are released from cane baskets by railway porters at the end of the quieter platforms on Saturdays; the owners, flat-capped and with an eye cocked upwards and a stop-watch ready, wait for their pigeons to come softly out of the Saturday dusk.

Much of the foregoing might be taken to indicate no more than a sort of resistance, not any more positive adaptation. But there are also strikingly numerous and varied communal activities among young people, founded on more than the street group; Youth Clubs, Young People's Institutes. Y.M.C.A.s and Y.W.C.A.s, Community Centres, Works' Sports and Hobbies Clubs, football, rugby, and cricket clubs (some of these last are still based on districts and have no official backing), and a host of local leagues for these and other sports. Many of these activities are sponsored by 'Them', but they would not survive were they not supported by a strong and genuine enthusiasm from working-people. To them can be added other instances not officially sponsored, such as the adoption of the 'chara' trip, a striking instance of spontaneous urban adaptation. Or we may think of the way urban working-class people still make use of the public baths. Go into them after four o'clock during the schools' term or on Saturdays. They are smelly with cleaning chemicals, chillingly angular, and slippery-scummy at the edges. But they ring shatteringly with the voices of working-class children throwing themselves and their friends in repeatedly, fighting in bunches in the water and blue with cold because they almost all stay in much too long.

There is, too, the still strong popularity of 'getting out into the country', especially during the great spring festivals. In the thirties the craze was for 'hiking', and though that seemed to me to affect the lower middle-classes more than others, the working-classes went too, on to the dales and hills and moors, which luckily are not far from most of the large towns. If walking is not markedly typical of working-class people, then cycling is. A sign of arrival at real adolescence is the agreement from one's parents to the buying of a bike on the hire-purchase system, paid for out of weekly wages. Then one goes out on it at weekends, with a friend who bought a bike at the same time, or with one of those mixed clubs which sweep every Sunday through town and out past the quiet tram terminus. Many young people insist that they 'like their bed' on a Sunday morning, but a good number are out in this way. The membership figures of the two main cycling clubs give no real indication of the numbers who are out, but rather of those who have more seriously taken up cycling; yet even they have a quarter of a million members. For those who want club companionship, exercise, 'a good day out', there is the Cyclists' Touring Club (and many another local club whose members are not in the C.T.C.); and there is the National Cyclists' Union for those who go in for racing, with specially selected tubing, wheels, and saddles, and an aluminium bottle in a cage on dropped handlebars. The N.C.U. members may often seem scarcely to know whether the road passes through a town or a National Park; but sightseeing is not their purpose. The C.T.C. members, talking as they ride or playing with a ball on the grass, seem to pay little attention to the countryside or the ancient monuments they visit. But they get what they come for – companionship, hard exercise, and fresh air. Both these clubs were founded in 1878, and since then cycling as a working-class hobby has enormously increased in popularity. It is valuable evidence that urban working-class people can still react positively to both the challenge of their environment and the useful possibilities of cheap mass-production.

Perhaps these items will seem little enough to put in the scales against all the forces described above, but I think they indicate great strengths. Working-class people survived the change from a rural to an urban life without becoming a dull *lumpen-proletariat*: in the last half-century they have survived, and in large measure still survive, dangers just as great. Recalling all that they have been asked to endure, one finds oneself adapting words from *King Lear*. 'The wonder is they have endured so long.' Marvelling at this greatest of all instances of 'putting up with things', recalling all that has been said here about the positive way in which these challenges have sometimes been met, one realizes again that it is not simply a matter of endurance but of a more positive response. The wonder is, not that so much remains, but that so much is newly born with each generation.

B. *Summary of Present Tendencies in Mass Culture*

The resilience to be found in individuals and local groups is healthy and important. But it can clearly be another form of democratic self-indulgence to over-stress this resilience, to brush aside any suggestion of increasingly dangerous pressures by a reference to the innate right-headedness of man; to point out that people do still persist in living lives by no means as rootless and shallow as the new influences seem to invite, and from that to assume that this will always be so, that 'human nature will always save itself', that 'you can trust in ordinary decency', to save people from the worst effects, that the resilience of human nature will ensure that 'people will always be people'.

It remains to sum up the general lines on which a mass culture seems to be at present developing. As throughout, I shall draw most of the illustrations from publications. But with suitable modifications of detail the conclusions would apply also to the tendencies encouraged by the cinema, sound broadcasting and television (particularly when these are commercially sponsored), and large-scale advertising.

There has been, particularly during the last few decades, a great increase in the consumption of many kinds of material designed to entertain; there has been an absolute increase, not simply one proportionate to the increase in population. Something of this was inevitable, as the technical capacity to provide entertainment on a large scale and as the money available to the majority of people for its purchase both increased. An increase is not in itself necessarily to be deplored; there was room for one. But to some extent the size of the increase appears to have been decided, not so much by the need to satisfy previously unsatisfied appetites, as by the stronger persuasions of those who provide the entertainment.

Thus, within the last hundred years the total number of publications of all types in Great Britain has risen from perhaps one thousand to over five thousand. Undoubtedly, a considerable increase was inevitable during a century in which a large nation became literate and highly industrialized. But the major part of this increase is due to a comparatively recent growth in the number of magazines and periodicals. Or, to take changes over a recent decade; the total circulation of national and provincial dailies increased by one-half between 1937 and 1947. During the same period the total circulation of Sunday newspapers almost doubled itself. Magazines and periodicals had a circulation of about twenty-six millions in 1938, and probably more than forty millions in 1952. Between 1947 and 1952 the total circulation of national morning papers rose by half a million, and that of Sunday papers by nearly two and a half millions. Daily newspapers are produced now at a rate of two copies for every household in the country. From the Hulton Survey for 1953 it appears that two out of three in the adult population read more than one Sunday newspaper, and more than one out of four read three or more Sunday papers. The estimated number of copies of daily newspapers issued per one thousand of the population is higher in the United Kingdom than in any other country in the world.

There have been concurrent increases in what I have been calling serious reading, just as there have been increases in the audiences for some more serious pursuits generally. Book production in the

United Kingdom is higher than in any other country. A large number are works of fiction, but there has been a substantial increase during recent years in titles of technical and educational books. And we all know of the success since the thirties of the Penguin and Pelican series. There has been a very great increase in the number of books issued from public libraries, especially during the past twenty-five years. During a Gallup Poll in 1950, 55 per cent of those interviewed said they were currently reading a book; this proportion was higher than that found in, for instance, the U.S.A. or Sweden. There have been increases in the sales of several of the decent periodicals.

These details of more solid reading are encouraging, but need to be qualified. What proportions of the issues from public libraries are of worthless fiction or of that kind of non-fiction which is really only a sort of fiction with the added pleasure of a 'true-life story'? A statistical answer cannot be given, since the question involves distinctions of value. The Derby Survey suggests that fiction of one sort or another accounts for between 75 and 80 per cent of public library issues; and most librarians would say, I think, that much of this fiction is of a very poor kind. There is no virtue in the habit of reading for itself; however unexceptionable its subjects and presentation may be, it can become as much an addiction, as separated from the reality of life, as the reading of some of the more occasional literature I have described earlier. The commercial libraries probably issue between 150 and 200 million volumes per year. Of those issued by the two largest libraries, probably about 90 per cent are fiction; of those issued by the 2d to 4d libraries, probably almost 100 per cent are fiction. In the public libraries the issues of the class 'history, biography, travel' form the biggest single non-fiction group, probably accounting now for a quarter to one-third of all non-fiction issues. Again, many librarians would say, I believe, that the books included in that general heading are often of little value. Qualifications of this kind could be raised for a long time. I raise them not to reduce the value of the genuine gains in serious reading, but to make sure that the gains are not assumed to be much greater than they are.

The situation seems to be that a small proportion of keen readers are taking good advantage of their opportunities and that their number is being somewhat increased, but that the great body of people is not only unaffected by such changes, but is affected by quite different tendencies. There seems little likelihood of substantial increases in serious readership, partly because serious reading and popular reading tend to attract different kinds of people (a point to which I shall return), and partly because the great block of popular readers is subject to a different kind of pressure than are the serious readers. There are many movements towards increasing and improving the minority; there are much larger and on the whole more successful movements towards strengthening the hold of a few dominant popular publications on the great majority of people.

I have probably sufficiently shown in earlier chapters that for the really popular publications there must be a constant struggle to expand, to seek very big sales. Thus, it seems as though from year to year the minimum economic circulation of a national newspaper becomes higher, as though each success pushes up the minimum for everyone else. As long ago as 1946 Francis Williams thought it likely that:

> To exist, a modern national paper in Britain must secure a circulation of at the very least close upon a million and a half and preferably one of over two millions (which means that it must regularly be of a kind to appeal to between five and a quarter million and seven million people).

One result of this process appears to have been an increasing centralization or concentration in popular reading, proceeding at the same time as the considerable increase in the actual reading of popular papers. In short, we seem to be reading fewer different papers, but yet to be reading a greater number; to be reading more often, that is, the same papers as each other. Although the circulation of the daily Press has much increased, the total number of newspapers published in this country has declined during the last thirty years. In most forms of popular publication today a very small number of organs is acquiring very large sales indeed; there is usually a sharp drop thereafter to the circulations of all other organs in that form. In a typical instance, the number of publications in this lower group will be greater than that in the higher group; yet the total sales of the upper few will be greater than those of all in the lower group combined. Thus, in one case two publications have more than half of all sales in their field and six or eight others share the rest. So far as can be seen, this process has not yet exhausted itself; a few organs are progressively acquiring a larger proportion than ever before of the total readers in their fields. This process makes the increases in some 'quality' publications seem hardly relevant to the much bigger problem of increased consumption and increased centralization of a few huge popular publications. It is occasionally announced, and always seems slightly disingenuous, that a 'quality' publication has increased its circulation by, say, 15 per cent in a year and that no popular publication can show an increase of more than 3 or 4 per cent. But, of course, with a circulation as large as that of the more famous popular journals there is not much room for large percentage increases. The combined increases made by the two best examples of one type of 'quality' publication in a recent year – though they were considerable when expressed as a percentage – amounted to only one-third of the increased sales recorded in the same period by a single popular publication in the same field. The case is typical; the advance by the 'quality' journals is useful, but does not offset the increasing concentration on the mass popular journals.

Indeed, the special difficulties in maintaining circulation are not so much those of the 'quality' papers as those of the popular papers which try to preserve more sober standards in reporting, comment, and layout. The General Council of the Press makes this point, but introduces it by placing the onus of responsibility on 'the public'; here, as elsewhere, the General Council of the Press seems readier to indicate the responsibility of readers for the present quantitative and qualitative changes in the Press than to analyse the nature of Press responsibility;

As an indication of the trend of public taste in a free and highly competitive market, it is significant that for every additional copy gained by the *Daily Telegraph* during the past year the tabloid newspapers added three. Furthermore, the increased sales of the tabloids were almost exactly counterbalanced by the combined losses of the *Daily Mail*, *Daily Herald* and *News Chronicle* – the *Daily Express* having remained steady.

As the possibilities of further large expansions in their existing publications become more limited, it is inevitable that the mass-publishing organizations should turn to other publications. The appearance of Junior Editions of some popular dailies in 1954 was a logical step next in the process, though this particular experiment seems to have failed. Presumably it was hoped that they would provide not only a new field for expansion but one in which readers could be cultivated for eventual transference to the version for adults.

In spite of the increases in the sales of some more serious publications, there appear to be indications that the greater concentration in popular publications makes existence harder for smaller-circulation papers, unless they have a firm audience willing to pay well for them, or are subsidized. The two most recently founded cultural journals, *Encounter* and *London Magazine*, have some financial backing, the latter from the *Daily Mirror* organization. I suggested above that concentration pushes up the economic minimum at which a paper can be produced. Thus there may be financial problems even though the actual circulation of the paper has not fallen. The death of *John O' London's Weekly* in 1954, when there was said to have been no significant loss in readership, may well be a case in point.

A considerable absolute increase in the amount of material produced, an increasing concentration in the organs supplying the material, consequent greater difficulties for minorities: these seem the main features in the organizational development of popular entertainments and publications. What, in equally brief summary, are likely to be their effects?

The readers of the more popular papers are clearly not only working-class people, though working-class people are likely to form a majority if only because they are a majority of the total population. No doubt these journals realize that the biggest single group to which they can address themselves is that comprising the three-quarters of the population who today leave school finally at the age of fifteen. In this connexion it may be useful to say something more about a matter I hinted at earlier – that is, about one possible effect of the scholarship system. The relation between the intellectual minority in the working-classes and those classes as a whole is an immensely complicated subject which I can discuss only tentatively. It is obviously important not to confuse the intellectual minority with the 'earnest' minority: a sense of social purpose does not necessarily accompany the possession of brains. Nor do all those who enjoy advanced education leave their class emotionally or physically. Nevertheless, the intellectual minority, with particular effect during the latter part of the nineteenth century, used to stay within the working-classes more than it does today. Its members formed some of the fermenting elements in their groups, and were an important part of that 'working-class movement' which, as I have already noted, help to bring about considerable improvements in the material lot and status of all working-class people. They were able to help to improve conditions partly because they were among the few who were able to meet and engage the managers in other classes with their own weapons, those of the intellect.

Today many of them are selected at the age of eleven and are often translated, by a process of education, into membership of other classes. At present, roughly one in five of the children of all classes go to grammar-schools. The home background of some lower middle-class or middle-class children may make it easier for them to win scholarships; and a few working-class children can still not take up scholarships, or they leave the grammar-schools early, because of financial pressure. But I was the poorest boy in my class and went to the grammar-school along with the next poorest boy and a few others; grants are higher today, working-class people are in general better off, and education is still valued by many working-class people. It therefore seems a large exaggeration to say of 'the best working-class lads', as the Vice-Principal of Ruskin College said recently, 'The majority are still driven by economic pressure to add to the family income as soon as possible.' Of those who go to the grammar-schools, not all leave their class, but a substantial proportion do.

The examination at eleven-plus may be in many things clumsy, but it does with a fair measure of success select intellectually agile children. Is it not therefore likely to cause the working-classes now to lose many of the critical tentacles which they would have retained years ago? It hardly helps to conclude that this proves only that we must stop speaking or thinking in terms of 'classes', that now each does the work he is best fitted for, and the clever son of poor parents takes up his position in that part of a democratic society where he can be of most value. Few people are likely to regret that clever children in the working-classes now have a greater chance of obtaining posts appropriate to their abilities. But even if the title 'working-classes' is not used, there exists a great body of people who have to perform the less interesting, the more mechanical jobs. It is a matter of some importance that they are likely to include a smaller proportion of the critically minded than they have hitherto included. For this is happening at a time when many who seek the money and favour of working-people approach them constantly along the lines to which they are most receptive and exposed, with material whose effect is likely to be debilitating. By the interaction of these two important factors in contemporary life we might eventually find ourselves moving towards a kind of new caste system, one at least as firm as the old.

I suggested earlier that it would be a mistake to regard the cultural struggle now going on as a straight fight between, say what *The Times* and the picture-dailies respectively represent. To wish that a majority of the population will ever read *The Times* is to wish that human beings were constitutionally different, and is to fall into an intellectual snobbery. The ability to read the decent weeklies is not a *sine qua non* of the good life. It seems unlikely at any time, and is certainly not likely in any period which those of us now alive are likely to know that a majority in any class will have strongly intellectual pursuits. There are other ways of being in the truth. The strongest objection to the more trivial popular entertainments is not that they prevent their readers from becoming highbrow, but that they make it harder for people without an intellectual bent to become wise in their own way.

The fact that changes in English society over the last fifty years have greatly increased the opportunities for further education available to the few people who will seek it has, therefore, little direct compensatory bearing on the fact that concurrent changes are bringing about an increased trivialization in productions for the majority. Most readers of a popular modern newspaper/magazine are unlikely ever to read a 'quality' paper, but they used to read an old-style weekly which was in some respects better than their newspaper/magazine. The new-style popular publications fail not because they are poor substitutes for *The Times* but because they are only bloodless imitations of what they purport to be, because they are pallid but slicked-up extensions even of nineteenth-century sensationalism, and a considerable decline from the sinewy sensationalism of Elizabethan vernacular writers. They can be accused (as can all else for which they stand as examples: the thin *bonhomie* of many television programmes, the popular film, much in commercial radio), not of failing to be highbrow, but of not being truly concrete and personal. The quality of life, the kind of response, the rootedness in a wisdom and maturity which a popular and non-highbrow art can possess may be as valuable in their own ways as those of a highbrow art. These productions do not contribute to a sounder popular art but discourage it. They make their audience less likely to arrive at a wisdom derived from an inner, felt discrimination in their sense of people and their attitude to experience. It is easier to kill the old roots than to replace them with anything comparable. Popular publicists always tell their audience that they need not be ashamed of not being highbrow, that they have their own kinds of maturity. This is true, but it becomes false the moment such people say it, because of the way they say it; that is, because their manner of approach seriously distorts the assumption.

Every tendency I have analysed in popular publications is to be found in some forms of broadcasting – especially in those with commercial connexions – and in some ways more strikingly than in publications. There is the appeal to old decencies, as in programmes with titles like, 'For Your Feeling Heart'; there are the new emphases, the stress on the acquisitive and the novel – 'For Your Feeling Heart – in this programme You may Make Your Pile'. There is the high-powered modern combination of these two, in programmes where intimate personal problems are exposed before an immense audience and the person afflicted 'wins' some money for his participation. There is the lowbrow-gang-spirit of some gramophone-record features in which young men, accompanying their items with a stream of pally patter, offer programmes whose whole composition assumes that whatever the greatest number like most is best and the rest are the aberrations of 'eggheads'. Always the apologists for these programmes make the usual defence – that they are 'in good taste – homely – full of the pathos and joy of ordinary lives'; and that they are also, 'new – arresting – startling – sensational – full of gusto – and handsomely endowed with prizes'.

Most mass-entertainments are in the end what D. H. Lawrence described as 'anti-life'. They are full of a corrupt brightness, of improper appeals and moral evasions. To recall instances: they tend towards a view of the world in which progress is conceived as a seeking of material possessions, equality as a moral levelling, and freedom as the ground for endless irresponsible pleasure. These productions belong to a vicarious, spectators' world; they offer nothing which can really grip the brain or heart. They assist a gradual drying-up of the more positive, the fuller, the more co-operative kinds of enjoyment, in which one gains much by giving much. They have intolerable pretensions; and pander to the wish to have things both ways, to do as we want and accept no consequences. A handful of such productions reaches daily the great majority of the population: their effect is both widespread and uniform.

They tend towards uniformity rather than towards anonymity. I have suggested that working-people are not so much visited by a feeling of anonymity as might appear to those who observe them from outside. Nor do I think that working-people have yet a strong *sense* of uniformity: they are nevertheless being presented continually with encouragements towards an unconscious uniformity. This has not yet been found hollow by most people because it is expressed most commonly as an invitation to share in a kind of palliness, even though in a huge and centralized palliness. Most people will respond to such an appeal the more readily because it seems to have much in common with some older working-class attitudes. The result is a high degree of passive acceptance, an acceptance often only apparent and often qualified at present, but which is a ground for more dangerous extensions. From this point of view it sometimes appears that the type of emerging common man will be one who tends, by three simple gestures, a highly complicated machine, and who keeps in a centrally-heated locker a copy of the latest mass-produced sex-and-violence novel – *Some Dames Don't Strip Easy*, to coin a characteristic title – for reading in those parts of the allotted intervals when he is not listening to a radio 'gang' show.

The fact that illiteracy as it is normally measured has been largely removed only points towards the next and probably more difficult problem. A new word is needed to describe the nature of the response invited by the popular material I have discussed, a word indicating a social change which takes advantage of and thrives on basic literacy. All this needs to be considered with special urgency today because it is in continuous and increasingly rapid development. The analysis of changes in some popular publications during the last thirty or forty years should have illustrated the dubious quality of the life such things promote, their greatly increased powers of dissemination, and the accelerated speed of their development. The arrival of television is only the latest goad to popular publications; there is not likely to be any halt if matters are left to take their normal commercial course. The General Council of the Press regrets what it calls 'immoderate condemnation' of popular papers, and continues, speaking of the general situation:

To maintain the circulations on which their existence depends, newspapers have to flavour themselves according to their public's requirements and to compete hourly with others catering for a similar public . . . with millions of the less cultivated in the land now buying a paper there is a proper and important place for what, without priggishness, can be termed a vulgar press.

Such sonorous generalization, meant to serve as a partial justification for much of the process described in this book, surely deserves to be called 'immoderate apologetics'.

I have continually stressed the way in which newer forces are adapting and modifying elements in what was a fairly distinctive working-class culture. No doubt something similar could be demonstrated in the culture of other classes, if only because the newer productions appeal to more than working-class people. This throws further light on the claim to an emerging classlessness which I questioned at the very beginning of this essay. We may now see that in at least one sense we are indeed becoming classless – that is, the great majority of us are being merged into one class. We are becoming culturally classless. The newer women's magazines are in this sense 'classless' whereas the older kind belonged to particular social groups. Mass publications cannot reach an audience of the size they need by cutting across class boundaries. No doubt many of them have a special warmth for the 'little folk' – the working- and lower middle-classes. This is not because they belong to their audience in the way that older working-class publications often did, nor simply because their producers subscribe to one of the more flattering democratic assumptions, but because that audience forms the majority of their potential readers, because, though they would like to attract many others, they must have this group as the basis of their sales.

From one point of view the old social-class distinction still has some force. It is possible to say that the new mass audience is roughly formed of the total of twenty million or so adults who read the most popular daily newspapers: and then to point out that nevertheless these papers are in some things different, that they can loosely be called either working-class or lower middle- to middle-class. Though this may be true it serves only to underline the general trend. Before the war one could reasonably speak of six or eight popular papers as though they were all more or less level in their effectiveness. If the present trend continues, we shall soon be able to speak only of two or three. Concentration has gone a long way but has had to pause at the rough boundaries of the present most important division in social class, that between the working-classes and the middle-classes. But from reading these papers it is plain that their differences are largely superficial, that they are chiefly differences of tone and 'properties'. Indisputably, these differences are important to the readers; as to the wider effects which the papers will have, the differences are less important than the similarities, than the fact that the kinds of culture which each paper embodies, the assumptions and appeals, are largely the same. The emerging classless class is likely to be a compound of these two audiences; at present it is held in a separation which is becoming less meaningful from year to year. Many factors are helping to make it less significant. To those already discussed another may be added, a further instance of a possible interplay between material improvement and cultural loss: that it is probably easier to merge working-class people into a larger, culturally characterless class when they no longer have such strong economic pressure as makes them feel the great importance of loyal membership of their known groups. No doubt many of the old barriers of class should be broken down. But at present the older, the more narrow but also more genuine class culture is being eroded in favour of the mass opinion, the mass recreational product and the generalized emotional response. The world of club-singing is being gradually replaced by that of typical radio dance-music and crooning, television cabaret and commercial-radio variety. The uniform national type which the popular papers help to produce is writ even larger in the uniform international type which the film-studios of Hollywood present. The old forms of class culture are in danger of being replaced by a poorer kind of classless, or by what I was led earlier to describe as a 'faceless', culture, and this is to be regretted.

Finally, it has been clear to me throughout this essay, as it must have been to a reader, that issues much more difficult than those I have directly treated were being approached – issues in philosophy, to name only one example. These are issues I am not qualified to pursue. In order to be able to till my own part of the field I felt I could reasonably take for granted a general agreement on certain assumptions, an agreement sufficient to allow me to use, without closer definition than emerges from the detailed illustrations, words such as 'decent', 'healthy', 'serious', 'valuable', 'poor', 'weakening', 'hollow', and 'trivial'. This is one individual view of some trends in the present cultural situation, based partly on personal experience and partly on specialist interests, and can only be a contribution to a much wider discussion, a single diagnosis offered for scrutiny.

There arise also many questions of a more specific kind, questions about possible direct action in the present situation; for instance, as to the extent and nature of permissible official interference with cultural matters in a democracy, and so on. These are not easy to answer, and perhaps they can best be discussed pragmatically, when from time to time decisions of this kind have to be made (as with commercial television). It would be pointless for me to try to enunciate general principles here. But there may be some point in putting forward two considerations about common attitudes to such questions today.

It often seems to me that many of the people who do know something of the process described here have too easy a tolerance towards it. There are many who feel that they 'know all the arguments about cultural debasement', and yet can take it all remarkably easily. Sometimes they confess to a rather pleasant ability to go culturally slumming, to 'enjoy looking at the — now and again'. I wonder how often this ease arises from the fact that, though they may know all the arguments, they do not really know the material, are not closely and consistently acquainted with the mass-produced entertainment which daily visits most people. In this way it is possible to live in a sort of clever man's paradise, without any real notion of the force of the assault outside.

Again, to define the limits of freedom in any single case is, I have admitted, extremely difficult. But many of us seem so anxious to avoid the charge of authoritarianism that we will think hardly at all about the problem of definition. Meanwhile, the freedom from official interference enjoyed in this kind of society, coupled with the tolerance we ourselves are so happy to show, seems to be allowing cultural developments as dangerous in their own way as those we are shocked at in totalitarian societies.

It seems best to end on a note that has occurred throughout, on the peculiarly inner and individual nature of this crisis. This is illustrated most briefly in the recurrent observation that working-class people, though they are being in a sense exploited today, at least have now to be approached for their consent. The force of environment and the powers of persuasion count for a great deal but are not irresistible, and there are many instances of the power of free action. Working-people may in much give their consent easily, but that is often because they think themselves assenting to certain key-ideas which they have traditionally known as the informing ideas for social and spiritual improvement. These ideas have a moral origin, and that part of them is still not altogether dead. Democratic egalitarianism has one source in the assumption that all are of equal worth in a much more valuable sense; overweening freedom owes much to the idea that we must try to be responsible for our own fate and decisions; the apparent valuelessness of the permanent open mind rests in part on a refusal to be fanatic, to let the heart ('the feeling heart') become 'enchanted to a stone'. The choice today should therefore be clearer than it was before: it begins from a somewhat freer ground, one less cluttered with material hindrances.

So much is profoundly encouraging. And it may be that a concentration of false lights is unavoidable at this stage of development in a democracy which from year to year becomes more technologically competent and centralized, and yet seeks to remain a free and 'open' society. Yet the problem is acute and pressing – how that freedom may be kept as in any sense a meaningful thing whilst the processes of centralization and technological development continue. This is a particularly intricate challenge because, even if substantial inner freedom were lost, the great new classless class would be unlikely to know it: its members would still regard themselves as free and be told that they were free.

NOTES AND REFERENCES

A. *Quoted Speech*

▶ The problem was to come close to the sound of urban working-class speech without either puzzling a reader or giving a misleadingly quaint air. Phonetic spelling would have had the first disadvantage and dialect the second. I have therefore used forms of spelling which roughly approximate to the spoken sound and should be immediately intelligible. Thus 'you' is usually shown as 'y', though probably a nearer spelling of the sound required would be 'yĕ' or 'yŭ'. 'Yer' is used where the following word begins with a vowel. Again, in working-class speech 'I' sounds like æ (as in 'apple'). 'Ah' has the disadvantage of slightly suggesting the Deep South, but is less puzzling than æ and more accurate than 'I', and so has had to serve. Almost every aitch had been dropped, and some readers will protest that not everyone in the working-classes drops the aitch. Yet almost everyone does, and it is more accurate to omit it in general than to include it. But here, as with 'you' and 'I', I have deliberately been inconsistent and used the normal forms occasionally.

B. *Details of Readership*

Unless otherwise described, all details of readership, in both the text and the notes, are drawn directly from or are based on the tables in the *Hulton Readership Survey*.

The *Hulton Readership Survey* (*HRS*) employs a socio-economic division into five groups. The compilers are particularly careful to point out (1955) that 'the division is primarily a social rather than an economic one. However, there is some correlation between social class and income and so we offer the following very rough guides to the range of income typical of a head of household in each class'. The groups are:

    A. The well-to-do, 4% of all informants
        (probably more than £1300 p.a.).
    B. The middle-class, 8% of all informants
        (probably between £800 and £1300 p.a.).
    C. The lower middle-class, 17% of all informants
        (probably between £450 and £800 p.a.).
    D. The working-class, 64% of all informants
        (probably between £250 and £450 p.a.).
    E. The poor, 7% of all informants
        (probably less than £250 p.a.).

Such a grouping can provide only a rough guide to types of reader-ship as they are discussed in this essay, particularly in groups D–E, which will include both the working-classes and many in the lower middle-classes as I have used the terms. But I have used statistics only as secondary supporting evidence, so these figures will be of some value.

The distinction between circulation (actual sales) and readership (estimated actual number of readers) should be clear from the text. Several authorities estimate that $3\frac{1}{2}$ people read each copy of a publi-cation sold; others think that $2\frac{1}{2}$ is a truer figure. The figure in *HRS* are of the estimated actual number of readers over the age of sixteen; the estimated population over sixteen is thirty-seven millions.

c. *The Derby Survey*

This term has been used, both in the text and notes, to refer to *The Communication of Ideas*, by Cauter and Downham.

The Derby Survey divides the population in this way:

Upper-class	3%
Middle-class	25%
Working-class	72%

D. *Miscellaneous*

(i) If a book reference has been given in full in the bibliography a shortened form has been used in the notes and epigraphs.

(ii) A.B.C. is an abbreviation for the Audit Bureau of Circulation.

CHAPTER I

Sec. B

p. 10   a hierarchy of specialization: Professor Asa Briggs, who has a particularly close knowledge of the smaller West Riding urban centres, reminded me of this feature. I am inclined to think that working-class life can more easily have dignity in these places than in the big cities. Many of the men and women are skilled craftsmen in one fine trade (usually some aspect of tex-tiles). The hills are still only just at the back of the streets of stone houses, and the links with preceding rural generations more evident. There is less likely, I think, to be an underlying sense of being part of a large and socially separated body of workers in various heavy industries. Professor Briggs also thinks that working-class people in these areas may move more easily than do those in the cities. Perhaps there is less sense of having finally 'landed up' than there is in one of the big workers' areas in the cities.

p. 12   'some rather mistily conceived pastoral tradition . . .': Some writers seem to me to make our own times blacker by exaggerating the pleasures of the life of the poor before the Industrial Revolution. Dorothy Marshall's *The English Poor in the Eighteenth Century* is a useful corrective here. After a study of the diaries of some eighteenth-century country-dwellers, Leonard Woolf summarized their life as one of 'laborious employment, narrow dreariness and boisterous brutality' (*After the Deluge*, vol. I, p. 152). The more 'comely' features did exist, of course.

p. 13   growth of the towns: Middlesbrough is a good example of the nineteenth-century boom town. In 1821 it was a village with 40 inhabitants; by 1841 there were 5,500; by 1861, 19,000; by 1881, 56,000 and by 1901, 91,000. Such increases were not simply caused by migration from the countryside; the total population was increasing rapidly. By 1861 it was 20 millions, more than double what it had been in 1801.

p. 14   'ready-packeted proprietary drugs . . .': There is still enormous faith in them. By now a few are so well-established in the minds of working-people that they are no longer regarded as proprietary products but almost as natural remedies.

CHAPTER 2

Sec. A

p. 15   'What are the roots . . .': T. S. Eliot, *The Waste Land*, Faber and Faber.

p. 18   the folklore of whist-drives: Related by a man who has been M.C. at 3,000 drives (*Reveille*, 2 Oct. 1953).

Sec. B

p. 22   the gregariousness of the family group: Before the appearance of sound radio and television, family card-games were very popular, with whist as the favourite. Even after they had lost much of their popularity, the one-man game of 'patience' still had a strong following. One of my aunts played it regularly in the thirties.

p. 22   dogs and cats: *HRS 1955* suggests that dogs are more popular
with the upper- than with the middle- and lower-classes, but
that the lower-classes (gps. D–E) have more cats, proportionately, than others.

p. 24   the popularity of pork-pies: A friend of mine recently heard
a young working-class couple discussing a pork-shop window.
'Eh, yer a pork-pie fanatic, aren't y'?' she said fondly.

p. 25   tinned salmon for tea: This was sometimes felt to be an extravagance: 'They're bringing t'salmon out for 'im now'
was a phrase used to indicate that a suitor had been accepted
by the parents.

Sec. C

p. 27   'I know . . .': Dylan Thomas, *After the Funeral*, Dent (New
Directions, N.Y., U.S.A.).

p. 28   Rowntree's poverty-cycle: Rowntree distinguished three
troughs of poverty in the usual working-class life, thus: born
in poverty; in poverty again during the time in which the
children were growing up; last, in poverty after the children
had married and the father retired from work.

p. 30   'looking well after the wage-earners, particularly in food . . .':
E.g. the number of wives who gave up most of their meat and
bacon rations to their husbands because they were 'so fond of
a bit of meat'.

p. 34   Anglo-Saxon poem: From *The Seafarer*, trans. R. K. Gordon,
Everyman edition of 1926 (E. P. Dutton and Co., Inc., N.Y.,
U.S.A.).

p. 34   Dr Zweig: See F. Zweig, *Women's Life and Labour*, *The British
Worker*, and *Labour, Life and Poverty*. Dr Zweig's books have
been useful general reminders throughout the whole of this
section.

p. 35   going to dances: Ballroom dancing is the second largest entertainment industry in the country (after the cinema). There are
probably between 450 and 500 ballrooms, and many more halls
which are used for dancing among other purposes. Attendances
are estimated at 200 million a year and the money involved at
about £25 million (a quarter of the amount involved in cinema-
going). The age-range is roughly 17–25 (details from 'Saturday
Night at the Palais', *Economist*, 14 Feb. 1953. This observer par-

ticularly noted the 'respectable' tone of most halls and the earnestness of the dancers' interest in the pursuit).

p. 37   'spare-time money-making is so often regarded as for their own pockets': Noted by Dr Zweig, *Women's Life and Labour*.

Sec. D

p. 39   husbands in charge of the money: There are differences even in other parts of the North: e.g. with married women weavers in Lancashire, in many cases.

p. 39   men's smoking: *HRS 1955* confirms what observation suggests, that cigarettes are the most popular form of smoking among working-class people. 68 per cent of working-class men smoke cigarettes and only 17 per cent smoke pipes; this is a rather higher proportion of cigarette-smokers than in other classes. Expenditure on smoking seems roughly uniform throughout the classes; thus it will, in general, account for a higher proportion of working-class incomes. The report on Consumers' Expenditure in the United Kingdom (see notes to Chapter 3) indicates that, as the expenditure on drink has declined, that on smoking (especially of cigarettes) has increased in all classes.

Sec. E

p. 42   't' Moor': My originals are Hunslet and Holbeck 'Moors' in Leeds. I believe both have now been transformed with soil, shrubs, and flowering plants.

p. 43   'scour her window-ledges and steps twice a week': There are interesting differences in practice from town to town. The women of South Leeds use yellow scouring-stone; those of Sheffield use, I think, white.

p. 45   'Nor does he travel a great deal'; The Derby Survey (p. 113) supports this. Among those interviewed, 1 in 4 of those in the middle-classes had made a journey out of Derby in 1952, but only 1 in 10 of those in the working-classes (day or two-day trips were excluded).

p. 45   'perhaps an annual holiday . . .': This may well be with relatives, since such an arrangement is not only cheaper but more homely.

p. 46   'diddlems': A form of club or 'draw' usually with weekly payments-in by all members, and a withdrawal by one member, normally chosen by lot, in each week ('Me diddlem's come up').

p. 47   the pleasure of eating fish-and-chips: A friend of mine had a very unhappy home during adolescence, and on one occasion expressed doubts whether life was worth living to his French master. The master, a poor Jew from Manchester, 'bade me think of the smell of fish-and-chips *with vinegar on*, and I was won for the living-on as surely as Goethe's Faust was by the sound of the Easter hymns'.

p. 50   Public Reading-Rooms: They were much sadder places in the thirties. Among others, the newspaper canvassers – out-of-work clerks and salesmen and a few graduates – used them as places in which to eat their sandwiches and make up their lists.

   Miss Sargaison's *Growing Old in Common Lodgings* is relevant and valuable here. Of the old men in a Belfast Reading-Room she notes, 'Some of the aged students take the opportunity of surreptitiously drying their socks on the hot pipes, but banishment to the cold outside is the penalty if discovered.'

CHAPTER 3

Sec A

p. 55   North-Country Magistrates' Court: Some of the material used here appeared in a different form, in an essay I contributed to *Tribune* (4 Oct. 1946).

p. 56   the 'Orlick' spirit: The reference is to Dickens's *Great Expectations*.

p. 59   'Oh, reason not the need . . .': Shakespeare, *King Lear*, II, iv, 268.

Sec. B

p. 60   the provisional committee of the National Union of Gas Workers: See *My Life's Battles*, Will Thorne, Newnes, 1925.

p. 62   'Lack of scope for the growth of ambition . . .': The point is also made by Dr Zweig.

p. 62   Matthew Arnold: *Culture and Anarchy*, chapter 2.

p. 65   'There's such a thing as mass thought . . .': A working-man, reported in Reaveley and Winnington, *Democracy and Industry*, p. 60.

p. 66   'emollient phrases . . .': I owe this pleasant epithet to T. H. Pear; see his *Voice and Personality*.

p. 67   rows: I was reminded of some details here by Professor Asa Briggs.

Sec. C

p. 74 'much less drinking of all kinds . . .': The turning-point in the consumption of alcohol came in 1900. Before then, consumption was rising; afterwards, it began to fall. Since the early thirties the consumption of alcohol per head has been less than half what it was in 1900 (see Prest and Adams, *Consumers' Expenditure in the United Kingdom, 1900–19*; *Report of the Commissioners of Customs and Excise, 1951–2* (Cmd. 8727); and *The Brewers' Almanack*, 1953 [p. 89]).

p. 75 'shyness about some aspects of sex . . .': The Kinsey Report gives this a wider corroboration.

CHAPTER 4

Sec. A

p. 81 'Adjusted to the local needs . . .': W. H. Auden, 'In Praise of Limestone', *Nones*, Faber and Faber, 1952 (Random House, N.Y., U.S.A.).

p. 84 sport: I am again indebted to Dr Zweig and Professor Asa Briggs for some of the detail here.

p. 85 'Regard your body . . .': R. M. N. Tisdall, *The Young Athlete*, quoted Harold Stovin, *Totem, the Exploitation of Youth*, p. 55.

p. 87 *Silver Star*; 27 May 1953.

Sec. B

p. 88 'freedom to leave Sunday school and read the *News of the World* . . .': Miss L. Fenwick confirms that this is still a custom, in *Periodicals and Adolescent Girls*.

The Derby Survey (p. 53) showed that 63 per cent of children between 4 and 10 and 56 per cent of children between 11 and 15 go to Sunday school in that town. Church and chapel attendances by adults are, of course, much below these figures (though 98 per cent of adults made a nominal profession of membership of a religious body).

p. 88 no active hostility towards the parson: Rowntree and Lavers, in *English Life and Leisure*, come to an opposite conclusion. I find myself wondering whether this may be due to listening more to what is said than to how it is said.

p. 91 concern with morals, not metaphysics: Professor Asa Briggs, whose background is in many ways similar to mine, thinks I

K

may be generalizing from too limited an experience here. His experience does not support my point.

p. 92   phrases indicating what is understood by religion: I owe some refreshment of memory here to Mass Observation's *Puzzled People*.

Sec. C

p. 94   *Thomson's Weekly News: HRS 1945* shows that this paper has the following readership:

> Classes A–B roughly 1 in 55
> Class C   roughly 1 in 19
> Classes D–E roughly 1 in 13

p. 94   the Sunday gossip–with–sensation papers . . . special favourites of the working-classes: They are very popular with other classes, of course; but working-class people, as compared with those in the middle-class, make more of their Sunday papers and less of their dailies (see *HRS*).

p. 95   De Rougemont: In *Passion and Society*.

p. 95   'some magazines . . . predominantly read by working-class women . . .': Most of the figures of the total readership of these magazines given in *HRS 1953* are rough approximations. They show:

TITLE	TOTAL ESTIMATED READERSHIP (*Women only*)	WORKING-CLASS READERSHIP (*Women only*)
Red Letter	750,000	700,000
Silver Star	650,000	620,000
Lucky Star	600,000	560,000
Red Star Weekly	570,000	530,000
Glamour	570,000	530,000
Secrets	No figures for women women in gps. A, B, and C. Readership there is too small.	350,000
Oracle	ditto	320,000
Family Star	ditto	350,000

The figures in the right-hand column are for Hulton's groups D–E, that is, for 71 per cent of the population. I should guess that the concentration is even heavier in the working-classes as I have sought to define them.

p. 95   age of the 'older' magazines: All are weeklies and at the time
of writing have reached the following serial numbers, approximately:

      Secrets 950: *Red Star Weekly*, 1,100: *Miracle*, 970: *Silver Star*,
      600: *Oracle*, 1,050: *Lucky Star*, 680.

p. 96   'Almost all are produced by three large commercial organizations . . .':

      Newnes publish *Lucky Star*, *Silver Star*, and *Glamour*.

      Amalgamated Press, which was known as Harmsworth Bros.
Ltd until just after the turn of the century and is the largest of
the periodical houses, publishes *Oracle* and *Miracle*.

      Thomson and Leng, two family groups which make up the
largest publishing organization for magazines and periodicals
outside London, publish *Red Star Weekly* and *Secrets*.

      D. C. Thomson, the Managing Director of Thomson's, died
on 12 Oct. 1954, aged 93, at Dundee. He seems to have been
a provincial Harmsworth, taking brilliantly the opportunities
offered by universal education. His father was a ship-owner who
acquired the Dundee *Courier* in 1884 and put him in charge of it.
Thereafter he constantly expanded, by buying other publications and amalgamating, until he controlled one of the largest
newspaper and periodical businesses in Great Britain. He directed
Scottish morning and evening newspapers, women's magazines
and children's comics (e.g. *Beano* and *Dandy*, which sell about
$1\frac{1}{4}$ million copies each), and several other kinds of publication.
(Most of this detail is from an obituary notice in the *Manchester
Guardian*, 13 Oct. 1954.)

p. 98   De Rougemont: 236–9.

p. 100 'As Stella Kay . . .': *Silver Star*, 27 May 1953.

p. 100 'Mother's Night Out': *Secrets*, 13 June 1953.

p. 100 *Oracle*: 27 Sept. 1952.

p. 100 *Lucky Star*: 'The Dream', 18 May 1953.

p. 101 'the case against "stock responses" . . .': It quickly becomes evident that the most commonly used contemporary cultural
division – into high-, low- and middle-brows – is of very
limited use, and soon becomes positively misleading.

p. 101 Christmas and Birthday card verses: The new style is arriving
here, too. As elsewhere, it is usually much slicker, in designs
and scripts.

p. 102   'Happiness is made up . . .': By A. E. P., *Silver Star*, 27 May 1953.

p. 103   '*The Sorrows of Satan* – a "classic" to my aunts . . .': So was Hall Caine's *The Deemster*, which had appeared a few years earlier, in 1887.

CHAPTER 5

Sec. A

p. 105   'There's but . . .': A workman in *Foma Gordyeef*, Maxim Gorki.

p. 109   'Working-class people . . . are fond of a gamble . . .': Figures in the *Report of the Royal Commission on Betting, Lotteries and Gaming* (Appendix II, p. 150, Table 6) suggest that the percentage of men in the working-classes who bet on the 'pools' is higher than the percentage of those doing so in other classes. This does not imply that their average stake is any more.

Sec. B

p. 112   the 'Baroque': I owe this use of the word to Lambert and Marx's *English Popular Art*.

p. 115   love of a high polish and of skill: French polishing used to be held in high regard. There was usually a local man who practised the craft in his spare time. I suppose the shinier modern furniture has helped to take away his customers.

p. 116   'The lovely stylized horses have almost gone . . .'; But they are now coming back, as very popular period pieces.

p. 119   'They make nothing of Scandinavian simplicities . . .': The 'contemporary' furniture which is available from shops catering for the working-classes has usually undergone a remarkable transformation. It retains the main 'contemporary' outlines, but is rather elaborate, rather overdone even in its 'contemporary' characteristics.

Sec. C

p. 120   'song-books sold by some stationers . . .': These are perhaps the modern counterparts of the Victorian 'long-songs' – 'Three yards a penny'.

p. 121   attention paid to working-men's club customs: There has been a B.B.C. programme called *Club Night*.

p. 121   working-men's clubs: The authors of the Derby Survey (pp. 63 and 72) point out that for every four cinemas throughout the country there are three working-men's clubs. They estimate that the male membership of these clubs is equivalent to one working-class man in seven throughout the whole country. I should guess that the proportion is much higher in the areas from which I have drawn my material: members of other classes do join the clubs, but in these districts they seem to be a small minority.

pp. 123-4 styles of singing – drawing out the words: This is slightly related emotionally to 'gridling' as described by W. H. Davies in *The Autobiography of a Super-Tramp*, ch. XXIII (first published 1908). (Cape, quoted by permission of Mrs H. M. Davies.) The old 'gridler' advises:

> Draw out the easy low notes to a greater length, and cut the difficult high notes short, as though you had spasms in the side.

I owe this reference to Mr R. Nettel.

p. 125 'The finest period in English urban popular song . . .': Some of the detail here is drawn from Christopher Pulling's *They Were Singing*.

p. 126 'If those lips . . .': Francis, Day, and Hunter, Ltd.

p. 129 'Paper Doll': Peter Maurice Music Co., Ltd.

p. 130 'Home': Peter Maurice Music Co., Ltd.

p. 131 'Comrades': Francis, Day, and Hunter, Ltd.

p. 131 Noël Coward's *Private Lives*: Act 1, French, 1930. I was reminded of this by *They Were Singing*.

p. 131 'to quote Cecil Sharp . . .': In *English Folksong – Some Conclusions*. I defend the songs against Mr Sharp's abrupt dismissal but do not claim that they will bear comparison with rural folk-songs.

p. 131 moving easily from comic to religious songs: Variety comedians used to do something similar, when they closed a turn with a 'serious monologue', which was always very well received.

p. 132 'Bless This House': by Helen Taylor (by permission), Boosey and Hawkes, Ltd.

p. 132 love of religious and 'classical' songs: Dame Clara Butt's singing of this type of song used to be very popular. It is some years since I heard a recording of her voice but, if I remember correctly, it was a peculiarly rich contralto – and this heavy and velvety quality would commend it to working-class people.

CHAPTER 6

Sec. A

p. 137 'By this means, . . .': *Democracy in America*, p. 403.

p. 141 'We speak of the bad taste . . .': Julien Benda, *Belphégor*, quoted Wyndham Lewis, *Time and Western Man*, pp. 292–2.

Sec. B

p. 142 Locke: *The Essay concerning Human Understanding*, 1690, bk IV, ch. 16, sec. 4.
        Paine: *The Rights of Man*, 1791, pt I, p. 65. Everyman ed.

p. 144–5 Tolerant phrases: I have been reminded of some of these by *Puzzled People*, pp. 83–4.

Sec. C

p. 145 'this phenomenon . . . is not new . . .': Dibdin, for example, in describing the Press of his time, the late eighteenth century, speaks of 'a sort of *levelling* gentlemen' (my italics), and also of the forerunners of our own ersatz sensationalists, who produce 'high-flown paragraphical descriptions of trifles'. In fact, the popular Press is true to itself through the centuries: but the pace alters.

        I am indebted for this reference to R. Nettel, who allowed me to see an unpublished MS. on Charles Dibdin's *Musical Tour* (published by Gales of the *Sheffield Register* in 1788).

p. 146 easy 'democratic' competitions: The same quality may be found in some radio quiz programmes.

p. 149 'We praise . . .': Dewey, *Individualism, Old and New*, p. 17, G. Allen and Unwin, Ltd, 1931 (Minton, Balch and Co., Ltd, N.Y., U.S.A.).

p. 149 'problems no smiling . . .': Auden, 'The Managers', *Nones*, Faber and Faber, 1952 (Random House, N.Y., U.S.A.).

p. 150 'the elemental odours . . .': Gilbert Harding, *Along My Line*.

p. 150–1 'Let us . . .': J. B. Priestley, in a Home Service broadcast, June, 1951; reprinted in the *Listener*.

p. 151 *ducdame*; Shakespeare, *As You Like It*, II, v. 60.

p. 152 outspoken broadcasters: As an allegorical figure such a person seems to have two main rôles *to his audience*:
        (*a*) The 'card' in a modern form – that is, the idiosyncratic hero, outspoken and debunking.

(b) The 'Honest Joe' who share the values of his audience, who hates humbug and official pretence, who has generous instincts and a warm heart.

Mr Gilbert Harding's illuminating autobiography suggests another aspect of such a reputation. He speaks there of what he calls the shallownesses and shams of such a life and of its lack of pattern, of the shortness of the public's memory and of the artificial inflated reputations which radio can make.

p. 153 'He'll look without . . .': Quoted Stovin, p. 139.

Sec. D

p. 154 De Tocqueville: pp. 410 and 311.

p. 155 'the notion of unlimited progress survives with the popular publicist . . .': It survives and dazzles at many levels, and often shows itself as an admiration of power, apparently made stronger by the insecurities of the writers. This is evident in the tone of many biographies of contemporary magnates, e.g. of such men as Lord Northcliffe.

p. 155 improvements in the teaching of history in schools: But often some of the approaches express a progressivism running away with itself: e.g., some of the Social Studies themes, 'Transport through the Ages', and so on – 'Every day, in every way . . .'.

p. 156 'They see visions . . .': Newman, *The Idea of a University*, Discourse VI, ed. C. F. Harrold, Longmans, Green, 1947, p. 120.

Newman is speaking of sailors, to distinguish between 'acquisition' and 'philosophy'.

My attention was drawn to this Discourse by a reading of J. L. Hammond's Hobhouse Memorial Lecture, 'The Growth of Common Enjoyment'.

p. 158 'Democratic nations care . . .': De Tocqueville, *Democracy in America*, p. 343.

Sec. E

p. 164 sales of American comics here: The most thorough analysis of American comic-books is to be found in Frederick Wertham's *The Seduction of the Innocent*.

p. 165 Tolstoy's Levin: *Anna Karenina*, ch. 28.

p. 165 increase of scrappy radio programmes: But there seems also to have been an increase in the programmes which wittily and quietly observe English manners, e.g. in the work of Eric Barker, Johnny Morris, and Al Read.

p. 166 *Maria Marten*: An edition, reprinted at least as late as 1946, is published by John Lane, The Bodley Head.

p. 167 'Above all, we will not be boring . . .': But the advertisements from some 'quality' papers make similar appeals, often coupled with cultural snobbery, i.e. how proud we should be to be seen reading a newspaper which is both serious and bright.

CHAPTER 7

Sec. A

p. 169 Wordsworth: *Lyrical Ballads*, 1798–1805, Preface.
Arnold: *Culture and Anarchy*, ch. 1.
Dostoyevsky: *The Brothers Karamazov*, trans. by Constance Garnett, bk v, ch. v, Heinemann.

p. 170 'Among democratic nations . . .': De Tocqueville, p. 332.

p. 171 'Every culture lives . . .': The phrase is Lewis Mumford's.

p. 171 an instinctive sense of the audience: Of J. S. Elias, who built the fortunes of Odhams Press, R. J. Minney says, 'He knew instinctively what they liked, because it was what he liked himself' (*Viscount Southwood*, p. 245).
A. P. Ryan, a biographer of Harmsworth, makes this kind of point several times, e.g. '[Harmsworth] believed in himself.' He also says, 'There was no streak of piety in him, or any sign of moral or intellectual fervour.'

p. 171 sincerity and cynicism: See the statements by some popular novelists in Mrs Q. D. Leavis's *Fiction and the Reading Public*.

p. 172 'I was once present . . .': Lawrence Dunning, 'Film Notes', *The European*, No. 1, March 1953.

p. 172 'I just go . . .': 'Her Hobby's Murder', *Picture Post*, 24 Jan. 1948. This authoress's books are not of the type called 'sex-and-violence novelettes' in chapter 8.

Sec. B

p. 173 Ryan: *Lord Northcliffe*, p. 14.

p. 174 'A few still survive with little change . . .': The *News of the World* has much the largest readership of all papers. Its estimated actual number of readers over sixteen is seventeen millions, or nearly one-half of the population. By groups it is read, approximately:

> by A–B   1 in 7½
>   C   1 in 3
> D–E   1 in 2

(in groups D–E it is read roughly equally by
men and women, at all ages).

For comparison, *Empire News* is read by approximately 1 in 9½ over the whole population; in groups A–B by 1 in 30, in group C by 1 in 14 and in groups D–E by 1 in 8 (*HRS 1955*).

p. 175 'presenting a vision of life for the working-classes just as "nice" as that of the middle-classes ...': It may be objected that this has long been the case with popular literature, e.g. in the works of Mrs Henry Wood. The point is that the view of a middle-class life usually presented now is more possession-laden or tinselly 'nice' than that in *East Lynne*.

p. 178 Ryan: *Lord Northcliffe*, p. 50.

p. 181 'gimmick': A smart 'line' or 'ploy', usually employed as an opening.

Sec. C

p. 183 'The will of God ...': The full text may be found in the *Oxford Book of Light Verse*, chosen by W. H. Auden, O.U.P., 1938.

p. 183 Arthur Morrison: In *The Hole in the Wall*, 1902.

p. 185 'If you're tired ...': 'The End of the Road', Francis, Day, and Hunter, Ltd.

p. 186 decline in the vigorous treatment of songs: There are some exceptions, notably in the programmes by Billy Cotton's band.

p. 186 'I can't give you ...': Lawrence Wright Music Co., Ltd.

p. 190 'strangulato': This manner may often be heard, in the mid-fifties, in renderings of 'Some Enchanted Evening'.

Sec. D

p. 191 'For our sense ...': Josef Pieper, *Leisure the Basis of Culture*, p. 131.

p. 192 ersatz sensationalism: If it is not ersatz it is likely to be vicarious, as in 'all-in' wrestling and stock-car racing.

p. 194 'Tears were streaming ...': Mrs Henry Wood, *East Lynne* (1861), ch. XVIII.

p. 194 'On the other hand . . .' George Eliot, *Adam Bede*, bk 1, ch. 5.

p. 199 'the basic facts about the nature of popular publications . . .':
'They have become great industrial enterprises,' says Francis
Williams, in *Press, Parliament and People*, 'governed by their
need to make profits on the large capital sums invested in them
and interested primarily in commercial success' (p. 146). He
adds that this is a generalization and so not altogether true.
Later he says, 'Primarily the mass circulation newspaper sets out
to entertain' (p. 161).

p. 201 pressure to be bright: R. J. Minney, in *Viscount Southwood*, gives
the point of view of the late managing director of Odhams
Press. J. S. Elias, as he was then, urged Francis Williams, no
doubt with complete conviction: 'Make them smile. Cheer
them up. The news is grim enough' (p. 287).

CHAPTER 8

Sec. A

p. 202 juke-boxes: known by the Board of Trade as 'coin-operated
phonographs'.

p. 203 schoolchildren reading these magazines: Incidental evidence is
easily found. I know of one secondary modern school where
they are exchanged in the playground.

p. 204 Samuel Butler's ploughboys: *The Way of All Flesh*, 1903,
ch. 14.

p. 208 Bacon on 'the farthest end of knowledge': The passage deserves
quoting at greater length, for its relevance here and to chapters
10 and 11:

'But the greatest error of all the rest is the mistaking or misplacing of
the last or farthest end of knowledge: for men have entered into a
desire of learning and knowledge, sometimes upon a natural curiosity
and inquisitive appetite; sometimes to entertain their minds with
variety and delight; sometimes for ornament and reputation; and
sometimes to enable them to the victory of wit and contradiction;
and most times for lucre and profession; and seldom sincerely to give
a true account of their gift of reason, to the benefit and use of men:
as if there were sought in knowledge a couch whereupon to rest a
searching and restless spirit; or a tarrasse, for a wandering and variable
mind to walk up and down with a fair prospect; or a tower of state,
for a proud mind to raise itself upon; or a fort or commanding
ground, for strife and contention; or a shop, for profit or sale; and

not a rich storehouse, for the glory of the Creator and the relief of man's estate. But this is that which will indeed dignify and exalt knowledge, if contemplation and action may be more nearly and straightly conjoined and united together than they have been' (*The Advancement of Learning*, 1605, bk I, sec. II, pp. 34–5 in Everyman edition).

p. 208 'spicy' magazines for working-class and lower middle-class readers: There is also a group of smart professional-class 'spicy magazines'.

Sec. C

p. 211 De Rougemont: p. 244.

p. 211 sex-and-violence novels: A little of the material in this section appeared, in a different form, in an article I contributed to *Tribune* ('The Bookstall', 29 Oct. 1948).

Readers of George Orwell's 'Raffles and Miss Blandish' (*Critical Essays*, Secker, 1946) will notice a general debt to him here.

p. 213 James M. Cain: See also *Serenade* (1937). Mr Cain can claim more serious literary attention than his debtors here.

p. 214 'one thinks of Nashe's *Unfortunate Traveller* ...': E.g. of Diamante, the wife of Castaldo:

'A pretie rounde faced wench was it with blacke eie browes, a high forehead, a little mouth, and a sharpe nose, as fat and plum everie part of her as a plover, a skin as slike and soft as the backe of a swan, it doth me good when I remember her. Like a bird she tript on the grounde, and bare out her belly as maiesticall as an Estrich. With a licorous rouling eie fixt piercing on the earth, and sometimes scornfully darted on the tone side. . . .'

or of the rape of Heraclide:

'He graspt her by the yvorie throat, and shooke her as a mastiffe would shake a yong bear, swearing and staring he would teare out her weasand if shee refused. . . . Backward he dragd her even as a man backwarde would plucke a tree downe by the twigs, and then like a traitor that is drawen to execution on a hurdle, he traileth her up and down the chamber by those tender untwisted braids, and setting his barbarous foote on her bare snowy breast, bad her yeld or have her winde stampt out. . . . Dismissing her hair from his fingers, and pinnioning her elbowes therewithall, she strugled, she wrested, but all was in vaine. . . . On the hard boords he threw her, and used his knee as an yron ramme to beat ope the two leavd gate of her chastitie . . .' (*The Unfortunate Traveller*, 1594. Edition of 1948 by John Lehmann, pp. 61 and 88–9).'

p. 219 'She drank beer ...' William Faulkner, *Sanctuary*, 1931, ch. XVIII, Chatto and Windus (Random House, N.Y., U.S.A.).

p. 223 Kafka – Hemingway – : I believe there are similarities in some contemporary French writing, notably in novels whose chief character, a *déclassé* middle-class man, engages in a life of violent but purposeless action.

p. 223 'You can't come in now ...': Ernest Hemingway, *A Farewell to Arms*, Cape, 1929 (Charles Scribner's Sons, N.Y., U.S.A.).

CHAPTER 9

Sec. A

p. 225 De Tocqueville: Preface to Part I.

p. 226 'In its newer uses ...': A somewhat similar point is made by Lewis Way, in *Man's Quest for Significance*.

p. 226 'wide': Date from *Shorter Oxford English Dictionary*.

p. 229 cynicism towards the newspapers: A. P. Ryan supports my rough chronology of the change. He says that 'You can't believe what you read in the newspapers' became a current phrase after the First Great War (*Lord Northcliffe*, p. 140).

Sec. B

p. 236 quotation from William Morris 'The Art of the People', a lecture, 1879; in *Hopes and Fears for Art*, p. 44, vol. XXII of the *Collected Works of William Morris*, Longmans, Green, 1914. I am indebted to the late Dr F. D. Klingender for drawing my attention to this passage.

p. 239 'intellectual sadism': The phrase is Sir Richard Livingstone's.

p. 240 'It's all very well ...': From a social survey.

CHAPTER 10

p. 241 Tchekov: Letter to A. S. Souvorin, 7 Jan. 1889, *The Life and Letters of A. Tchekov*, p. 114, trans. and ed. S. S. Koteliansky and Philip Tomlinson, Cassell, 1925 (Doubleday, Doran, and Co., Inc., N.Y., U.S.A.).
Turgenev: *Fathers and Sons*, trans. Constance Garnett, 1895, Heinemann, reprint of 1951, p. 32.

Sec. A

p. 241 George Eliot: *Middlemarch*, 1872, bk 3, ch. 29.

p. 244 difficulties of home environment See *Early Leaving*, pp. 19 and 36.

p. 244 isolation of working-class scholarship boys: see *Early Leaving*, p. 32.

few scholarships from 'elementary' schools in working-class areas: But see chapter 11 (B) below, and P.E.P. pamphlet 'Background of the University Student', *Planning*, vol. xx, No. 373, 8 Nov. 1954, on the increased proportion of working-class children at universities.

p. 247 'The established systems . . .': H. Spencer, *Autobiography*, 1904, i; Watts' reprint of 1926, p. 338.

p. 247 'Men do not become . . .': *The Life of Thomas Holcroft*, contd by William Hazlitt, ed. Elbridge Colby, Constable, 1925, vol. II, p. 82.

p. 247 slower development of scholarship boy: The contrast often seems to me even more marked in girls: compare a typical secondary modern schoolgirl of fourteen or fifteen with a grammar-school girl of that age.

p. 248 not taking up spare-time work: Dr F. D. Klingender's survey of the students at Hull University College, *Students in a Changing World 1951–2*, suggests that this is ceasing to be so. Of those giving information, 58 per cent of the men and 26 per cent of the women had done some spare-time work.

p. 249 'Pale, shabby, . . .': Graham Greene, *It's a Battlefield*, Heinemann, 1934, ch. 2. Of Conrad Drover.

p. 251 'a self-taught working-man . . .': 'I'm reminded . . .': Both from Virginia Woolf, *A Writer's Diary*, Hogarth, 1953, pp. 47 and 49 (Harcourt Brace and Co., N.Y., U.S.A.).

p. 252 'He will have put himself . . .': Arnold J. Toynbee, *A Study of History*, abridged by D. C. Somervell, p. 313, O.U.P., 1946.

p. 252 'You are gifted . . .': Tchekov, Letter to his brother Nicolay, Moscow, 1886; *The Life and Letters of A. Tchekov*, p. 80.

p. 252 'the discrepancy . . .': W. Trotter, *Instincts of the Herd in Peace and War*, T. Fisher Unwin, imp. of 1923, p. 67.

Sec. B

p. 253 *Notes from Underground*: trans. Constance Garnett, Heinemann, *White Nights*, imp. of 1950.

p. 257 advertisements in a 'quality' weekly: In case these proportions were not for a typical week I made a similar examination of the same journal's advertisement page for the week in which this chapter was revised:

3¼ columns, of 7 advertisements, were occupied with advertisements of the kind I am discussing. The remaining ¾ column, of 2 advertisements, was occupied with border-line advertisements.

p. 260 'She knew the type . . .': E. M. Forster, *Howards End*, Arnold, 1910.

p. 260 'But in each class . . .': Arnold, *Culture and Anarchy*, ch. 3.

p. 261 'everything is below . . .': George Eliot, *Middlemarch*. Of Casaubon.

p. 263 'they "sit in darkness . . ." ': Psalm cvii. 10.

p. 263 'We would rather be ruined . . .': W. H. Auden, *The Age of Anxiety*, Faber and Faber, 1948 (Random House, N.Y., U.S.A.).

p. 263 'these few . . .': How few, though? 30,000 people bought the first number of *London Magazine*. I should guess that a substantial proportion were people of this kind. *HRS 1954* suggests that approximately 30,000 unmarried men under 35 in Groups D–E are readers of the *Listener*.

p. 263 'The number of those . . .': Quoted by Matthew Arnold, *Culture and Anarchy*, ch. 3.

CHAPTER 11

Sec. A

p. 264 Wordsworth: *Lyrical Ballads, 1798–1805*, Preface.
Muir: 'The Combat', Faber and Faber (Grove Press, U.S.A.).

p. 265 politically active working-class people: Margaret McCarthy's *Generation in Revolt* is a good autobiographical account of a life of this kind during the twenties and thirties, chiefly in Lancashire.

p. 265 Mechanics' Institutes: By 1861 there were over 1,000 Institutes in England, with a membership of 200,000.

p. 265 Macaulay's *History*: Figures of sales from David Thompson, *England in the Nineteenth Century, 1815–1914*.

p. 265 *Outline of History*: 1920.
Science of Life: with Prof. J. S. Huxley and G. P. Wells.
Work, Wealth and Happiness of Mankind; 1932.

p. 265 Thinker's Library: More than 3 million copies of this series have been sold. I understand that there is a growing demand for these books in colonies moving towards self-government.

p. 266 expansion in further and part-time education: In Great Britain during 1952 approximately 1 in 45 of the population engaged in some form of non-vocational further education (though not necessarily in the study of what are classed as the 'liberal' subjects) (Derby Survey, pp. 34–7).

p. 266 W.E.A. student numbers: From *The Organization and Finance of Adult Education* ('The Ashby Report') p. 14 (by permission).

p. 267 'few grounds for satisfaction ...': There are some encouraging features; e.g. much in the character of the *Listener*, or the fact that several decent weekly or Sunday papers have one or two reviewers each, whose approach is admirably suited to the need I have outlined, or some sound and television broadcasting on social and political affairs.

p. 267 'earnest minority' thinking too exclusively of immediate political and economic objectives: Two recent instances come to mind:
(*a*) A W.E.A. student was refused a small bursary to study literature at a Summer School, because his trade-union education committee thought the subject irrelevant to trade-union interests.
(*b*) A proposed class for dockers on philosophy had aroused interest locally but was refused by the relevant body in London, because 'the subject would not help dockers'.

p. 271 'odd-jobbery': The recent considerable increases in the provision of materials and equipment to 'do-it-yourself', which improved techniques and centralization have brought about, seem so far to have been taken up chiefly by lower middle-class men and by skilled working-men, but not to have much affected the majority of working-men.

p. 272 interest in allotments declining a little: See *HRS 1952*, p. 42.

p. 272 pigeon-fancying: Clubs include the National Homing Union and the National Flying Club; there are Scottish and Welsh Unions and a North of England Union. The magazine, *The*

Racing Pigeon, has a net sale of 43,500 (*1956 Advertisers' Annual*). More than £2 million a year are spent on this 'fancy' in Great Britain. The editor of *The Racing Pigeon* tells me that one manual of instruction has sold an estimated 110,000 copies. (Some details from 'The Winged Fancy', by Edgar Ainsworth, *Picture Post*, 21 Nov. 1953.)

p. 273 cycling: *HRS 1952–55* suggests that there had been a slight drop in the popularity of cycling among all classes during the last few years. The men in groups D–E remain the most common users in all classes (40 per cent); women in groups D–E use cycles slightly less than women in other classes.

Sec. B

p. 275 increase in entertainments: *The cinema*; in this country in 1952 the average number of attendances over the whole population was twenty-seven, which was higher than the U.S.A. average. Expenditure on the cinema in 1952 was nearly 3s per week for every family in the country. There are approximately 4,600 cinemas in Great Britain. The group going most frequently to the cinema is that composed of working-class people aged 16–24 (see Derby Survey, pp. 121–3).

p. 275 one thousand to five thousand publications: Derby Survey, p. 164.

p. 275 increases between 1937 and 1947:

Nat. and prov. dailies: 17,800,000 to 28,503,000.
Sunday newspapers: 15,500,000 to 29,300,000.

Figures from *Report of the Royal Commission on the Press, 1947–9*, pp. 5–6 (by permission). A part of these increases might be explained by conditions peculiar to the war-period. But the war has now been over for more than ten years, and total readership has not begun to drop significantly.

p. 275 magazines and periodicals between 1938 and 1952: P.E.P. *Planning*, XXI, 384.

p. 275 increases between 1947 and 1952:

Nat. morning papers: 15,600,000 to 16,100,000.
Sunday papers rose to 31,700,000 in 1952.

Derby Survey, Table 51, p. 168. The authors comment (p. 163), 'Even when allowance is made for rising prices, we bought more reading material in 1952 than in 1948 (when expenditure was almost exactly double that of ten years earlier)'. It seems as though, in general, the 1937–47 rate of increase did not continue between 1947 and 1955. But, again in general, the new high levels of 1947 were maintained (see P.E.P. *Planning*, XXI, 388).

p. 276   two daily newspapers per household: Derby Survey, p. 166. Two out of three adults read more than one Sunday newspaper: quoted in Derby Survey, p. 170.

p. 276   number of daily newspapers per 1,000 people:
         Estimated number of copies of daily newspapers per 1000 in the population:

U.K. 611	France 239	Mexico 48
Sweden 490	Italy 107	Turkey 32
U.S.A. 353	Argentina 100	

See *The Daily Press*, UNESCO.

p. 276   book production in U.K.: During 1953, more than 18,000 titles were issued here as compared with about 12,000 titles for the U.S.A. which has a population three times as large. One should add that we have a large export trade in books, and that not all the titles listed in any year are of new books. Thus, of the titles issued during 1953, roughly 12,750 were of new books (the U.S.A. had 9,000 new books). One in five of the new books published in England was a work of fiction. Figures from the Derby Survey, pp. 182–3, and *Basic Facts and Figures*, UNESCO.

p. 276   increase in public library issues: During 1952–3 seven books were issued per head of the population as compared with five in 1939. The Derby Survey suggests that, in Derby, 1 person in 6 from the working-classes and those with elementary education, and 1 person in 4 from the middle-classes and those with secondary and further education, borrow one book a week from the public library (Derby Survey, pp. 165 and 198). As to the buying of books, including the paper-backed series, it is probable that between 125 and 190 million separate volumes are sold in each year (Derby Survey, p. 185).

p. 276   55 per cent reading a book: Quoted in Derby Survey, p. 184. In that survey (p. 190), one-third of those interviewed said they were currently reading a book. A Mass Observation survey in Tottenham, for the British Institute of Public Opinion, gave roughly the same result as the Gallup Poll quoted above.

p. 276   sales of 'quality' periodicals: In most cases the increase has not been continuous. There was, rather, an increase for a few years after the war and then a slight drop or a steadying. But over pre-war or immediate post-war figures the circulations of most 'quality' periodicals show an increase (see Wadsworth, *Newspaper Circulations*).

The following A.B.C. figures are from the *Newspaper Press Directory*, 1955:

Observer	534,752	*Sunday Times*	577,869
Times	220,834	(audited, not A.B.C.)	
New Statesman	70,598	*Spectator*	38,353

As examples of recent increases: the *Manchester Guardian* showed 127,083 for 1953, and 146,146 for 1955. The *Listener* has roughly doubled its sales since the war. The *Observer's* A.B.C. figure for the period Jan. to June, 1956, was 601,402.

Literary Reviews:

Encounter had a circulation in mid-1954 of about 15,000, and *London Magazine*, which was started at almost the same time, one of about 18,000 (*Observer*, 18 July 1954.) By mid-1956 the circulation of each magazine had dropped considerably, and it was announced that *London Magazine* was likely to lose its financial backing.

p. 276 75 to 80 per cent fiction: Derby Survey, pp. 186–7.

p. 276 commercial library figures: Derby Survey, p. 185.

'a small proportion of keen readers ...': The Derby Survey lends some support to this view, and speaks more than once of 'a substantial minority of keen book readers'. Were one to omit the number of those whose reading is almost entirely light-weight, one would be left, I think, simply with 'a minority'.

p. 276 'To exist ...': Williams, *Press, Parliament and People*, p. 175.

p. 277 decline in the total number of newspapers:

We have	122 daily papers for	51 million population			
U.S.A.	1,865	,,	,,	,, 157	,,	,,
Sweden	160	,,	,,	,, 7	,,	,,
Switzerland	127	,,	,,	,, 5	,,	,,
Mexico	162	,,	,,	,, 27	,,	,,
Argentina	140	,,	,,	,, 18	,,	,,
Turkey	116	,,	,,	,, 22	,,	,,
France	151	,,	,,	,, 42½	,,	,,
Italy	107	,,	,,	,, 47	,,	,,

(Figures from *The Daily Press*, UNESCO.)

The total number of different newspapers now published here is in most cases proportionately, and in many cases absolutely, smaller than that of other literate nations. Syndication will reduce the force of some of the disparities, but not enough to invalidate the general point. A decline in the total number of different newspapers is not, of course, peculiar to the United Kingdom: in the U.S.A. the total dropped by about one-third between 1909 and 1954.

p. 277 centralization of reading: The centralization on to national, as distinct from regional, papers has taken place most markedly in the morning and Sunday papers. In the evening papers, the provincial press still keeps much more of its strength. Most people will have noticed that one result of the present trend is a deterioration in some provincial papers. With syndicated material they try to ape the brightness of Fleet Street, and interlard with that their unconvincing local references. Such papers have the vices of the popular London Press with a drabness wholly their own. Details of centralization may be found in the *Report of the Royal Commission on the Press*, Kayser's *One Week's News* and Wadsworth's *Newspaper Circulations*.

p. 278 'As an indication ..': *The Press and the People*, pp. 12–13. The report adds that serious newspapers still represent only about 3 per cent of total Sunday sales.

p. 280 attendance at secondary grammar schools: See *The Organisation of Secondary Education*, W. P. Alexander (Councils and Education Press Ltd), and *Secondary Education Survey*, Joan Thompson, Fabian Research Series (Gollancz, 1952).

p. 280 scholarships for working-class children: 'In summary, despite the educational and social changes of recent years, the chances of attendance at a grammar-school increase with social level.' From 'Selection for Secondary Education and Achievement in Four Grammar Schools', A. H. Halsey and L. Gardner, *British Journal of Sociology*, vol. IV, No. 1, March 1953, pp. 60–75 (see also *Early Leaving*).

p. 280 Vice-Principal of Ruskin College: Letter to the *Observer*, 6 June 1954.

p. 281 a new caste system: After writing this I was interested to see a somewhat similar point put forward by Prof. Glass in the introduction to *Social Mobility in Britain* (pp. 25–7). He notes that he is there expressing personal views which 'have a value basis'.

p. 283   the popular Press and the arrival of T.V.: 'Increasing competition from radio and television is affecting the character of the press' (*The Press and the People*, p. 9). Thinking of the popularity of cinema, sound radio, television, and comic strips, one sometimes feels like hazarding the speculation that by the end of the twentieth century the impact of the written word on the majority of the population will be seen to have been a short and almost negligible interlude: that by then the largely oral and local culture dominant until the latter half of the nineteenth century will have been replaced by one that is again oral, but is also visual and massively public.

p. 284   'To maintain . . .' *The Press and the People*, p. 5.

p. 285   the new classless class: Presumably the large central groups the publicists have in view is roughly what *HRS* calls groups D–E, sometimes with C added. Groups D–E account for 71 per cent of the population; with C added, for 88 per cent.

SELECT BIBLIOGRAPHY

Unless otherwise stated the books listed have been published in London.

A. STUDIES IN HISTORY, ECONOMICS, SOCIOLOGY, PSYCHOLOGY, AND EDUCATION

MARSHALL, Dorothy. *The English Poor in the Eighteenth Century*, Routledge, 1926.

HAMMOND, J. L., and Barbara. *The Town Labourer 1760–1832*, Longmans, Green, 1932 (first pub. 1917).

HAMMOND, J. L., and Barbara. *The Skilled Labourer 1760–1832*, Longmans, Green, 1919.

HAMMOND, J. L., and Barbara. *The Bleak Age*, rev. ed., Penguin Books, Harmondsworth, 1947 (first published 1934).

COLE, G. D. H. *A Short History of the British Working-Class Movement 1787–1947*, G. Allen and Unwin, ed. of 1947.

COLE, G. D. H. *British Working-Class Politics 1832–1914*, Routledge, 1941

COLE, G. D. H., and POSTGATE, R. *The Common People 1746–1946*, Methuen, ed. of 1949 (first pub. 1938).

LYND, H. M. *England in the Eighteen-Eighties*, O.U.P., 1945.

THOMPSON, David. *England in the Nineteenth Century, 1815–1914*, Pelican History of England, vol. 8, Penguin Books, Harmondsworth, 1950.

WEBB, R. K. *The British Working-Class Reader, 1790–1848*, G. Allen and Unwin, 1955.

ROYAL COMMISSION REPORT on *Betting, Lotteries and Gaming, 1949–51*, Cmd. 8190, H.M.S.O., 1951.

PREST, A. R., with ADAMS, A. A. *Consumers' Expenditure in the United Kingdom 1900–19*, Studies in the National Income and Expenditure of the United Kingdom, Cambridge University Press, 1954.

CARR-SAUNDERS, A. M., and CARADOG JONES, D. *A Survey of the Social Structure of England and Wales*, Oxford University Press, 2nd ed. 1937 (first pub. 1927).

KUPER, Leo (Ed.). *Living in Towns*, Cresset, 1953.

CAUTER, T., and DOWNHAM, J. S. *The Communication of Ideas, a Study of Contemporary Influences on Urban Life*, Chatto and Windus, for The Readers' Digest Association, Ltd, 1954.

HULTON RESEARCH, *Patterns of British Life*, Hulton Press, 1950.

ABRAMS, Mark. *The Condition of the British People, 1911–45*, Gollancz, for the Fabian Society, 1946.

GLASS, D. V. (Ed.). *Social Mobility in Britain*, International Library of Sociology and Social Reconstruction, Routledge and Kegan Paul, 1954.

BRENNAN, T., COONEY, E. W., and POLLINS, H. *Social Change in South-West Wales*, Watts, 1954.

MASS OBSERVATION. *The Pub and The People, A Worktown Study*, Gollancz, 1943.

MASS OBSERVATION. *Puzzled People*, Gollancz, 1947.

ROWNTREE, B. Seebohm, and LAVERS, G. R. *English Life and Leisure*, Longmans, Green, 1951.

GORER, G. *Exploring English Character*, Cresset Press, 1955 (published too late to be consulted in the writing of this book, but demands a place in the bibliography because of its special relevance).

RICE, Margery Spring. *Working-Class Wives*, Penguin Books, Harmondsworth, 1939.

ZWEIG, F. *Labour, Life and Poverty*, Gollancz, 1948.

ZWEIG, F. *Men in the Pits*, Gollancz, 1948.

ZWEIG, F. *Women's Life and Labour*, Gollancz, 1952.

ZWEIG, F. *The British Worker*, Penguin Books, Harmondsworth, 1952.

REAVELEY, G., and WINNINGTON, J. *Democracy and Industry*, Chatto and Windus, 1947 (O.U.P., Toronto).

SARGAISON, E. Miriam. *Growing Old in Common Lodgings*, Nuffield Provincial Hospitals Trust, 1954.

SLATER, Eliot, and WOODSIDE, Moya. *Patterns of Marriage, a Study of Marriage Relationships in the Urban Working-Classes*, Cassell, 1951.

SPROTT, W. J. H. *Social Psychology*, Manuals of Modern Psychology, Methuen, 1952.

SPINLEY, B. M. *The Deprived and the Privileged*, Routledge and Kegan Paul, 1952.

PEAR, T. H. *Voice and Personality*, Chapman Hall, 1931.

LEWIS, M. M. *The Importance of Illiteracy*, Harrap, 1953.

KLINGENDER, F. D. *Students in a Changing World, 1951–2*, Yorkshire Bulletin of Economic and Social Research, vol. 6, Nos. 1 and 2, Feb. and Sept. 1954, University of Hull.

MINISTRY OF EDUCATION. *The Organisation and Finance of Adult Education*, H.M.S.O., 1954.

MINISTRY OF EDUCATION. *Early Leaving*, a report of the Central Advisory Council for Education (England), H.M.S.O., 1954.

B. ASPECTS OF WORKING-CLASS LIFE

BOURNE, George. *Change in the Village*, Duckworth, 1912.

BOURNE, George. *A Small Boy in the 'Sixties*, Cambridge University Press, 1927.

QUENNELL, J. P. *Mayhew's Characters*, Kimber, 1951 (Mayhew pub., 1864).

ESCOTT, T. H. S. *England, Its People, Polity and Pursuits*, 2 vols., Cassell, 1883.

ESCOTT, T. H. S. *Social Transformations of the Victorian Age*, Seeley, 1897.

BELL, Lady. *At the Works*, Arnold, 1907.

LOANE, M. *The Next Street But One*, Arnold, 1907.

LOANE, M. *From their Point of View*, Arnold, 1908.

REYNOLDS, Stephen. *A Poor Man's House*, Macmillan, 1911 (first pub. 1908).

FREEMAN, Gwendolen. *The Houses Behind*, G. Allen and Unwin, 1947.

ORWELL, George. *Shooting an Elephant*, Secker and Warburg, 1950.

ORWELL, George. *The Road to Wigan Pier*, Gollancz, 1937.

COMMON, Jack. *Kiddar's Luck*, Turnstile, 1951.

MCCARTHY, Margaret. *Generation in Revolt*, Heinemann, 1953.

SHARP, Cecil. *English Folksong – Some Conclusions*, 3rd ed., revised by Maud Karpeles, Methuen, 1954 (first pub. 1907) (H. W. Gray Co., N.Y., U.S.A.).

Ballads and Broadsides, a folio collection from the Manchester district, Central Reference Library, Manchester.

HENDERSON, W. (Ed.). *Victorian Street Ballads*, Country Life, 1937.

Curiosities of Street Literature, Reeves and Turner, 1871.

NETTEL, R. *Music in the Five Towns, 1840–1914*, Oxford University Press, 1944.

NETTEL, R. *Seven Centuries of Popular Song*, Phoenix, 1956.

PULLING, Christopher. *They were Singing*, Harrap, 1952.

JONES, Barbara. *The Unsophisticated Arts*, Architectural Press, 1951.

LAMBERT, M., and MARX, Enid. *English Popular Art*, Batsford, 1951.

C. THE PRESS, MASS PUBLICATIONS, AND ADVERTISING

HULTON RESEARCH, *Hulton Readership Survey, 1952–5*, Hulton Press.

Newspaper Press Directory, 1955. Benn Brothers.

Willing's Press Guide, 80th annual issue, Willing's Press Service, Ltd, 1954.

UNESCO. *Basic Facts and Figures*, 1952. (H.M.S.O.)

UNESCO. *The Daily Press, A Survey of the World Situation in 1952*, No. 7 of Reports and Papers on Mass Communication, 1953. (H.M.S.O.)

KAYSER, Jacques. *One Week's News*, Unesco, 1953. (H.M.S.O.)

REPORT OF THE ROYAL COMMISSION ON THE PRESS, 1947–9. Cmd. 7700, H.M.S.O., 1949.

P.E.P. *Planning*, XXI, issues 384 ('Balance Sheet of the Press') and 388 ('Ownership of the Press'), 1955.

GENERAL COUNCIL OF THE PRESS. *The Press and the People*, 1st Annual Report, 1954.

WADSWORTH, A. P. *Newspaper Circulations, 1800–1954* (pamphlet), Manchester Statistical Society, 1955.

ANGELL, Norman. *The Press and the Organisation of Society*, Labour Publishing Co., 1922.

ANGELL, Norman, *The Public Mind*, Douglas, 1926.

SOAMES, Jane. *The English Press*, Lindsay Drummond, 1936.

WILLIAMS, Francis, *Press, Parliament and People*, Heinemann, 1946 (Ryerson Press, Toronto).

RYAN, A. P. *Lord Northcliffe*, Collins, 1953 (Macmillan Co., N.Y., U.S.A.).

CUDLIPP, Hugh. *Publish and Be Damned*, Dakers, 1953.

NINNEY, R. J. *Viscount Southwood*, Odhams, 1954.

BRITISH COUNCIL STAFF ASSOCIATION. *The Beaverbrook Press and the British Council*, 1954.

FENWICK, L. 'Periodicals and Adolescent Girls', *Studies in Education*, VOL. II, No. 1, University College, Hull, 1953.

LEAVIS, Q. D. *Fiction and the Reading Public*, Chatto and Windus, 1932.

STEVENS, G., UNWIN, S., and SWINNERTON, F. *Best Sellers – are they Born or Made?* G. Allen and Unwin, 1939.

MELLERS, W. H. 'Searchlight on Tin Pan Alley', *Scrutiny*, vol. 8, 1939–40, pp. 390–405. Deighton, Bell, Cambridge.

Advertisers' Annual, 1956. Business Publications Ltd.

MCLUHAN, H. M. *The Mechanical Bride*, Vanguard, New York, 1951.

WERTHAM, Fredric. *The Seduction of the Innocent*, Museum Press, 1955.

WAGNER, Geoffrey. *Parade of Pleasure*, Verschoyle, 1954.

D. GENERAL PHILOSOPHICAL AND CULTURAL ASPECTS

DE TOCQUEVILLE, Alexis. *Democracy in America*, World's Classics ed., Oxford University Press, 1946 (first pub. 1935).

ARNOLD, Matthew. *Culture and Anarchy*, 1869.

BURY, J. B. *The Idea of Progress*, Macmillan, 1920.

LEWIS, Wyndham. *Time and Western Man*, Chatto and Windus, 1928.

DAWSON, Christopher. *Progress and Religion*, Sheed and Ward, 1929.

WOOLF, Leonard. *After the Deluge, A Study of Communal Psychology*, vol. I (1931); vol II (1939), Hogarth, reprint of 1953.

WOOLF, Leonard. *Principia Politica*, vol. 3 of *After the Deluge*, Hogarth, 1953.

WOOLF, Leonard. *Quack, Quack*, Hogarth, 1935.

LEAVIS, F. R., and THOMPSON, Denys. *Culture and Environment*, Chatto and Windus, 1933.

STOVIN, Harold. *Totem – the Exploitation of Youth*, Methuen, 1935.

DE ROUGEMONT, Denis. *Passion and Society*, trans. Montgomery Belgion, Faber, 1940 (Pantheon Books, Inc., N.Y., U.S.A.).

HOBHOUSE MEMORIAL LECTURES, 1930–40. Oxford University Press, 1938.

WAY, Lewis. *Man's Quest for Significance*, G. Allen and Unwin, 1948.

CHURCHILL, R. C. *Disagreements*, Secker and Warburg, 1950.

CHURCHILL, R. C. *The English Sunday*, Watts, 1954.

WEIL, Simone. *The Need for Roots*, Routledge and Kegan Paul, 1952.

PIEPER, Josef. *Leisure the Basis of Culture*, Faber, 1952 (Pantheon Books, Inc., N.Y., U.S.A.).

HARDING, Gilbert. *Along My Line*, Putnam, 1953.

ROLT, L. T. C. *Winterstoke*, Constable, 1954.

INDEX

The insertion of 'and n.' after a page-number or group of page-numbers indicates that the subject is mentioned both on the pages and in the 'Notes and References' to those pages. 'Notes to' indicates that a subject is mentioned in the 'Notes and References' to a page without being mentioned on the page itself.

The qualification 'working-class' should be assumed before the themes and attitudes indexed, unless they are otherwise described.